Titles in the same collection

No. 1 Promoting the policy debate on social exclusion from a comparative perspective (ISBN: 978-92-871-4920-6, €8 / US$12)

No. 2 Trends and developments in old-age pension and health-care financing in Europe during the 1990s (ISBN: 978-92-871-4921-3, €8 / US$12)

No. 3 Using social benefits to combat poverty and social exclusion: opportunities and problems from a comparative perspective (ISBN: 978-92-871-4937-4, €13 / US$20)

No. 4 New social demands: the challenges of governance (ISBN: 978-92-871-5012-7, €19 / US$29)

No. 5 Combating poverty and access to social rights in the countries of the South Caucasus: a territorial approach (ISBN: 978-92-871-5096-7, €15 / US$23)

No. 6 The state and new social responsibilities in a globalising world (ISBN: 978-92-871-5168-1, €15 / US$23)

No. 7 Civil society and new social responsibilities based on ethical foundations (ISBN: 978-92-871-5309-8, €13 / US$20)

No. 8 Youth and exclusion in disadvantaged urban areas: addressing the causes of violence (ISBN: 978-92-871-5389-0, €25 / US$38)

No. 9 Youth and exclusion in disadvantaged urban areas: policy approaches in six European cities (ISBN: 978-92-871-5512-2, €15 / US$23)

No. 10 Security through social cohesion: proposals for a new socio-economic governance (ISBN: 978-92-871-5491-0, €17 / US$26)

No. 11 Security through social cohesion: deconstructing fear (of others) by going beyond stereotypes (ISBN: 978-92-871-5544-3, €10 / US$15)

No. 12 Ethical, solidarity-based citizen involvement in the economy: a prerequisite for social cohesion (ISBN: 978-92-871-5558-0, €10 / US$15)

No. 13 Retirement income: recent developments and proposals (ISBN: 978-92-871-5705-8, €13 / US$20)

No. 14 Solidarity-based choices in the marketplace: a vital contribution to social cohesion (ISBN: 978-92-871-5761-4, €30 / US$45)

No. 15 Reconciling labour flexibility with social cohesion – Facing the challenge (ISBN: 978-92-871-5813-0, €35 / US$53)

No. 16 Reconciling labour flexibility with social cohesion – Ideas for political action (ISBN: 978-92-871-6014-0, €35 / US$53)

No. 17 Reconciling labour flexibility with social cohesion – The experiences and specificities of central and eastern Europe (ISBN: 978-92-871-6151-2, €39/ US$59)

No. 18 Achieving social cohesion in a multicultural Europe – Concepts, situation and developments (ISBN: 978-92-871-6033-1, €37 / US$56)

No. 19 Reconciling migrants' well-being and the public interest – Welfare state, firms and citizenship in transition (ISBN 978-92-871-6285-4, €44 /88$US)

Well-being for all
Concepts and tools for social cohesion

Trends in social cohesion, No. 20

Council of Europe Publishing

Cover design: Graphic Design Studio, Council of Europe

Council of Europe Publishing
F-67075 Strasbourg Cedex
http://book.coe.int

ISBN 978-92-871-6505-3
© Council of Europe, November 2008
Printed in Belgium

CONTENTS

Foreword 9
Alexander Vladychenko

Introduction 11
Gilda Farrell

**Part I – Well-being for all and citizens' involvement:
the approach of the Council of Europe**...................... 15

I. **Well-being for all as the objective
of social cohesion** 15
Gilda Farrell

1. Well-being and well-being for all: the differences..............................16

2. The benefits of the concept of well-being for all 17

3. A better understanding of the relationship between
subjective and objective well-being 24

4. Well-being for all as a means of improving life
in the community...27

Conclusion 29

References..31

Appendix: tables 32

II. **Involving citizens in defining and measuring well-being
and progress** 35
Samuel Thirion

Introduction 35

1. The proposed framework of our study 37

2. How to approach the question of well-being
(epistemological issues) 48

3. Working with citizens to develop knowledge
for societal progress – First findings from research............................55

4. Reflections on the key elements
of well-being for all..62

Conclusions..71

References..75

Appendix: methodology...76

Part II – The understanding and perception of well-being: individuals and goods..79

I. Understanding well-being to ensure that it is equitably accessible..79
Jean-Luc Dubois

Introduction...79

1. A general aspiration to well-being...80
2. Ensuring well-being: in search of a new ethics.........................87

Conclusion...94

References..96

Further reading..97

II. Well-being: perception and measurement................................99
Wolfgang Glatzer

Introduction...99

1. Well-being and its perception...99
2. Measurement of well-being..103
3. Public goods, context characteristics and national well-being in the social state.....................107
4. Private-public differentiation and well-being.........................108

Conclusions..114

References..116

Further reading..118

Part III – Well-being and responsibilities.............................119

I. The common good, well-being and the responsibility of local authorities...119
Iuli Nascimento

1. The common good and the public interest..............................119

2. Well-being and globalisation...122

3. Local authorities' role and responsibilities
and the tools at their disposal – The example of France
and the Île-de-France region 128

Conclusion 136

References...138

Further reading...138

II. **From ill-being to well-being: individual and
collective responsibilities** 141
Catherine Redelsperger

Introduction 141

1. Proposed definitions 142

2. Learning processes for a person's return to well-being:
individual and collective dimensions 145

3. The learning process of well-being/ill-being
as it affects wage-earners 151

Conclusion 159

**Part IV – The case for a society focusing on the common
good as a condition for well-being**............................161

From welfare state to welfare society 161
Bruno Amoroso

1. Collective imagination and well-being: the two utopias 161

2. Welfare society as a new project for well-being..............................169

Conclusion: access to, and the use of, resources and rights 180

References...182

FOREWORD

Well-being is a fashionable topic today, seen on advertising billboards as well as in numerous philosophical or scientific writings on the subject. This seems natural in a society seeking to procure complete satisfaction for all its members. Thus, after a period of strong economic growth granting easy access to mass consumption, citizens' concerns are shifting towards the purpose that it arguably defeats: well-being.

A distinction should now be drawn between individual well-being, as presented for example in advertisements, and well-being for all people. The latter concept, introduced by the Council of Europe in its revised Strategy for Social Cohesion as the ultimate goal of modern society, emphasises the fact that well-being cannot be attained unless it is shared. The well-being of one part of humanity is unattainable if another part is in a state of ill-being or if it is to be achieved at the expense of future generations, who thereby inherit an uncertain world stripped of resources.

This truth is increasingly obvious in a globalised world characterised by interdependence between peoples and generations and springs from the expression of the citizens themselves. Thus, in projects developed between the Council of Europe and certain municipalities and local players giving residents, workers, secondary-level students and others the opportunity to talk about their own well-being, some key dimensions of this concept invariably turn out to be the relationship with others, social balance and forms of responsibility and commitment.

Four years after the adoption of the revised Strategy for Social Cohesion and its development by a High-Level Task Force on Social Cohesion in the 21st Century, it is plain to see that the pursuit of common well-being in consultation and participation is an essential avenue for consolidating a society based on right and shared responsibilities. The present volume in the series "Trends in Social Cohesion" provides an overview of this question, grounded both in the results of the work conducted by the Social Cohesion Development Division and in research carried out elsewhere.

Alexander Vladychenko

Director General of Social Cohesion
Council of Europe

INTRODUCTION

In its Strategy for Social Cohesion[1] the Council of Europe defines social cohesion as the capacity of a society to ensure well-being for all its members, minimising disparities, and accentuates the importance of "social actors" joint responsibility for its attainment.

Four years after the adoption of this strategy (and one year after it was outlined in the conclusions of the High-Level Task Force on Social Cohesion in the 21st Century[2]), the current issue of "Trends in social cohesion" presents an initial appraisal of the worth of the key concepts fundamental to the strategy, particularly well-being for all and joint responsibility. The first two articles deal with some of the results of the work of analysis and research conducted by the Social Cohesion Development Division.[3] The other five are the outcome of reflections pursued elsewhere in various contexts, which the Council of Europe has collected together in order to make them known and to proclaim the importance for our Europe of well-being, construed as everyone's right.

The first article by Gilda Farrell, Head of the Social Cohesion Development Division at the Council of Europe, examines the implications of the concept of "well-being for all" as a societal goal. She demonstrates in particular how it differs from the concept of individual well-being and adds a new dimension to the concepts of freedom, choices and preferences. She clarifies the relationship between objectivity and subjectivity and also points to opportunities for mobilising each individual's potential and for learning to appreciate the value of intangible aspects in the evolution of official policies on social cohesion.

A second article takes stock of research completed and in progress to define and measure well-being for all and social cohesion at local level (territorial entity or structure) in conjunction with the players concerned and the citizens; this is the work of Samuel Thirion, Administrative Officer in the Social Cohesion Development Division. He proposes an

---

1. Council of Europe Strategy for Social Cohesion, revised version, approved by the Committee of Ministers on 31 March 2004.

2. Report on the conclusions of the High-Level Task Force on Social Cohesion in the 21st Century, 2007.

3. Work carried out subsequent to the publication of *Concerted Development of Social Cohesion Indicators – Methodological Guide*, Council of Europe, 2005.

interpretation sequence which provides a link with the concept of societal progress and its measurement, while exploring the relationship between assets and well-being.

These two articles, the product of the work carried out by the Council of Europe, advocate an endogenous approach in understanding well-being, one which proceeds from the citizens themselves and forms an indispensable counterpart to more exogenous approaches that involve analysing well-being through specific research of a philosophical or scientific nature. Besides its relevance, given the intrinsic subjectivity and interactivity of the concepts of well-being and well-being for all, this approach has many advantages (transversal perspective, mutual learning processes, low costs and ease of implementation) and shows that the concept of well-being for all is multidimensional.

However, as Jean-Luc Dubois demonstrates in a third article in this volume, if one surveys the exogenous approaches to well-being in the various fields (philosophical, economic and psychological), one still encounters the same multidimensional quality of the concept of well-being.

These two types of approach to well-being, endogenous or exogenous, thus converge and bring out the importance of the intangible dimensions – to be more precise, the "recognition" of each person as a player in society. This recognition is the key for furthering processes conducive to well-being which are founded on joint responsibility or mutual responsibility.

The pattern of apportionment of responsibilities and, more generally, everything to do with governance and human relations, has a crucial function. This is certainly one of the factors accounting for the discrepancies observed in modern societies between the sense of well-being (commonly referred to as "subjective well-being") and the material aspects of well-being (usually termed "objective well-being"). Wolfang Glatzer examines these questions in detail in the fourth article, drawing some essential inferences from them.

The next question is how to apply approaches relying on joint responsibility and more inclusive governance in a context of globalisation which does not make it easy. In the fifth article, Iuli Nascimento identifies avenues in this direction both at European level and at that of local and regional authorities, taking the Île-de-France region as an example.

The fact remains that such approaches are often difficult to achieve, if not well-nigh impossible in certain contexts, especially where they target people in difficulties who, after undergoing successive cycles of exclusion, have developed withdrawal mechanisms sometimes constituting real inhibitions. In the sixth article, Catherine Redelsperger, relying on her coaching experience with people affected by long-term unemployment and over-indebtedness, comes up with devices for rebuilding a path of trust and inclusion and gradually stimulating the desire to share responsibilities.

All these thoughts prompt the question of the assets needed to fuel processes generating well-being for everyone. Over and above the private or public material assets which are obvious and have no doubt often gained inordinate importance in developed societies, these analyses reveal the importance of intangible assets (there come to mind, of course, human rights, democracy, rule of law and all the regulatory mechanisms that allow their existence). Bruno Amoroso's cogitations in the final article of this volume thus concern the value and the function of the common good as the mainstay of a true ethic of conviviality (in the sense of living communally or together in one world) and of a social vision of the future.

In conclusion, while this volume confirms the aptness of the concepts proposed by the Council of Europe as regards social cohesion, it also allows the efforts made elsewhere to be appreciated. Above all, it demonstrates that securing well-being for everyone, and for future generations, requires new paradigms and new perceptions shared by the players, including the citizens as individuals.

Gilda Farrell

Head of the Social Cohesion Development Division
DG Social Cohesion
Council of Europe

PART I – WELL-BEING FOR ALL AND CITIZENS' INVOLVEMENT: THE APPROACH OF THE COUNCIL OF EUROPE

I. Well-being for all as the objective of social cohesion

Gilda Farrell[1]

> "The notion of preferences only has meaning in the context of unanimous preferences" (De Finetti, 1952).

This paper considers the notion of well-being for all as one of the objectives of social cohesion. It is based on research conducted by the Council of Europe in several European towns and cities, a multinational firm and a senior secondary school, or *lycée*. The research consisted of inviting ordinary citizens, whether employees or students, to consider three questions from the standpoint of interpersonal co-operation: what does well-being mean for you, what constitutes malaise or discontent and what are you prepared to do to contribute to well-being?[2] The fundamental difference between this and other studies lies less in the questions asked than in the fact that they were put to "groups of citizens". Such an approach, which emphasises the inter-relationships between their individual life circumstances and the social, economic and institutional changes in their environment, has enabled us to "objectivise" individual perceptions and achieve a consensus on what is essential for everyone. Even though well-being is essentially experienced individually,[3] when it is considered jointly it becomes a social objective. The Council of Europe therefore believes that discussing well-being for all is an essential element of living in a community.

---

1. Head of the Social Cohesion Development Division, DG Social Cohesion, Council of Europe.
2. The research was conducted in three European towns and cities: Mulhouse (France), Rovereto (Italy) and Timişoara (Romania), in the Strasbourg branch of a Finnish multinational firm (UPM) and in a Mulhouse *lycée*.
3. See article by Samuel Thirion.

1. Well-being and the well-being for all: the differences

> "Happiness is only real when shared." (Christopher McCandless, the young character in the film *Into the Wild*).[4]

As commonly understood, well-being is currently associated with what is ultimately good and thus, by implication, what is good for the individual. Various approaches can be distinguished, including hedonism (seeking the most positive balance between pleasure and pain), desire theory (satisfaction of preferences and the best possible life) and objective lists (of material and immaterial goods). Nowadays, we often associate well-being with products and forms of treatment capable of securing harmony between body and spirit, in accordance with certain standards of beauty. For evidence, it is simply necessary to enter "well-being" into a search engine. In this approach, individual well-being is closely linked to consumption.

We will use the term in a broader sense and refer to "well-being for all", as a concept that encompasses all of humanity, including future generations. The result of extending well-being to everyone is that the reference area, and the range and types of "goods" for achieving it, become universal and include interactions beyond purely local ones. The concept of well-being for all has to be a properly thought out construct, subject to constraints, consultations and mutual concessions. It embodies elements of equity and empathy and must be viewed over the long term.

If it is to become operational, that is subject to political intervention, the concept of well-being for all must apply within a defined area, such as a neighbourhood, town or factory. Nevertheless, in determining its components and the conditions that make it possible, account must be taken of the division of responsibilities between geographical areas and of the sometimes random elements of well-being that cannot be controlled at the level where the exercise is carried out.

Treating well-being for all as a universal right is not to deny those aspects that apply to individual well-being but simply shifts the focus of how it is perceived from the satisfaction of individual preferences to the

---

4. Book by Jon Krakauer, 1996, adapted for cinema in 2007 by Sean Penn.

formulation of agreed, or unanimous, preferences.[5] This approach also leads to the conclusion that individual well-being is a consequence not just of satisfaction and possession but also of sharing, and as such is the product of interactions: "Happiness is only real when shared". Here, the Greek word *eudaimonia*, or human flourishing, takes on a practical meaning in the form of a careful consideration of what constitute the fundamental aspects of well-being for all. This approach entails a quest for the answer to the question as to how to "be well" in society, involving an aspect of well-being likely to influence the formulation of knowledge and policies in areas such as creativity, expression, belonging, responsibility and solidarity.

The moral connotation of well-being, or how to achieve the well-being of others while still seeking one's own, thereby takes on another meaning, which is not that of virtue/goodness or obligation but rather that of understanding the interdependence between individual well-being and goods that are available to all. This approach is concerned less with maximising each individual's well-being than with inclusive optimisation, based on choices that are necessarily made in concert.

Finally, the aesthetic dimension and beauty – the capacity to transform the various spheres of community and personal lives – play leading parts as manifestations of human potential. "Making beautiful things" was one of the criteria of well-being identified by our groups of citizens. Beauty is one component of well-being.

2. The benefits of the concept of well-being for all

a. A shared vision

"Vision" is at the very heart of the definition of well-being for all. For example, the concept may not be confused with the accumulation and possession of goods, even if such assets do contribute to well-being. Without a vision, society can produce goods without adding to well-being. It is not an easy task to consider the question of vision against a

---

5. By unanimous preferences we mean ones about which there is a consensus, while recognising that there can always be conflicts on this question, particularly concerning the objectives of well-being of different groups of the population.

background of increasing individuality and a growing distance between how public/common and private goods are viewed.

First, however, it should be borne in mind that the Council of Europe's approach to defining well-being with ordinary citizens reintroduced an ethic of mutual responsibility, in which the participants stood aside from their individuality and immediate interests and developed their perceptions through a process of exchange. This contradicts the received view that our fellow citizens are unable to subscribe to shared visions. Emphasising a negative and egotistical individuality that condemns human beings to an exclusive concern for their own interests probably reflects an ideological viewpoint that seeks to reject each individual's potential for solidarity and sharing.

b. Another view of liberty

It is agreed that individual liberty depends on the ability to make choices and exercise responsibility. However, the dominant view, borrowed from neoclassical economics, reduces this freedom to choice in the market place. This confines the discussion to characteristics of goods that reflect individual tastes or constraints, such as price, colour or composition. It is a form of constrained or specific freedom since many of the components of goods remain invisible, opaque or not open to choice. This applies to such elements as human rights, preservation of the environment or decent working conditions, whereas taking these elements into account would lead to a more complex form of freedom of choice or a capacity for overall judgment. Because the choice of goods to maximise certain forms of utility or individual preferences is only concerned with specific elements it is not necessarily transformed into a choice of well-being. Paradoxically, too much choice or excessive fragmentation of supply may actually be to the detriment of individual freedom, since no one can choose satisfactorily from an unlimited range of goods. Moreover, this freedom is exhausted in the act of buying.

Our approach to well-being for all must reconsider the question of freedom from two standpoints:

- How can market choice be transformed into a potential creator of well-being? For example, when citizens agree to abide by collective decisions to buy local or green energy products by accepting seasonal or loyalty constraints, these "reasoned" constraints actually create freedom. They enable those concerned to discover previously unexplored means of expressing preferences that enrich each individual's capacity for overall judgment, thus increasing the impact on well-being for all.

- How can the capacity for choice in the civic or democratic arena be enhanced through the exercise of responsibility? This amounts to bridging the growing gap between ever more market choice and reduced choice in the public domain.[6]

c. *Another approach to the concept of goods*

Well-being for all is not just the exercise of a complex and reasoned form of freedom but is also rooted in the preservation and production of common goods.

A distinction must be drawn between public interest goods, such as universal self-fulfilment as a political objective,[7] involving the removal of barriers to achieving this goal, common goods and public goods.

Generally speaking, common goods are ones that are non-competitive, because their use by one person does not exclude others from benefiting at the same time, and non-excludable, in the sense that once produced consumers cannot easily be prevented from enjoying them.[8] (Pure) public goods – which by definition are non-exclusive and non-subtractive – are a particular category of common goods. Nevertheless, common goods are not all public or community goods in the broader sense. Instead, human communities find suitable combined methods of endogenous management to avoid conflict.

We shall consider material and immaterial common goods to be ones that society inherits or produces and then maintains in common. Material goods include the land, the environment, public utility services and water, while immaterial ones include knowledge, security, legality, confidence in social relationships, forms of recognition, market regulations and communal life. They are critical for well-being because increases or decreases in their supply directly affect the well-being of everyone (Donolo, 1997). They therefore point to an egalitarian vision of well-being. Awareness of their

---

6. For the impact of the exercise of democracy on well-being, see the works of Bruno Frey, including Frey and Stutzer, 2000.
7. Article 3 of the Italian Constitution.
8. See the article by Bruno Amoroso.

value leads to a rejection of inequalities and abuses that threaten individual well-being. To have equal well-being is to enjoy the same capacity to participate in general activities (Negri, 2006) and this is only possible if common goods continue to be produced and maintained.

In contrast to studies based on data from individual surveys, which highlight the widening gap between how people perceive their own and national assets and well-being, those taking part in the Council of Europe exercise are aware that a reduced level of common goods damages well-being (though they may be less aware of the growing gap between private affluence and public squalor).[9] They were concerned by the depletion of common goods resulting from excess pollution, green belt speculation, inadequate transport and nurseries, lack of meeting places, exclusion from the exercise of responsibilities and so on. They also recognised that the value of individual incomes varied according to the availability of common goods (Arena, 2008) and supported policies to prevent their decline and encourage their growth through active citizen participation.

These reactions suggest that, as Galbraith correctly points out (Galbraith, 2004), the perceived gap between personal and national well-being is due in part to the dominant myth of two sectors, which ascribes much higher value to private than to public assets – the personal vacuum cleaner rather than the people who collect the rubbish – but it also arises from the confusion between public and common goods. This confusion leaves citizens feeling isolated from the management of their communities.

Public goods are ones administered by the state while the very notion of a common good implies active citizen participation and responsibility. In Rovereto, for example, as part of their commitment to well-being, local citizens have offered to take responsibility for a neighbourhood of the town so that they can look after common goods and public buildings, where everyone can meet. Transparency in public administration is also considered to be a key component of well-being and an essential means of securing citizen commitment to raising the level of well-being for all. Our vision of well-being therefore implies a strong link between public and common goods, but they should not be seen as identical.

---

9. See the article by Wolfgang Glatzer.

d. The key role of non-material elements in the sense of well-being

The citizen studies have shown that well-being has both material and non-material dimensions and that the latter are very important.[10]

In traditional theory, non-material aspects are practically ignored and are confined to a sense of well-being or level of satisfaction. How this so-called "subjective well-being" is measured depends on the subject. Subjective well-being is therefore usually taken to mean the satisfaction of preferences and the general conditions of life that individuals obtain from their choices and includes the notion of maximising pleasure. However, since other non-material components of well-being, such as recognition, empathy/solidarity and civic spirit, are also subjective measures, we prefer to use the term "sense of", rather than "subjective" well-being.

How do traditional approaches deal with this sense of well-being?

The relationship between economic growth, individual happiness and a sense of personal peace has been examined in various contexts and countries. Most of these studies have been based on individual surveys, with a hedonistic approach – the balance of pleasure and pain – as the common thread.

Individual responses on overall satisfaction may vary according to circumstances and different factors (Kahneman and Krueger, 2006), such as the weather, the feeling of being lucky or recent press coverage of a particular crime. Various methods have therefore been proposed to measure long-term well-being. First, a distinction is made between the retrospective and the real, using the concepts of "momentary utility" and "experienced utility" (Kahneman and Thaler, 2006). Second, in order to identify particular episodes while avoiding general assessments of respondents' lives, those concerned are asked to concentrate on specific facts or events without reference to the context, for example using the so-called day reconstruction method. The resulting U-index, which measures the proportion of time that people spend in an unpleasant state, has been proposed as a measure of society's well-being (Kahneman and Kruger, 2006: 18-21).

---

10. See article by Samuel Thirion.

Some of the conclusions on how this U-index can be used to measure sense of well-being (*ibidem*: 22)[11] coincide with ones we have drawn from the exercises with citizens, particularly regarding the possible influence of public policies on individuals' choices:

- First is the idea that the sense of well-being may be increased by moving from policies that encourage greater consumption to ones that promote and reinforce social contacts and relationships. In the absence of "relational goods" (Becchetti, 2005),[12] citizens call for policies that encourage the establishment of meeting places and contact points, including ones with foreign nationals and migrants, and may even propose that public buildings be set aside for that purpose.

- Then there is the notion that the sense of well-being will be assisted by a switch from policies that implicitly or explicitly emphasise the importance of income to personal well-being to ones that acknowledge individuals' worth and their contribution to society. In the absence of genuine democratic forums in which each individual's dignity and contribution is properly acknowledged, citizens claim a right of recognition and to have their voice heard in the public arena.

- Finally, there is the idea that even if people are reasonably adaptable and have fairly stable levels of satisfaction, their sense of well-being is affected by changes in the use of time. People realise that inability to manage stress is destabilising and a source of discontent and therefore view cities and towns on a human scale – accessible without too much investment in time and with properly functioning public transport and reasonably flexible and efficient bureaucracy that avoids long queues – as genuine constituents of well-being. Notions such as receiving services without queuing, doing things without feeling pressurised or having the right to make mistakes show that control of one's time is a key aspect of a sense of well-being. They show how much pressure results from the time and

---

11. The authors speak of "maximising subjective well-being".

12. Becchetti argues that individual and collective well-being depend not just on production and consumption but also on the ability to enjoy relational and environmental goods, which are deemed to be goods in their own right and not just inputs to the productive process.

energy invested in – for example – avoiding social disapproval of mistakes ... as if there was no longer any time to rectify them.

Nevertheless, despite these areas of convergence, other dimensions of the relationship between sense of well-being and living environment fail to emerge from the individual approach. Moreover, its very significance and the conclusions to be drawn from it need to be questioned. The "reasoned and shared" approach mobilises the human potential that is essential to achieving well-being for all and at the same time requires us to formulate the preconditions of well-being as explicit rights, that is ones that are applicable to all. These two aspects are considered below.

First, however, we should consider two aspects of the sense of well-being that affect the right to privacy and the right to exercise responsibility:

- Citizens believe that outside interference in their lives is increasing, with a consequent diminution of their freedom of choice. The sources of discontent that they cite include safety measures that prevent risk taking and being under constant surveillance or subject to constant influence. One means of achieving a sense of well-being is to develop ways of improving social and personal confidence to counter the feeling that individuals' behaviour is excessively influenced by fear and/or advertising.

- Citizens' groups have also said that there is no worse form of alienation than that of not exercising responsibility. This shows just how intolerable they find it to be denied any forum for exercising responsibility in order to influence the future direction of society. Failure to exercise such responsibility creates a feeling of personal incompleteness and inability to affect the future. A combination of universal welfare policies and policies to promote active participation in public life should contribute to a sense of well-being.

To summarise, it is difficult to resolve the issue – from a policy perspective – of what constitutes an individual sense of well-being without taking account of non-material aspects such as the opportunity to take initiatives, the exercise of responsibility, the right to make mistakes and the right to recognition. This is shown by the findings of studies in which persons have been interviewed in isolation, where suggestions on how to achieve satisfaction have concentrated on the policy area, in other words the necessary changes to public life. If the areas for change are situated in the very core of public life, surely it would make sense to employ methods right from the start which allow the communities themselves to define what those aspects of immaterial well-being are? If everyone is to enjoy a sense of well-being, there have to be changes to and extensions of rights – that is, these universal forms of recognition – and common goods.

Well-being for all is therefore much more than the sum of individuals' well-being, so to think it can be achieved without the active commitment of those concerned, namely ordinary citizens, is in some ways to deny the very essence of the concept. Agreement on what constitutes well-being opens the way to a form of community preference, based on unanimity or at least potential unanimity, which is more than just the aggregate of individual goods or preferences. Citizens have a vision of well-being in which some of the "goods" that comprise it are the product of interaction between individuals and the community, between citizens and their environment. In the studies, the participants saw well-being in terms of "meaning", "lack of fear of the future", "life projects", "exercising responsibility", "recognition of everyone's worth" and "the value of participation in the public arena", thus emphasising the interactive nature of the process.

3. A better understanding of the relationship between subjective and objective well-being

Numerous works and writers refer to the disparity between subjective and objective well-being. However, it would be more accurate to speak of the difference between the material aspects of well-being and a sense of well-being. Individuals' adaptability means that material improvements have only a short-term effect on their subjective perception of well-being. In the long term, therefore, higher income or greater wealth have no identifiable effect. There are various examples to show why the rising expectations that accompany real changes in average purchasing power nullify any sense of improvement in subjective well-being.[13]

Studies of the economy of the welfare state have already shown that there is no direct or linear relationship between objective and subjective indicators of well-being. The difference is apparently the result of a disparity that is inherent in all human kind, namely that the individual standpoint may not necessarily coincide with public experience, which is objective, because it is common to all (Da Fonseca, 2001). Nevertheless,

---

13. For example, in China, where average income rose by 250% between 1994 and 2005 the percentage of persons satisfied fell and the percentage of those dissatisfied rose (see Kahneman and Krueger, 2006: 16).

there seems to be confusion about the difference between objective and subjective well-being. The research carried out with citizens should be considered from three standpoints:

- The actual concept of well-being is by its nature subjective, in that it is the subject him- or herself who has to define it.[14] Nevertheless, the concept of well-being for all is a social construction.

- How can well-being be measured? The material components may be measured objectively, such as average income per head or square metres of living space per person. However, most of the non-material elements are essentially subjective, particularly where they reflect perceptions, feelings, types of use, interactions and so on.

- Finally, there are the criteria of well-being. An objective criterion is one on which there is consensus, or unanimity, and which forms part of a shared vision with others. For example, there is unanimity about housing as a key component of well-being – making it "objective". However, within this heading, criteria may differ from one person to another. Roma/Gypsies see places for their caravans as criteria whereas for others a roof over their heads is essential.

As a result, the close correlation between objective and quantitative is only relevant when "objective" is defined as being independent of the subject, whereas when "objective" also corresponds to "unanimous", the measure may also become qualitative.

The feeling of well-being as the result of complex inter-relationships

The observation, noted by numerous researchers, that an increase in wealth may coincide with fewer persons expressing satisfaction and a rise in the number who are dissatisfied, thus a lower level of perceived well-being, is the result of attempts to equate a simple, quantitative and national measurement – the increase in traded goods and services as measured by their price – with a complex, qualitative and individual phenomenon – the sense of well-being.

---

14. See article by Samuel Thirion.

In studies of the economics of happiness[15] – defined by Richard Layard as "feeling good, enjoying life and wanting this feeling to continue" – the measurement of well-being includes non-quantitative elements on which there is unanimity, such as security, stability and efficient public services (Layard, 2005). Other writers have emphasised the importance of other non-quantitative elements of well-being linked to public affairs, such as the exercise of democratic rights (Frey and Stutzer, 2000). All these studies point to a complex and multidimensional definition of well-being, particularly well-being for all. We will return to this question with particular reference to the problem of how to bridge the gap between changes in material conditions and the perception of well-being.

However, there are other explanations for the disparity between rising incomes and satisfaction levels, particularly ones linked to how individuals view their past and future. According to certain writers (Easterlin, 2001), individuals tend to view the past with bitterness and the future with optimism on the assumption that their income will rise, as a result of which they adjust their aspirations. Their previous standard of life is deemed unsatisfactory in the light of current aspirations. On the other hand, future prospects are seen as positive because their rising aspirations can be met. It has also been argued that the weight of past experience declines, at the expense of social comparisons – so-called relativism – particularly when a certain income level is reached. Beyond such a level, individuals are concerned not just with their absolute well-being but also with their relative position in society.

These observations are mainly based on surveys that assume a certain element of determinism in the life cycle and are guided by an ideology that gives little thought to alternative uses of resources – both time and income – and is strictly confined to rising consumption. They are also confined to individuals' own life cycles and take no account of intergenerational relationships. Thus, they do not consider the well-being that may flow from the ability to influence the well-being of future generations.

The evidence does not support such assumptions. In Italy, for example, recent studies have shown that the new generations consider themselves to be less well-off than the previous ones and that their material well-being will not be greater than that of their parents. This breakdown of

---

15. See article by Jean-Luc Dubois for a discussion on the meaning of happiness and well-being.

certainty about the future poses a challenge to determinist theories about how individuals view the past and what is to come.

4. Well-being for all as a means of improving life in the community

The foregoing discussions raise the issue of whether there is a hierarchy of material and non-material components of well-being for all, or in other words whether there are priorities for improving life in the community and how best to frame the question.

This is a perfectly meaningful question when well-being for all is considered in all its complexity and multiple aspects. Thus, the Council of Europe's research shows that there are numerous criteria of well-being and that they reflect various dimensions of life in society: equitable access to rights and resources; good environmental conditions (including aesthetic aspects); the conditions for legality; relations with institutions; personal and collective relationships; time management; opportunities for everyone to develop their potential for responsibility and solidarity and their competences. How possible is it to establish hierarchies of these dimensions and where is the best place to start?

We would maintain that, by itself, no material improvement can totally satisfy individuals, though consideration must also be given to individuals and groups made vulnerable by economic processes. The well-being of the poor does depend on their access to decent material living conditions, on which there is unanimous agreement, thus making them both objectives and priorities.

However, once such unanimously agreed objective material conditions are satisfied, "recognition" becomes an acknowledged priority. "Recognition" is what our democratic societies promise and focuses on individual rights. Failure to take account of this criterion of well-being demotivates citizens in all areas of social and economic life.[16]

This can be illustrated by our analysis of well-being in a firm.[17] Here, managers and other employees drew up criteria for defining well-being

---

16. Our argument here is based not on material relativism but on the idea that in societies where needs are satisfied, people compare themselves in terms of degree of recognition.

17. The exercise took place in Stracel – a branch of UPM in Strasbourg.

and indicators to measure it (Table 1) and then allocated various values to those indicators in the light of the firm's policies (Table 2). Table 2 shows that the largest gap between indicators concerns employees' perception of their commitment, over and above their obligations, compared with the level of the wage or salary received in exchange for the contracted duties. Even if the salary is acknowledged to be fair in the local context, it does not satisfy the need for recognition of the efforts made. Among the priorities[18] for increasing well-being in the firm put forward at the end of the analysis, the participants identified the need for internal management policies to improve hierarchical relationships, greater recognition for employee ideas and suggestions and more transparent and efficient communication (including orders). Admittedly, they also sought a more individually tailored pay structure, in other words one that recognised individual productive effort.

As in the case of the firm, some 30 indicators emerged unanimously from the study of well-being in local areas, and the Council of Europe has grouped these into eight families.[19] This multidimensionality is a plus for social cohesion because it opens up numerous policy options and makes it clear that any government action can be assessed on the basis of its effects on well-being, rather than purely in terms of immediate impact, therefore creating virtuous circles of well-being through the operation of induced effects. Such an approach may result in the design and application of government actions themselves being revised at an early stage.[20]

a. Well-being for all as a motivating factor

Giving priority to raising average income as a means of increasing well-being ignores the social fragmentation and resulting social immobility that growing disparities bring about, whereas well-being for all is a much more motivating concept. A discussion-based approach to defining well-being for all draws on each individual's potential to contribute to community

---

18. Following the participative construction of indicators of well-being in Stracel, an action plan was prepared to deal with deficiencies in well-being, particularly in the non-material domain. For information/contact see:
http://w3.upm-kymmene.com/upm/internet/cms/upmcmsfr.nsf/$all/AF429D46A847 490FC2257069003E5287?Open&qm=menu,0,0,0.

19. These are: means of life (individual rights); living environment; institutional relationships; social relationships; perceptions/feelings; social equilibrium; individual equilibrium; participation/commitment.

20. See article by Samuel Thirion.

life. The fact that everyone can participate makes it an inclusive concept in the real sense of the term, and includes the dimension of tolerance or the right to make mistakes.

An emphasis on general, rather than just individual, well-being means that people can work together to improve it and offers a greater insight into how interaction can help to create well-being, including the element of personal fulfilment.

b. Defining well-being in terms of rights applicable to all

One of the most important consequences of the Council of Europe research is an awareness of the need for inclusivity. Such an inclusive approach requires the criteria of well-being to be expressed in terms of "rights", in other words ones that are valid for everyone, irrespective of other circumstances. It should be noted that the rights claimed by citizens in connection with well-being go beyond existing recognised and formalised fundamental rights, because the latter are primarily material in character whereas the former also include non-material aspects. They include, for example, the right to make mistakes, to privacy, to a second chance, to exercise responsibility, to take risks without fear for one's safety, to be recognised, to express oneself in public and be heard, to influence decisions affecting the community, to equal treatment and so on. They reflect people's reaction to the failure of democracy to keep its promises or its descent into bureaucratic procedures that nullify the potential of individual participation and responsibility. If well-being is to be a universal entitlement it will need public forums in which everyone's opinions will be given their due weight.

Conclusion

Well-being for all is the product of a multiplicity of personal, occupational and economic interactions that are always subject to change. It therefore often appears unstable. The Council of Europe considers that to maintain the stability of well-being for all in the long term requires not the elimination of day-to-day hazards but the production and continuing availability of common goods, including means of offering individuals recognition, as intrinsic elements of democracy and social rights. A society that enjoys well-being has a vision of common goods that serve the dual purpose of reducing individual vulnerability and fears and increasing and protecting the scope for active participation in public life. According to Hannah Arendt and Margaret Canovan (1998), there are only two ways of countering the fear of irreversibility: forgiveness, including from our point of view the right to make mistakes, and standing by promises and commitments, including recognition of each individual and his or her potential for responsibility. Common goods are a key element of keeping the promises and meeting the commitments of well-being, as means of ensuring that everyone has a stake in and can participate in the community, including its aesthetic dimension.

The research conducted or supported by the Council of Europe offers one way forward. Even so, it has its limits. In identifying criteria, citizens do not reveal the full potential of well-being for all, which may suddenly emerge from changes in their individual relationships with markets, particularly in the field of consumption. "Consumption" is nearly always seen as a factor for personal satisfaction, apart from its environmental consequences, particularly in connection with waste disposal. It will not be possible to take on board all the different dimensions of human interaction until the production of goods ceases to take precedence over well-being for all.

References

Arena, Gregorio, "La 'tragedia dei beni comuni'", Labsus, Laboratorio per la sussidiarietà, 3 March 2008, http://www.labsus.org.

Arendt, Hannah and Canovan, Margaret, *The Human Condition* (second edition), University of Chicago Press, 1998.

Becchetti, Leonardo, *La Felicita Sostenibile – Economia della responsabilità sociale*, Donzelli Editori, 2005.

Donolo, Carlo, *L'intelligenza delle istituzioni*, Feltrinelli, 1997.

Easterlin, R.A., "Income and Happiness: Towards a Unified Theory", *Economic Journal*, Vol. 111, No. 473, July 2001, pp. 465-484.

De Finetti, Bruno, "Sulle preferibilità", *Giornale degli Economisti*, Vol. XI, 1952, pp. 685-709, cited by Rosaria Adriani, "Bruno de Finetti e la geometria del benessere", Università di Pisa, Dipartimento d'Economia, www.dse.ec.unipi.it/seminari/lunch/Paper_pdf/Adriani.pdf.

Da Fonseca, Eduardo Giannetti, "Economia e felicità", https://nextonline. it/archivio/13/index/htm. Next No. 13, 2001.

Frey, Bruno S. and Stutzer, Alois, "Happiness, Economy and Institutions", *Economic Journal*, Vol. 110, No. 466, 2000, pp. 918-938.

Galbraith, J.K., *The Economics of Innocent Fraud*, Houghton Mifflin, 2004.

Kahneman, Daniel and Krueger, Alan B., "Developments in the Measurement of Subjective Well-being". *Journal of Economic Perspectives,* Vol. 20, No. 1, Winter 2006, pp. 3-24.

Kahneman, Daniel and Thaler, Richard H., "Anomalies: Utility Maximization and Experienced Utility", *Journal of Economic Perspectives*, Vol. 20, No. 1, Winter 2006, pp. 221-234.

Layard, Richard, *Happiness: Lessons From a New Science*, Allen Lane, London, 2005.

Negri, Antonio, *Goodbye Mr Socialism,* Feltrinelli, 2006.

Appendix: tables

Table 1 – Indicators of well-being in employment

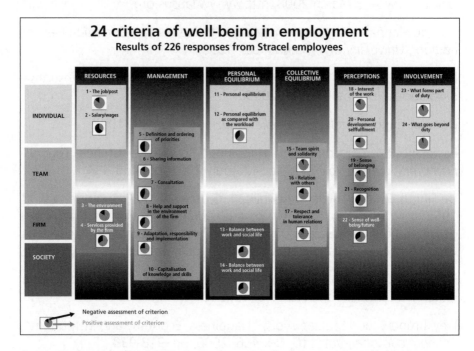

Source: "Indicators of Well-being in Employment", final report prepared by Cathy Fanton, consultant to the agreement between Stracel, the Council of Europe and the Strasbourg and Bas-Rhin Chamber of Commerce and Industry.

Table 2 – Employee assessment of indicators of well-being in employment

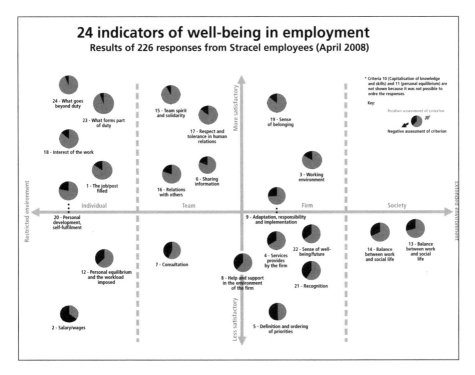

24 indicators of well-being in employment
Results of 226 responses from Stracel employees (April 2008)

Source: "Indicators of Well-being in Employment", final report prepared by Cathy Fanton, consultant to the agreement between Stracel, the Council of Europe and the Strasbourg and Bas-Rhin Chamber of Commerce and Industry.

II. Involving citizens in defining and measuring well-being and progress

Samuel Thirion[1]

Introduction

a. *The need for a review of social progress indicators*

Since national statistics began to be kept, gross domestic product (GDP) growth has served as the reference indicator for measuring the progress made by modern societies, chosen on the basis of a very widely accepted notion that economic growth *per se* brings greater overall well-being to humankind. This widespread belief, however, has now been cast into doubt by the realisation that growth, judged solely by this yardstick, has negative side-effects, and that populations' subjective indicators of well-being are stationary, or even in decline, as are many social and environmental indicators, while GDP continues to climb.

These contradictions necessitate a new definition of progress, making it a question for society as a whole. Thanks to the Organisation for Economic Co-operation and Development (OECD),[2] discussion of this issue has been given new impetus through the participation of a wide range of public institutions, some at international level. The fact remains that, as this is a question for society as a whole, a wide-ranging democratic debate on the subject needs to be possible, with citizens themselves as its starting point.

b. *Well-being for all as a reference point*

When giving thought to progress, it is quite logical to use as a reference point well-being for all.[3] Well-being is in fact defined as a reflection of the satisfaction to which all human beings aspire, as do living creatures in general. Well-being for all, future generations included (and, by a process

---

1. Administrative Officer, Social Cohesion Development Division, DG Social Cohesion, Council of Europe.
2. See, *inter alia*, OECD: "Global Project on Measuring the Progress of Societies – Towards a Strategic Action Plan", currently in preparation.
3. See Gilda Farrell's article in this volume.

of deduction, that of the planet), is thus a reflection of society's ultimate objective in a globalised context. It must be possible for any progress indicator to refer to this objective.

The fundamental question which then arises is that of how to approach the subject of well-being: how it is to be defined, measured and used as a basis for developing social progress indicators. This question is far from banal, for it takes us into the realms of epistemology, well beyond the search for appropriate techniques to use for surveys or for composite indices. If we fail to raise the question at this level, we shall have to continue to use conventional approaches inappropriate to the nature of well-being.

This is why, once we have set out the framework of our study (part one of this article), we shall endeavour to grasp the nature of the concept of well-being, and what this implies for the way in which we define and tackle it (part two). Hence our re-examination of study methods and our devising of an appropriate approach based, de facto, on citizens themselves.

c. The approach taken by the Council of Europe: one possible response

This is precisely the approach that the Council of Europe decided to take in its Strategy for Social Cohesion,[4] which is based on the realisation that the developments that began in the 1970s in Europe and elsewhere and the increasing globalisation of the economy make it impossible to continue to consider human rights, especially social and economic rights, as matters for which states alone are responsible (as they are understood to be in the welfare state context), for they now have to be regarded as the responsibility of society as a whole. The shift from a welfare state to a welfare society brings with it shared responsibility for the players.[5] Therefore the Council of Europe defines social cohesion as "the capacity of a society to ensure the welfare of all its members, minimising disparities" and places emphasis on the shared responsibility of the various stakeholders in society which is necessary to achieve this. The promotion of shared responsibility for the welfare of all presupposes that well-being can be defined as a shared objective; hence the idea of a concerted effort to devise indicators of well-being and of social cohesion.

---

4. Revised version of 2004.
5. See article by Bruno Amoroso.

The *Concerted Development of Social Cohesion Indicators – Methodological Guide* (hereinafter referred to as "the methodological guide") was prepared and published in 2005 (Council of Europe, 2005), and has subsequently been put to use in a number of local and regional contexts (cities, neighbourhoods, local communities) and institutions (businesses, schools, etc.), and we shall report on these applications in the third part of this article. The early results show how many dimensions there are to the concept of well-being for all. They give the concept greater meaning and enable the first pointers to be given to an understanding of its complexity. They reveal the interactive and systemic nature of the various component parts of well-being, resulting in, depending on the circumstances, either virtuous circles (generating well-being) or vicious circles (generating ill-being).

This overall, systemic view of well-being, still a very general one, is being gradually fine-tuned by the experience now being gained and through comparison with the research being done by various writers, some crucial examples of which are described in the other articles in this volume. Without making any claim to certainty about positions which are still merely theoretical, we shall, in part four, present the main conclusions and questions which emerge from our study of well-being.

1. The proposed framework of our study

a. *The key components of well-being: initial assumptions*

The methodological guide puts forward a view of social cohesion which encompasses three components (together forming a social cohesion "tree"), each with its own objective:

- the first component is the situation of individuals, represented by the foliage; the objective at this level is well-being for all;

- the second is human activities, represented by the tree trunk; the objective is shared responsibility;

- the third is social capital (trust, bonds, shared values, knowledge, etc.), represented by the tree roots; the objective is to get the tree firmly and permanently established, enabling it to withstand the conditions prevailing at any given time.

A number of key elements[6] crucial to the development of a virtuous circle of well-being have been identified (Council of Europe, 2005: 49-58) in respect of each of these components:

- component one has four: fair access; dignity and recognition of each person in his or her diversity; autonomy and personal, family and occupational development; commitment/participation of citizens;

- component two depends on responsibility being shared among the players, and on the conditions for that sharing (shared objective of well-being, citizenship, associative approach, democratic skills and an economy geared to individual and community well-being);

- component three depends on the values of citizenship (sense of justice and the common good, solidarity and responsibility, tolerance of/openness to/interest in difference), transverse links, trust and shared knowledge.

Following the research carried out by the Council of Europe in various areas and institutions in order, with the help of citizens, to produce indicators of well-being, these theories have proved particularly useful, casting light on the interaction between different dimensions of well-being (see part four of this article).

b. Well-being and (common) goods

An analysis of the factors in, and conditions of, the maximisation of well-being and minimisation of ill-being throws up the question of the resources that can be used to develop well-being, widely referred to as goods.

Bearing in mind that, by definition, a good is any resource useful to well-being for all, we need to view goods in terms of their societal function. They may be of a particular (usually private) nature, things like clothes, diaries, personal computers and so on, or they may be common goods, such as air, mutual trust, shared identities, social rights and social protec-

---

6. When the methodological guide was written, identification of these key elements was not based on any systematic or scientific analysis, but on general observations and thoughts which were both a matter of common sense and widely acknowledged within the Council of Europe and elsewhere; hence their status as assumptions, albeit ones which are regarded as likely and fairly logical. They cannot really be said to have been systematically verified, nor their meaning and reasons wholly understood.

tion. There are several levels within the category of common goods: a park is a common good shared by all who live nearby, whereas the air is a common good for the whole of humankind and the other creatures living on the planet.

On the basis of this definition, we shall consider six kinds of goods,[7] the first two of which take physical form, while the other four are not material goods.

The six are:

- economic goods (infrastructure, equipment, businesses, markets, etc.);

- environmental goods (soil and subsoil, water, the biosphere – namely, living beings, biodiversity and ecosystems – and air);

- human capital (population, knowledge, skills, etc.);

- social capital (human relations and bonds, trust);

- cultural capital (shared values, knowledge of history, sciences, etc.);

- institutional and political capital (democratic institutions, human rights, rules, regulatory arrangements, etc.).

Taking another look now at the social cohesion tree already referred to, let us consider the same image again, but without limiting the tree roots to social capital. We shall regard each of the six kinds of goods/capital as forming one root, with each root in turn being subdivided. What we now see is a tree depicting sustainable development, defined as society's capacity to ensure well-being for all, including future generations, in a relationship of equity, through the sharing of responsibility among the various stakeholders.

---

7. It should be noted that the word "capital" may be preferred to "goods" (especially when referring to non-physical aspects). "Capital" is a word which suggests something useful that accumulates and remains over a period of time to be put to good use. As we shall see from our analysis of the interaction between different dimensions of well-being, this is the characteristic which provides the fundamental distinction between good and well-being, so that they are no longer regarded as the two ends of a linear chain of cause and effect, with goods at one end and well-being at the other, but as two kinds of element interactive in a non-linear system.

The main feature of this image to be borne in mind is the three-stage structure, which is extremely helpful to anyone wishing to grasp the inter-relationship between goods and well-being (see Diagram 1).

Each of the three stages is of a different kind (state, action, resources) and it is the relationship between the three and the activities in the centre that reveals the relations between goods and well-being. We see that, to a greater or lesser degree, every human activity of any kind (manufacturing, creation, services, consumption, leisure activities, etc.) leads to the consumption of some goods and the generation of other goods and well-being. The other side of the coin is that, clearly, well-being/ill-being has its own effect on activities.

Diagram 1 – The three stages of the "sustainable development tree"

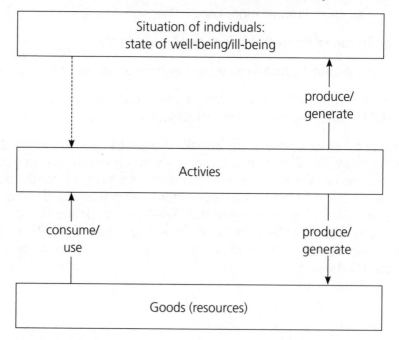

c. Well-being, goods and progress indicators

The concept of progress bears within it the idea of drawing closer to a goal, a state that one is endeavouring to achieve. Progress along a road, for instance, is impossible to imagine unless the destination is known. Someone who is walking along may have no other ambition than to go for a walk, in which case he or she will not speak of progress, but of moving along, and of the pleasure given by the activity of walking. Even if the whereabouts and exact appearance of the objective are unknown, there must at least be some awareness of its existence and a desire to get there, before we can refer to progress. And the more precisely the objective, the direction of travel and the available paths are known, the more possible it will be to assess and to measure progress and to create appropriate indicators.

If we apply the same argument to society, we can see that, unless we have agreed on society's ultimate objective, any effort to create progress indicators is likely to be unsuccessful and unclear, or even misleading. It would be rather like picking up a tape measure to establish the distance covered without knowing which direction to take the measurement in. And the ease with which a measurement can be taken in a given direction does not make that one the right direction!

Looking back to our earlier thoughts, we could say that society's ultimate objective is to be able to ensure the well-being of both present and future generations. If we link this up to goods, we might say that it is society's ability to ensure well-being for all and the production and preservation of the requisite goods.

In order to measure progress towards that objective, therefore, we must establish the extent to which society is capable of engaging in (and effectively engages in) activities (in terms of production, consumption, leisure activities, etc.) which ensure well-being for all, while generating and preserving the necessary goods. The question arises not only of the knowledge of the situation at a given time – t (progress indicator) – but also of the knowledge of the action taken in the direction of progress: what needs to be done, in a given situation, so that society effectively engages in activities which ensure well-being for all, while generating and preserving the requisite goods.

We might therefore subdivide these questions as shown below (Table 1), highlighting the logical relationships between six questions relating to the progress of society.

Table 1 – The six questions relating to the progress of society

Knowledge of the situation in terms of progress (progress indicators)		Knowledge of what still needs to be done	
1. To what extent do human activities ensure:	1.a. well-being for all?	2. What needs to be done so that human activities ensure:	2.a. well-being for all?
	1.b. the production of the requisite goods?		2.b. the production of the requisite goods?
	1.c. the preservation and beneficial use of the goods, and thus at least a balance between goods lost (e.g. through use) and goods regenerated?		2.c. the preservation and beneficial use of the goods, and thus at least a balance between goods lost (e.g. through use) and goods regenerated?

These questions make it easier to grasp both the benefits and limitations of GDP and the additional progress indicators that need to be developed. GDP, a measurement of economic activity in monetary terms, is in fact an indicator that can be applied only to question 1.b, and only in part: in practice it measures the goods produced that can be traded on the market, the price of which can therefore be measured, to the exclusion of all other goods (such as non-physical public property in the form of human rights, social protection, social capital, etc.). This is not the only limitation: measuring a good by its price brings several different angles into play (no account is taken of domestic or voluntary work; prices vary in the light of supply and demand; productivity improvements are not taken into account and so on), and GDP remains an overall performance indicator relating to the production of goods (annual quantities produced), thus providing indirect information about the capacity to produce goods (only those measurable in terms of price).

The progress of society measured solely in terms of GDP is subject to a great imbalance in respect of the questions already referred to where well-being for all is concerned: while considerable progress has been made in terms of the production of tradable goods (as reflected in dramatic productivity gains and the quantities of material goods available in the modern world), performance in terms of preservation is very poor, jeopardising the supply of environmental, but also other equally important, goods essential to the well-being of future generations. Performance in terms of the generation of well-being also remains well below what would be achievable with the goods available. We shall come back to this later.

There are a number of ways in which GDP can be adjusted to make it a more appropriate progress indicator, one being the Genuine Progress Indicator (GPI), while other new indicators have also been introduced, such as the Human Development Index (HDI).[8] As Takayoshi Kusago (2007: 89) points out, however, it is impossible to build up a system of progress indicators without reference to the question of overall satisfaction. It would also be difficult to create a satisfactory system of progress indicators simply by making a series of adjustments to GDP, without taking as the starting point some new thinking about the objectives.

Several conclusions have been drawn.

Firstly, if we give thought to the objectives, we come up with a number of questions and knowledge needs. The objective for society proposed above implies six questions, each of which arises at two levels:

- at the level of each human activity: to what extent does an activity contribute to well-being, generate goods (beneficial to well-being) and help to preserve goods, and what needs to be done in order for it to make such a contribution?

- at the level of society as a whole: to what extent do all activities make it possible in general terms to ensure well-being for all and the production and preservation of the requisite goods and what needs to be done to achieve this? A fundamental subsidiary question is how the players share out responsibility for this overall performance.

In order to answer these questions, it is necessary to:

- know how to define well-being;

- be able to identify the goods that are necessary to well-being.

An overview of this "cascade" of logical relationships appears in Table 2 below.

---

8. See article by Wolfgang Glatzer.

Table 2 – Relationships between the objective for society, the questions raised and the knowledge needs for progress

Objective for society		Society's capacity to ensure well-being for all and the production and preservation of the requisite goods
Six questions	Three questions to measure progress vis-à-vis the objective for society	1. To what extent do human activities ensure i. well-being for all, ii. the production of the requisite goods and iii. their preservation?
	Three questions to find out what must be done to achieve the objective for society	2. What needs to be done so that human activities ensure i. well-being for all, ii. the production of the requisite goods and iii. their preservation?
Two levels at which these questions arise		– at the level of every human activity – at the level of all activities.
Basic knowledge needed to answer these questions		– definition of well-being – identification of the goods necessary to well-being – knowledge of the conditions of their production and preservation.

The result is 12 kinds of knowledge that need to be built up for progress:

1. definition of what constitutes well-being for all (objective of the society);

2. knowledge of current situations of well-being/ill-being (overall contribution of human activities);

3. knowledge of the contribution made by existing activities;

4. knowledge of the possible improvements of existing activities;

5. knowledge of the overall improvements to be made;

6. identification/choice of the most relevant/efficient new actions to be implemented for progress towards well-being of all;

7. knowledge of the goods necessary for well-being;

8. knowledge of existing goods (overall contribution of activities to the production and preservation of goods);

9. contribution of existing activities to the production and preservation of goods;

10. knowledge of what should be done to reconcile the generation of well-being with the production and preservation of goods for existing activities;

11. knowledge of the overall improvements to be made to reconcile the objective of well-being of all with the production and preservation of the requisite goods;

12. identification/choice of the most relevant/efficient new actions to be implemented for progress towards well-being of all and production and preservation of the requisite goods.

Thus it is possible to define 12 kinds of knowledge for the progress of societies. Numbered 1 to 12, these are shown in the diagram below.

The first six kinds relate to progress in terms of well-being and the remaining six to progress in terms of goods.[9] It should be noted that these are kinds of knowledge for progress rather than stages in the process of progress, since the development of these kinds of knowledge is partially iterative. For example, immaterial goods required for progress are considered throughout the process. In addition, these kinds of knowledge do not concern the implementation and follow-up to new activities.

Secondly, these questions and challenges lead to a rethink of the very functionality of the progress indicators. Because of its complexity, progress implies several kinds of regulatory action, each dovetailing with the others. In order to be feasible, each of these forms of regulatory action needs at least one indicator. A single progress indicator is thus inadequate and can only indicate the overall result; it cannot help in respect of all the interaction needed to obtain this result.

---

9. Without claiming to know the answer in every case, we shall endeavour to show how the research exercises conducted with citizens are casting light on the appropriate approach and on the important answers to these questions (see parts three and four of this article).

Diagram 2 – Schematic representation of the 12 knowledge requirements for progress

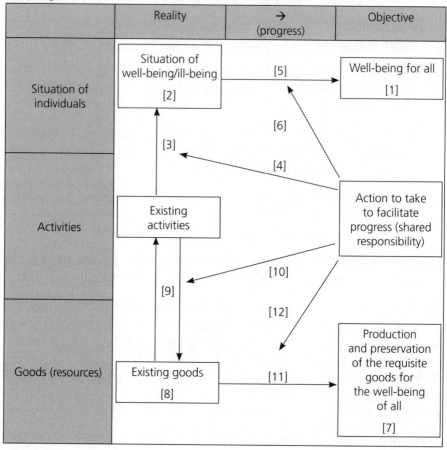

	Reality	→ (progress)	Objective
Situation of individuals	Situation of well-being/ill-being [2]	[5]	Well-being for all [1]
		[6]	
		[3] [4]	
Activities	Existing activities		Action to take to facilitate progress (shared responsibility)
		[10] [9]	
		[12]	
Goods (resources)	Existing goods [8]	[11]	Production and preservation of the requisite goods for the well-being of all [7]

NB: The figures in square brackets are the numbers of the 12 kinds of knowledge referred to above.

On the other hand, a single indicator performs a vital service by showing overall performance and drawing attention to any advances or regression. It functions as a confirmatory or warning indicator.

This leads to the conclusion that, for society to progress towards its ultimate objective, an indicator of overall progress is needed, accompanied by a series of more specific indicators for each of the requisite kinds of regulatory action. By way of comparison, a good overall indicator in the health sphere would be the life expectancy of the population born in good health (health-adjusted life expectancy). This indicator gives an overall result, but provides no information about the various contributory factors. In order to make progress in the health sphere, another set of indicators is needed to point to strengths and weaknesses, so that appropriate action may be taken.

The third conclusion relates to the very nature of the progress indicators used. Progress towards an objective cannot be measured solely in terms of an open-ended quantitative indicator (such as GDP or the more appropriate GPI), without reference to an evaluation scale not based solely on relative progress (one country is more advanced than another because its GDP is higher and a country is progressing if its GDP grows and regressing if it falls). It must be possible to assess it in relation to the desired (ideal) objective and, on the other hand, in relation to the worst-case scenario, which the aim is to avoid. The United Nations' HDI, on a scale limited by a maximum and a minimum for each of its three components (income, education, health), comes closer to the concept of progress, but the figure obtained (of between 0 and 1) remains fairly abstract, for it, too, is essentially used to compare countries or make comparisons over a period of time.

In order for progress indicators to become genuine tools for detection, reflection and joint responsibility, we propose that they should be linked to a scale of evaluation which is discussed as widely and democratically as possible. In order to devise such a scale, we need to define for each indicator the ideal, good, fairly good, fairly poor and poor situation. Such a scale (in this case based on five levels, but the number of levels could be reduced or increased at will) offers the advantage of being applicable to all kinds of indicators, quantitative and qualitative. It also makes possible the adoption of qualitative indicators, each based on a number of criteria, which are vital for taking account of progress in its various dimensions. And, by using such a scale, "benchmarks" of progress in fields such as governance can be expressed as indicators.

In this article, we shall put forward a few examples of experimental application of the scale, especially in the context of work with citizens on creating indicators of well-being. Looking beyond the specific nature of each example, some transverse reference points emerge in relation to what is generally called an ideal, good, fairly good, fairly poor or poor situation. An ideal situation, for instance, is one in which not only the objective, but also its permanence (and thereby future security/sustainability/peace of mind) is achieved, whereas a poor situation is one in which not only is the objective far from being achieved, but a very high risk exists of steady deterioration and/or irreversibility of the situation. Intermediate situations involve combinations of several variables.

Taking this general principle as the starting point, we obtain a very rough impression of a possible progress indicator reflecting the general position vis-à-vis the desired objective:

- an ideal situation is that of a society capable of ensuring well-being for all, in every dimension and over the long term, meaning that it has the capacity to produce/generate and preserve the requisite goods;

- a good situation might be one in which the capacity exists to produce/generate and preserve the goods required for well-being, but without yet having achieved the ideal in terms of well-being for all;

- a fairly good situation might be one in which a certain well-being is ensured, but with the goods available neither expanding nor deteriorating;

- a fairly poor situation might be one in which well-being is obtained at the cost of deterioration/destruction of goods and resources, the renewal of which cannot be guaranteed, but without the point of irreversibility having been reached;

- a poor situation is one entailing deterioration in which irreversibility is a strong risk and the long-term costs to future generations will be high.

This definition must of course be regarded as a very general example illustrating what an overall indicator might be like. In view of its importance, such an indicator would require a more accurate and more detailed scale and, in particular, would need to be supplemented by other indicators.

2. How to approach the question of well-being (epistemological issues)

As we have already said, the definition and analysis of well-being encompasses aspects which go well beyond technical and methodological questions. The very nature of the concept invites us to take our thinking into the epistemological field. Without engaging in complex considerations, let us look at three key ideas which will point us conclusively in the right direction to deal with well-being.

The first of these ideas is that well-being is by definition a subjective concept which only the person concerned can define.

Well-being is not an ordinary item that might be studied in the same way as others through a conventional scientific approach and unless the specific characteristics of the concept are taken into account, the whole enterprise may get off on the wrong footing.

Firstly, well-being is an intrinsically subjective concept in that only the person concerned can define and assess it. This does not mean that it cannot be measured objectively, for it can if a person claims to be in a state of well-being because his or her house is large enough for his or her whole family – the amount of space being quantifiable in square metres. A distinction has to be made, however, between well-being as a concept and well-being as actually measured. That measurement may be objective or it may be subjective, depending on whether the criteria are measurable objectively (especially those relating to access to material resources) or subjectively (whenever it is a matter of somebody's opinion and especially in relation to non-material criteria, such as trust, recognition, etc.). The concept of well-being itself, however, is subjective by nature.

It is in fact impossible to say on somebody else's behalf whether he or she is in a situation of ill-being or well-being, in the same way as it is impossible to know whether somebody is in pain or not, or whether he or she feels pleasure or not. Even if it were possible to identify the specific area of the brain where pleasure or well-being is felt, and to measure the corresponding activity by electroencephalogram,[10] and even if what the person says is contradicted by evidence from the part of the brain that is active, it would not be possible to say that the person is wrong about his or her pleasure, well-being or lack thereof. At most he or she could be suspected of telling a lie. And if he or she is telling the truth, the inevitable conclusion is that well-being sometimes manifests itself in unexpected ways, for well-being is by nature a personal experience which

---

10. The University of Wisconsin, for instance, has come up with a series of clinical tests involving study of the different areas and intensities of brain activity, using magnetic resonance imaging (MRI) to measure the degree of happiness of the persons subjected to the tests. Clearly, the underlying theory relates to the areas of the brain which are usually active and the intensity of that activity, established in advance on an experimental basis (statistical repetition of the results of the experiment). If the actual feeling expressed by a test subject conflicts with the theory, it is the theory which needs to be revised or adjusted and not the subject's judgment, provided that he or she is telling the truth about his or her feeling.

cannot be described independently of the person. Thus it is impossible to define well-being from the outside and the fact that only the person concerned can define his or her own well-being has considerable implications, both scientifically and politically.

On the scientific level, it has to be recognised that all knowledge of well-being has to emanate from what the individuals concerned (citizens) say about the concept. Any attempt to predefine well-being in principle, even partially, is an intellectual exercise based on a misconception. That is what occurs whenever people's well-being is measured through their answers to specific questions about their satisfaction level in various predefined categories (housing, education, income, health, etc.).

In the political sphere, if we consider that well-being for all, society's ultimate objective, must originate with citizens themselves, it becomes obvious that they must be involved in the definition of objectives before policies are devised. It is as if a new Copernicus had announced his findings and revolutionised governance, for policy can no longer be considered and devised in terms of pre-set categories, but must have its objectives thoroughly revised and achieved on the basis of parameters defined with citizens themselves.

The second idea is that subjective does not mean irrational. Reason may be applied to the subjective.

There are nevertheless many reasons why well-being is not studied in this way, but more on the basis of predetermined definitions which impose an exogenous framework (that is, produced by the research scientist, statistician or politician) on research subjects.

The main reason for this is the tendency, often an unconscious one, to regard well-being as a momentary feeling, a variable depending on the conditions at the relevant time. This is clear, for example, in certain approaches, as in the U-index[11] method, which divides the day according to type of activities and asks the research subjects whether or not they feel well-being as they engage in each one.

This conception of well-being is based on the principle that well-being, as a subjective matter, is not connected with reason and is merely an overall response to a set of immediate endogenous and/or exogenous stimuli,

---

11. See article by Gilda Farrell.

comparable with a light that burns more brightly if the electric current is stronger.

From our own experience, all of us know that well-being is something far more complex, determined by a wide range of factors. Neurologists highlight the fact that satisfaction level does not depend solely on conditions at the time, but also derives from a process in which not only feelings, but also memory and reason play their part. Some findings cast interesting light on the interaction between feelings, memory, reason and satisfaction level.[12]

It is a dangerous mistake to regard well-being as unconnected with reason, for this entails a passive conception of the subject, as found in the idea of the subject as consumer (of goods for the sake of his or her well-being), leaving aside all the endogenous processes whereby we create our own individual well-being, as well as the active and collective processes whereby citizens work for well-being for all.

This tendency to dissociate well-being from reason probably stems from a degree of amalgamation between the subjective, feelings and the irrational. This very common short cut itself stems from the distinction made between, on the one hand, the objective and rational, subject to reasoning, and, on the other, the subjective and irrational, as if there could be no reasoning about what is subjective.

We shall not, in this article, detail the deep-rooted cultural and historical reasons for the highlighting of this distinction in contemporary thinking. It is enough to say that the distinction is made, albeit without any justification. Quite the contrary, for philosophers, followed by psychologists and neurologists, have demonstrated that the subjective, our feelings and emotions are completely bound up with our reason. Thus the satisfaction level beyond which individuals consider themselves happy or feel happy is often established, or at least strongly influenced, by their own reason.

Control through reason of our satisfaction level and feeling of happiness is something that every individual can try out, as suggested by Matthieu Ricard, a Tibetan monk of French origin shown by neurological tests to be

---

12. See, for instance, Klingler and Théodule (2008).

"the happiest man in the world". His advice to anyone seeking happiness is to change his or her "own base line" through mind training.[13]

Reason, which plays its part in our relationship with the world in which we live, is crucial to the feeling of well-being (happiness) or ill-being (sadness).[14] It is, to some extent, what determines the rules of the game and acts as the referee, like a teacher awarding marks to pupils' test papers. The teacher, too, may decide to mark more harshly or less, or to raise or lower his or her expectations, in the light of many factors which play a part in his or her reasoning: for example the level of the test, the pupil's previous record, whether or not encouragement needs to be given, progression and so forth. The parallel drawn is a striking one, for in the same way that a teacher's character influences the decision taken on degree of harshness and tolerance, all of us as individuals have a natural tendency to react with our own level of positiveness (feeling of well-being) or negativeness (feeling of ill-being) to a given situation.

In both cases, the person's own history plays a crucial role. In the same way as the teacher can change his or her outlook (applying reason, sensitivity, etc.), the individual can work on his or her reaction level ("own base line"). In the same way as every teacher tends to apply personal criteria when marking and may assess the pupils that he or she regards as best differently from another teacher (within the bounds of certain basic common parameters), individuals will take different views of the situations which give rise to well-being, despite the points common to (almost) all individuals, which correspond to human characteristics in general (few people, for instance, would take the view that a situation of great physical suffering or constant stress gives rise to well-being).

The third idea is that well-being as an objective of society must be the subject of a reasoned democratic debate.

It is very important to take account of the fact that reason plays a vital role in well-being, as it has numerous consequences, starting in the economic field.

---

13. "The important thing with mind training – probably a more useful term than meditation – is that you change your own base line. This is very different from the temporary sensation of feeling good that you might experience when you watch a Marx Brothers film. What you have to do is raise that base line". Extract from Robert Chalmers' interview with Matthieu Ricard: "Meet Mr Happy", 2007.

14. See article by Jean-Luc Dubois.

Reason casts some doubt on the assumption, expressed more explicitly by some economic scientists than others, that there is an intrinsic correlation between standard of living (and therefore purchasing power and consumption capacity) and well-being. If we take the view that reason plays a vital role in well-being, we need to rethink our economic theories, restoring reason to its proper place as a factor which generates well-being, like any other factor that plays a part in production or growth. Several fundamental facts, set out below, emerge from this.

Firstly, it places the use of progress indicators in addition to GDP in an interesting light. Whereas GDP takes account quite specifically of just total and average per capita income, and therefore purchasing power and consumption capacity (to the exclusion of public activity), it is clear that account should also be taken of individuals' capacity to reason about their own well-being and therefore to live well, individually and collectively. Growth in this capacity is in practice a fundamental criterion of progress which goes beyond GDP on its own. We shall return to this subject.

Secondly, we need to take a different view of human intelligence. If, from the economic viewpoint, we consider that only purchasing power is really important and therefore the productive capacity which enables it to progress, human intelligence – meaning the ability to meet humankind's needs – is regarded primarily in terms of technical and technological intelligence or economic intelligence in the conventional sense. If we start to consider that reason applied to well-being is also part of the economic cycle leading from resources (goods) to well-being, human intelligence will no longer be viewed solely in terms of knowledge and know-how, but also in terms of interpersonal and practical skills.

Thirdly, and probably most importantly, the application of reason to well-being cannot be solely at individual level, but must take place in a collective and societal dimension. It is all the more important to be aware of this because there is currently a new crop of reasoned approaches to well-being which are mainly of an individual nature; while these are very useful, they are certainly inadequate. One example is the "positive psychology" which offers a certain amount of advice, together with principles, rules and practices, to help each and every person to achieve happiness. Devised by Martin Seligman and Christopher Peterson, this approach saw a list drawn up in 2004 of six virtues and 24 character strengths which contribute to happiness.

To consider that well-being can be achieved through individual thinking is to ignore the role of the thinking done in interaction with others. There are, however, several reasons why it is vital to go beyond a purely individual to an interactive approach when producing a formal definition of well-being:

- Firstly, for the sake of accuracy, well-being has a very strong interactive dimension and to ignore this would give rise to an extremely incomplete vision, as shown by all the research carried out on the subject. Happiness is "only real when shared", as the young hero of the film *Into the Wild* concludes after leaving his own family, where he was unhappy, to go and live in the wilds of nature in quest of true happiness.

- It brings certain direct advantages and especially contributes to the well-being of every individual: discussions of well-being cast light on each person's position relative to others, as well as being extremely helpful in terms of distinguishing between the objective and the subjective and re-establishing some degree of consistency between the two.

- Finally, there is a political reason, as part of an essential process of clarification of the objectives of society, enabling a shared vision of well-being to be created and changes to be made to short-term visions, which are often influenced by clichés or immediate impressions, without reason being applied. In this respect, what takes place is a fundamental exercise in concerted action and democracy in order to affirm a single shared and reasoned vision. So well-being for all, as an objective of society, must be able to be discussed in an open and democratic manner.

Conclusion

In conclusion, the specific nature of well-being makes it impossible to define and grasp completely other than through a two-dimensional reasoned approach that is both individual and interactive between different individuals. If statistical and neurological approaches are taken, or an approach based wholly on individual reflection, only one aspect of well-being can be dealt with, giving results which are partial, or even truncated and misleading. In other words, well-being is a subjective concept which must be able to be grasped not just by each individual, but also by all the members of a group (living in a given territory, working in a given firm, etc.).

The definition of well-being for all is thus fundamentally democratic in nature. It must be possible for citizens to play their part in the definition process.

The conventional scientific approach, for its part, will produce material relating to additional aspects, such as comparative analysis of the criteria for well-being according to context or social category, any correlation that exists between the criteria and other matters which may cast light on the factors which play a crucial role in well-being and ill-being.

3. Working with citizens to develop knowledge for societal progress – First findings from research

a. Defining well-being

On the basis of the concept of well-being described above and the shared responsibility of the relevant stakeholders for well-being for all, the Council of Europe has drawn up a method to develop, in conjunction with citizens, well-being criteria and indicators. This method has been piloted and fine-tuned in a number of areas[15] with the municipalities and local players concerned.

The fundamental principle behind this method (described in greater detail in the Appendix) is to give citizens total freedom in defining their own well-being criteria, with a link being made between individual and inter-active reflection:

- individual, so as to uphold everyone's right to self-determination;

- interactive, so as to ensure a shared approach and include the social dimensions of well-being.

Application of this uncomplicated method revealed a wide range of criteria for well-being (and ill-being), highlighting the many dimensions of well-being (see below).

---

15. These include Mulhouse in France, Timişoara in Romania, Rovereto in Italy and the 14th *arrondissement* in Paris, in a variety of environments (companies, schools, etc.).

b. Understanding situations of well-being/ill-being

These criteria give an idea of what constitutes well-being in an ideal situation and therefore make it possible to define the objective of well-being for all, where each criterion is fully satisfied.

The next stage is to be able to measure the differential between the actual situation and the objective, which is why it is essential to have indicators showing progress towards reaching this objective.

In view of the fact that the ideal situation (the objective) is one in which all the criteria are satisfied, the worst situation would be one in which none of the well-being criteria are met. Of course, there would also be a number of intermediate situations in which some of the criteria were fulfilled and others not at all or only partly fulfilled. For example, the criterion of having friends could be fulfilled (having many friends), not fulfilled (having no friends) or partly fulfilled (having just a few friends). In the case of well-being criteria, the focus will be on the satisfaction aspect, breaking this down into two positions: "having a sufficient number of friends" (positive position) or "not having a sufficient number of friends" (negative position).

These combinations of fulfilled and unfulfilled criteria presuppose a correlation between them. In some cases, these correlations are obvious, for example the correlation between "having a place to live" and "having access to running water" (it is not possible to have access to running water at home if you do not have somewhere to live). In other cases, the correlations are linked to local contexts. They may also be based on priority choices.

In any event, the criteria must be grouped together according to subject matter. There would be no sense in seeking to establish correlations between criteria relating to different spheres (for example, there is no intrinsic correlation between a housing criterion and an employment one). This is why the criteria have been grouped together in indicators (for example an employment indicator with all the employment-related criteria) and for each indicator there is a five-level progress scale: the ideal situation is one where all the criteria have been fulfilled, the worst situation where none of the criteria has been fulfilled and lastly the various intermediate situations in which some criteria have been satisfied and others not, bearing in mind the logical or contextual correlations between them.

Table 3 – Example of progress indicator for well-being: employment indicator

Criteria expressed in the meetings and corresponding variables for developing the indicator	Value scale for the indicator to describe the situation:					
	0 – Zero (for reference)	1 – Very poor	2 – Poor	3 – Average	4 – Good	5 – Ideal (objective achieved)
• equity in employment • fulfilling employment → Variables: 1. Job security 2. Possibilities of career advancement 3. Quality of employment (fulfilling employment – suitable working hours, fair remuneration)	Those permanently excluded from employment	Long-term unemployed having little chance of finding a job	Insecure jobs interspersed with periods of unemployment with no opportunities for career advancement – poor quality employment	Lack of job security: temporary or part-time employment but fairly easy to find other jobs and to develop professionally – poor quality employment	Permanent job but few opportunities for career change or advancement – average quality employment	Permanent job with varied work, fulfilling, suitable working hours, well paid and good opportunities for career change or advancement

Source: results of the trial carried out in Mulhouse.

This example shows the advantages of a well-being progress indicator geared to an assessment scale:

- It provides a more accurate picture of the actual situation by taking several criteria into account (for example, in the case of employment, several criteria come into play in order to assess well-being and not just a single criterion such as the unemployment rate in conventional indicators).

- It makes it possible to analyse the full range of diverse social situations without being limited to the average situation, by identifying who or what type of people correspond to each of the situations in the steps of the scale.

- It defines a progression which is readily understandable and usable by citizens and other players.

- It makes for democratic debate and consensus on the choice of steps.

The development of these indicators also makes it possible to reduce the number of well-being indicators from 100 or several hundred to some 30 or 40, broken down among seven or eight categories, as can be seen in the following example, showing the list of indicators drawn up in Timişoara (Romania).

Using these indicators, it is possible to take a snapshot of the well-being situation. The main problem at this level is the availability of data, of which there are generally very little at local level. To offset this, it is necessary to canvass citizens themselves, using a range of tools.[16] The participation of citizens and local stakeholders in general in data production has a three-fold advantage: it is a means of collecting and turning to account existing knowledge (both subjective and objective), it helps reduce costs and, perhaps most importantly, it generates a common pool of knowledge which in turn contributes to social cohesion and shared responsibility.

---

16. These techniques will be explained in greater detail in the future methodological guide on involving citizens/communities in measuring and fostering well-being and progress: towards new concepts and tools (focus groups, surveys carried out by the stakeholders involved, etc.).

Table 4 – Summary of well-being indicators in Timişoara (Romania)

1 – Access to essential resources	2 – Living environment	3 – Relations with institutions	4 – Relations between persons	5 – Individual and social balance	6 – Feelings	7 – Participation
1.1. Employment	2.1. Environment and public areas	3.1. Institution-citizen relationships	4.1. Respect	5.1. Family	6.1. Confidence	7.1. Civic responsibility
1.2. Purchasing power	2.2. Security	3.2. Upholding of rights and non-discrimination in access to rights	4.2. Non-discrimination in human relations	5.2. Time and stress management	6.2. Fear/ calm	7.2. Involvement in civic life
1.3. Housing		3.3. Respect for and application of lawfulness	4.3. Empathy and solidarity	5.3. Personal development	6.3. Feeling of belonging	7.3. Responsibility
1.4. Health		3.4. Institutional assistance/social services	4.4. Social harmony	5.4. Social equity		7.4. Respect for public assets/the common good
1.5. Food		3.5. Civic dialogue and consultation in the decision-making process		5.5. Peace and prosperity		
1.6. Education/ training						
1.7. Culture and leisure						
1.8. Information						
1.9. Transport						

c. Understanding the contribution of each activity to well-being for all

There are two complementary ways in which the contribution of a given activity to well-being for all can be assessed:

- by analysing the impact of the activity on each indicator identified. This could be done simply by assigning a value +1, -1 or 0 depending on whether it has a positive, negative or neutral impact on each of the well-being criteria identified with citizens (this scale could be extended if greater differentiation between the levels of impact were required). The advantage in such a method, trialled in Mulhouse, is that by involving all the relevant parties it ensures that the players concerned are much more familiar with the process and, conse-quently, are better prepared for shared responsibility;

- by analysing the relevance of the activity in relation to the situations of ill-being identified: to what extent is the activity relevant to the criteria and groups of people for whom there are genuine situations of ill-being?

This dual analysis offers an interesting perspective since it enables the overall impact to be seen and not merely the impact in relation to a specific objective. For example, in a traditional approach, a school is assessed in terms of education, a company in terms of efficiency and economic viability, a social measure in terms of integration and so forth. Taking well-being into account highlights the multiple nature of the impact of each action.

This exercise, trialled in Mulhouse, showed, for example, how certain measures, conceived originally as social, could have equally significant effects in economic terms, and vice versa.

d. Identifying the possible improvements of each activity analysed

The other advantage in this method is that it makes it possible to find forms of improvement which go beyond the specific objective of the measure and relate to other dimensions of well-being. In Mulhouse, for example, as part of the municipal health education plan, one measure had been devised to address obesity among the most disadvantaged groups, a factor in ill-being. Basically, it involved providing support and advice to the people concerned in the choice of the food they bought and their cooking practices. The multidimensional analysis on the basis of well-being criteria highlighted the fact that it was extremely well focused on its specific objective (balanced diet) but that it made only a slight contribution to other aspects of well-being which it could otherwise have done had it been carried out in a different way.[17]

The multidimensional approach focusing on well-being for all as a societal objective therefore makes it possible to assess and devise measures in a cross-sectoral way, so as to develop linkages between different approaches which will be mutually reinforced. It is, *per se*, a factor in promoting shared responsibility between the relevant stakeholders, making it possible to go beyond sectoral policies which are often too compartmentalised in view of their predefined specific objectives.

e. Understanding the overall improvements to be made

What is the best way of moving from an improvement approach focused on specific activities to a more general approach relating to all activities?

One way would be to aggregate the impacts and relevance of the different activities that had been or were being carried out. This makes it possible to identify:

- the well-being criteria for which there is little impact and which therefore require greater attention;

- the situations of groups experiencing ill-being where no response has been provided; here new measures need to be devised or current activities adjusted.

It is in this second case that this way of proceeding is at its most meaningful. However, in the first case, two questions need to be asked:

- To what extent is it possible to amalgamate the impact of measures on each of the well-being criteria so as to assess the overall effect?

- To what extent does improvement of well-being relate solely to a balancing of the criteria?

---

17. For example, if instead of buying everything in a supermarket, part of the shopping had been done from alternative sources such as via collective and solidarity-based farming initiatives, the measure would have helped encourage social bonds, citizen participation, greater familiarity with local produce, etc., and would therefore have contributed to the social inclusion and well-being of those involved.

This raises the question of the independence (that is, lack of interdependence) of well-being criteria and indicators. Supposing that the various dimensions of well-being were independent of each other, it would be possible to make a linear analysis of the impact on well-being of any measure by studying it separately for each criterion and then carrying out a matrix aggregation between measures to ascertain the overall impact.

The individual impacts can be consolidated quite simply by amalgamating the values assigned at the point where each well-being criterion and measure converges, in line with the method described above. The exercise carried out in Mulhouse, based on an impact analysis of 70 measures chosen relatively randomly, helped identify the criteria for which there were insufficient measures and among these, the ones requiring urgent attention, that is, for which the assessment of the situation revealed a negative or very poor result. In this way, three critical situations were identified: insufficient equity, inadequate social mix and insufficient equality of opportunities. Accordingly, any concerted action plan should focus on remedial action.

However, this approach does not hold if we take into account the interactions between the different dimensions of well-being, where they exist. There is no evidence in these circumstances that, for example, the shortage of social mix could be filled by measures specifically targeted to this aspect, such as this criterion being taken into account in the construction of new housing units. It would doubtless have a short-term effect, but in the long term thought must be given to the interactions with other dimensions of well-being, such as recognition, non-discrimination, the creation of social bonds between social layers or dialogue.

4. Reflections on the key elements of well-being for all

It is therefore not possible to advance any further in the methods for building up knowledge for social progress without highlighting the interdependence of the various dimensions of well-being.

Accordingly, we shall focus on a comparative analysis of well-being based on the results of the research carried out.

a. Nature of the dimensions of well-being

Clearly, the exercise of developing well-being criteria and indicators will yield results that differ from one area or institution to another. Nonetheless, above and beyond the diversity of criteria and, to a lesser extent, of indicators, between seven and 10 key dimensions of well-being are seen as being constant, constituting seven to 10 categories of indicators. This would imply that they are universal dimensions of well-being, relating to the very nature of human societies. They cover very different aspects, both tangible and intangible, individual and collective, with a strong relational and social dimension. They include:

- the living environment: surroundings, living and meeting spaces, social mix and, more generally, spatial planning;

- access to the essential resources of life (socio-economic rights): food, housing, health, education, employment, income, culture, transport, etc;

- relations with public institutions: forms of dialogue and consultation, citizens' voices being heard, transparency, quality of services, etc;

- human relations, whether at a general level (recognition, solidarity, social harmony, etc.) or a more personal level (friendship, family, etc.);

- personal balance: balance between family life, working life and life as a citizen, absence of constant stress;

- social balance: equity in access to resources, social mobility, etc;

- citizen participation and commitment and manifestation of individual and collective responsibility;

- lastly, the dimensions relating to the feeling of well-being or ill-being, such as fear, calm, self-confidence, confidence in the future, etc.

In order to understand the links between these dimensions of well-being, we need to look more closely at the specific features of each one:

- The essential resources of life constitute the fundamental conditions of well-being: no one can experience well-being if they are hungry, sick, homeless, have no access to education, etc.

- The concept of balance is fundamental in well-being and is present in virtually all situations. It expresses the need for diversity and the contribution of several factors in well-being, for example the balance between family life, working life and life as a citizen, the balance between different types of activity, the balance between the level of demands made on an individual and his or her own capacity to respond, etc.

- The concept of balance goes beyond the individual level to cover the social level as well. It plays a fundamental role because the unfair distribution of resources, injustice and no possibility of upward social mobility for those on the bottom rungs are the first factors in provoking feelings of ill-being. Faced with situations in which there is no justification for certain citizens having considerably greater advantages than others, the feeling of exclusion takes hold and saps any possibility of improved well-being. This is the main explanation for the divergence that can be seen in certain wealthy countries between the increase in objective well-being (in terms of income and access to resources necessary to live) and the decrease in subjective well-being (growing feeling of ill-being).

- Social balance/imbalance encompasses relations (between persons and with institutions), governance and everything relating to each individual's participation and commitment, three other dimensions of well-being. These highlight the fundamentally societal aspect of human nature: the feeling of belonging to a community, collective responsibility and responsibility to others and practices of sharing are key factors in the ability to regulate behaviour on the basis of community interest and not merely on the individual interest which is prevalent in the animal world. Humankind has particularly developed this awareness of others, challenging the still current idea of *homo economicus* whose sole reasoning is based on self-interest.

- One's surroundings play a key role in the different dimensions of well-being, whether in terms of access to resources (housing, infrastructure, culture and information, lack of pollution), balance (towns of a manageable size, well-connected services such as the different types of transport, balanced spatial development, quality of life) or human relations (social areas, social mix, forums for meetings and discussion, etc.).

This rapid analysis throws up a number of conclusions on the significance and implications of well-being:

- An analysis in conjunction with citizens of the well-being criteria highlights the fact that well-being is not to be found solely in results but also in processes (the way things are done).

- The concept of balance illustrates the universal importance of seeking the optimum rather than the maximum. Not only does seeking maximum income no longer produce well-being but it gives rise to a feeling of ill-being because of the injustice it generates.

- Rethinking income (and the other dimensions) in terms of the optimum on the basis of the multidimensional nature of well-being leads to a reappraisal of economic reasoning. A typical example will suffice to illustrate this: viewing consumption solely in relation to its usefulness in terms of access to the essential resources of life leads one to maximise consumption in line with the income available. If other criteria were taken into account, such as responsibility, equity and the pleasure of sharing, consumer choices would no longer be geared to the maximum but to an optimum, whereby all these different criteria could be satisfied. This is what happens in daily life: in many situations we prefer to share and have less ourselves than have a great deal without the pleasure of sharing.

b. Fine-tuning the Council of Europe hypotheses in the light of the results of the research

It is therefore clear from looking at the different dimensions of well-being that the inter-relations are highly complex and can consequently be fully perceived only by approaching them as a whole rather than individually.

To this end, let us take another look at the Council of Europe hypotheses relating to the key elements of well-being. Underlying this concept is the idea that a process can develop positively or negatively depending on the "key elements" which play a decisive role. It can be seen that between these different dimensions of well-being there are chain reactions which have knock-on effects fostering either well-being or a growing sense of ill-being. We refer to virtuous circles of well-being and vicious circles of ill-being.

How can we verify that the key elements which will bring about a virtuous as opposed to a vicious circle are the ones put forward in the Council of Europe guide? Knock-on effects may occur between different dimensions of well-being, in particular between access to essential resources, the relations set up by the relevant players to guarantee everyone such access, the resulting personal and social balances, the feeling of well-being or ill-being to which this gives rise and the readiness for commitment and participation fostered in consequence, which in turn can improve relations between persons and with institutions and the personal and collective balances.

These interactions are represented (as virtuous or vicious circles) in Diagram 3.

Two key ideas emerge from this diagram:

- the central role of the relations in the interactions between the components of well-being, linking the tangible (access to essential resources and living environment) and intangible dimensions;

- the fact that there may be a virtuous or a vicious circle between the components in the upper part of the diagram.

This would tend to show that the key elements of well-being are to be found at the level of relations between persons and with institutions. They are closely linked to the way in which society and activities in general are managed, in other words governance. This could explain any disconnection between objective well-being (primarily tangible, in the lower part of the diagram) and subjective well-being (upper part), as highlighted by Wolfgang Glatzer.[18] In other words, even where all the material conditions are satisfied, poor governance may give rise to imbalances which lead to feelings of dissatisfaction and introversion.

So what are the features of governance and human relations that are conducive to positive interactions (virtuous circle) and what are those that are likely to lead to a vicious circle and ill-being?

Some of the results of the research taking place could help us in attempting to answer this question.

For example, recognition (being acknowledged and listened to) is invariably the most frequent well-being criteria cited by citizens. Being acknowledged and listened to as a person and as a citizen can be found in all types of relations whether between persons or with institutions. It is a sign of inclusion in society (not merely economic inclusion, but social/societal inclusion in the sense of taking part in the way it is run). Governance

---

18. See his article in this volume.

Diagram 3 – Interactions between dimensions of well-being with examples of indicators

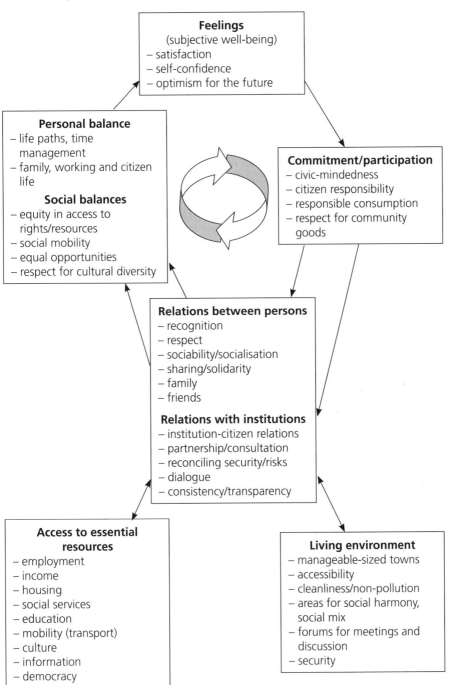

Feelings
(subjective well-being)
– satisfaction
– self-confidence
– optimism for the future

Personal balance
– life paths, time management
– family, working and citizen life

Social balances
– equity in access to rights/resources
– social mobility
– equal opportunities
– respect for cultural diversity

Commitment/participation
– civic-mindedness
– citizen responsibility
– responsible consumption
– respect for community goods

Relations between persons
– recognition
– respect
– sociability/socialisation
– sharing/solidarity
– family
– friends

Relations with institutions
– institution-citizen relations
– partnership/consultation
– reconciling security/risks
– dialogue
– consistency/transparency

Access to essential resources
– employment
– income
– housing
– social services
– education
– mobility (transport)
– culture
– information
– democracy

Living environment
– manageable-sized towns
– accessibility
– cleanliness/non-pollution
– areas for social harmony, social mix
– forums for meetings and discussion
– security

which fosters well-being is therefore inclusive governance where everyone is a stakeholder in the management of society at his or her own level and is recognised as such, whereas governance which fosters ill-being is one which does not enable this or which makes it difficult.

Second, there are many criteria relating to balance (personal or social) which emerge in all exercises. This is understandable if one takes the view (as suggested in the diagram) that feelings of well-being or ill-being can be traced back to questions of balance. The idea of recognition also plays a part here: it is not merely a question of recognising citizens as stakeholders in the society (or institution) but as individuals who, like any other, have the right to a life path and needs in terms of personal balance (time management, etc.). Social balances (equity in access to rights and resources and its corollaries: social mobility, equal opportunities, respect for cultural differences) are the very reflection of the recognition of everyone, without discrimination, as fully-fledged persons.

Returning to the hypotheses on key elements set out in the methodological guide, shared responsibility for well-being for all appropriately expresses the idea of inclusive governance geared towards each individual's social and personal balances. Shared responsibility is the very embodiment of the idea of everybody's interests being taken into account by everybody and, therefore, of governance based on everybody's commitment and participation so that all can find their place in accordance with their needs and abilities. The concept of shared responsibility can be seen as signifying harmonious co-existence or a relationship between co-subjects where each subject considers, along with the others, all humans and living beings and not only themselves. It ties in with the idea of the associative approach at the level of each individual living space, institution, territory or indeed the planet as a whole (a concept also set out in the methodological guide as a key element of social cohesion).

The four key elements concerning individual situations relate to the objectives pursued by a virtuous circle of well-being in terms of its four dimensions: recognition in human relations and governance; autonomy and personal, family and occupational development in personal balances; equity in access for social balances; and participation/commitment. The feeling of well-being is the outcome of achieving these four objectives.

In conclusion, shared responsibility is a means of linking material aspects, forming balances and subjective perceptions. It consolidates citizen participation and commitment and signifies the idea of harmonious co-existence or a relationship between co-subjects. Based on this, one could, in a manner of speaking, reformulate Stefan Klein's "magic triangle" made up of a sense of civic duty, social balance and mastery of one's own fate (Klein, 2006), adding that all these aspects need a regulatory function both regarding material matters and in respect of the acknowledgement of everybody's contribution.

c. Breaking free from the "vicious circle"

The key elements of well-being relating to the concept of shared responsibility point the way towards an ideal "well-being for all" situation. However, they do not shed any light on how to overcome certain obstacles in order to be able to break free from a situation of ill-being.

Vicious circles of ill-being comprise stumbling blocks that require special action. For example, as Catherine Redelsperger points out,[19] individuals either in long-term unemployment, who experience severe problems in their work, or who suffer from over-indebtedness (all of which are processes giving rise to ill-being) tend to withdraw into themselves to avoid repeating a negative experience. One of the most extreme cases is that of the "self-exclusion" of persons drawn into repeated processes of exclusion from a feeling of guilt.

In such cases, the way out requires another person to listen, not pass judgment, and to suggest other paths. Here again, the key elements for the way out of ill-being are to be found in relations with others, dialogue, empathy, solidarity, everything inherent in the co-subject relationship discussed above.

However, the obstacles to the exercise of (shared) responsibility at the level of society are immense. Particularly in the case of the poor and the victims of exclusion, apportioning the blame for their situation on them obviates the need to admit mutual responsibility; blaming others is the first stage in abdicating one's own responsibility and is therefore the opposite of co-responsibility.

In addition to apportioning blame, other social phenomena lead to individuals being stuck in ill-being: one's contribution to society not being recognised, one's voice in the public arena counting for little unless one belongs to the groups in power, information in the hands of a monopoly and others.

---

19. See her article in this volume.

d. Shared responsibility as an ethical stance

Allocating blame and denying people the opportunity to exercise responsibility are to be found in several spheres of life in society. In the social field in particular, the theories and practices based on attributing responsibility for poverty to poor people themselves are taking over from the idea of the social state and citizen solidarity.

To understand why, we need to look at the legitimisation of these negative trends, that is, those reflecting selfishness, egocentrism and defence of one's own interests above those of others (dissociative approaches) rather than empathy and solidarity (associative approaches). Once these trends and practices are acknowledged as legitimate and there are no rules outlawing or forbidding them, they easily take root as they are a much easier choice than shared responsibility.

In the history of humanity, there have been examples of periods where the legitimisation of (or simply failure to condemn) these trends has led to regression and sometimes disaster, followed by periods where, learning lessons from these outcomes, society incorporated new rules and forms of regulation based on responsible co-existence. The most telling example in modern European history is the period 1920 to 1945 when the legitimisation of non-tolerance and dictatorship led to great atrocities. This was followed by a period of learning respect for difference, the dignity and autonomy of every individual and citizen participation, as a result of the emphasis on human rights and the whole process which ensued, in which the Council of Europe and other national and international institutions have played a key role.

Today, legitimisation of abdication of responsibility and its corollary, attributing blame, leads to situations of widespread ill-being which, in turn, gives rise to rejection and negligence bringing with it the risk of disaster if the paucity of resources requires increased capacity for sharing and co-existence. More than ever, there is a need for a new ethical stance of shared responsibility for well-being for all, a complementary aspect of human rights for co-existence.

Whereas human rights and the associated rules are legal and institutional in nature and fall above all into the public sphere, a matter for states and governmental or intergovernmental organisations, shared responsibility is a matter of ethics, because it is inseparable from inter-player relations: it cannot therefore be decreed but has to be learned empirically from rules and practices. Ethics here means knowledge developed in a reasoned way, from the interaction between subjects and structures. In a manner of speaking, it is the ability to live together harmoniously, based on rules between players (in a local, regional or national setting, or in an institution – company, department, etc.) among themselves and/or in their dealings with the outside world. This could be termed reasoned ethics, developed in an interaction between subjects, differentiated from morality which is rather a set of rules generally laid down by a higher entity.

Conclusions

The above analysis gives us a clearer idea of how to respond to the knowledge requirements for progress.

Let us first of all look again at the knowledge requirements relating to well-being (see Diagram 2). Taking account of the key elements of well-being introduces a second dimension into the analysis of the relevance of activities (either already existing or new activities), that is, relevance in terms of helping strengthen these key elements. This is a particularly important assessment criterion as it highlights the particular added value of activities which give rise to shared responsibility and other related key elements, especially equity in access. It also gives some guidance for identifying the improvements to be made to each activity taken individually. Lastly, it involves consideration being given to two dimensions in seeking consistency among activities (understanding the overall improvements to be made):

- to ensure that situations of ill-being are indeed taken into account;

- to enable full expression of shared responsibility for well-being for all.

With regard to knowledge for progress in terms of goods, the research carried out since 2006 have not yet reached the point where answers to methodological questions are clearly available. Nonetheless, a number of methodological approaches to be followed have clearly emerged.

For example, with regard to the knowledge of the goods necessary for well-being, the analysis above has demonstrated the vital role played by intangible assets, particularly vision and the rules which subjects (citizens, stakeholders) draw up and lay down to ensure together well-being for all. It is these common rules and vision which make it possible to identify what is necessary for well-being and to respond to questions relating to goods. In contrast, without vision, everybody would be functioning individually, "blindly" seeking forms of compensation for non-material ill-being in material goods, without any real understanding of what it is they are looking for.

This is much more than just rules, it is a genuine culture of harmonious co-existence. It is built up gradually. The processes of reflecting on well-being for all and the way of achieving this together, as described above, can act as catalysts.

However, as we have already seen, this culture of harmonious co-existence is fragile. Abdication of responsibility and attributing blame can gain the upper hand, especially in times of tension, and give rise to ill-being. More generally, all forms of non-recognition, discrimination, contempt, lack of transparency or unjust access to resources or similar can give rise to vicious circles leading to ill-being (distrust, insecurity, etc.), run counter to the ability to live together harmoniously and can, in a very short space of time, destroy years of effort.

This is why, if well-being for all is to be secured in a sustainable way, harmonious co-existence cannot be limited to an informal common culture. It must be formalised with precision, providing for socio-institutional bodies and instruments of practical implementation, monitoring and remedy.

Human rights and the associated rights (democracy, rule of law) are a fundamental achievement in this regard as they lay down the limits which must not be overstepped in order to avoid falling into vicious circles of ill-being and the destruction of common goods.

However, as we have said, rights are just one facet of the rules of harmonious co-existence. They have to be supplemented by responsibilities which are the other side of the coin and which must be developed in line with a reasoned ethical stance by the interactions inherent in a form of governance that makes room for shared responsibility and, in particular, consultation and the principle of autonomy versus responsibility.

In addition to intangible goods, well-being presupposes the preservation of material goods and the conditions which will allow each human community to secure access by all to basic needs (housing, education, health, employment, etc.).

Identifying the goods necessary for well-being is a complex but essential task, so as to have a reference framework (ideal situation) in order to assess existing goods (stage seven). The differential between what exists and what is required must be determined not only in static terms but also in terms of trends (tendency towards optimisation or, in contrast, deterioration), so as to be able to assess the impact and relevance of existing activities and identify what has to be done, either for each activity or at the overall level.

At this point two fundamental questions are raised:

- How should one allocate responsibilities for the production and preservation of goods? Here the concept of equity in access to goods and in responsibility for preserving them is key. It lies at the foundation of shared responsibility in consumption, production and preservation, one of the major challenges facing society today (responsible consumption and production).

- How can one reconcile the production and preservation of goods with the generation of well-being? This question already lies at the very heart of discussions when work on well-being criteria and indicators in conjunction with citizens is carried out in institutions whose output is tangible or intangible goods (companies, schools, etc.). While at the outset this may appear a difficult equation to resolve, since the effort exerted on production of goods is often associated with the idea of sacrifice and ill-being (ill-being at work, educational effort, etc.), it subsequently emerges, in applying this method, that well-being for all is a performance factor in the production of goods, placing this question of reconciliation in a win-win context.

In conclusion, the process of constructing shared responsibility for well-being for all opens up the prospect of a new, more associative form of governance, creating bridges not only between stakeholders, institutions and citizens, but also cutting across the different sectors and between major societal objectives which for a long time may have been viewed as difficult to reconcile.

The research being carried out have pinpointed key avenues to explore, whether in the context of a local area or within institutions (companies, schools). This article has sought to make an initial assessment, while at the same time highlighting the many questions still to be addressed. In some ways it is a progress report. In particular, developing the progress indicators concerning goods is an essential task which still needs to be carried out.

Nonetheless, we now have a simple method for defining criteria and constructing indicators for well-being for all, which can be easily applied and passed on, so that in the coming years it should be possible to transfer this method on a much larger scale.[20]

---

20. See Resolution 226 (2007) and Recommendation 207 (2007) of the Congress of Local and Regional Authorities of the Council of Europe on the development of social cohesion indicators: the concerted local and regional approach.

References

Chalmers, Robert, "Matthieu Ricard: Meet Mr Happy", published in *the Independent*, Sunday 18 February 2007.

Council of Europe, *Concerted Development of Social Cohesion Indicators – Methodological Guide*, Council of Europe Publishing, Strasbourg, 2005.

Klein, Stefan, *The Science of Happiness: How Our Brains Make Us Happy – And What We Can Do To Get Happier*, Marlowe and Co., March 2006.

Klingler, Cécile and Théodule, Marie-Laure, "Pourquoi le cerveau devient dépendant", *La Recherche*, No. 417, March 2008, p. 36.

Kusago, Takayoshi, "Rethinking of Economic Growth and Life Satisfaction in Post-World War II Japan – A Fresh Approach", *Social Indicators Research*, March 2007.

Appendix: methodology

Defining well-being criteria in conjunction with citizens

Well-being criteria can be defined in conjunction with citizens in a three-hour session with a large number of citizens (at least 60) using a group-based methodology based on the world cafés used in the "future search" approach,[21] adapting this method to reflection on well-being.

To begin with, citizens are asked to divide up into small groups of eight to 10 people of similar age, sex, ethnic origin and/or occupational categories (for example a group of young people, a group of immigrants, a group of people with disabilities, a group of elderly people, a group of housewives or an ethnic minority group). Each of these groups defines its own well-being criteria on the basis of three questions:

- What does well-being mean for you?

- What does ill-being mean for you?

- What do you or can you do as regards your well-being?

(The questions may be slightly different depending on the case, but taking care never to predefine the categories of well-being.[22])

Within each group, members first of all think about these questions on their own, writing down their criteria on post-it stickers. A group reflection phase follows with all the individual stickers put on a large sheet or table visible by all, and then a group summary is produced. In all, this should take about an hour.

Then "multi-profile" groups are formed with one person from each of the single-profile groups. Supposing one had eight single-profile groups of eight people, it would be possible to form eight multi-profile groups, which will attempt to define the criteria of well-being for all, summarising in an inclusive way the criteria identified in the single-profile groups,

---

21. Method used amongst others by the Neighborhood Assemblies Network: www.sfnan.org/.

22. A fourth question was added in the latest experiments (Trento, Paris) asking "What should be done to foster well-being?" The advantage of this question, which falls perhaps outside the definition of well-being, is that it encourages people to think about what would constitute an ideal situation and therefore makes it possible to broaden the scale of indicators (see below).

ensuring that diversity is taken into account. For example, if one of the criteria relating to housing is to have sufficiently spacious permanent housing and if a Roma-profile group had mentioned the possibility of living in caravans, the consolidated result should take both situations into account. In this way, it should be possible to reconcile different points of view, such as reconciling young people's desire to have places where they can celebrate late at night and the desire of older people to have peace and quiet, by identifying as a criterion for well-being for all the existence of physically separate areas.

I. Understanding well-being to ensure that it is equitably accessible

Jean-Luc Dubois[1]

Introduction

Worldwide growth has led to the emergence of new players in the international arena. This arouses great hopes for the sustainable improvement of living conditions and more generally of well-being for millions of human beings hitherto deprived of it. But it also has a cost, since the ensuing increase in pollution, the growth of domestic and industrial waste and the effects on biodiversity and climate generate new risks – reflecting the environmental costs. In social terms, while extreme long-term poverty is on the wane, there is a parallel increase in the different forms of inequality, a growing vulnerability to these new risks and a permanent lack of financial security which fosters new poverty traps engendering social exclusion. In human terms, there is a certain malaise due to the collectively shared obligation to succeed and be productive, to forms of social disintegration and to the appearance of new forms of loneliness, whose psychological consequences affect the most privileged population groups as much as the others.

In this context, the pursuit of economic growth raises a number of questions. Can we protect a natural environment damaged by our modes of production to the extent that biodiversity is declining and ecological equilibria are endangered? What arrangements should we make for living together in such a way as to equitably combat inequalities and the

1. Centre d'Economie et d'Ethique pour l'Environnement et le Développement (C3ED) de l'Université de Versailles Saint Quentin-en-Yvelines (UVSQ) and Institut de Recherche pour le Développement (IRD). The author's thanks to François-Régis Mahieu, Professor emeritus at the C3ED, for his advice on the outline of this study and Hanitra Randrianasolo, Ph.D., at the C3ED, for her support in the final drafting of the text.

gradual loss of social cohesion in a globalised world? How can we counter individual ill-being, in human terms, by enhancing people's potential and promoting their capability for innovation? To answer these questions, we need to think about a form of growth that would aim to meet these challenges while continuing to improve well-being.

There is an aspiration to well-being which seems to be universally shared and at the same time turns out to be a remarkable engine for change, in societies and in the organisation of social ties and relationships. This requires us to agree on the actual definition of "well-being", then to ask ourselves how to improve it while ensuring that it is equitably distributed.

In this article I shall attempt to address both these questions, in two parts. The first part will discuss the definition of well-being, seeing how it relates to happiness as conceived by philosophers and the search for meaning as conceived by psychologists. The second part will look at how we might introduce processes of collective action involving the responsibility of social players, in an attempt to equitably satisfy all human beings' aspiration to well-being.

1. A general aspiration to well-being

There is currently a universal aspiration to reach a level of well-being perceived as satisfactory. It arouses such a strong demand that it is disrupting demographic, economic, social, ecological and other equilibria. It results in development strategies that galvanise the international community, such as the millennium objectives on the reduction of poverty and some forms of inequality.

In actual fact, this pursuit of well-being is part of a long-standing philosophical tradition concerning the "quest for happiness". The earliest thinkers of ancient times, whether Greek, Chinese or Indian, studied this question as early as the 5th century BC. But most modern economists have kept in mind only a simplistic view of it, emphasising the optimal management of goods and services stemming from market balance. Yet many authors have introduced the concepts of public goods, basic needs, social ties, achievements and even freedom to achieve, thus broadening the economic view of well-being.

Recent studies in psychology take the issue still further, incorporating personal life into the analysis of well-being. They aim to confer "meaning" on the concept of well-being by providing tools to counter the ill-being which is developing in parallel to the increase in material well-being. The psychological concept of "meaning" therefore links together the economic concept of "well-being" and the philosophical one of "happiness".

a. Starting with the philosophical view of happiness

The first people to ask questions about happiness were the philosophers of Antiquity. The Greek Aristotle (382-322 BC) observed that all human beings wanted to be happy, but that they did not all agree on how to achieve this or on the approaches to adopt for the purpose. Quite similar views were expressed elsewhere, particularly in China, by thinkers such as Mencius (Mèng Zí, 371-289 BC) and Mo Zi, (479-392 BC).

On this human aspiration to happiness, regarded as universal, two opposite schools of thought soon developed, proposing different definitions of what happiness should be.

The first, known as the "hedonist school", emphasised the pursuit of pleasure as the source of happiness. It was based on the hedonist philosophy (Aristippus, 435-356 BC) which held that life could be considered good only if it afforded the greatest possible pleasure or satisfaction. The Epicurean definition (Epicurus, 342-271 BC), a milder version of this view, held that happiness was the outcome of a well-thought-out balance between the positive dimension deriving from pleasure and a negative dimension associated with suffering. It was for the individual human being to be able to manage this balance between the two wisely, across time and space.

This view influenced the utilitarian philosophy (Bentham, 1748-1832), which contended that the individual's behaviour was the outcome of a hedonist calculation designed to maximise the amount of pleasure and minimise the amount of pain, so that happiness was defined as the difference between the two. In collective terms, universal happiness then derived from the sum of individual happinesses and the best society was that capable of providing "the greatest happiness of the greatest number".

Stuart Mill (1806-73) placed this theory on an economic footing and turned it into a philosophy capable of assessing, in terms of utility, the consequences of people's acts for well-being. Utility, or objective satisfaction, reflects the fact that a good or act can generate well-being in the form of pleasure, joy, benefits and so on, leading even indirectly to happiness. This means regarding well-being and happiness as equivalent. The purpose of all acts is then to pursue the greatest possible satisfaction in order to maximise well-being for all. What is important is the overall amount of well-being produced, irrespective of how it is distributed among individuals. In this context, all individuals are of equal worth and each one's happiness depends on that of the others. So we need to consider the well-being of everyone, not that of a few individuals in particular.

Current economic thinking, while featuring many non-orthodox trends, remains strongly influenced by this view. It considers that the growth of consumption and income is the prerequisite for improving well-being, and that utility always measures the capacity of a good to satisfy an economic agent's needs. Decision theory, for example, which uses cost-benefit analysis techniques to assess projects and public policies, always refers to a hedonist-type calculation.

Aristotle's view is at the opposite end of the spectrum from this utilitarian view with its strong hedonist underpinnings. His school of thought, known as "eudaemonist", focuses on personal or social achievement as the source of happiness, referring to ethical values such as prudence and generosity. In Aristotle's view, what is important is to establish, together with others, an ethics of what is possible in the *polis* or city-state, in order to achieve common goals on the basis of a concerted approach and, by this form of freedom, to improve the happiness of living in the city-state. This philosophy of "the good life" rejects the idea that the balance of pleasures is the sole criterion for defining happiness and relies on the fact that if the individual is an autonomous, rational and reasonable subject, he/she must also be able to establish a link between his/her own capability for action and the possibility of achieving happiness by means of acts suited to his/her social and natural environment.

The philosopher Robert Misrahi (2003) clearly illustrates this viewpoint, particularly in his thinking on happiness. Happiness is not the spontaneous result of pleasant events occurring in life, but rather the outcome of a considered personal construction. It is for the individual to build happiness through his/her own acts. However, there can be no access to happiness unless society first provides individuals with the basic social and economic opportunities that will allow them to lead normal lives.

This view is similar to that expounded by Sen (1999), who shows that in the economic sphere, it is "capability for action" in a free environment – what he calls agency – that enables individuals to achieve the aims they consider important. The role of public policies is then to ensure access to resources and opportunities that allow individuals to choose from a range of possible achievements, those likely to lead to a fulfilling life.

Still in the same frame of thought, individuals can then be regarded as incorporated into networks of rights and social obligations, which compels them to combine their freedom of choice with responsibility for their social obligations (Ballet et al., Dubois and Mahieu, 2005). This means broadening "agency", or the individual's capability for action, to include personal responsibilities, over and above the individual's freedoms and goals alone. This additional contribution refers to the phenomenological approach, which views social interaction in connection with individuals' existential intentions, the forms of responsibility they assume and the power struggles or dominant/dominated relationships in which they are involved in a given context. This is a more relevant way of addressing the complexity of human beings' aspiration to happiness.

In conclusion, this philosophy of "the good life" shows that by means of a reasoned, structured approach based on responsibility, it is possible to ensure that people's individual and collective capability for achieve-ment results in the capability to build a fulfilled life, which is a source of common happiness. In this sense, Ricœur talks of "the good life, with and for others, in just institutions" (Ricœur, 1995).

b. Broadening the very restrictive view of economic well-being

While philosophers reason in terms of happiness, economists use the concept of well-being, defined as the result of a balanced management of material goods and services, either consumed or accumulated in the form of capital. The definition has been broadened with the recent intro-duction of relations between individuals and their social environment, particularly incorporating the concepts of social capital and altruism.

To reach a certain level of well-being, decisions must be taken on the allocation of available resources, given the many technical constraints and people's social behaviour. As economic reasoning is based chiefly on goods and services, one can look into ways of efficiently allocating one's limited resources to purposes that have previously been evaluated, usually in monetary terms. In this context, the economic approach means managing the available resources in the best possible way by deciding where to allocate them in order to achieve a given purpose, such as increasing well-being, as swiftly as possible.

The utilitarian view is upheld by the theory of general equilibrium and that of welfare economics. Both seek to answer this question: which of several possible economic situations, each featuring a certain distribution of resources and incomes, can be considered the best? This is a fundamental question in public sector economics, which looks at individual behaviour in order to analyse issues relating to public goods, taxation, collective choices, the social optimum, the treatment of forms of poverty and inequalities and issues surrounding justice and equity (Jarret and Mahieu, 1998).

On the basis of various hypotheses, the theory of general equilibrium demonstrates that when consumers rationally maximise their individual satisfactions despite income constraints, and producers likewise maximise their production despite technical constraints, the outcome is a single system of prices and quantities which ensures equilibrium between supply and demand on all markets, the optimal satisfaction of economic agents and the most efficient possible technical production. The hypotheses concern the behaviour of individuals, which is assumed to be selfish and rational, in a system of pure and perfect competition. Furthermore, according to welfare economics, this situation of equilibrium can be regarded as optimal (in the sense conferred on the term by Pareto): in other words, the satisfaction of one economic agent cannot be increased without that of another being reduced.

This formalised monetary approach, which is interesting because of its rigour and consistency, is based on extremely restrictive hypotheses. These are individualist in terms of both consumers and producers, so they do not incorporate forms of social interaction such as commitment to others or alliances between producers, which are nonetheless conducive to social innovation and technical progress and consequently generate increases in output. Of course such models are of interest in helping us to understand, on a didactic basis, how different variables can interact in a coherent framework, but there is a risk that the theory will be completely disconnected from real experience. When it comes to predicting public policies, this can lead to targeting errors in terms of the well-being of the population groups concerned.

In this frame of thought, gross national product (GNP) and national income per head serve as indicators to measure the level of well-being in macro-economic terms. They have many weaknesses: although they take proper account of goods and services consumption and of the production-generated income that ensures this consumption, they do not take account of the nature of the goods produced or consumed, or of the adverse side-effects of production (urban congestion, social costs, insecurity), and they also disregard many forms of production such as domestic work and voluntary work.

Unlike this utilitarian view, the view of the good life focuses on people's attainments in terms of living conditions, on their behaviour and on the achievements that may result. What is important is not so much the satisfaction obtained as people's capability to act, that is their capability to perform a number of acts (or functionings) which enable them to reach a goal that is not necessarily the pursuit of their own well-being, but reflects a degree of personal achievement (Sen, 1985).

This "capability approach" moves beyond economics based solely on the management of resources, particularly goods and services consumed; it devises a form of economics that focuses on people's potential and functionings so that they will be more capable of making the life choices they want, for themselves and with others. This amounts to incorporating a discussion of behaviour into economic analysis, alongside the usual discussion of living standards and conditions.

By definition, this "capability" of the individual comprises two components. The first reflects what the person is actually capable of achieving in the current context, given the constraints and opportunities he/she encounters, on the basis of his/her own characteristics and with the use of the resources available. This can be measured by standard indicators, deriving in particular from household surveys. The second component – and this is its original feature – expresses a person's potential capability, that is what he/she could achieve in a different context and which would demonstrate his/her capability to choose and perform specific acts which were not initially planned. This in fact reflects the person's degree of freedom to choose to achieve what he/she aspires to do. It is a form of "freedom to do and be" which proves much harder to measure with indicators, but enables the person's "capability" to be viewed as his/her freedom to achieve.

In this frame of thought, poverty expresses the deprivation of capabilities and even of freedom of choice, and combating poverty means pursuing economic policies designed to increase people's capabilities so that they can be free to lead the lives they want. Sustainable human development, as advocated by United Nations Development Programme (UNDP), is part of this thinking. It aims to reinforce individual and collective capabilities through ties with others, while countering intra- and inter-generational inequalities in capability which put a brake on poverty reduction.

Likewise, a person's vulnerability stems from a shortage of the capabilities he/she would need to muster in order to cope with the consequences of risks that occur. Increasing one's range of individual and collective capabilities would improve one's capability for resilience in the face of unexpected setbacks.

In this context, well-being is part of a multidimensional view which contrasts with monetary well-being or "welfare", a reflection of utility. The fight against poverty, taken in the multidimensional rather than the exclusively monetary sense, the reduction of vulnerability, the fight against exclusion and so on are part of this process, which places the accent on development (Perroux, 1952) and sustainable human development (UNDP, 2005) rather than on economic growth alone, as expressed by GNP.

This economic view of well-being more closely reflects the human realities observed, in which economic relations such as those of production, consumption and savings take place between individuals belonging to social networks, who have to meet obligations and constraints. It takes account of their capability for compassion or commitment, which makes them reasonable social players, responsible citizens or people capable of looking beyond themselves. This approach is concerned as much with people's social ties and achievements as with management of the goods and services that allow those achievements to come about. The individual's capability to act and achieve thus becomes the source of well-being, much more than satisfaction or utility (Sen, 1999).

The macro-economic measurement of this well-being is the Human Development Index (HDI), which also has many limitations. It refers to a small number of essential achievements relating to income, education (literacy, schooling) and health (life expectancy). The advantage of these few achievements is that they can be evaluated in all the countries in the world, so that HDI can be regularly compared to GNP.

c. The necessary contributions of psychology

With the various currents of positive, clinical and social psychology, psychologists add a new dimension to the idea of well-being, broadening the economic view and linking it up to the philosophical concept of happiness. The positive or humanist current, represented by Eric Fromm,

Abraham Maslow, Carl Rodgers and Victor Frankl, looks at people's capability to give life "meaning" (Lecomte, 2007) through the intensity of their social relationships, reference to a number of values and skills, and their personal or collective capability for action. Happiness, in the philosophical sense, is then constructed by a combination of well-being, in the sense used by economists, and "meaning".

In clinical psychology, as in psychoanalysis, the accent is placed rather on seeking out the underlying causes of ill-being and of the ensuing suffering, which obstructs the possibility of well-being. While some advocate medication to combat ill-being (Layard, 2005), it is clear that many such situations stem from difficult human relationships in terms of hierarchy and information-sharing, in a context marked by the use of more sophisticated technologies, increased international competition and new modes of communication.

Social psychology studies the effects of the social environment and institutions on people's behaviour, taking account of factors such as individuals' interaction in groups, people's perceptions and motivations in society, the influence of social representations and conflict situations.

These different approaches give us a clearer picture of the concepts of well-being, meaning and happiness. We can therefore avoid equating well-being with happiness, as the utilitarians do, and consider that people construct happiness via the pursuit of well-being, expressed in terms of living standards, living conditions and social ties, together with the pursuit of meaning, which is based on people's capability for achievement. Some go so far as to speak of "human well-being" to reflect this broader view of well-being which incorporates the economic and psychological aspects and thus comes closer to the idea of happiness.

This expression tallies with the very pertinent question put by the sociologist Edgar Morin, who wondered whether it was not preferable to talk of "good living" (*bien-vivre*) rather than well-being.

2. Ensuring well-being: in search of a new ethics

In the 18th century (Sismondi, 1773-1842), the introduction of the first public policies provided a response to the universal aspiration to well-being. This continued in the 20th century with the pursuit of regular economic growth and planned development. The idea was that growth would benefit everyone, regardless of the redistribution mechanisms envisaged. But the 19th-century social question in the industrialised countries, then development issues in Third World countries and lastly European integration at the end of the 20th century made it quite clear that only growth policies coupled with deliberate redistribution mechanisms could ensure that everyone had access to basic levels of well-being.

By means of specific social redistribution mechanisms, the welfare state upheld this strategy with a concern to protect the most vulnerable. The state thus bore part of the responsibility for access to well-being by firstly guaranteeing the resources to ensure the regular rise of living standards and improve living conditions, and secondly reducing the risk of poverty and remedying inequalities through appropriate redistribution mechanisms. Policies of this kind have served to regularly reduce poverty and in many countries, to foster the emergence of a new middle class.

At present, however, while growth continues worldwide, inequalities are rising sharply, to the extent of curbing poverty reduction, although it is the prerequisite for gaining access to well-being. Moreover, beyond a certain threshold, this growth is no longer coupled with an improvement in people's subjective perception of well-being, as if economic growth were no longer helping to improve well-being.

a. Economic growth no longer ensures well-being

Surveys assessing well-being on a subjective basis, using questions to individuals, show that while the feeling of well-being increases very sharply when people leave poverty behind, as a result of their increased consumption of goods and services, the feeling then wanes steadily as their consumption grows.

It is as if economic growth improves the subjective feeling of well-being as long as it allows people to escape poverty and reach a living standard they perceive as decent. Beyond this level, improvements in income or consumption levels have little impact on the level of well-being experienced (Lecomte, 2007).

The findings are similar in all the rich countries, whether in the United States, where this trend became apparent in the mid-1960s, or in Britain and Japan, where it emerged later, towards the late 1970s.[2] This discon-

---

2. Comparative country analysis shows that above a threshold in national income per head of about US$20 000, the subjective feeling of well-being ceases to grow with the increase of income (Layard, 2005).

nection may also be due to the fact that the pursuit of economic growth generates additional social and human costs which are increasingly rejected. To increase this well-being, we need to look into its broader form, particularly in view of the psychological evidence discussed above that additional well-being can be found in the intensity of social relationships, in access to knowledge and the practice of certain values and in people's capability to act – all elements that provide people with meaning and a feeling of achievement. In other words, involvement in social networks, with the commitment, compassion, obligations and responsibilities this entails, helps to increase the subjective feeling of well-being.

This nevertheless raises the difficult question of how to handle the shift from an approach geared to individual well-being to a situation of collective well-being, taking account of social interaction. This is a serious aggregation problem, which collective choice economists, among others, study closely. For the moment, however, there is no universal solution because it remains difficult to assess the well-being stemming from interaction between several people otherwise than by taking a specific look at each situation.

When it comes to measuring well-being, the question is how to describe it and how to assess levels of well-being. There are of course income and consumption indicators, but they turn out to be inadequate. The solution is a pragmatic approach, referring to the different aspects of well-being in the broad sense and adding the aspects of ill-being.[3]

To assess people's capability for action and achievement, and the difficulties and constraints they encounter in achieving them, the list of basic capabilities proposed by the philosopher Nussbaum (2000) can serve as a reference for exploring new avenues. Lastly, the psychological approach, which is closer to existential concerns, requires us to consider factors such as social interaction, perceptions, trust, aspects of ill-being and social comparisons and representations.

b. Ensuring equity in reducing poverty and inequalities

Escaping poverty can be regarded as the priority achievement sought in the aspiration to well-being. The same is true of social exclusion, especially bearing in mind that it is due to the impossibility of gaining access to certain goods, services and social relationships. The different

---

3.   On this point, see the article by Samuel Thirion.

forms of exclusion derive from this deprivation of access (Dubois and Mahieu, 2002).

Economic growth is an effective way to reduce poverty. However, it has been demonstrated, particularly in monetary terms, that growth reduces poverty much less effectively if inequalities increase at the same time. In other words, at a given level of growth, the increase in inequalities curbs poverty reduction, since the additional income is not transferred to the poorest groups. To remedy this situation, specific redistribution mechanisms must be put into operation so that the benefits of this growth enable people to escape poverty.

The problem is that there are many forms of inequality – social, spatial, gender-based and so on. They are reflected in differences in access to goods and services, discrepancies in the building of assets and potential, unequal opportunities, inequality in terms of capability to function, differences in outcome and so on. All these forms of inequality often collect around the same groups, shaping structures of inequality which are hard to remedy with the use of redistribution mechanisms.

Given the range of socio-economic situations, the problem is which inequalities to focus on and which ones to combat first. Furthermore, depending on the areas of action chosen, the fact of reducing particular forms of inequality occasionally has the effect of generating or heightening others.

The concept of equity resolves this dilemma because it draws a distinction between inequalities: those that are considered unacceptable because they are unjust or unjustified, and those that can be considered acceptable at a given time because they are tolerated for social reasons or recognised as producing generally positive benefits.

The principles of equity determine spheres of justice in which trust can be established between social players, facilitating the emergence of innovative individual or collective initiatives. Clearly, equity is of fundamental importance. In a setting of permanent growth and development, it is a way of combining action to reduce poverty and inequalities with respect for the freedom of social players.

In this context, the prime objective is to ensure equitable access to well-being. This means guaranteeing basic access to essential goods and services for everyone, then ensuring that each individual has the wherewithal to aim for a situation of well-being that he/she considers decent.

Then it will be a question of tackling situations of ill-being and the factors underlying them.

c. *Relying on an ethics of responsibility*

Setting in motion processes designed to promote well-being, especially equitable access to well-being, raises issues of moral responsibility – responsibility towards those who have been promised an improvement in their situation and who are expecting results in view of their aspirations, but also responsibility as the joint authors of equity rules, or processes, for the achievement and distribution of well-being. These two forms of responsibility suggest a distinction between two views of responsibility reflected in the terms "being answerable to others" and "being answerable for others" (Thirion, 2004).

"Being answerable to others" refers to one's responsibility for one's own acts and therefore for their a posteriori consequences (the term would be *ex-post* in economics). This kind of responsibility is normally defined by social practices, which is why it can be described as social or retrospective responsibility (Jonas, 1979). What is important in this case is the person's freedom of action, which makes them responsible to others.

When it comes to "being answerable for others", the important point is responsibility for meeting obligations, which may be imposed by a particular status, by others or by oneself. This is a priori responsibility (the term would be *ex-ante* in economics). The model here is parental responsibility. This can be described as personal or prospective responsibility, which effectively reduces the person's own freedom.

Explicitly at least, an author such as Sen considers only retrospective responsibility, because that is where it is easiest to measure a posteriori the consequences of the acts performed. Conversely, philosophers Jonas, Levinas and Ricœur emphasise prospective or personal responsibility as the most appropriate element for dealing with the natural and social challenges of today's world. It is a fact that apart from a few precisely defined situations such as parental responsibility, the responsibility of company directors and sometimes political responsibility, there is no general moral rule covering all the cases reflected in this form of responsibility.

Expanding on the example of parental responsibility, Jonas (1979) stresses responsibility towards future generations and towards a natural environment undermined by sophisticated technologies born of technical progress – a situation calling for a principle of responsibility which can be implemented with the introduction of precautionary or prudential principles. This brings us back to Aristotle's virtuous view, in which prudence was the virtue associated with all capabilities for action.

Levinas (1982) takes the same attitude. Our encounter with the most fragile and vulnerable individuals, whether we already know them or not, requires us to give them priority and therefore to restrict our own freedom. Personal responsibility to others thus takes precedence over personal freedom of action.

Ricœur clarifies responsibility in relation to people's capability to act. In his view, situations of vulnerability are due to individuals' fallibility, to the fact that they can make mistakes. Carrying the two previous authors' thinking further, he shows that prospective responsibility means being capable of assigning oneself a priori responsibility with regard to specific acts and individuals, considering oneself "responsible for ...". This leads to a voluntary process of restricting one's own freedom to meet social obligations that take priority, as it were. This voluntary capacity to impose constraints on oneself is a characteristic of the individual as a responsible subject.

Behind these three authors' concurrent thinking lies the understanding approach of phenomenological thought, which focuses on people's intentions and social interaction and the connections between their rights and obligations in order to ensure the cohesion of a socially and culturally identified society.

The emphasis on personal responsibility thus results in a departure from the strict definition of the utilitarian individual, who seeks to rationally maximise his/her interests, and a move towards a broader definition, that of the individual capable of transcendence, that is of looking beyond him/herself for the benefit of others, especially the most vulnerable. The individual becomes the most comprehensive subject of analysis, being simultaneously capable of rationality, reason, responsibility and transcending the self.

On the spectrum between the rational individual, as perceived in economics, and the person capable of transcending the self, there are many different ways of considering the subject in action – as an economic agent, a reasonable social player or a responsible citizen, for example.

Nowadays, what makes personal responsibility increasingly important by comparison with social responsibility, although the latter is more clearly defined and more firmly established, is the need to confront the great natural and social challenges of today's world. Given the scale of the problems to be resolved in this much more complex society, a wide range of players are affected by the existing risks, and a preventive approach, adopted a priori, becomes preferable to an approach consisting in remedying the consequences a posteriori – which in some cases even proves impossible.

At the same time, the various social players are growing increasingly aware of the challenges threatening well-being in its broader form. This raises the wider issue of how to share out responsibility between the different players concerned. In addition to the usual role of the state and formal institutions, there are now individuals, various social groups, local authorities and a range of associations concerned with environmental issues, poverty reduction, the rise of inequalities, social cohesion and so on. All these aspects have to be taken into account by those involved in the process of improving well-being.

In any event, the sharing out of responsibilities must be addressed. It can be done on the basis of a legal and institutional framework determining each player's particular responsibilities. Alternatively, the players' shared responsibility can be viewed as a process better suited to prospective responsibility because it allows the players to feel responsible in terms of rules they have established themselves. This process can be applied to the equitable promotion of well-being in the broad sense. It is thus conducive to the establishment of "just institutions" in the sense advocated by Ricœur, that is institutions which, because they feel jointly responsible, take care to promote well-being equitably, particularly by reinforcing people's capability to act.

In this context, distribution criteria are not established by law or by institutions and can therefore derive only from an agreement between the different players concerned, after discussion. The ethics of discussion (Habermas, 2003) then provides the conditions for a debate between the stakeholders, resulting in a compromise solution to the problem of sustainable distribution.

Thanks to this approach, important collective decisions can be taken, such as agreement on the aspects of well-being or ill-being, on the priorities for reinforcing capabilities in order to link up freedoms and responsibilities, or on the equity criteria for distributing well-being. Debate on these issues serves to build a capability for collective action, in the form of co-operation and commitment, on the basis of the stakeholders' capabilities, while taking account of their choice of values. Debate then becomes a formidable tool for effectively determining the level of shared responsibility between the various players concerned.

Nevertheless, efforts to implement this approach will undeniably run into a number of difficulties due to situations of exclusion, discrimination, power structure and unequal access to information, which are features of all societies. Special skills, held mainly by psycho-sociologists and social coaching specialists, help to overcome the corresponding risks of deadlock.

Conclusion

In view of the universally shared aspirations to well-being, the state and institutions can ensure that a basic level of well-being is available to everyone and that the resources and capabilities for achieving this well-being are equitably distributed. The pursuit of happiness, on the basis of the broader view combining economic well-being and psychological meaning, is more a matter for individuals and social players, who, by their choices, can take advantage of the opportunities directly offered to them by growth and technical progress to work towards greater achievement.

Taking people's aspirations and means of expression as a starting point in order to inspire concerted public policies thus seems to be a plausible approach if well-being does not amount exclusively to the pursuit of personal satisfactions arising from the consumption of goods and services, but incorporates the aspects of individual and collective achievement deriving from a system of mutual rights and obligations. This also confers meaning on the steps taken.

This brings us back to Ricœur's ethical statement on the establishment of a "good life, with and for others, in just institutions". It provides the ethical framework justifying the equitable promotion of a view of well-being in the broad sense, on the basis of shared responsibility between social players. This view can generate a practice based on the concerted expression of ideas by stakeholders regarded as sharing responsibility for situations of well-being and ill-being, who, in line with a bottom-up approach, carry out processes for improving and distributing well-being.

On this basis, taking a pragmatic approach and relying on debate, we can identify the range of indicators for characterising situations of well-being and ill-being. And we can then consider public measures and policies aimed at influencing the factors for improving well-being while combating those that cause ill-being.

Putting this vision into practice, however, still poses many theoretical and empirical problems. For example, the discussion of economic subjects regarded as responsible individuals because they are capable of restricting their freedom to comply with their social and economic obligations entails assessing the costs of this kind of responsibility by taking specific measurements.

Likewise, the fact that people can together take collective steps to improve their well-being entails knowing how to resolve the problem of aggregating the effects of these steps, since improving well-being at local level should preferably also help to improve well-being at a wider level.

These methodological investments need to be made; they are legitimised by the new conceptual discussions in the field of phenomenology which aim to incorporate social players' perceptions, aspirations and intentions into economic analysis. The emphasis on social interaction thus brings us back to the more comprehensive view of socially sustainable development, with its direct concern for responsibility and equity (Ballet, Dubois and Mahieu, 2005).

References

Ballet, J. and Mahieu, F.-R., *Ethique Economique*, Ellipses, Paris, 2003.

Ballet, J., Dubois, J.-L. and Mahieu, F.-R., *L'autre développement, le développement socialement soutenable*, L'Harmattan, Paris, 2005.

Dubois, J.-L. and Mahieu, F.-R., "La dimension sociale du développement durable: lutte contre la pauvreté ou durabilité sociale?" in Martin, J.-Y. (ed.), *Développement durable? Doctrines, pratiques, évaluations*, IRD, Paris, 2002, pp. 73-94.

Habermas, J., *L'éthique de la discussion et la question de la vérité*, Grasset, Paris, 2003.

Jarret, M.-F. and Mahieu, F.-R., *Economie publique: théories économiques de l'interaction sociale*, Ellipses, Paris, 1998.

Jonas, H., *Le principe responsabilité*, Champs, Flammarion, Paris (French translation, 1990, of *Das Prinzip Verantwortung*, Insel Verlag, Frankfurt, 1979).

Layard, R., *Happiness: Lessons from a New Science*, Penguin Books, New York, 2005.

Lecomte, J., *Donner un sens à sa vie*, Odile Jacob, Paris, 2007.

Levinas, E., *Ethique et Infini*, Fayard, Paris, 1982.

Misrahi, R., *Le sujet et son désir*, Editions Pleins Feux, Paris, 2003.

Nussbaum, M., *Women and Human Development: The Capabilities Approach*, Cambridge University Press, Cambridge, 2000.

Perroux, F., *L'économie du XXe siècle*, PUF, Paris, 1952.

Ricœur, P., *Le Juste*, Esprit, Paris, 1995.

Sen, A.K., *Commodities and Capabilities*, Elsevier, Amsterdam, 1985.

Sen, A.K., *Un nouveau modèle économique: développement, justice et liberté*, Odile Jacob, Paris (French translation, 2000, of *Development as Freedom*, Knopf, New York, 1999).

Thirion, S., "Social Cohesion Indicators and the Contribution of a Solidarity-based Economy", *Ethical Solidarity-based Citizen Involvement in the Economy: a Prerequisite for Social Cohesion*, Trends in social cohesion, No. 12, Council of Europe Publishing, Strasbourg, 2004.

UNDP, *15 Years of Human Development Reports 1990-2004,* CD-Rom statistical database, United Nations Development Programme, New York, 2005.

Further reading

Aristote, *Ethique à Nicomaque*, Garnier-Flammarion, 1965 edition, Paris.

Ballet, J., Dubois, J.-L., Bigo, V. and Mahieu, F.-R., "Happiness, Responsibility and Preference Perturbations", in Ballet, J. and Bazin, D. (eds.), *Essays on Positive Ethics in Economics*, Transaction Publishers, London, 2006, pp. 225-238.

Bebbington, A., Danis, A., de Haan, A. and Walton, M., *Institutional Pathways to Equity: Addressing Inequality Traps*, The World Bank, Washington DC, 2008.

Beck, U., *La société du risque. Sur la voie d'une autre modernité* (French translation, 2001), Flammarion, Paris, 1986.

Deneulin, S., Nebel, M. and Sagovsky, N. (eds.), *Transforming Unjust Structures*: *The Capability Approach*, Springer, Dordrecht, the Netherlands, 2006.

Mahieu, F.-R., *Responsabilité et crimes économiques*, L'Harmattan, Paris, 2008.

Misrahi, R., "Construire son bonheur", in *Philosophies de notre temps*, Editions Sciences Humaines, Paris, 2000, pp. 287-289.

Ricœur, P., *Parcours de la reconnaissance*, Stock, Paris, (translation, 2005, of *The Course of Recognition*, Harvard University Press, Cambridge, MA, 2004).

Sen, A.K., "Equality of What?" in *Choice, Welfare and Measurement*, Blackwell, Oxford, re-edited Harvard University Press, 1982, pp. 353-369.

II. Well-being: perception and measurement

Wolfgang Glatzer[1]

Introduction

The concepts of well-being and quality of life are rather similar in respect to the basic idea that they are conceived as fundamental societal goals much broader than material welfare. Both are conceived in terms of "objective" living conditions and their "subjective" perception by individuals. When different components of "objective" and "subjective" provenance are interconnected then the picture of society always shows some complexity. The perception of public goods, in particular, seems to follow its own rules and is of apparent significance for the social cohesion of the population. Depending on the type of goods, the state has more or less influence on their provision and different types of welfare state use this influence in different ways. The problem will be illustrated by three examples: firstly, by the difference in the ratings of private and public goods; secondly, by the difference in the evaluation between individual and aggregate characteristics and, thirdly, when the difference of levels between personal and national well-being is taken into account. In all these cases we find a lower estimation of and satisfaction with components which are outside the responsibility of the individual. The problem of the evaluation of public goods by the population is demonstrated and the challenge to avoid negative social consequences is articulated.

1. Well-being and its perception

a. The concepts of well-being and quality of life

Among the ultimate goals of humankind well-being or social well-being is discussed and considerably emphasised, although the concept itself is historically not very old. As far as can be seen it was the Organisation for Economic Co-operation and Development (OECD, 1973, 1976) who developed the term and the concept of well-being in the early 1970s and used it until recently. As well as the OECD there were some American authors (notably Andrews and Withey, 1976) who particularly chose well-

---

1. Professor Dr Wolfgang Glatzer, J. W. Goethe-Universität, Frankfurt-on-Main – Institut für Gesellschafts- und Politikanalyse.

being as their guiding term and presented investigations related to well-being and quality of life. These terms seem to be interchangeable and they were used without clear separation in books and papers.

Of course the subject of well-being has existed and been discussed since ancient times, but often with different terminology and different concerns. The OECD stated that "the term social well-being is used as a shorthand for the aggregate well-being of individuals. ... The heart of the problem is the well-being of individual human beings and the way in which it is affected by their relations with other human beings and the physical environment" (OECD, 1976: 12). The broader frame of reference for well-being is the context of research into social indicators and among the first 17 articles of *Citation Classics from Social Indicators Research* (Michalos, 2005) one finds seven times the concept of (subjective) well-being. Well-being is related to objective reality as well as to subjective perception and evaluation. Soon afterwards, however, the *Subjective Elements of Well-Being* (OECD, 1973) or more concise *Subjective Well-Being* (Strack, Argyle and Schwarz, 1990) came more and more to the attention of research and politics. The concept is so successful that editors spoke recently of "the universality of subjective well-being indicators" (Gullone and Cummins, 2002).

Well-being in its broad sense is defined basically as a constellation of components which can consist of objective living conditions and/or of subjective perceived aspects of life.

The objective living conditions are usually monitored by experts from the social and natural sciences; these objective conditions exist independent of the awareness of the population exposed to them. Their range may vary from narrow personal conditions through the community domain to the world's environmental conditions. Some approaches prefer to focus on social problems, preferably on poverty and social exclusion and not least on social inequality (see Figure 1).

Figure 1 – Components of well-being and quality of life

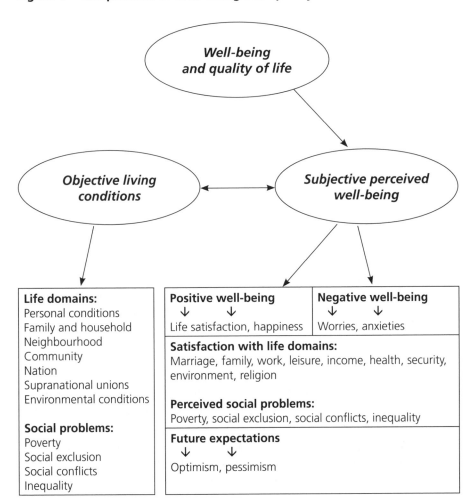

Subjectively perceived well-being consists of perceptions and evalua-tions from individuals; subjective quality of life is here in the eye of the beholder. Investigations into the subjective perceptions of well-being have demonstrated that it is a multifaceted concept. It has a positive side, mostly described in terms of satisfaction, happiness or similar, and there is a negative side in terms of worries, anxieties and further aspects.

For the subjectively perceived aspects of life there are comprehen-sive concepts such as satisfaction with life as a whole and happiness. These concepts can be deconstructed down to many specific life domains. Several investigations have shown that negative well-being is only modestly correlated with positive well-being. This means some people are satisfied and happy although they have a high burden of worries and others are unhappy although they have only few worries. Subjective well-being is obviously a rather complicated and ambivalent concept.

The relationship between objective conditions and subjective perceptions is not very strong and many investigations have been done into this problem. One approach is related to typical combinations between good and bad levels. Consistent types are "well-being" and "deprivation"; inconsistent types are "dissonance" and "adaptation". For example, the case of "adaptation" is characterised by poor living conditions with relatively positive well-being of the people exposed to them (Glatzer and Zapf, 1984).

In order to achieve a full picture of social well-being in addition to the positive and negative dimensions, another dimension has to be taken into account, namely future expectations. It makes a big difference if somebody is in a bad situation and looks optimistically into the future as opposed to someone who sees no way out of a difficult situation. This is the reason to also emphasise future expectations as a component of well-being. Thus, optimism and pessimism became an essential part of the concept of well-being.

The problem of defining well-being was solved in rather different ways, due to the challenges of the different contexts. In the United States a strong preference for the subjective approach to well-being gained acceptance, while in Europe – at least in Scandinavia and to a certain degree in other parts of Europe – there was more emphasis laid upon objective indicators which measure social conditions in the eyes of statistical experts. In Germany the researchers took up a position in between and preferred a combination of objective and subjective data (Zapf, 1987). Only recently has the subjective approach been adopted for developing countries (Camfield, 2004). In Europe the monitoring of well-being gained increasing awareness and is now an established and respected part of social sciences.

The concept of well-being is related to goals which are of high significance for our society: freedom[2] and democracy, social security and safety, solidarity and political participation, equity and sustainability and suchlike.

---

2. In analogy to measurement of quality of life there are nowadays measures for freedom and similar concepts; see, for example, Holmes, Feulner and O'Grady, 2008.

Among the value concepts of our society, well-being has a position among the values of highest importance.

b. The objective-subjective difference

The distinction between objective and subjective aspects (respective components) is fundamental in research into well-being. The emerging problem is that we do not have a clear decision as to what is right or wrong about the two views of society. Are the objective aspects of reality more correct than the subjective ones or is the contrary true? If somebody decides that both are relevant, the question arises as to whether they have equal weight or if one has more significance than the other. In the course of time different pragmatic solutions to operationalise and measure objective and subjective concepts have been developed. Having a number of objective and subjective indicators on the table – as is the situation nowadays – we get a view of the gaps and discrepancies. On different levels – the world, nations, individuals – the objective components do not show exactly the same as the subjective components.

2. Measurement of well-being

a. Measurement of well-being in different countries

The new measures of well-being on the objective side are the Human Development Index (HDI), the Human Wellbeing Index (HWI) and the Weighted Index of Social Progress (WISP). In the HDI, which has basically three components, the traditional GDP has the weight of one third. The HWI is strongly oriented towards environmental goals and contains 10 components. The WISP is an index of 40 components and includes more aspects of a social state. On the subjective side we find the Overall Satisfaction with Life index (OSL) and the Affect Balance Scale (ABS). OSL is a single-item index and ABS is a 10-item index which is explicitly related to positive and negative daily experiences. Finally, there is the Happy Life Expectancy index (HLE) a mixed index containing objective and subjective aspects in one index. Length of life and satisfaction with life are included in one index. These seem to me to be the most important measures of well-being and quality of life but there are additional ones in scientific and public literature, though sometimes they are insufficiently documented.

To attain a certain picture, the overview (Figure 2) is restricted to a selection of countries. The countries which were selected for the comparison are always two representing a larger area: two from northern Europe (Norway, Denmark), two from central Europe (Germany, France), two from southern Europe (Italy, Spain) and two from eastern Europe (Poland, Romania). In addition to the European countries there are two other countries (United States, Japan) from the developed world.

Figure 2 – Quality of life indicators for selected countries

Indicator	HDI	HWI	WISP	OSL	ABS	HLE
Norway	1 0.97	1 82	2 104	3 79	1 2.31	2 59.4
Denmark	3 0.94	2 81	1 107	1 86	3 1.93	1 62.7
Germany	6 0.93	4 77	3 100	2 80	4 1.47	4 56.1
France	4 0.94	5 75	6 94	6 66	6 1.33	8 51.4
Italy	5 0.93	6 74	4 98	5 70	7 1.24	5 54.2
Spain	7 0.93	7 73	5 96	7 65	8 0.73	6 53.4
Poland	9 0.89	8 65	7 85	8 50	5 1.47	9 43.2
Romania	10 0.83	9 50	10 77	10 38	9 0.71	10 38.0
United States	2 0.94	7 73	7 85	3 79	2 2.21	3 57.0
Japan	8 0.92	3 80	7 85 (1995)	9 53	10 0.93	7 53.0

HDI: Human Development Index (UNDP, 2005)
HWI: Human Wellbeing Index (Prescott-Allen, 2001)
WISP: Weighted Index of Social Progress (Estes, 2004)
OSL: Overall Satisfaction with Life (Halman et al., 2008)
ABS: Affect Balance Scale (Bradburn, 1969; Veenhoven, 2008)
HLE: Happy Life Expectancy (Veenhoven, 1996)

According to the construction of well-being indices, the results for the positions of the 10 nations are the following. The best values on each scale were attained mostly by Norway and Denmark. The Scandinavian and northern European countries are all exceptional according to all the well-being indices. Only the United States sometimes has evaluations as high as the northern European countries. Europe as a whole shows a bias in favour of northern and central Europe as opposed to southern and eastern Europe. Comparison countries such as the United States are sometimes in the upper part of the scale but Japan is mostly in the lower part of the ranking list. The US has the strongest changes in positions from two on the HDI to seven on the WISP. There is more often continuity rather than strong changes and the gaps between the upper and lower positions are constant over time. The HDI results are quite close to those of the OSL and the discrepancies, all in all, are lower then one might expect. It should be added that time series data are always very stable over time for whole countries, and it is obvious that the societies in countries exert an influence on quality of life (Böhnke, 2008).

b. Measurement of well-being within countries

The measurement of well-being contributes to a better understanding of the differences between nations but also within nations, where the distribution of well-being is often described in terms of gaps. Gaps can be defined as the existence of a significant long-running discrepancy between two variables and these exist in many forms. We often come across a gender gap, age gaps, intergenerational gaps, educational gaps, regional gaps (Bergheim, 2007), unemployment gap (Luechinger, Meier and Stutzer, 2008), migration gap and gaps related to family composition. There are comprehensive maps of the distribution of well-being for whole countries (Bergheim, 2007).

Figure 3 – Living conditions and social exclusion in Europe, 2003

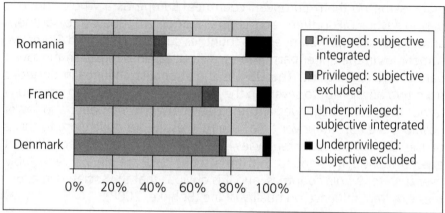

Privileged and underprivileged conditions: index of objective conditions
Subjective integration and subjective exclusion: index of feelings of social exclusion

Source: Böhnke (2008: 22) according to Alber and Fahey, European survey: percentage of population in the age between 15 and 65.

It is obvious that we have a lot of well-off people who are privileged in life and who feel socially integrated (see Figure 3). At the same time we have a pattern of underprivileged people who feel excluded. Most interesting now is that there are inconsistencies: people who are in the privileged group and feel subjectively excluded and people who are underprivileged and feel subjectively integrated. A rich country like Denmark still has around 25% and a poorer country like Romania has 60%. The underprivileged who feel subjectively integrated are many more than the privileged who feel subjectively excluded and this favours the social integration of society.

There are many gaps like these and each aspect of social inequality can attain significance in objective and subjective terms. Gaps inside a society are characterised by the social consequences they have on societal development. The point at which objective differences turn into subjective articulated discrepancies varies according to societies and cultures.

c. *Individual well-being*

In a third context, the concept of gaps is related to the individual and their perception process. This has been a very broad discussion since the beginning of well-being research (see mainly Michalos, 2005; Diener and Lucas, 2000). A common hypothesis is that behind the dissatisfaction of an individual there is always a gap between what the individual has and what the individual wants. Both need to be defined: the individual defines how the situation is and how it would be preferred. Between both reference points is a gap which determines the level of satisfaction. There are a number of reference points: expectations/aspirations, past experience, future expectations, the situation of relatives, friends and neighbours, the average citizen, the poor and the rich. There is some ongoing research into this problem but the gap is currently the most important theory to explain satisfaction and dissatisfaction.[3]

3. Public goods, context characteristics and national well-being in the social state

Within the approach of measuring well-being it is a normal procedure to include the perception of goods and characteristics beyond just market goods and domestic products. In our opinion these are public and common goods such as the transport system and social security, environment characteristics such as the average health in the region, as well as national well-being, for example the satisfaction reflected by national performance indicators.

Goods, as well as their opposite the "bads", are a result of the process of welfare production. Goods and services are produced through one of four institutions: the market with its enterprises, the state with its activities, the households with their household production and the intermediate organisations concerned with the provision of services. Each good is mainly produced by one provider, for example the market is responsible for market goods, but often we find combinations of producers, for example care is provided both by the state and by the private sector. This joint production is often regarded as especially productive. Political goods are goods which are provided by the state or sometimes in co-operation with the state.

There is a complex discussion on various types of goods: public goods, common goods, collective goods, social goods, merit goods, political goods and others, such as infrastructural goods and environmental goods. All these goods are defined in some way in contrast to private goods, personal goods, individual goods and market goods. A good is everything which is a positive contribution to life in the material or

---

3. The most discussed non-gap theory is set theory.

symbolic sense; the opposite are "bads", which have a negative impact on life. The significance of "bads" for inequality in society is as high as for goods, although they are much less mentioned. In the classic sense the criteria for public goods and common goods is related to non-rivalry and non-exclusiveness. Sometimes public goods are conceived as non-rival and common goods as non-exclusive, but this is a theoretical definition. If we want to look at the goods provided by the state we would speak of political goods.

Some goods are shared by the whole population, for example air, climate, social security or the transport system. The average conditions in a country are also similar to a common good: the average standard of living, the average satisfaction level and so on. We could speak of context goods which act as a framework for individual goods. The opposite are personal goods which are accessible only by the individual whereas the common goods are for everybody. Common goods are a result of the aggregation of individual goods.

The social state is an institution, established during the last century, which offers a broad range of public goods and services to the population and especially symbolic goods such as solidarity and justice. There are different types of welfare state: conservative, social democratic or liberal. Another terminology distinguishes between the poor and restricted welfare state and the more developed one. It is hard to detect the influence of the welfare state on well-being because there are direct and indirect influences. The more developed welfare state is intertwined with the social structure and is guaranteed and shaped by the social state.

4. Private-public differentiation and well-being

The significance of public and common goods for well-being is not in doubt in principle but in practice it is an unsolved problem. There is no comprehensive book or article which gives an informative overview of this problem, but certain aspects can be found in various places and many datasets include hidden data about this problem. In this article three examples are presented which throw light on the private-public differentiation from different perspectives. A broad systematic survey would go beyond the possibilities of this report. Only some illustrative pointers can be given here.

The pioneer studies on well-being (Andrews and Withey, 1976: 433) and quality of life (Campbell and Converse, 1976: 63) already touched on the problem of low satisfaction with governmental concerns. The indicators show "that the great majority of people in this country were content with life in the United States today" but they also demonstrate the "presence of millions of Americans who had serious complaints about their society" (*ibidem*: 285-6). This was mentioned but did not become a significant point presumably because only very few public dimensions were included in the questionnaires. Similar results can be found in various studies. There is one study in Europe looking explicitly at *The Quality of the Public Sector* (Social and Cultural Planning Office of the Netherlands, 2002). Many dimensions of the public sector are investigated but the comparison with the private sector is very brief. All in all, moderate satisfaction with public goods is supported: "It is not difficult to tap a large reservoir of dissatisfaction among the population towards the public sector in the Netherlands" (*ibidem*: 56). The following example is related to the comparison of private and public domains (Table 1).

a. *Private well-being versus public well-being*

In the investigation of life domains and societal areas there are topics which seem more private and others which seem more public. Without reservation, it is obvious that there is generally a clear division: the private ratings are higher and the public ratings are lower. The data comes from the welfare survey (1998), which is representative of the German population, because in the course of the interview more domains than elsewhere are counted. The distinction between western Germany and eastern Germany was made because the data for eastern Germany have a special underlying rationality although the public-private division is the same.

Table 1 shows that the margins for the general average are between 8.8 and 5.8 with a difference of 3.0 between the relatively high and relatively low domains. Results of over 7.0 include satisfaction with marriage/partner, family, living area, working position, living standard, housing, health and household income. Below 7.0 are social security, democracy, political participation, public security and environmental protection. The first impression is without doubt a lower satisfaction in public areas and a higher satisfaction in private areas.

Table 1 – Satisfaction in private and public life domains for population groups in western Germany, 1998

Satisfaction* with ___ for total population and subgroups	Total	Gender		Age			Education			Status of occupation			Income		Citizenship	
		M	F	18-34	35-59	60+	Secondary school certificate	Middle degree	High school	Employed	Unemployed	Pensioner	Lower quintile	Upper quintile	German	Other
Marriage/ partnership	8.8	9.0	8.6	8.8	8.7	8.9	8.8	8.8	8.6	8.8	8.5	9.0	8.7	8.7	8.8	8.8
Family	8.5	8.7	8.4	8.3	8.5	8.9	8.6	8.7	8.3	8.6	7.5	8.9	8.3	8.6	8.5	8.5
Housing	8.3	8.1	8.3	7.8	8.2	8.8	8.3	8.2	8.2	8.1	7.2	8.7	7.6	8.5	8.3	7.3
Residential area	8.1	8.0	8.1	7.6	8.0	8.5	8.1	8.0	8.0	8.0	7.0	8.4	7.9	8.1	8.1	7.3
Employment position	7.7	7.7	7.6	7.6	7.6	8.5	7.6	7.7	7.6	7.7	-	-	6.7	8.1	7.7	7.1
Leisure time	7.6	7.6	7.5	7.2	7.2	8.3	7.6	7.5	7.5	7.2	6.7	8.4	7.3	7.7	7.6	7.0
Economic status	7.4	7.4	7.4	7.1	7.3	7.7	7.2	7.4	7.8	7.5	5.2	7.7	5.3	8.3	7.4	7.0
Health	7.4	7.6	7.3	8.4	7.3	6.5	7.0	7.8	7.9	8.0	7.4	6.2	7.0	7.6	7.4	7.9
Income	7.0	7.0	7.0	6.7	7.0	7.4	6.8	7.0	7.3	7.1	4.9	7.4	5.0	8.2	7.0	6.2
Social security	6.5	6.6	6.4	6.2	6.4	7.0	6.5	6.5	6.6	6.4	5.5	7.1	6.4	6.9	6.5	7.0
Democracy	6.5	6.7	6.3	6.4	6.5	6.7	6.3	6.4	6.8	6.6	5.9	6.7	6.3	6.9	6.5	6.6
Environment protection	6.1	6.3	6.0	6.0	6.1	6.4	6.3	6.1	5.9	6.2	6.2	6.3	6.0	6.3	6.1	6.5
Public safety	5.9	6.0	5.9	6.1	5.9	5.9	5.8	5.8	6.2	6.0	5.6	5.9	5.9	5.9	5.9	6.3
Political participation	5.8	6.0	5.5	5.5	5.8	6.0	5.5	5.8	6.3	5.9	4.7	6.0	4.9	6.3	5.8	4.4

* Average on satisfaction scale from 0 (completely dissatisfied) to 10 (completely satisfied).
Database: Wohlfahrtssurvey, 1998.
Source: Statistisches Bundesamt, 2000: 432 et seq.

This result is not unique for a certain time context. It is stable over time (in Germany since 1978) and another type of data also hints at the same direction. In the socio-economic panel in a series of domains, social security shows the lowest value (Statistisches Bundesamt, 2006: 445). Again the developments over time are of special interest: certain domains have lower satisfaction, especially environmental protection and, in recent years, social security.

Different population groups often show the same satisfaction level, but some population groups are different in their satisfaction levels. Women are less satisfied than men in respect to satisfaction with democracy and political participation, which could be explained by historical developments. The older generation are more satisfied with social security, probably because they profit more from it. There are no big differences with regard to educational levels. The pensioners are most satisfied with social security, the unemployed least of all. The upper quintile is more satisfied with social security, democracy and political participation than the lower quintile. The German people are more satisfied with their political participation, less with social security. It seems that conditions that influence satisfaction depend on the interests of the people. The reasons will be discussed in the final section. It is an unexpected result that richer people are more satisfied with public goods than poorer ones. Presumably they can compensate for deficits in public goods by using their private income.

b. Individual characteristics versus aggregate characteristics

In each collective entity there are characteristics of individuals and characteristics of the aggregate, for example the wealth of an individual and the wealth of the collective. Each individual can have a perception of the individual characteristics and a perception of the aggregate characteristics.

The most popular example is the individual's perception of their own situation versus the aggregate situation. The problem is that there is a tendency to rate the individual situation better than the aggregate. Public goods are in the same category as aggregate goods, more distant from the individual and their influence. Examples of the differences between individual and aggregate characteristics can be:

- personal satisfaction with one's own life versus national levels of satisfaction with life;

- personal feeling of justice versus evaluation of justice in the country;

- evaluation of personal economic conditions versus national economic conditions;

- perception of personal conflicts versus the general intensity of conflicts;

- satisfaction with own social security and satisfaction with general social security of the region.

Whatever is asked, there will always be different results for the individual characteristics and for the aggregate characteristics, and there is a clear tendency to evaluate the personal conditions better than the aggregate ones.

c. *Personal well-being and national well-being*

In the debates about well-being there are always voices saying that a single item is not sufficient to describe subjective well-being. Indeed one item alone can never meet the differentiation and intricacy of subjective well-being but it gives a rough picture and shows the main message. A small number of items could give a more informative representation of subjective well-being. One of the interesting approaches to deconstruction of well-being is the Personal Well-Being Index (PWI) and its complement, the National Well-Being Index (NWI) (Cummins, 2007: Figure 4). The PWI consists of seven items which concern the perception of an individual's life whereas the six items of the NWI are related to questions of life in the nation in general.

Figure 4 – Personal and national well-being indices

Personal well-being is represented by seven items based on the question:
How satisfied are you with

❏ your standard of living?	77.8
❏ your health?	75.1
❏ what you have achieved in life?	74.8
❏ your personal relationships?	81.3
❏ how safe you feel?	79.0
❏ feeling part of your community?	71.2
❏ your future security?	71.4
Personal Well-Being Index	**75.8**

There are six questions on national well-being:
How satisfied are you with

❏ the economic situation in your country?	66.1
❏ the state of the natural environment in your country?	59.6
❏ the social conditions in your country?	62.6
❏ the government in your country?	55.8
❏ business in your country?	60.9
❏ national security in your country?	65.2
National Well-Being Index	**61.6**

Source: Cummins, 2007.

The answers are given on an 11-point scale from zero to 10 in which zero means completely dissatisfied and 10 means completely satisfied. Several tests in a variety of countries were conducted using this measurement instrument and they showed good measurement capacities for the scale, as it seems the items on the scale are more or less of relevance in all countries (Lau, Cummins and McPherson, 2005).

The interesting point is the differentiation between personal well-being and national well-being. National well-being is on average somewhat below personal well-being and the highest value of the NWI is always below the lowest value of the PWI. The components of the PWI and those of the NWI are not on the same level but are spread over the whole range.

At present, the PWI is available in Australia and a few other European countries. What can be shown is that the order of European countries is the same as for general life satisfaction. The PWI of Ireland is above Italy and Spain and both are above Romania; in each country the NWI is below the PWI.

Conclusions

The data presented here and many additional data demonstrate the fact that perceptions of goods and characteristics are different: goods close to the individual are highly estimated and goods distant from the individual have a low level of estimation. The problem is expressed through different terminologies: the satisfaction level relating to public goods is below the level of private goods, the satisfaction with aggregate characteristics is below that of individual characteristics, the level of national well-being is below the level of personal well-being. There is obviously an imbalanced perception which remains over time and is stable between population groups. It seems as if something which is in a social sense far from the individual is less satisfying than something which is close to the individual. There are some hypotheses which could explain these differences:

- The different degrees of satisfaction could show differences in the real level of provision, that is, private affluence and public poverty. Public goods are more often scarcer than private goods and therefore the satisfaction with the public area is lower. It is also remarkable that public goods show average satisfaction scores above the numerical midpoint of the satisfaction scale: people tend in general to be rather satisfied. It should not be overlooked, however, that some public goods attain higher and others attain lower ratings and this means that there are differences between the satisfaction levels of various public goods.

- What could make the difference between private and public goods is that private goods are bought according to the individual's wishes whereas the public goods are given. As far as private goods are concerned one can choose within the restrictions of one's own budget, but the provision of public goods is mostly a political decision which is not influenced directly.

- Private goods cost something whereas public goods are paid for indirectly through taxes or social contributions but to use them is free. It is an old theory that something which is free is less appreciated whereas something which is expensive is highly appreciated.

- It could be that aspirations and expectations are higher for public goods than for private ones. Because public goods cost nothing there is no budgetary limit to act as a brake on individual expectations.

- There is a theory that the attribution process is important for satisfaction ratings. An individual who does not see a good as being relevant to their field of activity is more easily dissatisfied than those who do. If the individual is involved, it can change their perception of the situation. Again this could be the reason for higher satisfaction.

- It is easy to escape from private goods which are not liked, be they an old car or an unhappy marriage. In each case it is possible to escape the dangers of the car or the unhappy marriage. In the case of public goods it is not usually possible to escape or to improve the situation through individual actions.

- There is also the question of information. Interpretation of private goods is usually through direct experience or direct observation. Public goods are only used under special conditions: the kindergarten if there are small children, the pension if somebody is old enough and so on. Often people have to answer questions about the distant future, especially those relating to pensions, but they may have only vague ideas about what might happen in thirty or forty years time. People often have the wrong idea about public goods and this could be the reason that they are so dissatisfied.

- Knowledge about public goods and other features outside the individual field is influenced by the media. One rule of the media is to prefer negative messages because they gain more attention so this unavoidably contributes to low satisfaction with public goods.

- Despite all these irritating factors, it is obvious that there exist differences in public satisfaction between population groups as well as at different points in time, which should be taken into account in the political process. It should be of relevance for different types of welfare state and – right or wrong – what people think has an impact on politics and society. It is obviously significant for social cohesion. So the evaluation of public goods is a challenge for research and the development of policies.

References

Alber, Jens and Fahey, Tony, "Wahrnehmung der Lebensbedingungen in einem erweiterten Europa", *Europäische Stiftung zur Verbesserung der Lebens- und Arbeitsbedingungen*, Dublin, 2004.

Andrews, Frank M. and Withey, Stephen B., *Social Indicators of Well-being*, Plenum Press, New York and London, 1976.

Bergheim, Stefan, "Deutschland zum Wohlfühlen", *Deutsche Bank Research*, 14 November 2007.

Böhnke, Petra, "Does Society Matter? Life Satisfaction in the Enlarged Europe", *Social Indicators Research*, Springer, 2008, pp. 189-210.

Bradburn, Norman M., *The Structure of Psychological Well-Being*, Aldine, Chicago, 1969.

Camfield, Laura, "Subjective Measures of Well-being in Developing countries", in Glatzer, Wolfgang, von Below, Susanne and Stoffregen, Matthias, *Challenges for Quality of Life in the Contemporary World*, Social Indicators Series, Vol. 24, Kluwer Academic Publisher, Dordrecht/Boston/London, 2004, pp. 45-60.

Campbell, Angus, Converse, Philipp E. and Rodgers, Willard L., *The Quality of American Life. Perceptions, Evaluations and Satisfactions,* Russell Sage Foundation, New York, 1976.

Cummins, Robert A., *Australian Unity Wellbeing Index – Survey 18*, Deakin University and Australian Unity Limited, 2007.

Diener, Ed and Lucas, Richard E., "Subjective Emotional Well-being", in Lewis, M. and Haviland, J.M. (eds.), *Handbook of Emotions* (second edition), Guilford, New York, 2000, p. 325.

Estes, Richard, "Development Challenges of the 'New Europe'", *Social Indicators Research*, Kluwer Academic Publishers, 2004, pp. 123-166.

Glatzer, Wolfgang and Zapf, Wolfgang, *Lebensqualität in der Bundesrepublik Deutschland*, Campus Verlag, Frankfurt/New York, 1984, p. 25.

Gullone, Eleonora and Cummins, Robert A. (eds.), *The Universality of Subjective Well-being Indicators*, Social Indicators Series, Vol. 16, Kluwer Academic Publisher, Dordrecht/Boston/London, 2002.

Halman, Loek et al., *Changing Values and Beliefs in 85 Countries. Trends from the Values Surveys from 1981 to 2004*, Brill, Leiden/Boston, 2008.

Holmes, Kim R., Feulner, Edwin J. and O'Grady, Mary Anastasia, *The 2008 Index of Economic Freedom*, Dow Jones Company, New York, 2008.

Lau, Anna L.D., Cummins, Robert A. and McPherson, Wenda, "An Investigation into the Cross-cultural Equivalence of the Personal Well-Being Index", *Social Indicators Research*, No. 72, 2005, pp. 403-430.

Luechinger, Simon, Meier, Stephan and Stutzer, Alois, "Why Does Unemployment Hurt the Employed? Evidence from the Life Satisfaction Gap Between the Public and the Private Sector", Boston Public Policy Discussion Paper, No. O8-1, 2008.

Michalos, Alex C. (ed.), *Citation Classics from Social Indicators Research*, Springer, Dordrecht, 2005.

OECD, "Subjective Elements of Well-being", OECD Social Indicator Development Programme. Papers presented at an OECD seminar, Paris, 1973.

OECD, *Measuring Social Well-being,* Paris, 1976.

Prescott-Allen, Robert, *The Wellbeing of Nations. A Country-by-Country Index of Quality of Life and the Environment*, Island Press, Washington/Covelo/London, 2001.

Social and Cultural Planning Office of the Netherlands, *The Quality of the Public Sector*, The Hague, 2002.

Statistisches Bundesamt (ed.), *Datenreport 1999*, Bonn, 2000.

Statistisches Bundesamt (ed.), *Datenreport 2006*, Bonn, 2006.

Strack, Fritz, Argyle, Michael and Schwarz, Norbert, *Subjective Well-Being*, Pergamon Press, Oxford, 1990.

United Nations Development Programme, *Human Development Report*, New York, 2005.

Veenhoven, Ruut, "Happy Life-expectancy. A Comprehensive Measure of Quality of Life in Nations", *Social Indicators Research*, Vol. 39, 1996, pp. 1-58.

Veenhoven, Ruut, *World Database of Happiness*, 2008.

Zapf, Wolfgang, "German Social Report. Living Conditions and Subjective Well-being", *Social Indicators Research*, Vol. 19, No. 1, 1987, pp. 1-171.

Further reading

Böhnke, Petra and Kohler, Ulrich, "Well-being and Inequality", WZB Discussion Paper SP I 2008-201, 2008.

Ferris, Abbott L., "The 2008 Index of Economic Freedom", *SINET*, No. 93, 2008, pp. 1-3.

Glatzer, Wolfgang, "Quality of Life in the European Union and the United States of America. Evidence from Comprehensive Indices", *Applied Research of Quality of Life*, Vol. 1, 2006, pp. 169-188.

Glatzer, Wolfgang, "Der Sozialstaat und die wahrgenommene Qualität der Gesellschaft", *Zeitschrift für Bevölkerungswissenschaft*, 2006, pp. 183-204.

Glatzer, Wolfgang, von Below, Susanne and Stoffregen, Matthias, *Challenges for Quality of Life in the Contemporary World*, Social Indicators Series, Vol. 24, Kluwer Academic Publisher, Dordrecht/Boston/London, 2004.

OECD, *Society at a Glance – OECD Social Indicators*, OECD Publishing, 2006.

Veenhoven, Ruut, "Return of Inequality in Modern Society?", paper presented at WIDER Conference on Inequality, Poverty and Human Well-being, Helsinki, 2003.

PART III – WELL-BEING AND RESPONSIBILITIES

I. The common good, well-being and the responsibility of local authorities

Iuli Nascimento[1]

1. The common good and the public interest

Social crises and rifts between citizens and their representatives are now a feature of the political arena in most European countries. Members of the public feel less and less well represented by the system of political representation. The abstention rate has nearly doubled since the 1970s for every type of election – presidential elections, general elections, municipal elections and European elections (and even regional elections since 1986, when they were introduced), with the result, in France at least, that citizens have become less involved in the system of political representation. This rift affects all sections of the population and is massive in the areas where the working classes, those hardest hit by the social crisis, are concentrated (Dapaquit, 2007). Citizen involvement in the participatory and social cohesion process is thus running out of steam.

Does this really mean that citizens are becoming apolitical or is it that they do not identify with the system for their political representation and with the current social development model? Might it not also mean that individuals have lost confidence in the body politic as a result of rising unemployment and growing social inequality?

Although the aim here is not to provide exhaustive answers to these questions, it would seem that this rift stems from the fact that the existing system of political power, its authority, its effectiveness and its results are being called into question, as is the integrity of political representatives. As cultural precepts change, the old models of political representativeness are disintegrating. In several European countries we are witnessing, at each level of political representation, efforts to put participatory democracy in place.

---

1.   Institut d'Aménagement et d'Urbanisme de la Région d'Île-de-France (Île-de-France Regional and Town Planning Institute), IAURIF.

Local authorities' aspirations to introduce participatory democracy must not, however, be announced merely for political effect and remain a dead letter. They must usher in a new learning process so that new theories and new information systems can be devised to address the changes in society.

The aim must be to give citizens a proper place in the decision-making process in order to answer their genuine questions and meet their expectations. Local authorities have a responsibility here to help establish a framework conducive to sustainable development, in which the notion of the common good and the public interest is no longer confined to the local population but extends to the current world population and to future generations under the banner of solidarity between generations. Local authorities must help to avert any threat of society's disintegration, precisely in order to ensure social cohesion and hence citizen well-being. The social cohesion of a modern society depends on its ability to secure the long-term well-being of all its members, including equitable access to available resources, respect for human dignity with due regard for diversity, personal and collective autonomy and responsible participation (Council of Europe, 2005).

Society is changing increasingly fast, as people lose their old bearings and new ones emerge. The current crisis is an identity crisis and we need to understand its mechanisms rather than merely establish a correlation between, for example, rising unemployment and urban violence, or globalisation and the disintegration of society. Transformations have always taken place in societies. They invariably necessitate changes and may therefore create problems for human communities. In order to adapt to and address these changes, local authorities must therefore rise to the challenges of these transformations.

In the current context of globalisation, the economic model does not lead to transparency of the democratic management of local authorities and it undermines the legitimacy of their action at local level. The global economy and the exercise of democracy operate at different paces and are based on different things. The former needs a global market and is developing fast. The latter requires a well-defined, geographically localised territory, which develops slowly. The contrast between the two rates of development and the geographical scope of each, whether in economic or social terms, can sap confidence in a high-quality personal and collective future and bring the social development of the poorest sections of the population virtually to a standstill. The growth of ill-controlled free trade in the absence of regulatory instruments can plunge modern societies into uncertainty and put paid to collective strategies that could mobilise the population.

Generally speaking, with economic globalisation, rapid growth should generate extra output, maximise consumer benefit and increase population well-being. But the imperfections of the market prevent this extra output from delivering the anticipated benefits to the world population as a whole. Firstly, producers of goods and services can play with the argument of "improving the efficiency" of production and increase their profits to the detriment of consumers. Secondly, producers are increasingly concentrated in a small number of countries, unlike consumers, who are spread throughout the planet. This waters down the concept of the common good. In this context, care must therefore be taken to ensure that there are regulatory instruments to offset the shortcomings of the globalisation process.

Globalisation has thrown societies' conceptual frameworks into disarray, not only in cultural and societal terms but also on the trade and financial fronts. We are living in a world in which human activity is accelerating constantly, and in which the global economy has repercussions on life in society. This requires us to give thought to the changing content of the concepts of the common good and population well-being. To this end, new frames of reference need to be devised so that we can asses their consequences and ascertain whether they meet our requirements and those of future generations. It is thus essential to rethink the concept of the common good in the current globalisation context in order to preserve social cohesion within our societies.

The concept of the common good is similar to that of the public interest. It implies meeting the needs of people living in a given area who share the same vision. The common good is the result of their own individual actions within and outside this area. The members of this community voluntarily display solidarity towards the outside world and depend on it in practice, just as it depends on them. The shared living area in which they consume and meet their needs must be commensurate with the level at which decisions are taken by economic operators, who, in turn, will be responsible for these exchanges between different communities or societies. The common good is therefore what gives meaning to society and hence to human beings as individuals and members of society (Rochet, 2001). Local and regional authorities have an important role to play here.

2. Well-being and globalisation

a. *Economic globalisation, a process that began a very long time ago*

The idea here is not to try to explain the situation in terms of historical events or to show that globalisation inevitably affects population well-being. A brief look at how the economic globalisation process came into being is nevertheless called for. Globalisation is the result of a process that began a very long time ago. The planet went through successive phases during which the economy became more international. The first covered the period from 1840 to 1914, which was marked by an attempt to standardise the price of commodities and by such phenomena as human migration and movement of capital within the Atlantic area and on the Asian markets. This phase came to an end with the 1914-18 war. At the time, this first stage in the globalisation process called for numerous sacrifices, but many consumers benefited from the resulting market. During the post-war years and up till 1945, there was a backlash, with the emergence of ideological and trade wars, greater exploitation of the colonies and sharing of their natural resources, along with such tragedies as Auschwitz and Hiroshima. In order to regulate international economic relations, institutions were set up to introduce trade, monetary and financial regulations. In 1947 a new economic globalisation phase began, and some 20 states signed the Havana Charter,[2] which liberalised trade within a multilateral framework. Since the charter was signed, 139 countries have joined GATT,[3] now known as the WTO,[4] with a view to making trade policies more flexible. The volume of trade has made an unprecedented contribution to the growth in world production since the agreement was signed.

---

2. The Havana Charter, signed on 24 March 1948, was proposed by the United States at the end of the Second World War. The rules were not observed immediately, but it provided for the establishment of a World Trade Organization (WTO). It was a proper agreement, setting up a genuine organisation.

3. General Agreement on Tariffs and Trade: an agreement signed in Geneva in 1947 in order to organise the customs policies of the signatories. In 1955, GATT was supplemented by the Organization for Trade Cooperation.

4. The World Trade Organization (WTO) is an international organisation responsible for rules governing trade between countries. It seeks to help importing and exporting countries to carry out their activities, by reducing obstacles to free trade and producers of goods and services.

Since the 1970s the economy has become increasingly international and nations have become aware of their interdependence. At the same time, companies have extended their activities beyond national borders. New connections of different kinds (telecommunications, transport, new technology, etc.) are now materialising, creating a grid across the whole planet. International, national, intergovernmental and non-governmental scientific, cultural and political agencies and organisations are mushrooming in the international arena. The development of communication technology is highlighting the growing role of multinational companies and declining role of the state in the global economy. In the 20th century the state played a leading part in introducing major innovations – free trade, road transport, the digging of canals, railways and the laying of cables across the ocean bed.

The result of this process is globalisation, as it emerged from the 1960s to the 1980s: the "global village" described by McLuhan in 1968, the "globalisation of markets" to which T. Levitt referred (1983) and the "world without borders" described by Ohmae (1999) – in other words, a diversified worldwide village shaped by the dwindling effect of distance and the universal availability of information; a world without barriers, in which there is a growing awareness of a heritage and of common values stemming from the benefits of scientific progress. The effects of the "progress" made since 1990 are casting doubt on this globalisation, for the abundance that world economic growth has provided for some has not brought well-being to the bulk of the planet's population. The fact is that globalisation is now something that transcends political and ideological systems and bears the hallmark of a world where capitalism, the market and neo-liberalism[5] hold sway and technology is constantly being developed in a quest for improved productivity. This state of affairs has led to rapid changes in relations between certain parts of the world and the globalised world as a whole.

Given the substantial changes taking place in the world as a result of free trade and market competition, we need to look at the relationship between economic globalisation and the common good, between globalisation and the general interest of populations and between globalisation and the role of states in addressing economic challenges. Does the "state of free trade" of the existing globalisation process create the requisite conditions for the economy to function in optimum fashion and thus

---

5.   Limited state intervention.

provide the population with maximum satisfaction? Does the scale of the conflicting interests that states have to reconcile for the benefit of the protagonists call into question the concept of the common good or public interest?

The advantages of free trade and of opening up the world to the global economy may be illustrated by the premise of a "competitive balance",[6] which entails a world without states, companies without market power and totally malleable production machinery. The imperfections of the international market and national regulations interfere with the balanced operation of free trade. The member states of the WTO are running a process that exposes political leaders to pressure from economic interest groups. In other words, the WTO is an intergovernmental agency in which the countries' official representatives have a twofold task: to negotiate in order to protect the interests of their own country as much as possible and to try to do away with the protectionist practices of their trading partners.

It should be stressed that present-day globalisation extends beyond phys- ical goods: it applies to international trade that includes a substantial proportion of service provision, which may or may not be linked to the provision of goods. The services in question depend on information trans- mitted by satellites, for which states are responsible. The intangible nature of the Internet undermines the effectiveness of any form of supervision of trade negotiations concerning financial services, transport services, the cultural industry, the film industry, intellectual property rights and so on. In such a context, where does one draw the line between what lies in the domain of governments and what is to be left to market forces? By dint of promoting free competition, globalisation thus prevents governments from providing financial aid for their respective countries' industrial poli- cies, as a result of which national economic policy can no longer be based on domestic demand because of the repercussions it may have on foreign trade. Moreover, the free movement of capital ties national governments' hands and restricts their room for manoeuvre in the area of fiscal and monetary policy.

---

6. The general balance achieved by perfect competition is said to lead to full employ- ment of all the factors of production. It is claimed, in other words, that it enables the entire workforce to be employed and all capital to be used to make it possible to meet all effective demand (Léon Walras – 1834-1910).

One of the paradoxes of globalisation as shaped by the WTO is that there is a constant demand for free access to foreign markets and yet import barriers are imposed unilaterally in defiance of the spirit of free trade. As a result, although globalisation admittedly sustains economic growth, it breeds inequality and social exclusion. Present-day society is witnessing three major transformations: in the power of the state, the allocation of responsibility for public choices and the content of the concept of the common good and the public interest.

In this context, all public services need to be rethought and reorganised in order to reconcile the civic and commercial dimensions of globalisation. It is this that constitutes the major challenge for participatory democracy. The fact that elected representatives are less and less representative because fewer citizens are voting in elections must be offset by another form of participation in public decision making so that the general interests of the public and public policy in general can be defended. User/consumer associations and non-governmental organisations (NGOs) are the logical partners for consultation between governments and the public. Through them, citizens can shoulder a substantial share of responsibility in the policy-making process.

b. Globalisation and the notion of "common-good"

One of the features of the current globalisation process is that growth is not the same in urban and rural areas and differs from one region, country and continent to another. This unequal distribution concerns growth of all kinds: economic and population growth as well as the increase in knowledge, income and life expectancy. The unequal distribution of the fruits of growth is affecting the lifestyles of populations and cannot be allowed to continue indefinitely (Dollfus, 2007).

In Europe, European Union directives are legally binding and yet this has in no way diminished the responsibilities of states. On the contrary, these responsibilities have become more complex as a result of the concept of the common good that emerges from these directives. Public services must reconcile their public interest mission with the requirement that they be open to competition. In the context of sustainable development, the concept of the common good and the public interest is no longer confined to the existing world population, but extends to future generations in the name of solidarity between generations. Pursuit of the common good therefore entails organising various components in connection with any project: material components (physical and financial resources), intangible components (identity and a feeling of belonging) and the project itself, which draws together the two in the light of long-term considerations.

The Lisbon Strategy set out, without success, to make the European economy more competitive by drawing on knowledge and technical innovation, with a view to ensuring a higher level of social protection and hence of well-being. Other avenues must continue to be explored in search of a "state of well-being" for the population. Some see the new European Treaty of Lisbon, as amended and signed in Lisbon on 13 December 2007 by the heads of state and government of the 27 member states of the European Union, as a missed opportunity, arguing that environmental issues were ignored and that none of the institutional reforms proposed will make it possible to do any more to avert the major crises that are looming, as is confirmed by one expert report after another.[7]

The Lisbon Strategy Report largely incorporates the earlier sustainable development provisions of the Treaty on European Union (Maastricht) without leaving any scope for European citizens to become involved in environmental issues. The only means of participation offered to Europe's citizens is the right of petition, and any petition requires a million signatures. This right merely enables citizens to submit proposals to the European Union but in no way obliges it to take account of them. On the other hand, where energy is concerned, Europe's clearly defined policy is to continue to promote the development of new and renewable forms of energy. Little scope is afforded to citizen participation in this context.

It has to be said that the latest edition of the UNDP *Human Development Report* shows that the world has never before produced so much wealth but that, paradoxically, poverty is on the increase, even in the most highly developed countries. Consideration of the common good should form part of all development strategies, be they European, national or regional, for it is this concept that makes society meaningful and allows human beings to exist as individuals and members of society.

The statistical tools currently at our disposal are incapable of measuring the advantages and genuine satisfaction that globalisation (free trade) provides in terms of the common good. Reality is more complex. Consumer (citizen) satisfaction and the concept of the common good cannot be reduced to the sum total of the interests of individuals or small groups

---

7.   *Le journal de l'environnement*, 14 December 2007.

that are separated from one another, to the detriment of the majority of the world population.

The point was recently made at France's major environmental conference (Grenelle de l'Environnement) that many of our activities generate greenhouse gases and therefore contribute to global warming. The French daily newspaper *Les Echos* published an article on 21 November 2007 entitled "Desertification is taking hold of fertile soil", showing that human activity was responsible for the deterioration of farmland throughout the world. This is a somewhat alarming finding: the desert is spreading considerably and soil erosion is becoming substantially worse. The International Soil Reference and Information Centre (ISRIC) reports that 200 000 square kilometres of soil are eroded every year, an area the size of the United Kingdom. Social and ecological balances are being destroyed and this is resulting in increasingly rapid and substantial disturbances, including:

- desertification;
- climate change (global warming);
- rapid, pronounced urban expansion (leading to a contrast between urban and rural areas);
- growing social exclusion (in terms of access to drinking water, health services, housing, education, etc.);
- substantial demographic change (ageing of the population, immigration and pressure from the growing world population);
- increasing world poverty;
- effects of pesticides on health and the environment;
- recurrent natural and technological disasters.

The global economy envisages several solutions to the worldwide crisis, in the form of the generation of renewable energy through the development of biofuels produced from vegetable oils and cereals, which is held up in some quarters as a miracle remedy. In order to develop fuels of this kind, the agricultural industry has to make massive use of chemical fertilisers and pesticides. This economic development model drives growth but does not provide a solution to the problems of social cohesion and population well-being, as is borne out by growing world poverty and hunger. The pace of change fuelled by technology is no longer conducive to the well-being and social cohesion of the socio-economic system as a whole. It is therefore high time the concept of the common good were refined and adapted to collective projects and that local authorities were recognised as being legitimately entitled to consider the future of the population and the means of improving its living environment and the future of the world in general.

3. Local authorities' role and responsibilities and the tools at their disposal – The example of France and the Île-de-France region

a. *Responsibilities of local authorities and the population's well-being*

Local authorities acquire a new sense of responsibility when they are required to put the concept of sustainable development into practice and its implementation enhances the effectiveness of efforts to introduce a fairer socio-economic development model, since the concept can be applied to numerous sectors. The notion of well-being, when it is based on a sufficiently comprehensive and polymorphous concept of sustainable development, can be applied to virtually all local public policies. A systemic approach to human activity across the planet, in its biophysical entirety, should provide an opportunity to give thought to the future of our societies and how to manage the various parts of the world in conjunction with the natural environment and human activity. This is the main message to emerge from the Earth Summit (Rio de Janeiro, 1992), and the main sustainable development challenge highlighted by the Rio Agenda 21, which spawned the local Agenda 21s.

The Île-de-France has been chosen as an example here, illustrated below by a description of the regulatory instruments the local authorities have at their disposal for assuring the population of an acceptable quality of life and level of well-being.

Two main regional instruments set out the role to be played by the Île-de-France region in ensuring its integrated development: the regional economic development strategy (*Schéma régional de développement économique*) and the Île-de-France regional planning blueprint (*Schéma directeur régional*). The first is designed to co-ordinate the economic development measures taken by the local authorities and their associations on the region's territory, except for those tasks for which central government is responsible. Under Article L. 1511-1 of the General Local and Regional Authorities Code, the state may entrust the regions with devising a regional economic development strategy. This experimental strategy sets out and promotes strategic guidelines designed to achieve balanced economic development and seeks to enhance the attractiveness of the region and to avert risks to the economic balance of the region as a whole, or parts of it. Once the strategy has been adopted by virtue of powers delegated by central government, the region becomes responsible for allocating aid to companies.

The purpose of the Île-de-France regional planning blueprint is to provide for the planning of the region as a whole. It may be amended by the Chair of the Regional Council with the consent of central government, provided the amendments do not run counter to the broad lines of the economic development strategy. After a public inquiry, the draft blueprint may be amended to take account of citizens' observations and the views of the public corporations consulted. It is adopted by the Regional Council and approved by the relevant administrative authority. If a *département* objects, the amendments are approved by a decree issued by the *Conseil d'Etat* (the supreme administrative court).

The "public interest declaration" or "strategy declaration" is issued once the validity of the blueprint has been examined in consultation with central government, the Île-de-France region, the regional economic and social council, the *départements* and the chambers of commerce and industry. The "public interest declaration" signifies that the new provisions of the Île-de-France blueprint have been approved. It is issued by *Conseil d'Etat* decree if the region objects. The "strategy declaration" cannot be issued until the administrative authority has rendered the blueprint compatible with requirements and, if the region objects, it is issued by *Conseil d'Etat* decree.[8] A two-month public inquiry is then opened, during which all parties concerned within the boundaries of the region may intervene in respect of the guidelines set out in the regional blueprint.

On the basis of the regional strategy and the regional blueprint, the concept of well-being can be addressed in terms of six main sustainable development themes that are a matter for local public policy: spatial organisation and planning; social development; the development of economic activities and employment, transport and mobility; ecological

---

8. Article 2 of the Town Planning Code L. 141-1-2 – *Projet de loi relatif aux libertés et responsabilités locales* (Freedoms and Responsibilities of Local Authorities Bill) (final text).

management of natural resources, energy and waste; and decentralised co-operation and measures to combat global threats. In the context of these main themes, it is possible to promote the concept of the common good and population well-being. Proper co-ordination of the regulatory instruments at the disposal of the local authorities should make it possible to clarify their responsibilities in respect of both these concepts and ensure that sustainable development is put into practice by the various tiers of government.

A number of existing spatial organisation and planning instruments in France may serve as effective tools for ensuring population well-being and fostering a sustainable development policy: the *Schéma de cohérence territoriale* (Territorial Cohesion Strategy) (SCOT), the *Plan local d'urbanisme* (Local Urban Development Plan) (PLU), the *Plan d'aménagement et de développement durable* (Municipal Planning and Sustainable Development Strategy) (PADD), the *Programme local d'habitation* (Local Housing Plan) (PLH), the *loi Solidarité et Renouvellement Urbain* (Solidarity and Urban Renewal Act) (SRU) and the *Plan de déplacements urbains* (Urban Transport Plan) (PDU).

The SCOT is drawn up by elected representatives and has replaced the old local town planning and urban development strategy. It is designed to co-ordinate town planning, housing, transport and commercial amenity policies within the urban area concerned. It sets town planning and urban development objectives in order to co-ordinate all planning and programming strategies. It is designed, on the one hand, to strike a balance between development, urban renewal and rural development and, on the other, to preserve farmland and forests and protect natural areas and landscapes. It must also respect the diversity of urban functions and ensure a social mix in housing and employment. In short, it seeks to ensure carefully managed, balanced development of urban, suburban, natural and rural areas.

The PLU has replaced the *Plan d'Occupation des Sols* (Land Use Plan) (POS) and determines the allocation of space at municipal or inter-municipal level. It must include a PADD setting out arrangements for the general organisation of municipal territory in town and spatial planning terms. It may provide specific information about the use to which certain areas or neighbourhoods are to be put. The document is drawn up at municipal level and provides a frame of reference for planning schemes concerning housing policy, public spaces and landscape conservation.

It also identifies sectors to be renovated or protected and provides for appropriate action.

The PLH is a planning tool specifying the required supply of social housing (and in particular the balance to be struck between social and other forms of housing) and sets out five-year plans for local authority new-build housing and housing rehabilitation. The SRU encourages the preparation of an inter-municipal PLU to allow housing policy to be framed on an appropriate geographical scale at the request of a "housing catchment area", in accordance with the SCOT. The SRU strengthens consultation procedures for the purpose of the revision of a PLU or POS.

In the area of social development, local authorities carry only a small share of responsibility for addressing such major social problems as poverty, unemployment, dilapidated or insanitary housing and violence. Unemployment and poverty are more a matter for national than local policy. This responsibility extends to problems in the environmental, economic and social fields. Environmental problems take several forms, such as exposure of households to noise, the presence of industrial wasteland, subsoil pollution, the presence of inert waste and the deterioration of the natural environment. Economic problems include rising unemployment and dwindling local finances. Among the social problems are the difficulty of redeploying former employees, the loss of vitality of the social fabric and growing poverty. Since the regions are responsible under Article L. 214-12 of the Education Code for implementing regional apprenticeship and vocational training policies for young people and adults in search of a job or change of career, they are expected to organise, on their territory, a network of centres providing information and advice about obtaining recognition for vocational experience and, at the same time, to organise schemes to meet apprenticeship and training needs.

The promotion of economic activity and employment is one of the major responsibilities of local and regional authorities and yet current practice does not involve an approach that takes account of environmental and social considerations when companies are sited or projects for the economic exploitation of local resources are devised.

Local authorities have considerable responsibility for transport and mobility. They have various means at their disposal, provided for in the PDU, for curbing the growing trend towards personal car use that has been apparent for several decades now.

The PDU, as provided for in the Air and Rational Energy Use Act, is compulsory for towns with over 100 000 inhabitants. Its long-term purpose is to reduce car travel in favour of public transport, cycling and walking.

Local authorities must therefore introduce a number of measures to strike a new balance in the area of transport and mobility. They are required:

- to introduce areas specifically designed for public transport, bicycles and pedestrians;

- to control parking by means of regulations, pricing and park-and-ride car parks;

- to optimise goods transport in town centres by setting up delivery logistics centres on the outskirts of towns and ensuring that non-polluting vehicles are used for deliveries;

- to co-ordinate urban development and transport by siting new areas to be developed near public transport infrastructure.

Local authorities have key responsibilities when it comes to achieving the objectives set in terms of the ecological management of natural resources, energy and waste. In particular, the aim is to control the impact of economic and social development on the environment. This responsibility requires local authorities to make efforts to protect vulnerable ecosystems by managing natural resources sparingly, reducing the consumption of raw materials and energy and cutting back on waste production.

Some of these measures directly affect the quality of life and well-being of the population. For instance, the conservation of natural areas (natural parks, green belts, suburban farmland, etc.) in town centres and/or on the outskirts helps to protect and enhance local fauna and flora, thus lessening the effects of air pollution.

These measures bring about a direct and very substantial improvement in the lives of city dwellers, as a result of the proximity of leisure areas and the possibility of procuring quality farm produce nearby. Other measures may seem less important, but they have indirect benefits, for example the sorting of waste, water-saving measures and steps to combat climate change and global warming.

Waste treatment measures have made it possible to reduce the amount of fly-tipping in France. Other measures that indirectly improve the quality of life include schemes to re-use waste (recycling, home composting, energy recovery) and energy-saving measures (housing insulation, environmentally sound house-building). Other examples are pilot renewable energy schemes (wind, biomass and solar energy), which contribute to the well-being of local communities.

A local plan to combat greenhouse gases can also bring significant benefits by combining measures to reduce polluting vehicle emissions with steps to save energy in housing and public buildings.

Under the decentralised co-operation scheme, a local authority may, in order to combat global threats, promote projects to boost the development of the least-favoured parts of the world. The production of electricity by such means as photovoltaic panels, water engineering micro-schemes, wind turbines and from biomass, along with training for local technicians, is an alternative to the installation of generators burning fossil fuels. It makes it possible to provide power for craft activities and reduce pollution while helping to improve the quality of life and well-being of a disadvantaged section of the population.

b. Improving sustainable development in the regions

Asserting a determination to strive for the common good is tantamount to affirming that people have the capacity to decide on their future and that of the planet. In taking account of the common good, companies also become more creative, productive and competitive. In order to devise a form of development that is genuinely sustainable, it is necessary to assess long-term benefits and avoid jumping to conclusions about the disappearance of borders, the liberalisation of trade in goods and services, the movement of capital and technological innovation. Technological innovation and globalisation can then become opportunities for cultural openness, provided they are tied to a well-thought-out form of liberalism.

Human societies are complex systems that are constantly evolving and subject to imbalances. If such systems are to work, they must be regularly adjusted. Local authorities must be responsible for ensuring that these systems operate properly in order to avoid social regression. Non-governmental organisations representing the public can and must help to ensure citizen well-being. The transfer of decision-making power to independent authorities can be quite damaging to local authorities. Care must be taken to ensure that the existing economic development model does not become increasingly complicated rather than merely complex, and to make sure that it is not only lobbies that are able to make their voices heard.

Here it is politics that is in greatest need of complexity. Ideas are being produced that increasingly simplify things and yet societies are more and more complex. Increasingly one-dimensional visions are being generated and yet societies are more and more multidimensional. Ideologies are being produced that increasingly rationalise things and yet the situation is ever more uncertain (Morin, 2004).

Human beings must be actively involved in, and responsible for, organising and managing their environment. The ties between human beings and their territory make it possible to take simultaneous account of individual interests and the public interest in terms of the long-term sustainability of the territory and the survival of the community living there. This cannot happen unless the activities of local authorities are co-ordinated with those of NGOs. The local Agenda 21s can therefore be a very useful means of introducing coherent sustainable development in the regions.

For the sake of sustainable development, there is no option but to consider population well-being and a high-quality ecosystem as objectives to be achieved at all levels. The regional tier of government plays a key role here. Setting well-being indicators is one means of achieving these objectives. This entails reorganising information systems at all levels (national, regional, *départemental*, municipal) and rendering them interoperable with one another and with ad hoc data so as to allow both in-depth technical approaches (particularly for the purposes of assessing the quality of the ecosystem) and simpler approaches designed to make the media and the general public aware of the various facets of human well-being.

This objective implies that systems for compiling statistics must be able to come up with a set of comparable data at the different levels. Apart from statistical analyses, it is essential, when regional plans are devised, to be able to define "areas of well-being" according to different criteria (for instance, calm, heritage, wild and domesticated biodiversity) in order to preserve the quality of life and well-being of the population in areas used for mixed purposes (the built and open urban environment, cultivated areas, nature in the wild, etc.). The quality of life and well-being indicator developed by the Île-de-France region is, along with other sustainable development indicators, an example of an effort made by a regional authority to acquire a better grasp of the notion of the common good and thus make the planned ecoregion more effective.

The composite indicator for well-being devised by the Île-de-France region is more than just an indicator: it is a proper tool which can be adapted to various territorial levels and which, by virtue of its transparent and evolving tree-like structure, makes it possible:

- to assess and compare territories at a given point in time;

- to monitor their development;

- to set well-being objectives and target the sectors and parties that can make their achievement possible;

- to carry out simulations, varying some or all of the component indices;

- to carry out an overall assessment of a policy on the basis of a set of sustainable development indicators and, more particularly, to shape a policy (by producing tree diagrams specifically designed for the purposes concerned).

The Regional Council's plan to make the Île-de-France into an ecoregion is an excellent opportunity to introduce sustainable development at regional level. Although, at first sight, the concept of sustainable development may seem somewhat vague, it has the merit of advocating an across-the-board approach to regional development, encompassing the economy and sociological and environmental considerations. This makes it both rich and complex. It also takes account of the long term, incorporating the concept of responsibility towards future generations, and of the principle of citizen participation and governance (political ecology). It is not always easy to translate the notion of sustainable development into practice in the regions, and its application requires a special effort on the part of specialists in the various disciplines. The human sciences, the earth sciences and sustainable development are sometimes at odds with sectoral objectives, but sustainable development provides an opportunity to acquire a better grasp of the way in which urban systems operate as a whole and to pursue a genuinely ecological approach – one that is fully in keeping with the Île-de-France inhabitants' desire to be responsible citizens.

Conclusion

In the 1970s, Nicholas Georgescu-Roegen (1995) demonstrated in his theory of "non-growth", based on thermodynamics[9] and system entropy,[10] that economic growth was the result of the productivity of a society and that this productivity depended on the availability of natural resources and the workforce used to transform those resources into consumer goods. It emerged from his work that natural resources were not inexhaustible and that they were not being used with due regard for the resilience[11] of habitats and the environment. As said above, the post-war economic development model has had serious consequences for present-day societies, including climate change, growing natural hazards, loss of biodiversity and the denial of survival necessities to a section of the world's population. Growth means an increase in economic activity and is not always reflected in the quality of the living environment and population well-being. Development, on the other hand, implies greater human fulfilment and requires us to consider the concept of the common good in greater depth.

The industrial-growth-based economic model has undeniably been damaging to rural economies and natural resources. Globalisation in its current form merely speeds up the process whereby small urban centres and rural areas are excluded from the global economic network. Care must therefore be taken to ensure that economic globalisation has positive externalities for all countries and regions of the world.

The Île-de-France region is seeking to ensure that rural areas do not remain isolated from the global economic network, without disrupting their economic and cultural balance. In order to reshape the model for the development of human activity at regional level, it is necessary to propose new means of organising space that are conducive to the well-being of the population. An ecoregion would seem to provide the appropriate spatial framework in which to achieve this objective.

An ecoregion is broken down into geographical sub-sectors (living areas), in which the well-being of the community can be fostered and enhanced. Together they form the regional ecosystem. These geographical sub-

---

9. The field of physics concerned with thermal phenomena.

10. In thermodynamics, entropy is a measure of the state of disorder of a system. It increases when disorder increases.

11. Here, resilience corresponds to the capacity of an environment to regenerate itself.

sectors are the basis of society and of all economic and cultural life within the territorial entity formed by the Île-de-France region. The region's balance stems both from its ability to meet the legitimate needs of its population and from its capacity to react to conduct on the part of the population that is detrimental to sustainable development. What we must do, therefore, is rethink the concept of the common good in the current globalisation context in order to maintain cohesive societies, for the common good is the result of individual and collective action within and outside the boundaries of a particular community.

References

Council of Europe, *Concerted Development of Social Cohesion Indicators – Methodological Guide*, Council of Europe Publishing, Strasbourg, 2005.

Dapaquit, Serge, *Crise sociale et fracture civique – Le système d'autorité en question*, Forum de la gauche citoyenne, February 2007.

Dollfus, Olivier, *La mondialisation*, La bibliothèque du citoyen, Presses de Sciences Po, 3rd edition, 2007.

Georgescu-Roegen, N., *Demain la décroissance*, Editions Pierre-Marcel Favre. Second edition, Sang de la terre, Lausanne and Paris, 1995.

Levitt, T., "The Globalization of Markets", *Harvard Business Review*, Vol. 61, No.3, 1983, pp. 92-102.

McLuhan M., Fire Q., *War and Peace in the Global Village*, Bantam, New York, 1968.

Morin, Edgar, *Pour rentrer dans le XXIᵉ siècle,* Le Seuil, April 2004.

Ohmae, K., *The Borderless World, Power and Strategy in the Interlinked Economy*, revised edition, HarperCollins Publishers, New York 1999.

Rochet, *Claude, Gouverner par le bien commun. Un précis d'incorrection politique à l'usage des jeunes générations*, Cahiers pour la liberté de l'esprit, François-Xavier de Guibert, 2001.

Further reading

Bienayme, Alain, *Bien commun, concurrence et mondialisation*, Montreal, May 2001.

Boyer, Robert, proceedings of the Colloquium on the "State and Social Regulation", 11-13 September 2006: *L'Etat social à la lumière des recherches régulatrices récentes*, Paris, 2006.

Brachet, Philippe, *Le "service public", enjeu de citoyenneté active*, Forum de la gauche citoyenne, September 2001.

Council of Europe, *Ethical, Solidarity-based Citizen Involvement in the Economy: a Prerequisite for Social Cohesion*, Trends in social cohesion, No. 12, Council of Europe Publishing, Strasbourg, December 2004.

Nascimento, Iuli, *Indicateurs stratégiques de développement durable, "Un indice de qualité de vie et de bien-être"*, IAURIF, November 2007.

Nascimento, Iuli, *L'Île-de-France et l'écorégion,* available at: www.notre-planete.info, June 2006.

O'Neill, William, "Remettre sur le métier le bien commun"; CERAS - revue Projet n° 268, December 2001, available at: http://www.ceras-projet.com/index.php?id=1868.

II. From ill-being to well-being: individual and collective responsibilities

Catherine Redelsperger[1]

Introduction

The world of work is a battlefield where forces striving to achieve solidarity, departitioning, dialogue, integration, symbolisation and shared vision contend with forces intent on classification according to categories, territory, narrow expertise, hermetic language, insularity and disintegration of what is communal.

On the premise that experience of the world of work can be helpful in understanding, querying and discovering avenues as regards the learning processes that internalise states of individual and collective balance or imbalance generating well-being or ill-being, the author proposes to define three key expressions:

- learning processes;

- states of individual and collective balance/imbalance;

- feelings of well-being/ill-being.

She will then present what she has learned about these processes in the context of job-seeking and that of the wage-earning community, in three dimensions: individual, collective and from the standpoint of someone coming from outside and acting upon the system.

---

1. Catherine Redelsperger trained as a Protestant theologian and now assists companies and associations in matters such as management, learner teams and governance through actions to coach individuals, teams and organisations. She has also written a philosophical mystery story on questions of paternity and bioethics, *Dayly, Texas*, Hachette littératures, 2007, a play *Le Sauvage* staged by the Nie Wiem troupe in April 2008, whose theme is the break-up of a society founded on fear of the other, and *Météo Mélancolique* to be published at the end of 2008 by EDON, graphics by Nicolas Famery.

1. Proposed definitions[2]

a. Learning processes

A learning process is the clarification (a priori for a known process, a posteriori for a random process) over time of the transformation of an initial condition into a final condition experienced by an individual:

- by observing and confronting the world at large, other people and him/herself; from his/her observations and confrontations he/she infers general laws and knowledge;

- by receiving knowledge and skills with which to interpret the facts.

The observations and knowledge are memorised and the individual acts and adapts both for better (improves, creates greater well-being for him/herself and others) and for worse (withdrawal, decline, dragging others into a vicious circle of ill-being).

Learning requires that the individual should be in liaison with another. One does not learn alone but in a state of interaction with another, who may even be an animal, an object or an imaginary invention.

A learning process is living: it consists of paths, detours, encounters, casting about, questioning, dialogues, tensions and errors or conflicts.

Learning processes differ between individuals. They are reversible and can branch out.

The content of the learning process can just as easily be ill-being as well-being. Ill-being is also learned.

b. States of individual and collective balance/imbalance

Balance will be spoken of as the proper combination of several "ingredients" for an individual or group. Let us take the example of how an individual combines working and private life.

---

2. The definitions offered here are based on the scientific dictionary "Le Trésor" edited by Michel Serre and Nayla Farouki (eds.) (Flammarion, 2000); Barbara Cassin's article on "esti" and "einai" in Parmenides' poem "On Nature" as found in the dictionary of European philosophical vocabulary (Le Seuil, 2004); on varied reading about complexity and systematics and on the author's professional experience.

If my working life monopolises and absorbs me through the amount of time I spend working (or lack of it in the event of unemployment) or due to stress or worries, and if in these instances my personal life is affected, I suffer from a general imbalance in my life.

Another example at the collective level is where a department of an enterprise chooses an open, participative approach starting from the shop floor for a project closely concerning the participants, since the aim is to plot the potential of their occupational careers according to the firm's future development and skills needs. Volunteers enter into this approach and discover the pleasure of working collectively and their own ability to shoulder responsibilities. The same department's day-to-day functioning is partitioned, hierarchical and infantilising. After a few months, the domination of the daily routine, of a nature discouraging responsibility, literally stifles the volunteers who experience imbalance and ill-being because of this contradiction.

This is an initial definition of an imbalance based on a combination of elements that are skewed by the wrongful domination of one element which generates ill-being, or a contradiction between two elements, or even the paradoxical injunction to be spontaneous. Balance is thus defined by a combination of ingredients of life, of living conditions whose effect on the individual or the system is to generate well-being.

The dynamics of the balance/imbalance correlation will also be embodied in our hypothesis.

According to scientists, the balance/imbalance correlation can be dynamic. This dynamic concept makes us aware that a type A balance can become a type B balance. Moreover, the transition from one to the other occurs via a transitional, or critical, imbalance. A very simple example may illustrate this argument: the crisis of adolescence, which is a state of physiological and psychological imbalance and a transition from childhood to adulthood.

The process of well-being needs this transitional imbalance: it strikes a particularly responsive note in Western culture where the creation myths tell of a creative separation – God dividing the waters from the heavens and the earth, or light from darkness. Psychoanalysis also tells us something self-evident: for a newborn infant to live, it must be severed from the mother by cutting the umbilical cord. This separation is a transitional imbalance allowing a new balance to be struck.

In the link between the individual and collective spheres, I make the assumption that if I am ill at ease with myself I have difficulty in generating well-being with others, but I can rebuild it with a person or persons who do generate it. This raises the question of who is proactive, in the sense of who initiates the dynamic of switching from imbalance to balance.

The regulation of states of collective balance/imbalance on a larger scale (organisation, institution) is performed by the law (in its various forms), whose amendment results from the meeting of individuals and their interests, for example wage parity between men and women in companies or through regulatory bodies.

c. Feeling of well-being/ill-being

Defining the sense of well-being and ill-being is complex. The question of being is one of European philosophy's major questions, through the exceptional use of the verb "to be" which has a syntactical and lexical use and serves to connect subject with predicate in language. The reference text is Parmenides' poem. From the interpretation of the poem by philosophers, I draw two maxims for subsequent examination:

- To be is to live, to develop, to dwell (in the sense of a home).

- To be is to exist, think and speak.

I infer that well-being must be in the realm of "it is" and ill-being in the realm of "it is not".

There remains the question of feeling. The "sense of well-being and ill-being" places us in the register of emotion, of appeal to the senses and of subjective representation of what is experienced as well-being and ill-being. The relativity of this feeling is immediately perceived.

Simply by considering the question of ill-treatment, it is very quickly understood that there are two realities: the one actually lived and the spoken one. As long as making children work was not said to be ill-treatment, it was not ill-treatment for anyone, least of all the person undergoing it, who did not have words to express it, and all of whose reference points were built on that normality. This means that the feelings of well-being and ill-being are subjective and social, making it necessary to lend an ear to the other, or others, waiving judgment. This is done on a variety of levels such as the subject who speaks, society speaking through the subject (what the subject purportedly says) and the strategy of the subject going through the process (intelligence harnessed to an over-indebted-ness strategy, for instance). But there is also knowledge of self, of one's own representations and experience of life compared to the well-being and ill-being ordained by practitioners, decision makers, thinkers and experts.

One question is important: who speaks and who ordains whether it is well-being or ill-being: do I speak, or is this spoken by someone else?

d. How these definitions are used

These proposed definitions are not final but open-ended, enriched by their dynamic quality and conceptual variety (scientific and philosophical standpoints). Moreover, the definitions are under construction. In the subsequent discussion, the reader will find links with one or more aspects of the proposed definitions. They are, as it were, a backdrop to what will be an illustrative, empirical argument.

2. Learning processes for a person's return to well-being: individual and collective dimensions

In line with the proposed definitions, I now set out to describe processes of transition from a state of ill-being to one of well-being. As ill-being is associated with imbalance (for instance, lack of work, lowered income, self-esteem and social life), so the learning process can momentarily generate an imbalance within the imbalance, that is a transitional imbalance (for example, overcoming the belief that one will no longer be able to find work). Well-being is associated with balance.

a. The individual dimension

Voicing of expectation and assumption of responsibility or how I escape from inevitability to regain control of my destiny

I have guided persons who have been out of work for over two years towards resumption of employment. It was hard for the regional directorate of the state employment agency (ANPE)[3] to find consultants who would accept this type of assignment. I accepted not because I was

---

3. ANPE: Agence nationale pour l'emploi: the French national employment agency.

supposedly a superwoman or a knight in shining armour, but because I knew that once a person enrols in a coaching scheme after two years of unemployment, he or she has some expectations (even if responding to coercion by a spouse or the ANPE). In any case, this is the person confronting the counsellor, not an ANPE official or a spouse. The first task in the process is to restore to the other person the ability to say what their expectation is and to shoulder their responsibilities. Thus the person escapes from their alignment of the planets, the disaster of fatalism, to express a desire for change in which they will be an agent. It is a first transition to well-being, a stage in regaining self-possession. Indeed, it should not be overlooked that human beings adapt to their misfortune. It is an effort in these circumstances to express the desire to live otherwise because of the huge risk.

Normalisation and ending self-condemnation, or how I understand what is happening to me

As our society is firmly founded on culpability rather than responsibility, the learning process operates by tracking down guilt. Guilt is a forceful emotion conducive to narcissism, self-centredness and inhibition. It is usually learned during one's upbringing and a person experiencing the sense of guilt lives though it as an ineradicable torment. What helps jobseekers is to help them understand what is happening to them, that they are not alone, that others are going through a similar sequence (fracture, affliction, reprogramming), and that they must take a share of responsibility in what is happening to them today as well as in their role in building their future. In short, the question of guilt is not addressed by delving into it and looking for the causes, but by centring oneself on responsibility conducive to action.

Self-esteem or how the other appreciates me and restores my self-esteem

Self-esteem is eroded:

- by people's opinions of me at the time of my break with the firm (on a ++ sliding scale if I did not leave by choice, and on a - - one if it was my choice);

- by the opinions of those around me (whether fantasised or real);

- by my own opinion of myself in relation to my system of values and world view.

When the erosion is very pronounced, a sense of exclusion is expressed. It may be associated with denial of the situation to those around one (untruthfulness about the real position), or with such dejection that the person dealt with has little hope of still being "worth" anything, or with such a violent spirit of vindictiveness as to become intolerable, or again with unappeased rebellion against the former employer.

Regaining self-esteem is a stage in learning the way back to a balanced state of well-being vis-à-vis oneself and others – to inclusion.

This rehabilitation requires a number of ingredients:

- an institution which recognises and is recognised by the person; here I note a difficulty: an institution such as the state employment agency (ANPE) by no means enjoys legitimate recognition by enterprises, or therefore with employees, and its staff themselves often have trouble with their self-esteem; the mirror of self-esteem does not work properly;

- a position and a person: the quantitative targets set for ANPE staff of number of appointments per day aggravate the difficulty of getting past the relationship of an official (counsellor) with a jobseeker, and thus of working within a relationship of a genuine, sincere person who recognises another person's worth;

- time for acquaintanceship is lacking: may I recall here that the process of recognition does not occur without an initial stage of getting to know the other person.

Let it be re-emphasised at this juncture, I am not speaking of the ANPE's prowess, in competition with private agencies, at conjuring up a return to work (equal success for both) but of what happens during the phase of exclusion from the active labour market.

Inclusion, or how I identify with a group

In this process, within a very brief space of time, the person is presented with a *modus operandi* under both individual and group conditions. The first group they face consists of their own peers, other unemployed people. The sweeping designation "unemployed" should not conceal the group's wide inner differences: people from different occupational backgrounds who did not mix with their counterparts in their previous jobs, people who are not in the same psychological state or people in differing positions of authority. It is an important first stage, even if unsettling and unpleasant for some (exposure to others, being forced out of one's personal sphere and habits). It is a first stage of inclusion, that is, coming to terms with and being disturbed by others.

Inclusion by re-skilling

For some, inclusion can only be achieved by re-skilling for another occupation. The person goes through renunciation of one occupation in order to re-programme themselves for another. There too, imbalance and the time of ill-being due to renunciation are necessary before one can re-immerse oneself drastically in something else. It is necessary so that the imbalance may be beneficial – a transitional imbalance. Another instance is literacy training (reading and simple arithmetic) without which an operative cannot take part in quality operations, follow instructions, and suchlike, or qualifying to drive (paying for and obtaining a licence) without which certain occupations are impossible, as is general mobility.

For others the situation is far more complicated. Here I refer to people who are rigid in their way of relating to others, who function in an unvarying one-to-one authoritarian register of subordination, whereas enterprises are looking more for people capable of working both in a chain of command and on a transversal plane or within a matrix structure. In this case, the mutation is painful but nonetheless decisive for a return to work.

b. The collective dimension

I propose to enlarge on this collective dimension in the same context of unemployment. In practice the collective dimension is organised in groups around a nucleus of 10 or so people – jobseekers and others, based on workshops (on CVs, letters of motivation, mailings, interview skills, phone canvassing, networks). The benefits of these workshops, apart from instruction in the use of methods or tools which trigger action, lie in generating a balance adjustment process during them.

Measuring oneself by the yardstick of others: taking one's bearings from degrees of well-being/ill-being

Normalisation, ending self-condemnation and regaining self-esteem, discussed above under the individual dimension, are amplified and speeded up by collective confrontation. Indeed, individuals can measure themselves through each other; they measure their misfortune, resources, chances and solutions. They devise a scale and position themselves on it. Often, moreover, their assessment changes as they come to understand what is happening where the others are concerned. A sensitiveness to others develops; gaps open in their reserve during these workshops, for there is nothing of interest at stake between them (except borderline cases of reversion to very strong competitive instincts when, for example, a large enrolment of computer technicians in the workshop coincides with a glut on the market).

Interaction with companies

In my own practice, I have observed that the approach is most workable when it includes the companies and thus is not confined to an ANPE officer as group leader or a private-sector operator and the group of jobseekers. During a telephone canvassing workshop, a period of instruction in method, testing and role-play leads to a real application during the workshop, with the jobseekers calling companies. The ability to win recruitment interviews during the workshop, in a mood of emulation among the group, is a powerful inclusive factor: "By my own proactiveness, I have succeeded in securing an appointment without anxiously waiting for a reply to land in my letterbox" (whether physical or virtual). The lightened brow and triumphant look of the one who secures an appointment is the sign of a return to self-esteem.

Divisive space: replication of social divisions in job-seeking

The question of space is ambivalent. Both the ANPE and the employment agencies play on the replication of social divisions in the world of work. Executives and non-executives are distinguished by the ANPE, and non-executives, executives and managerial executives by the employment agencies. In short, "everyone in their proper place". I mentioned space because the places are not identical; the space is shared with one's peers, the space made available is not the same and the benefits are different. The entirely positive effect is that the conditions are met for aiding recovery of self-esteem: people continue "playing in the same league", the "big league" (moreover, executives are often the most fragile in terms of self-image).

Yet the imperviousness remains surprising. One cannot help thinking that a director of human resources development could help non-executives in their search for employment through his/her advice and personal address book. However, to the best of my knowledge bridges of this type are hardly ever built (I would be glad to learn of experience with this). Such bridges could help change people's opinions once they find themselves caught up in the organisation of an enterprise: "I now know that a Director of Human Resources is not only the strong arm of the management, but also capable of helping"; "I know that a worker is not just one more registration number, I have seen the human being" or similar.

Solidarity over time: the amnesia of former jobseekers

It is a rare occurrence in the corporate environment for me to meet people ready to talk about their period of unemployment or to concern themselves with jobseekers or, in the case of recruiters, not to be intent on recruiting someone who is already working.

Former jobseekers are amnesic, with little patience for jobseekers, who they do not seem to trust, as if their own period of unemployment was suspect, as if it carried shame and stigma. This period is seldom valued as a phase of greater self-knowledge and of learning. Presenting it in this light is often perceived by those on the other side of the fence as window-dressing for self-promotion.

At the collective level there is a twofold loss: recognition of the learning is forfeited and likewise solidarity.

c. Specific case of over-indebtedness

I wish to bring up a specific, complex issue which is one of the possible effects of very protracted unemployment: over-indebtedness. It simultaneously involves elements of macrosystems (banks, lending agencies, laws, the employment market, etc.) and of the individual system bringing the over-indebted person's responsibility into play. May I firstly stress a conviction founded on my experience: I do not believe that all over-indebted persons feel they are in a state of ill-being or imbalance. They may have found in over-indebtedness a comfort zone with fringe benefits of some significance and they may choose an adaptive response to the prevailing rhetoric of ill-being. They may not attempt to reason differently or to devise other strategies, but they make tools of the new aid resources. A most important question arises: is an over-indebted person ready to change their stance?

Attaining a shared vision through confrontation

I find it essential that all "assistive" functions come together with the over-indebted person or couple in order to align the shared vision to the situation and the demand, avoiding word games such as "I tell you what you want to hear about me according to your role". This confrontation with reality is harsh for the professionals and for the over-indebted person or couple. Why? Because everyone at the table is forced to admit to themselves that they have been blind to the situation.

Unity of time and place counters the allure of mirror images

The confrontation occurs in a unity of time and place. It eliminates possibilities of triangular manipulations: "You understand me, but not the others" and replies targeted according to who is addressed.

The paradoxical question is how to succeed at being over-indebted

The systemic approaches reveal paradoxes in terms of learning and self-esteem. Indeed, through the disclosures about their successes, the over-indebted person's skills, qualities and strategies leading to over-indebtedness can be revealed, then these very same skills and qualities can be harnessed to another strategy to vanquish over-indebtedness, by way of all the proposed arrangements tried out under the multipartite social contract.

3. The learning process of well-being/ill-being as it affects wage-earners

I recall my initial premise that what happens as regards learning processes associated with states of balance/imbalance generating well-being or ill-being in the context of the enterprise gives us a perspective of society as a whole by analogy.

a. The individual dimension

Estrangement of employees from their companies

Ethnological studies of enterprises have established that employees are alert to and undeceived by the systems of marketing and propaganda set up in companies. They play the game, keep up the pretence and above all protect themselves by withholding their full intelligence, creativeness and culture from the enterprise. They build their path to happiness outside the enterprise. This phenomenon would seem to have intensified since the introduction of the thirty-five-hour week in France. For example, many fathers take their paternity leave at the birth of their child. This is still more blatant in the case of younger people who contemplate just passing through companies, using them as their parents were used by them (parents who experienced periods of unemployment, mothers tied down by part-time working hours making an absurd ordeal of their day-to-day lives). Private life is more important to them than working life.

Here I am describing an instance of individual balance which has been achieved but which generates significant collective weaknesses as well as withdrawal and pronounced individualism. Some enterprises try to develop what they call collective intelligence or joint responsibility, more or less successfully depending on the contradictions that exist; for example, developing joint responsibility when a manager will not acknowledge his/her mistakes renders the task impossible.

Some situations of "estrangement" are linked with a confusion causing ill-being and frustration, when an employee casts the enterprise in the role of complete power over his/her whole life. I have observed this in young single women trapped in working hours which they themselves have taken to crazy extremes (sixty or seventy hours per week). They end up blaming the enterprise for their inability to find a soul-mate and often consider it unappreciative of their professional dedication. Ending confusion, putting everything back in the right slot and restoring the individual's responsibility for his/her own problem is the most effective avenue. Here I am referring to situations where, under similar working conditions, some work within inordinately extended time bands while others find regulation mechanisms which are very easy to describe (simply working less) but hard to apply for someone "trapped".

The zones of non-being

We have been speaking of well-being and ill-being; now I take the liberty of introducing Virginia Woolf's idea of zones of non-being. I construe non-being as a kind of evanescence, loss of self, of passing time, of linkage with the world. In it, events are non-events. Nothing happens to me, nothing matters. This trivialisation of self makes me a nonentity.

This zone of non-being is an absence of being, neither well-being nor ill-being, a negation of being. As it implies suffering, one would be inclined to class it with ill-being. But that would be to overlook a concept pointing to a situation of self-effacement, like a situation of refuge, a bolt-hole, a zone of safety from the vicious circles of ill-being in society.

I sometimes find myself faced with people in a state of non-being when they work. They function mechanically but are "not there". This is a form of self-exclusion from the world. There too, by dialogue with another, the possibility of a link with oneself and the other is rebuilt. This dialogue restores a self-excluding person's perspective and appreciation of day-to-day events.

Materialism and individualism

The acquiescent sadness of disillusion in people with the potential for dedication and supportiveness, considering their competence and capacity for professional initiative, is questionable. I regularly come across executives approaching middle age who admit they are materialistic, individualistic and sad to be like that, while at the same time saying how clear-sighted they are about themselves. They like their comfort and do not wish to choose a path to greater happiness entailing a loss of income (to change occupations, set up a firm), since they use the money to purchase compensatory pleasures (their very words). It is hard to imagine these people who take a "preservative" attitude to themselves spontaneously taking the risk of caring for someone else. Yet they are aware of the socially excluded. The question remains as to how to stimulate their desire to activate change. There too, the key lies in encounters with another who does not judge them and offers them other avenues.

Saying no

In the learning process that leads towards well-being, learning to say no is one of the keys to resumption of proactiveness. Of course, the reverse happens, since acquiescence is also a key. On the whole, however, I meet people subjugated to their wish to please, to be perfect, obedient and overburdened. Sometimes when I meet them, weary and at odds with themselves, they have not realised it on their own because it had become their normal state. Another person (family member, manager, colleague) has pointed out that life could be different. The next step after gaining this awareness is learning to set oneself limits and make them clear to others, to force a change in one's doormat image. The learning may take place, *inter alia*, by inversion methods (I take the other's place and realise that to hear "no" does not trigger a conflict), through learning by rhetoric (reasoning the refusal).

b. The collective dimension

Here I propose to deal only with the principles that govern the learning processes of well-being by setting out the limits and the hardships of these learning processes. These principles mainly result from research within companies. They are being tried out more and more in varied contexts (associations, job creation schemes, companies, regions).

The diagonal approach

The word "diagonal" means offering people from different entities, levels of authority and cultures the possibility of becoming involved in seeking heterogeneity and creating conditions of parity, that is, in hierarchical organisations, in creating a-hierarchical or hetero-hierarchical areas. In the first case there is no more hierarchy, in the second the hierarchy revolves, each person taking their turn as leader. The advantage is in being able to create conditions of joint responsibility, empathy, inventiveness and implementation. For this to work, it requires that experts and decision makers strive for the humility to accept and heed people less knowledgeable than themselves but nonetheless to help seek solutions in which all would be involved.

Voluntary service

Voluntary service is also one of the keys to success and, in a group situation, has a knock-on effect. The limitation, in the corporate environment, is that at some stage the rule of voluntary service is pushed aside by short-sighted time constraints and in the end a decision maker chooses the volunteers.

Joint responsibility

Joint responsibility is another way of saying that all are players, all are interacting and all have effects on each other. Enterprises, like states, have high levels of complexity. To live this complexity to the full, not contemplate its dissolution, it is necessary for all players to realise that they are players. In practice, one of the keys is decentralisation.

Decentralisation

For there to be joint responsibility, there must be no more centre, or one that shifts according to the encounters, reflections and actions. As long as an individual or group of individuals can be identified constantly as the centre, the phenomenon reduces the possibilities for the players to see themselves in action; they so often become onlookers again that they end up leaving the action to the person or persons at the centre. In practice, this means circularity in the exercise of power (each in turn, with frequent change decreed not by a rule but by force of the real circumstances observed as one makes one's way along).

Making one's way

The foregoing does not generate well-being at the outset but unease, a disturbance of habits (stating one's opinion, listening to people different from oneself, making a commitment, breaking down barriers). One of the other features is the need to take account of reality. How do we act? How could we do otherwise? What kind of effect do we produce? This signifies leaving behind a pure planning logic to combine it with acceptance of contingencies, side-effects of greater interest than the results aimed at. This accommodation of reality, of what happens and of its consequences, confirms each group member's scope for action at their level. It is a process of experimentation, interesting in its peculiarity of being undergone by a particular group at a given time – "t".

Dialogue

The way people speak to each other is crucial in a learning process generating well-being. Several conditions are necessary:

- a person speaks, not the function or institution;
- it is not communication;

- it is the spoken word;

- there is suspension of judgment;

- the other must show hospitality;

- empathy must exist;

- curiosity must also be there;

- there must be association of ideas, etc.

All this is learned by doing but with initial guidance in order to develop this way of escaping from monologues of the deaf, from "I want to be in the right", from restrained parlour conversation.

Shared objectives and shared vision

Shared vision, a heavily used term in corporate parlance, implies the possibility of creating a common image, concept and logos.

The term is used to denote the possibility of collectively devising a common strategy (for example, on health for an enterprise making and marketing foodstuffs), a joint project (for example to build a car costing less than €10 000 for the "emerging" markets). In this dimension, the term "shared vision" denotes the activation of all in the implementation of the strategy or project, hence a way of bringing together different occupations, rationales and individuals.

A tendency for employees, customers and shareholders to join in creating value around the shared vision has been taking hold for the last ten years or so in very large enterprises. One example to illustrate this claim is an international agri-food firm quoted on the stock exchange which has "nutrition" as its strategy. Symbolically, the strategy embraces the shareholder (feeding the shareholder) and, in practice, the customer and the employees (with the idea of education). Aimed at the employees, a nutrition programme has been set up specifically for operatives working shifts, whose eating habits, linked with their working conditions alternating between night and day, are not optimum and may cause health problems. Moreover, companies alert to their "planetary responsibility" increasingly accommodate the natural environment (eco-responsibility).

At the same time, however, in some of these very large enterprises, the employees often perceive this drive for joint creation of value as a trendy way of asking them to accept further numerous changes under stressful conditions.

Yet shared vision is perceived in a perspective of rational philosophy. Shared vision does not go with the idea of literally "making" one's way. It is more a matter of the "mix" competing with the "logos". "Mix" is subterfuge, lateral thinking. It is a matter of heeding and sharing the mental representations and the goals of individuals and groups, of collectively setting up a common progression, an impetus towards future action.

Today in companies, these two rationales of "logos" and "mix" combine more or less successfully.

Here is an example of a success: an international enterprise manufacturing industrial components is merging two sites in a new location but 110 staff will be required to work 50 km from their present place of employment. The enterprise wished to secure every chance of causing as little ill-being as possible and took this occasion as an opportunity to develop employees' expression. The director-general, the factory manager, the human resources department, the works committee, the trade unions and all 110 staff (operatives and team leaders) went through a multiple experience six months before the move:

- personal interviews with all employees to understand their needs;

- other firms' transport experience (car-sharing, company buses, local transport authority buses);

- working from the road map to calculate costs (motorway toll);

- joint work with real-estate agents and architects.

This procedure was an extraordinary gamble which ended with the choice of the new site. This new factory construction site is an amazing adventure which, even years after this experience, welds the staff of the new factory together and has given them self-confidence. The workers felt they were heeded, considered and were agents of the decision. A shared choice could not possibly be jointly constructed like this in enterprises where planning and centralisation reign supreme. After cursory opinion polling of employees, the financial manager and the general director would decide and disclose their decision.

c. Keys?

Attitude of mentors: unknowing

The term "societal coaching" denotes a mentoring action at the level of the system, hence interactions between the elements thereof. Here the societal coach would be one of the players with other players. The mentor's stance is essentially unknowing.

The mentor has a low profile (conversely, a decision maker has a high profile), does not know what will be the solutions, the content or the outcome. His/her know-how concerns the conditions of success to be met (some of which are described herein) so that interactions within the system are rewoven, some of its elements disappear and other new ones are introduced to transform the system as a whole. The mentor is not the decision maker, or the expert on content.

Perception of the system: interactions

To look at the system is to look at its interactions, which is easily said but difficult to do. We tend to contemplate our own navels and to regard the other as a problem to be solved. Looking at interaction and the effects on myself generated by the other, and by myself on the other, demands great rigour, a search for a way out of self-delusion at the individual level. At the institutional level, looking at interactions requires us to look at them together and speak to each other about how we can manage to work together (well or badly).

A blind spot

The chief blind spot when a person undertakes to work in liaison with someone weaker and more destitute is their own generosity. Excessive generosity has adverse effects, for generosity is a way of making the other dependent on me, beholden to me, in short I derive pleasure from being generous, superior to the other. This generosity, very aptly described by Edgar Morin in *Éthique*,[4] must be counterbalanced by egocentricity and consciousness of the effects of one's generosity. This is one of the chief risks of blindness in mentors.

---

4. Morin, Edgar, *La méthode,* Vol. 6, Ethique, Le Seuil, 2004.

At the level of society, the flaunting of generosity with a strong undercurrent of self-interest may amount to forgetfulness of the equity of well-being for all. Indeed, this association of selfishness and generosity could be the seed of cronyism: "I am generous to you, but you will have to do me a good turn back one day." Anyone not equal to this or not wishing to play along is excluded.

Conclusion

The few examples given in this article show how the learning processes that lead to states of balance or imbalance generating well-being or ill-being are fraught with pitfalls, false appearances, paradoxes and illusion, and that vigilance and humility are indispensable qualities for any player involved in the process.

PART IV – THE CASE FOR A SOCIETY FOCUSING ON THE COMMON GOOD AS A CONDITION FOR WELL-BEING

From welfare state to welfare society

Bruno Amoroso[1]

1. Collective imagination and welfare: the two utopias

The collective imagination that nourishes people's plans for life and society is expressed by concepts such as education, instruction, culture and religion. It is reflected in the role of family, civil society, labour and institutions. The collective imagination has often given rise to new utopias when the old ones have declined or have been recaptured by old-new visions. Utopias are historically specific and promote the necessary conditions for a radical transformation. Utopias are needed because they enable the collective imagination to materialise in time and space. Any transformation – economic, political or religious – first requires a cultural revolution. Utopias can legitimise revolutions as well as counter-revolutions. The Keynesian revolution was sustained by the utopia of the social economy (fairness, efficiency and equality) in the same way as the neo-liberal counter-revolution was sustained by the utopia of globalisation (the "global village").

Globalisation has very quickly been shown to diverge from its promises. The global village has turned into global apartheid and the reactions to it are creating a new universe of visions, aspirations and dreams. The changes occurring on a day-to-day level at local and world scale (such as globalisation of the economy; the information and communication explosion; the growth of inequalities and social exclusion; economic marginalisation and political destabilisation of communities and countries; the biotechnological "revolution"; the renewed rise in unemployment and

---

1. Jean Monnet Chair, Docent Emeritus, Department of Society and Globalisation, Roskilde University, Denmark.

labour slavery in the North and in the South; environmental pollution; climatic change on a planetary scale) have reopened the need for a re-think of the present situation as well as of the overall objectives of our way of life.

Because globalisation has been introduced as the highest achievement of the Western modernisation model, "the landing point of human history", its discontents have re-opened the dossier not only of globalisation but of the whole system built up by more than two hundred years of European history. Once again collective imagination is creating a new utopia, "another world is possible", based on the revival of the communities and their cohabitation. Its benchmarking is provided by the reintegration of the markets into the communities, the deinstitutionalisation of its main functions which will be overtaken by civil society, the re-linking of education with instruction and training. Life, people, living together and creativity have again become major issues to be questioned, explored and investigated.

a. European utopia and globalisation

Since the 18th century European utopias have attributed a central role to science and technology, to the supremacy of the state over communities and of institutions over civil society. Furthermore globalisation defines itself as the "knowledge society", because its economy is considered to be increasingly driven by knowledge and the dominant tendency is to give primacy to a techno-scientific and utilitarian vision of research and education. First education and knowledge were expropriated from the family and community life (civil society) by the state (as the governor of a new umbrella called society), now they are being expropriated from societies and states by capitalist globalisation. Knowledge and its institutions (schools, universities, research centres) are becoming instrumental to the objectives of the capitalist market and its transformation from welfare to workfare (1980-90) and from workfare to warfare (2000-08).

The impact of these processes on universities and educational systems is obviously destabilising. Universities tend to specialise in "useful" fields and disciplines where they can better serve the economic interest of national competitiveness. This leads to increasingly close links with private companies in the financing of research "which produces returns" and in "cutting edge" training. In turn, this leads to an expansion in commercialisation and privatisation of higher education, particularly university education. Education no longer belongs to the field of non-commercial goods and services. Students are becoming customers and the various actors in the education field are regarded as "stakeholders" in the "educational enterprise" that the university is becoming.

Above all, they have to become functional to the objective of globalisation by educating the most qualified and competent "human resources" to enable companies to maintain and improve their competitiveness in the world markets. This means continuing with the process of "financialisation" and creation of a techno-structure that increasingly uses science and technology to orient production systems and consumer behaviour to its purpose and for the creation of unequal control by social groups and countries of the design, production and use of the new information and communication technologies (the Internet universe).

This process, called the "knowledge divide", refers also to the ever growing gap between individuals, social groups and countries which produce and those which do not produce the increasingly sophisticated and complex knowledge which fashions the military, space, biotechnological, agricultural and multimedia fields. Because of the power this capacity gives them, the former have little interest in sharing this knowledge. Their interest lies rather in using it to extend and consolidate their influence and control of the economy from a local to global scale. This explains the strategic importance acquired by intellectual property rights and, consequently, the race for patents.

b. European paths of emancipation

The communities' revival, identified by the will of millions of people in Europe and elsewhere to govern their own lives in coherence with their own choices and values, has been a recurrent event in European history. All forms of protest and revolt against the imposition of economic and political processes have been vital. At the centre there was a difficult relationship with modernity and the various forms of modernisation introduced at institutional level (state policies and practices) as well as at the economic one (commoditisation, "financiarisation" of market economies). Choices and decisions were always introduced as "constraints" – dictated by the needs of the economy and the promise of development by various social and political forces – to which people and local communities had only to submit.

Choices and decisions have been entrusted to God and to the interpretation of oracles in ancient times and to science and laboratories in modern times. Once the main routes for the future have been outlined, communities need only to adapt to them. Consequently, the transformation from "education to ..." to "training for ...", from experiences and knowledge to science and the need to make local demands consistent with the general interest became the accepted rules of the game. The traditional view, "think local and act global" (bottom-up), that has always been the natural basis for communities' sustainability, has been transformed into the opposite, "think global and act local" (top-down), with its inevitable impoverishment.

These approaches, reflected in the policy orientation of European and international organisations, as well as in various movements, can be summarised in two blocs:

- those who pursue the adaptation of local communities, regions and countries to the increasing demand for integration and industrial innovation imposed by globalisation; these are the positions of the European and international institutions that are also accepted by a number of governments;

- those who search for possible ways to adapt the processes of integration and technological innovation to the needs of communities; these positions, sustained by some governments and by the movements labelled "new-global", do not question the choices and orientations of the former but try to reduce their negative impact.

Both positions, despite their diversity, assume the direction and the content of development as given, and share an optimistic view about the outcomes of modernisation. The first considers the adaptation of the communities to the needs of industry a simple result of world development in which it is necessary to participate as much as possible. The second is more critical about the risks of social exclusion and its high social costs. However, it retains the possibility of overcoming these using appropriate policies. Common to these positions is the idea that local development is a residual factor consistent with more general objectives. A third position is taken by the "no-global" and "alter-global" movements that question globalisation as well as the more general concept of development. It is close to the approach of "mondialisation" that overturns the two previous positions, because it assumes the community to be the independent variable and industry and market the dependent ones.

The events that characterise the life of our communities and societies always follow at least two paths, parallel and often intertwined: the planned juridical and institutional one and the voluntaristic one of people, movements and associations. Diversity and interaction among the two create conflicts but also reciprocal influence and synergies and therefore they ought to be carefully analysed and monitored in order to verify the coherence of their respective objectives.

c. The rise and fall of the European social model

The welfare state was the social project applied through European policies over two decades after the Second World War and it has been a positive achievement of European societies. Its crisis is due to the lack of innovation during the 1960s and to the impact of globalisation since the 1970s. Its inner construction and dynamic were established with the "social pact", which gave the entrepreneurs the right to manage and organise production in order to achieve the efficiency of the system, and the labour movement the prerogative to govern and to provide the necessary public goods and an income re-distribution financed by a progressive tax system in order to achieve equity in income and welfare distribution.

However, the narrow path of social redistribution was dictated by the logic and intention to compensate for the "social costs" of capitalist development. The challenge posed by the economic system was not answered by policies trying to internalise social costs within the enterprises but, on the contrary, by reducing their negative impact on workers and citizens in general. Paradoxically, the state care on these matters and their partial compensation produced an enlarged externalisation of production costs by the enterprises.

Here are the roots of the failure of the welfare state – its inner crisis – illustrated by various authors (for example, Archibugi, 2000) in its various dimensions: i. fiscal crisis; ii. efficiency crisis; iii. crisis of affection. Its inability to react to these trends and the resistance met in implementing the needed reforms (industrial and economic democracy) made it easier for the new economic policies of the 1970s and 1980s (neo-liberalism) to undermine the legitimacy of the "social pacts" through the Washington Consensus, to dismantle the public goods supply through privatisation and to reintroduce "flat" tax systems.

In the meantime, the transformation of the production systems from Fordism to post-Fordism erased the systems that made possible the rise of the working class and middle class on which the system of democratic institutions and participation had been created. Therefore, because of these structural changes that have produced a power shift from industrial to finance and technology groups the reconstruction of the welfare system is not possible on the prerogatives of the previous one. As has been correctly noted:

> "From this point of view, then, the expression 'welfare society' could be considered not only *integrative* and *complementary* to that of the 'Welfare State' but it would become even *antinomic* to the latter: for the welfare society to exist it is necessary that first the Welfare State in one way or another is 'destroyed'; that state that until now has assumed the task of generalising well-being only through an ever-increasing *redistributive* function and/or the supply of productive functions of (divisible and indivisible; individual and collective well-being)" (Archibugi, 2000: 177).

The "common good" project arises because of the crisis of the welfare state, put down by the European Union Commission to democratic, economic and social deficits. This crisis is rooted in two problems of scarcity: economic scarcity expressed by the "financial crisis of the state"; and scarcity of resources due to the limited availability of natural resources.

Economic scarcity is caused by the welfare systems' inability to properly manage the processes of socialisation and democratisation that they had introduced (Caffè, 1986). The stated principles of economic sustainability (by the enterprises) and social sustainability (by the citizens), that ought to limit the impact of social costs on public finances and on people, did not produce the expected results. The behaviour inspired by the capitalist system produced the externalisation of the "social costs" ("the privatisation of profit and socialisation of costs"). The capitalist market became increasingly a "system of unpaid costs" (Kapp, 1950) that made the economy inefficient and public finance out of balance. The state support to enterprises was systematically used not to reinforce the real economy but to cover for structural deficits and management mistakes. The welfare measures were not used to improve the quality of life for families and people but to increase their dependency on the labour market. Furthermore, greater access to higher income and welfare did not improve the quality and the lifetime of the product but increased the people's propensity to consume and their behaviour as consumers.

Scarcity of resources has been caused by the conflict between the unlimited growth ideology and the limited nature of natural resources. During the 1970s a number of reports dealt with the problem of "limits to growth" (for example, the report produced for the Club of Rome:

Meadows et al., 1972) and increased the social consciousness of their worldwide dimension and interconnection. Various reports further raised awareness of the problem of distribution of resources (WCED, 1987) and regional disparities.

In recent years both phenomena have given rise to various movements and new organisations that have taken over the fulfilment of the above-mentioned objectives, widening their implication on forms of market organisation, production systems and international co-operation. The civil society mobilisation on these topics represents a constructive contribution to the problem of the welfare state but, at the same time, has accelerated the need for its reform and radical transformation. The awareness of the interconnection between people and communities – due to the growth of environmental problems, outrageous waste of energy and raw materials, increasing migration, conflicts and wars – is what we define as "mondiality". These interdependencies are reinforced and extended by the diffusion of new transport technologies, communication and new materials. Finally, the increase of immigrant communities within national states calls attention to the problems of cultural diversity and polycentrism in European countries.

d. The social state as a symbol of the common good, in the past and today

Prior to the objectives of the welfare society today under discussion, the European social project has for forty years been that of the welfare state. Its objectives and functions were articulated through public goods. The welfare state project was established during the last century to deal with the economic and political crisis of the capitalist system. After the Second World War, it was designed to deal with the reconstruction of much of the civil and economic infrastructure including education, health, transportation, post services, housing, and industry. At that time, governments, democratic or not, were the only authority in charge of those functions. The state, therefore, took over many of the functions of a market economy and introduced a "mixed economy" characterised by the presence of powerful, state-controlled enterprises in the main strategic sectors of the economy. The modernisation of the economy was mainly based on the Fordist system and its model of mass production and consumption.

This hegemonic industrialism introduced in European countries from the United States became the guideline for the newly established European reconstruction, penalising rural societies and traditions. The institutional and political framework (political parties, trade unions, etc.) was built around this new economic and state organisation: the industrial "trade union" and the "class" political party both derived from the large-scale model of the Fordist enterprise. Rural culture and traditions at the core of European societies were ignored during this process and marginalised as "pre-capitalistic" or "pre-modern" forms of social organisation.

The search for a new worldwide welfare consistent with the objective of "living together" on earth – with less government involvement and greater self-reliance and participation of citizens and the local community – started several decades ago. The limits of laissez-faire economics and liberalism and the need for the "common good" had already been emphasised by J.M. Keynes in his *National Self-reliance (1933)* and in *The Economic Possibilities for Our Grandchildren* (1932). During the 1960s Gunnar Myrdal pointed out the need for transition from welfare state to welfare society (Myrdal, 1960), while Gunnar Adler Karlsson denounced the "cultural barbarism" of consumerism and growth ideologies (Adler-Karlsson, 1976).

The need to overcome the national model of welfare redistribution has been analysed recently by Franco Archibugi:

> "Welfare Society is not integrative or complementary to the Welfare State but can only be born through its destruction: the limits of Welfare State are identified in the utopia of the functional dualism between social policy and economic system and in the need to put an end to the logic of compensation for the social costs produced by 'development'" (Archibugi, 2000: 177).

As stated by William Robson:

> "The welfare state is what the government does. The welfare society is what people do, feel and think about the general welfare. Unless people generally reflect the policies and the assumptions of the welfare state in their attitudes and in their actions it is impossible to attain the objectives of the welfare state… When an industrial nation becomes a welfare state, the need for a strong sense of individual, group and institutional responsibility, the need for social discipline, become very much greater" (*ibidem*: 303).

The importance and complexity of this paradigm shift are due to the fact that after three hundred years of European modernisation a new culture needs to be created. In many ways, the welfare state stands for the most developed form of economic and institutional transformation initiated by the French Revolution. The power shift introduced by the European bourgeoisies was achieved by the destabilisation of all existing forms of power based on civil society (family, religion, local communities, etc.) that transformed "persons" into "individuals" and liberated "citizens" from their communities' bonds and obligations. The vacuum created by this change was taken over by the state that took on the role of the previous community structures through the proclamation of individual rights and the establishment of the social state (in its various forms). This transformation individualised the relation between government and citizens and took away from individuals their social responsibility towards the community as a whole. The "collective interest" created by the sum of individual interests, replaced the "community common good". People's attitudes toward the concept of the common good were replaced by conflicts among "special interest groups".

The state thus became the provider of goods and services for its citizens "from the cradle to the grave". This situation explains why the crisis of the welfare state has been particularly dramatic in societies where the transformation has been most successful. Individuals have nothing to fall back on: in most cases they are driven to despair and, in some cases, try to re-establish new forms of community life. The recent rise of civil societies and the development of alternative economic systems based on community are an expression of this new demand for social transformation.

2. Welfare society as a new project for well-being

Welfare society is an alternative to globalisation, oriented by the communities' new vision of the common good and their capability of living together. It should find educational and operational methods coherent with its principles, based on local developments as the primary cells of worldwide networks of solidarity and on new co-operative institutions at meso-regional level re-establishing common boundaries that national states no longer represent. These methods ought to be participative from the drafting of the project to its implementation. Furthermore, they must be able to unify the segmented knowledge produced by specialisation into a trans-disciplinary perspective giving back a central position to intercultural dialogue, which today has been reduced from an approach involving listening to each other and real dialogue to simply teaching our own values and way of life to other cultures.

This new utopia of the common good is based on the principle that knowledge is the common heritage of humanity and that knowledge sharing has primary importance. The expropriation of the knowledge accumulated over years of collective effort by the communities and the privatisation of results produced thanks to public investment in education and research are against the logic of the common good and living together. Rewards for the achievements of researchers can be provided in other ways than by privatising research results, whose only real objective is to ensure the highest profit for the shareholders of the companies owning patents.

The common good of each community ought to be supported by the principle of "living together" in a worldwide polycentric system of communities and meso-regions able to co-operate at all levels, thus counteracting the 21st-century trend towards deepening conflicts and wars between states and between social groups within countries. The majority of these conflicts are rooted in economic, political and social systems that have created unsustainable "ways of life" putting people in opposition to each other in their confrontational rationale for survival. The promotion of these "ways of life" and the economic systems they rely on in a new form of civilisation, as well as the repeated statement that they can neither be the objects of bargaining or be shared because of their sustainability, has given rise to Western rhetoric that the world has entered an era of "wars between civilisations", a "war" between, on the one hand, a knowledge system considered to be evolved, modern and open and, on the other hand, an antiquated system accused of being backward, archaic and obscurantist.

The objectives of the common good and its utopia are different from those of globalisation. The unsustainability of globalisation is due to its attempt to create a global sustainability in the interest of 800 million people by the exclusion of more than 6 billion. The utopia of the common good is different: it is the project of "mondialisation" for the living together of 8 billion people. It is a project that fosters dialogue among communities and participation within them in order to create a worldwide system of various "ways of life" respectful of each other and "all concerned about the sustainable use of natural resources.

The question is whether the utopia of the common good be transformed into a worldwide project:

> "which enables a group of individuals to constitute a human community, 'to create society' and to live together in such a way as to ensure

and guarantee the right to a 'decent' life (in accordance with human dignity) to each member as well as collective safety; all this while respecting 'the other' and in solidarity with other human communities and future generations, while safeguarding life on the planet" ("The University for the Common Good", 2004).

The project is rooted in the theory and life praxis of millions of people around the world who, by opposing the response given to "mondiality" by globalisation, are establishing new forms of community life and co-operation ("mondialisation"). "Another world is possible" because it exists already in the life of communities, families and people that are today deprived of the possibility to express themselves, have been frustrated in their collective aspirations and have had the possibility to govern their own lives taken away from them. However, the rise of a worldwide "citizenship" has been manifested by the civil society movements during recent decades (Seattle, Prague, Göteborg, Genoa, Québec, Porto Alegre, Florence) despite difficulties and contradictions. The task is not easy. What is required is a responsible attempt to re-think the world's dynamics, to question the dominant paradigms, to open a discussion about the current worldwide cultural homologation and to act on the processes of globalisation. What is needed is to re-establish the ability to think about the common good at local and worldwide level; to redefine the foundation and the value of the world in coherence with different keywords; to reintroduce the "other" into the dynamics of interpersonal relations within human communities and in all relations of the world society and of the planetary ecosystem.

a. Links between well-being and resources/the common good

The project of the welfare society arises because an unsustainable system of production and consumption has been created despite the success of the previous project – the welfare state – which was unsustainable because of its brutal exploitation of natural resources and its unfair distribution of wealth and power. This requires a re-think of our production and consumption models as well as of the ideas behind our institutional setting. The former ought to be oriented towards sustainability and co-operation among states and communities. The latter ought to be reassessed in accordance with the need for increased self-reliance and participation at the local level in order to increase co-operation among neighbouring countries and meso-regional entities. The two basic elements of the common good are the reconciliation of human life with all other living species and their natural environment and their capability of living together.

The common good is neither the singular form of common goods nor the sum of individual wealth in a country but:

> *"the community spirit,* an invisible and inclusive third factor that cannot be reduced to the sum of the parts and cannot be owned by somebody. Therefore in this perspective nobody can be perceived as more important than anyone else. His identity includes the diversity of the other. It is an invisible and irreducible family relation that unify us despite our differences and because of them. It is a structure of reciprocity that prevents privatisation efforts and hinders competition, accumulation of wealth and exploitation and therefore the birth of social classes" (Vachon, 1988).

The common good is the essence of the project, the nucleus around which the economic, social and cultural objectives and activities of people and communities are articulated. The common good provides the values and principles that inspire the form and content for living together during a specific period of history, as well as the choice of common goods necessary for its implementation. As stated elsewhere:

> "By 'common good' we refer in their entirety to:
>
> - *principles* (such as the principle of the right to life for all, the principle of precaution, the principle of equal citizenship, the principle of the finiteness of most of the planet's resources ...);
>
> - *institutions* (such as representative democracy, local community institutions, free trade unions ...);
>
> - *resources* and *means* (such as air, water, land, education, information ...);
>
> - *practices* (the practices of common sharing, individual and collective solidarity ...)" ("The University for the Common Good", 2004).

b. *From welfare state to welfare society*

The transformation from welfare state to welfare societies, based on the new social pact for the common good, requires the correct definition of three areas: i. community welfare, ii. associative and co-operative welfare and iii. personal welfare.

i. Community welfare: "is constituted by the whole of principles, institutions, means and practices taken by society in order to guarantee for all its citizens the right to a human decent life and a peaceful, suitable and co-operative 'living together', to preserve one's own 'home' security, that is to say the sustainability of the local and global ecosystem, and overall taking into account the right to life of the future generations" (Petrella, 1999). The common good is the basis of the communities' welfare on which associative and personal welfare can be built.

ii. Associative and co-operative welfare: "is constituted by the whole of principles, institutions, means and practices taken by society in order to promote voluntary co-operation among people, and/or groups that pursue common objectives by putting at common disposal and sharing the material and immaterial resources following the practices of mutuality and co-operation" (ibidem). De-privatisation means the extension of the area of de-commodification to new forms of organisation of the private sector able to promote and establish co-operative and associative economic forms belonging to the concepts of "other economy", "economy of solidarity" and "districts of solidarity". These new areas of activity and socialisation, which include forms of production, consumption and services, can be developed if the community has access to an autonomous space, both inside and outside the market economy, where they are able to develop participation and various forms of social benefits which are consistent with the values that inspire them. These social forms of organisation and management of the economy should be able to avoid the juridical constraints introduced by institutions in order to protect monopolistic positions on the economic as well as the institutional side.

iii. Personal and private welfare: "individual welfare is constituted by the whole of principles, institutions, means and practices taken by society in order to permit to each individual, in competition with all the others, to optimise his own personal utility in terms of monetary wealth and freedom of action" (ibidem). This sector of the private economy should regain its strength in the market economy, re-establishing its links to the real economy by pursuing enterprise profit within production and service channels liberated from "bonds" and "constraints" imposed by the financial systems and by an unnecessarily excessive state burden on the enterprise's costs and management. The creation of an enterprise culture able to internalise social costs, to remain within the boundaries of non-war production, to contribute to the establishment of a fair relationship between production, distribution and consumption in society, open to dialogue with the community and the society it belongs to, seems to be a realistic objective.

These guidelines enable a group of individuals to constitute a human community, "to create society" and live together in such a way as to ensure the right to a "decent" life (in accordance with human dignity) to each member, as well as collective safety. All this is done while respecting "the other" and in solidarity with other human communities and future generations and while safeguarding life on the planet.

c. Establishing new tangible and intangible common assets in the pursuit of citizen well-being

The common goods are the instruments needed by a welfare society, which should reflect the content and form of the objective of solidarity for the achievement of the common good. They are the goods necessary for material life as well as for new activities and relations seen as of central importance in the life of the communities. Therefore, they should be characterised differently from private goods (commodities) where the principles are those of rivalry and exclusivity of access and use applied in the capitalist market system. The public economy and the co-operative economy function in a different way in the market economy than in the capitalist one.

A preliminary list of the common goods includes: air, water, state lands, seas and forests, space, energy, knowledge, transportation, education, health, communication and information, security, justice, basic financial activities and political institutions. Among the common goods we also find labour and culture whose roles, functions, times and forms are closely intertwined with other forms of social life. Common goods of world-wide importance should be matters for dialogue between communities regarding their maintenance and use within the perspective of "living together" (Table 1).

Table 1 – Common goods, actors and practices, well-being

Common goods	Actors and practices	Well-being
– air – water (from surface and underground, brackish and fresh water, not only for drinkable use but also for all other uses, such as agriculture, necessary to common existence – "green" energies, such as solar energy, wind power, etc.) – state lands and forests – the ether and extra-terrestrial space – knowledge (in all its various forms) – education (in all its forms) – habitat (from housing to the government of the territory) – health – culture (specifically cultural goods) – common transportation – communication and information – common security (police, army, civil protection) – justice – mutual financial insti-tutions (for example, the Treasury, popular saving banks) – political institutions (parliament, govern-ment, public administration).	Actors: – institutions (represent-ative democracy, local community institutions, free trade unions, etc.) – social enterprises (SMEs, co-operatives, social co-operatives, etc.) – civil society organisations (NGOs, associations, etc.). Practices: – principles (the prin-ciple of the right to life for all, the principle of precaution, the principle of equal citizenship, the principle of the finite-ness of most of the planet's resources, etc.) – practices (the practices of common sharing, individual and collective solidarity, etc.).	Sustainability: – environmental – social – cultural – political – economic.

The resources at the disposal of the welfare society project inspired by the common good are:

- values and principles;
- laws and institutions;
- finance;
- actors and practices.

The recent trend towards the segmentation of common goods to be managed by international agencies ("governance") reproduces the negative effects experienced with public goods administered by the state, followed by the "de-responsabilisation" of communities and peoples. Therefore the selection and the management of common goods should re-establish the principle of sovereignty at community level as opposed to the state, as well as to international institutions. This implies the introduction of new ownership and management forms based on a high level of self-government and participation able to mobilise local communities and civil societies.

The economy cannot remain outside and independent of this system, as in the case of the welfare state built on the dualism of state and market. This dualism is today challenged on two sides. Globalisation, by increasing privatisation, transforms dualism into a unified system based on the principle and supremacy of finance and technology with the marginalisation of increasing areas of society. An alternative answer to this problem is the common good, which overcomes the dualism of the previous system by re-establishing the centrality of community life based on its main components: territory, population, production systems and institutions (Figure 1).

The life of the communities inspired by the common good requires an overall cohesion and mobilisation of all its components and resources. The common goods create the basis for its overall functioning and within each of its main factors: territory, production systems, population and institutions. The diamond represents the necessary structure based on its main pillars. Globalisation is based on de-territorialised production systems, on nomadism of the population and on centralised institutions. The cells of welfare societies are the communities that demand, within their respective boundaries, the existence of their own institutions that govern a specific territory, population and production systems (Table 2).

Figure 1 – The diamond of the community

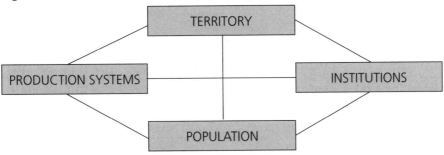

In comparison to globalisation, the common good pursues re-socialisation in order to extend the domain of de-commodification from the co-operative sector of the economy to other forms of private economy sensitive to the appeal of the "other economy", based on various forms of co-operation, solidarity networks, social districts, and similar. It is the creation of an economy reintegrated into the community, where the market regains a dependent service function for producers and consumers, liberated from the capitalist "for-profit" spirit and oriented by a surplus principle (not-for-profit) which enables it to maintain its sustainability. These new areas of activity and social relations can be developed in the autonomous space at local level, inside and outside the market economy.

Their success can also have positive effects on the behaviour of private enterprises. Therefore the success of this new economy has been extended to the private sector through the concept of "social enterprises"; that is to say, all enterprises that, independently from their chosen juridical forms, operate at local level and follow patterns of organisational behaviour that define their social function. The social enterprise, according to this definition, is rooted in its community and pursues its sustainability goals (economic, social, institutional and environmental).

In all forms of social organisation, the production system and the market can play an important role as instruments of social and cultural exchange of experience and as places to meet and develop new ideas. This can only take place, however, if a strong link is maintained between the territory, population, production systems and institutions without the decline or disappearance of any of these elements. Therefore the central position given to the local dimension in designing the new boundaries of the community (instead of the national state dimension) is not a choice of specialisation within a bigger domain, but the privileged areas of reference to which the other dimensions – such as the state, regions, international institutions – should be functionally related (Table 2).

Table 2 – Welfare state, globalisation and common good

	Welfare state	Globalisation	Welfare society
Objectives (a)	Individual and material	Individual – status	Social – relational
Objectives (b)	National growth	Global apartheid	Common good
Instruments	Public goods: – steel – electricity – transport – education – health	Private goods: – finance – technology – trade – knowledge society	Common goods: – water – environment – habitat – education – health – space
Actors	**Individual rights**	**Consumer choices**	**Individual membership**
Institutions	National state	Triadic power	Community, region, state and meso-region
	Government	Governance	Self-government and participation
	National development	From global to local	From local to meso-regional
Production systems	Public and private enterprises (big enterprises) Industrial districts	Transnationals (Toyota model)	Social enterprises SMEs Networks Public institutions

d. Role of collective ownership and shared heritage

The second half of the last century witnessed two stages in the development of European economies. The first two decades – 1950s and 1960s – experienced the planning system in central and eastern Europe and the capitalist market and mixed economies in western Europe. Both systems produced economic growth and a strong rise of public institutions and services. During this stage, planning and market economies were able to satisfy most of the demand for goods and services and almost no space was left for the development of other forms of economy. The existing co-operative movement in the East and in the West was squeezed between the market and the state and had to survive in a very narrow space often adapting itself to the behaviour of the prevailing economic system.

The situation changed radically in the following decades (1970-2000) because of globalisation that became the dominant paradigm in the economy and politics. The fall of the Berlin Wall unified eastern and western European societies favouring concentration of growth and squeezing the market along the lines of global apartheid (Amoroso, 2004). Furthermore, the implementation of the new neo-liberal policies put an end to Keynesian economic policies that sustained mass production and consumption during the stage of national capitalism. The public sector policies and their public goods were no longer needed and started to decline.

Paradoxically, these two negative events in the history of European societies are also the cause of the rise of the most innovative events of the new century. The withdrawal of capitalism from vast regions and sectors – because of its concentration on the rich segments of the markets (the capitalist answer to the problem of worldwide sustainability) – led to the opening up of opportunities for market and social activities. This has given rise to civil society mobilisation that, after a short period of resistance to globalisation in defence of the welfare system, decided to experience new ways of economic and institutional organisation. Hence the rise of social co-operatives and social enterprises together with a revitalisation of local development as the basis for the revival of communities (Amoroso and Zandonai, 2007). The slogan of globalisation "from global to local" was overturned into its opposite: "from local to global". The first assumes globalisation as the model for inspiration at local level. The local community should adapt to it. The second opposes this monocentric view with a polycentric one, where it is the sustainability of the single community and its social project that determines the forms and extension of the necessary dialogue with other communities for the achievement of the common good worldwide. Therefore within this new paradigm the social enterprise becomes the answer to the problem of sustainability in the production of goods and services for the new economy.

To sum up what has already been mentioned we can state that the qualifying elements of the social enterprise are:

- its territorial and local roots as a condition for an efficient choice of sector of activities and use of local resources;

- its belonging to the community, which can understand the demands made on it, as well as the social and productive impact on the community that it generates;

- the hybrid character of the resources and labour forms at the disposal of the entrepreneurial project, which is able to make use of all forms of employment beyond the boundaries of market-oriented juridical definition with reference to employment, as well as owner-ship forms;

- the involvement of all entrepreneurial actors through real forms of participation and co-decision making in the enterprise management;

- attention and adequate investment in inter-organisational relations at the local as well as the enlarged level, able to link local co-opera-tion with co-operation with producers and markets in other commu-nities and other countries.

The social enterprise model is a natural response to the problems raised by globalisation.

Conclusion: access to, and the use of, resources and rights

The topics of "access to", and "the use of", have been the keywords by which the efficiency of a democratic system has been monitored and measured in European policy as well as in the international organisations during recent years. They have been widely introduced to set up bench-marking for the processes of democratisation. During the period of the welfare state the procedures for their implementation were based on the supply by the public sector of the basic infrastructures needed to achieve these goals and by the strategy of "rights" to be guaranteed to all citizens by formal declarations (right to work, right to income, etc.). The strategy of rights has been widely intertwined at international level with the one of "human rights", sharing with it the underestimation of the problem posed in both cases by the "to" and by the "of" which are assumed to be clearly defined and well known.

However, some results have been achieved but nearly always below the level of expectation and, since the 1970s, problems that were finally considered solved – such has poverty, inequality, poor labour conditions, insecurity, and so forth – have reappeared on a greater scale. These have provoked various reactions from the people and their movements, who have expressed a general disaffection for institutions and politics as such and have sought initiatives from institutions and from civil society. The new slogan has become "participation", introduced on a vast scale at all level of institutions and tested also in some sectors of the economy. The limit of participation, however, is that it does not question the objectives and the forms of the existing political and economic institutions, but tries to create more support for their functioning. It can improve "access to" and "the use of" but does not question the objective and the forms for which participation is intended to work.

This brings us back to the central problem of form and content of the model of development to be chosen. The prevailing trend today, despite the declarations and policies that raise awareness of the problem of diversity in European development, rightly pointed out as a positive and specific European value, is a monocentric one (Eurocentrism and Westernisation). Diversity has not become the key to understanding the need for a polycentric development based on regions and communities – where values, objectives and forms are shared but remain different – but, as already mentioned, still goes from global to local by a process of adaptation of the latter to the former.

References

Adler-Karlsson G., *The Political Economy of East-West-South Co-Operation*, Springer-Verlag, New York, 1976.

Amoroso, B., *Global Apartheid,* Economics and Society, Federico Caffè Center, Roskilde, Città di Castello, 2004.

Amoroso, B. and Zandonai, F., *Oltre i confini: percorsi di internazionalizzazione dell'impresa sociale*, CGM Brescia, 2007.

Archibugi, F., *The Associative Economy*, Macmillan Press, London, 2000.

Caffè, F., "Umanesimo del welfare", *Micromega*, No. 1, 1986.

Kapp, K.W., *The Social Costs of Private Enterprise*, Harvard University Press, Cambridge, MA., 1950.

Keynes, J.M., "National Self-Sufficiency", *Yale Review*, 1933.

Keynes, J.M., "Economic Possibilities for our Grandchildren" in Keynes, J.M., *Essays in Persuasion*, 1932.

Meadows, D.H., Meadows, D.L., Randers, J. and Behrens, W.W., *Limits to Growth*, Universe Books, 1972.

Myrdal, G., *Beyond the Welfare State. Economic Planning and its International Implocations*, Yale University Press, New Haven, CT, 1960

Petrella, R., *Le manifeste de l'Eau*, Pour un Contrat Mondial, Lausanne, 1999.

"The University for the Common Good", Federico Caffè Center, Roskilde University, Denmark, 2004, www.ruc.dk/upload/application/pdf/f51d6748/The_UNIVERSITY_for_the_COMMON_GOOD.pdf.

Vachon, R., "La pensée de Dominique Temple", *Interculture*, No. 98, Montreal, 1988.

WCED (United Nations World Commission on Environment and Development), *Our Common Future*, Oxford University Press, 1987.

Le bien-être pour tous
Concepts et outils de la cohésion sociale

Tendances de la cohésion sociale, n° 20

Editions du Conseil de l'Europe

Couverture : Atelier de création graphique du Conseil de l'Europe

Editions du Conseil de l'Europe
F-67075 Strasbourg Cedex
http://book.coe.int

ISBN : 978-92-871-6505-3
© Conseil de l'Europe, novembre 2008
Imprimé en Belgique

Autres titres dans la même collection

n° 1   **Promouvoir d'un point de vue comparatif le débat politique sur l'exclusion sociale** (ISBN : 978-92-871-4920-6, 8€/12$US)

n° 2   **Le financement des systèmes de retraite et de santé en Europe : réformes et tendances au cours des années 1990** (ISBN : 978-92-871-4921-3, 8€/12$US)

n° 3   **Utiliser des aides sociales pour combattre la pauvreté et l'exclusion sociale : examen comparatif des opportunités et des problèmes** (ISBN : 978-92-871-4937-4, 13€/20$US)

n° 4   **Nouvelles demandes sociales : défis de la gouvernance** (ISBN : 978-92-871-5012-7, 19€/29$US)

n° 5   **Lutte contre la pauvreté et accès aux droits sociaux dans les pays du Sud-Caucase : une approche territoriale** (ISBN : 978-92-871-5096-7, 15€/23$US)

n° 6   **Etat et nouvelles responsabilités sociales dans un monde global** (ISBN : 978-92-871-5168-1, 15€/23$US)

n° 7   **Société civile et nouvelles responsabilités sociales sur des bases éthiques** (ISBN : 978-92-871-5309-8, 13€/20$US)

n° 8   **Les jeunes et l'exclusion dans les quartiers défavorisés : s'attaquer aux racines de la violence** (ISBN : 978-92-871-5389-0, 25€/38$US**)**

n° 9   **Les jeunes et l'exclusion dans les quartiers défavorisés : approches politiques dans six villes d'Europe** (ISBN : 978-92-871-5512-2, 15€/23$US)

n° 10   **L'approche de la sécurité par la cohésion sociale : propositions pour une nouvelle gouvernance socio-économique** (ISBN : 978-92-871-5491-0, 17€/26$US)

n° 11   **L'approche de la sécurité par la cohésion sociale : déconstruire la peur (des autres) en allant au-delà des stéréotypes** (ISBN : 978-92-871-5544-3, 10€/15$US)

n° 12   **Engagement éthique et solidaire des citoyens dans l'économie : une responsabilité pour la cohésion sociale** (ISBN : 978-92-871-5558-0, 10€/15$US)

n° 13   **Le revenu de la retraite : développements récents et propositions** (ISBN : 978-92-871-5705-8, 13€/20$US)

n° 14   **Les choix solidaires dans le marché : un apport vital à la cohésion sociale** (ISBN : 978-92-871-5761-4, 30€/45$US)

n° 15   **Concilier flexibilité du travail et cohésion sociale – Un défi à relever** (ISBN : 978-92-871-5813-0, 35€/53$US)

n° 16   **Concilier flexibilité du travail et cohésion sociale – Des idées pour l'action politique** (ISBN : 978-92-871-6014-0, 30€/45$US)

n° 17   Concilier flexibilité du travail et cohésion sociale – Les expériences et enjeux spécifiques de l'Europe centrale et orientale (ISBN : 978-92-871-6151-2, 39€/59$US)

n° 18   Quelle cohésion sociale dans une Europe multiculturelle ? Concepts, état des lieux et développements (ISBN : 978-92-871-6033-1, 37€/56$US)

n° 19   Concilier bien-être des migrants et intérêt collectif – Etat social, entreprises et citoyenneté en transformation (ISBN : 978-92-871-6285-4, 44€/88$US)

SOMMAIRE

Préface..9
Alexander Vladychenko

Introduction 11
Gilda Farrell

**Partie I – Bien-être de tous et implication des citoyens :
l'approche du Conseil de l'Europe** 15

**I. Le bien-être de tous :
objectif de la cohésion sociale** 15
Gilda Farrell

1. Bien-être et bien-être de tous : quelles différences? 16

2. Les apports du concept de bien-être de tous 17

3. Une meilleure compréhension des rapports entre
bien-être subjectif et bien-être objectif.........................25

4. Faire du bien-être de tous un levier pour améliorer la vie ensemble....27

Conclusion 30

Bibliographie 32

Annexe – Tableaux sur les indicateurs de bien-être en entreprise.............33

**II. Définir et mesurer le bien-être et le progrès
avec les citoyens** 35
Samuel Thirion

Introduction 35

1. Le cadre d'analyse proposé...............................37

2. Aborder la question du bien-être (questions épistémologiques)..........48

3. Construire la connaissance pour le progrès sociétal
avec les citoyens – Premiers résultats des expérimentations 55

4. Réflexions sur les éléments clés du bien-être de tous 64

Conclusions..73

Bibliographie 77

Annexe – Eléments de méthode 78

Partie II – Compréhension et perception du bien-être : les sujets et les biens 81

I. Comprendre le bien-être pour l'assurer de manière équitable 81
Jean-Luc Dubois

Introduction 81

1. Une aspiration générale au bien-être 82

2. Assurer le bien-être : à la recherche d'une nouvelle éthique 90

Conclusion 97

Bibliographie 99

II. Perception et mesure du bien-être 101
Wolfgang Glatzer

Introduction 101

1. Bien-être et perception du bien-être 102

2. Les mesures du bien-être 106

3. Biens publics, caractéristiques de l'environnement et bien-être national dans l'Etat social 109

4. Différenciation public/privé et bien-être 111

Conclusions 116

Bibliographie – Références bibliographiques 119

Biliographie – Pour en savoir plus 121

Partie III – Bien-être et responsabilités 123

I. Bien commun, bien-être et responsabilités des collectivités locales 123
Iuli Nascimento

1. Bien commun et intérêt général 123

2. Bien-être et mondialisation 126

3. Rôles, responsabilités et outils des collectivités territoriales – L'exemple de la France et de la région Ile-de-France 132

Conclusion 140

Bibliographie – Références bibliographiques 143

Biliographie – Pour en savoir plus 143

II. Du mal-être au bien-être :
   responsabilités personnelles et collectives 145
   Catherine Redelsperger

Introduction 145

1. Proposition de définitions 146

2. Processus apprenants pour un retour vers le bien-être :
   les dimensions personnelles et collectives 149

3. Le processus apprenant de bien-être/mal-être
   dans le contexte du salariat 156

Conclusion 164

Partie IV – Plaidoyer pour une société du bien commun
   au service du bien-être 165

De l'Etat providence à la société de bien-être 165
Bruno Amoroso

1. Imaginaire collectif et bien-être : deux utopies 165

2. La société du bien-être, un nouveau projet
   en faveur du bien-être 174

Conclusion : la question de l'accès aux ressources
et aux droits et de leur utilisation 186

Bibliographie 188

Préface

Le bien-être est aujourd'hui un thème à la mode, décliné tant sur les panneaux publicitaires que dans de nombreux écrits à caractère philosophique ou scientifique sur le sujet. Et cela semble naturel dans une société qui cherche à apporter pleine satisfaction à tous ses membres. Après une phase de forte croissance qui a permis l'accès à la consommation de masse, les préoccupations des citoyens se tournent vers ce que celle-ci est censée desservir : le bien-être.

Il faut distinguer à présent le bien-être individuel, évoqué par exemple par la publicité, et le bien-être de tous. Cette dernière notion introduite par le Conseil de l'Europe dans sa stratégie révisée de cohésion sociale comme objectif ultime de la société moderne met l'accent sur le fait que le bien-être ne peut être atteint s'il n'est pas partagé. Une partie de l'humanité ne peut vivre bien si l'autre est dans le mal-être ou si elle y parvient aux dépens des générations futures, en léguant à ses propres enfants et petits-enfants un monde incertain, aux ressources appauvries.

Cette vérité devient de plus en plus une évidence dans un monde globalisé, marqué par l'interdépendance entre les peuples et entre les générations, et jaillit de l'expression des citoyens eux-mêmes. Ainsi dans les projets développés par le Conseil de l'Europe avec certaines municipalités et acteurs locaux, donnant aux habitants, travailleurs, lycéens, etc. l'opportunité de s'exprimer sur leur bien-être, la relation à l'autre, les équilibres sociaux et les formes de responsabilité et d'engagement se manifestent toujours comme des dimensions clés du bien-être.

Quatre années après l'adoption de sa stratégie révisée de cohésion sociale et son approfondissement par une task force de haut niveau sur la cohésion sociale au XXIe siècle, la recherche du bien-être de tous dans la concertation et la participation s'affirme toujours davantage comme une voie essentielle pour asseoir une société de droit et de responsabilités partagées. Ce volume de « Tendances de la cohésion sociale » permet de faire un point sur cette question, en s'appuyant à la fois sur les résultats des travaux conduits par la Division pour le développement de la cohésion sociale et sur d'autres recherches réalisées par ailleurs.

Alexander Vladychenko

Directeur général de la cohésion sociale
Conseil de l'Europe

INTRODUCTION

Dans sa Stratégie de cohésion sociale[1], le Conseil de l'Europe définit cette dernière comme étant la capacité de la société à assurer le bien-être de tous et éviter les disparités, et met l'accent sur la nécessaire coresponsabilité des acteurs pour y parvenir.

Quatre années après l'adoption de cette stratégie (et un an après les conclusions de la task force de haut niveau sur la cohésion sociale au XXIe siècle qui en précise les contours[2]), ce numéro de «Tendances de la cohésion sociale» propose un premier bilan de l'intérêt des concepts clés qui en sont à la base, notamment ceux de bien-être de tous et de coresponsabilité. Les deux premiers articles portent sur certains des résultats des travaux d'analyses et des expérimentations qui ont été conduites par la Division pour le développement de la cohésion sociale[3]. Les cinq autres sont le produit des réflexions réalisées ailleurs, dans différents contextes, et que le Conseil de l'Europe a réunies dans le souci de les faire connaître et d'affirmer l'intérêt qu'a, pour notre Europe, le bien-être décliné en tant que droit pour tous.

Le premier article de Gilda Farrell, chef de la Division pour le développement de la cohésion sociale au Conseil de l'Europe, analyse la portée du concept de bien-être de tous en tant qu'objectif de société. Elle montre notamment en quoi il diffère de celui de bien-être individuel et apporte une nouvelle dimension aux notions de liberté, de choix et de préférences, clarifie le rapport entre objectif et subjectif et ouvre, également, des perspectives en termes de mobilisation du potentiel de chacun et d'apprentissage de la valeur des aspects immatériels pour l'évolution des politiques publiques de cohésion sociale.

Dans un deuxième article, un bilan des expérimentations réalisées – et en cours – pour définir et mesurer le bien-être de tous et la cohésion sociale au niveau local (territoire ou structure) avec les acteurs concernés et les citoyens est présenté par Samuel Thirion, administrateur au Conseil

---

1. Stratégie de cohésion sociale du Conseil de l'Europe, version révisée, approuvée par le Comité des Ministres le 31 mars 2004.

2. Rapport de la Conclusion de la task force de haut niveau pour la cohésion sociale, 2007.

3. Travaux réalisés dans la suite de la publication du *Guide méthodologique pour l'élaboration concertée des indicateurs de cohésion sociale*, Conseil de l'Europe, 2005.

de l'Europe. Il propose un chemin de lecture permettant de faire le lien avec la notion de progrès de la société et sa mesure, tout en abordant les relations entre biens et bien-être.

Ces deux articles, produit des travaux conduits par le Conseil de l'Europe, préconisent une approche endogène de la connaissance du bien-être, partant des citoyens eux-mêmes, comme complément indispensable des approches plus exogènes consistant à analyser le bien-être par des recherches spécifiques, à caractère philosophique ou scientifique. Outre la pertinence d'une telle approche, compte tenu du caractère intrinsèquement subjectif et interactif des concepts de bien-être et de bien-être de tous, elle présente de nombreux avantages (transversalité, apprentissages mutuels, coûts mineurs et facilité de mise en œuvre) et met en évidence la multidimensionnalité du concept de bien-être de tous.

Toutefois, comme le montre Jean-Luc Dubois dans le troisième article de ce volume, lorsqu'on fait le tour des approches exogènes du bien-être dans les différents domaines (philosophique, économique et psychologique), on retrouve également la même multidimensionnalité du concept de bien-être.

Ces deux types d'approche du bien-être, endogènes ou exogènes, convergent donc et mettent en évidence l'importance des dimensions immatérielles. Plus précisément la « reconnaissance » de chacun en tant qu'acteur de la société. Celle-ci est la clé pour faire avancer des processus conduisant au bien-être fondés sur la coresponsabilité ou responsabilité mutuelle.

Ce rôle déterminant de la façon dont les responsabilités sont réparties et, plus généralement, de tout ce qui concerne la gouvernance et les relations humaines, est sans doute un des éléments d'explication des écarts que l'on observe dans les sociétés modernes entre le sentiment de bien-être (couramment appelé « bien-être subjectif ») et les dimensions matérielles du bien-être (dénommé usuellement « bien-être objectif »). Wolfang Glatzer analyse en détail ces questions dans le quatrième article, en en tirant quelques enseignements essentiels.

La question se pose alors de savoir comment mettre en œuvre des approches de coresponsabilité et de gouvernance plus inclusive dans un contexte de mondialisation qui ne le rend pas aisé. Dans le cinquième article, Iuli Nascimento dégage des pistes dans ce sens tant au niveau européen que des collectivités territoriales avec l'exemple de la région Ile-de-France.

Reste que de telles approches sont souvent difficiles à réaliser, voire presque impossibles dans certains contextes, notamment avec les publics en difficulté qui, après des cycles d'exclusion successifs, ont développé des mécanismes de repli sur soi constituant parfois de véritables blocages. Dans le sixième article, Catherine Redelsperger, s'appuyant sur son expérience de coaching avec les chômeurs de longue durée et les surendettés, en dégage des leviers pour reconstruire un chemin de confiance et d'inclusion, et susciter progressivement le souhait de partager des responsabilités.

Ces réflexions conduisent à se poser la question des biens dont on a besoin pour pouvoir assurer des processus générateurs de bien-être de tous. Au-delà des biens matériels privés ou publics, qui sont une évidence et qui ont sans doute pris souvent une importance démesurée dans les sociétés développées, l'importance des biens immatériels ressort de ces analyses (on pense bien sûr aux droits de l'homme, à la démocratie, à l'Etat de droit et à toutes les régulations leur permettant d'exister). Les réflexions de Bruno Amoroso dans le dernier article de ce volume portent ainsi sur la valeur et le rôle des biens communs en tant que piliers d'une véritable éthique de la convivialité (dans le sens de co-vivre, ou vivre ensemble sur la même terre) et d'une vision sociale d'avenir.

En conclusion, si ce volume confirme la justesse des concepts qui sont proposés par le Conseil de l'Europe en matière de cohésion sociale, il permet aussi d'apprécier les efforts réalisés par ailleurs. Plus que tout il met en évidence qu'assurer le bien-être de tous et des générations futures, exige des nouveaux paradigmes et de nouvelles visions partagées par les acteurs, y compris les citoyens, individuellement.

Gilda Farrell

Chef de la Division pour le développement de la cohésion sociale
DG Cohésion sociale – Conseil de l'Europe

PARTIE I – BIEN-ÊTRE DE TOUS ET IMPLICATION DES CITOYENS : L'APPROCHE DU CONSEIL DE L'EUROPE

I. Le bien-être de tous : objectif de la cohésion sociale

Gilda Farrell[1]

« La seule signification des préférences non privée de sens est celle des préférences à l'unanimité. » (Bruno de Finetti, 1952)

L'analyse ici présentée porte sur le bien-être de tous en tant qu'objectif de cohésion sociale. Elle s'appuie fondamentalement sur un travail expérimental mené par le Conseil de l'Europe au niveau de plusieurs territoires européens (ainsi qu'au sein d'une entreprise multinationale et d'un lycée). L'expérience consistait à inviter des citoyens (ou travailleurs, étudiants, selon le cas) à réfléchir sur trois questions dans une logique d'interaction : Qu'est-ce que le bien-être pour vous ? Qu'est-ce que le mal-être ? Qu'êtes-vous prêt à faire pour contribuer au bien-être[2] ? La différence fondamentale entre cette expérimentation et d'autres ne réside pas dans le type de questions mais plutôt dans le fait de les avoir posées à des « groupes de citoyens ». En effet, cette dynamique – qui a mis en lumière les interrelations entre leurs conditions de vie en tant que personnes et les évolutions sociales, économiques et institutionnelles de leur environnement – a permis d'« objectiver » les perceptions individuelles et d'arriver à des consensus sur ce qui est essentiel pour tous. Même si le bien-être est par essence « ressenti » individuellement[3], lorsqu'il est abordé en commun, il devient objectif de société. Pour le Conseil de l'Europe s'interroger sur le bien-être de tous est ainsi essentiel à la gestion de la vie ensemble.

---

1. Chef de la Division pour le développement de la cohésion sociale, DG Cohésion sociale, Conseil de l'Europe.
2. L'expérimentation a été réalisée dans trois villes européennes : Mulhouse (France), Rovereto (Italie) et Timişoara (Roumanie), ainsi que dans une entreprise filiale strasbourgeoise d'un groupe multinational finlandais (UPM) et dans un lycée à Mulhouse.
3. Voir l'article de Samuel Thirion dans ce volume.

1. Bien-être et bien-être de tous : quelles différences ?

« Le bien-être n'est pas vrai s'il n'est pas partagé. » (Christopher McCandless, le jeune protagoniste du film *Into the wild*)[4]

Dans son acception la plus courante, le bien-être est associé à ce qui compte en définitive et fait sens dans ce qui est bien pour la personne : dans cette optique, on distingue les courants de pensée hédoniste (recherche du bilan le plus positif entre plaisir et douleur), du désir (satisfaction des choix ; la meilleure vie possible) et des listes objectives (des « biens » matériels ou immatériels). De nos jours, on associe assez souvent le « bien-être » à des traitements et à des produits capables de rendre l'harmonie entre corps et esprit et tout cela dans le cadre de certains standards de beauté. Il suffit de taper « bien-être » dans un moteur de recherche pour le découvrir. Dans cette approche, le bien-être individuel est étroitement lié à la consommation.

L'utilisation que nous allons faire du terme « bien-être » est plus large. Nous allons d'abord nous référer au « bien-être de tous » en tant que concept qui comprend l'humanité tout entière y compris les générations futures. En étendant le bien-être à tous, l'espace de référence – ainsi que le stock et le type des biens pour l'atteindre – devient universel et inclut des interactions au-delà de la proximité. Le concept de bien-être de tous conduit à l'idée qu'il s'agit d'une construction raisonnée, assujettie à des contraintes, à des concertations et à des concessions mutuelles. Il renferme des aspects d'équité, d'empathie et s'inscrit dans la durée.

Pour devenir opérationnel (c'est-à-dire susceptible d'intervention politique), le concept de bien-être de tous s'exprime nécessairement par rapport à un périmètre délimité : un quartier, une ville, une usine. Néanmoins, pour en établir les composantes et les conditions qui le rendent possible, il faut pouvoir prendre en compte l'articulation des responsabilités entre différents niveaux de pouvoir de décision et hiérarchies ainsi que la « partie » non maîtrisable et parfois aléatoire du bien-être au niveau où est réalisé l'exercice.

L'approche du bien-être de tous en tant que « droit » ne nie pas les aspects propres au bien-être de la personne, mais plutôt déplace l'axe de perception de la satisfaction des préférences individuelles vers l'élabora-

---

4. Krakauer, Jon, *Voyage au bout de la solitude*, 1996, adapté au cinéma en 2007 par Sean Penn.

tion de préférences concertées (unanimes[5]). Par ailleurs, cette approche amène au constat que le bien-être individuel résulte du partage (en plus de la satisfaction et de la possession) et qu'il est – dans ce sens – le produit d'interactions. « Le bien-être n'est pas vrai s'il n'est pas partagé. » Dans cette optique, le terme grec *eudaimonia* (épanouissement humain) trouve sa concrétisation dans un « raisonnement élaboré » sur les aspects fondamentaux du bien-être de tous. L'approche s'inscrit dans la quête de la réponse à la question : « Comment être bien en société ? », donc dans une conception du bien-être susceptible d'influencer les processus d'élaboration de la connaissance et des espaces politiques de création, d'expression, d'appartenance, de responsabilité, de solidarité.

La connotation morale du « bien-être », ou comment se pose la question du bien-être de l'autre tout en recherchant le sien, prend ainsi un autre sens : ce n'est pas celui de la vertu (bonté) ou de l'obligation, mais plutôt celui du raisonnement sur l'interdépendance entre bien-être individuel et biens accessibles à tous. Plutôt que de « maximisation » de bien-être de chacun, l'approche conduit à réfléchir sur une vision d'« optimisation inclusive », axée sur des choix qui sont nécessairement concertés.

Finalement, la dimension esthétique, la référence à la beauté en tant que capacité de transformer les diverses sphères de la vie commune et personnelle prennent toute leur place en tant que potentiel humain. « Faire des belles choses » a été un des critères de bien-être souligné par les citoyens.

2. Les apports du concept de bien-être de tous

a. Le partage d'une vision

La vision partagée est à la racine même de la définition du bien-être de tous. Ainsi ce concept ne peut pas être confondu avec accumulation et possession des biens, même si les biens ont leur fonction dans le bien-être. Sans vision, une société peut produire des biens sans pour autant produire du bien-être. Aborder la question de la vision dans un contexte

---

5. Lorsqu'on se réfère à des préférences unanimes on fait allusion à celles qui font le « consensus » tout en tenant compte que sur cette question il peut toujours y avoir des conflits, notamment par rapport aux objectifs de bien-être des différents groupes de population.

de démultiplication des individualités et de distance croissante entre l'appréciation des biens publics – communs et privés – n'est pas aisé.

Il faut néanmoins souligner que l'approche utilisée par le Conseil de l'Europe pour définir le bien-être avec les citoyens a permis de réintroduire une éthique de la responsabilité mutuelle conduisant les participants à s'extraire de leur individualité et intérêt immédiat pour affiner leurs perceptions par l'échange. Ce résultat met en cause le lieu commun qui affirme l'impossibilité de nos concitoyens d'adhérer à des visions partagées. La mise en avant d'une individualité négative et égoïste, qui condamne les humains à la recherche exclusive de leur seul intérêt, ne relèverait-elle pas du domaine idéologique, empêchant ainsi de mettre en valeur le potentiel de solidarité et de partage propre à chaque personne ?

b. Une autre lecture de la liberté

La liberté individuelle, on en convient, dépend de la capacité de faire des choix et d'exercer la responsabilité. Mais la pensée dominante, empruntée à l'économie néoclassique, réduit cette liberté aux choix dans les marchés. Elle se limiterait ainsi aux caractéristiques des biens qui répondent aux goûts ou aux contraintes personnels : les prix, les couleurs, ou encore la composition. C'est une sorte de liberté à périmètre délimité ou liberté spécifique puisque nombre de composantes des biens restent invisibles, opaques ou non ouvertes au choix. C'est notamment le cas de toutes les composantes reliées aux respects actifs des droits de l'homme, de la préservation de l'environnement ou encore des conditions décentes de travail, alors même que la prise en compte de ces éléments mènerait vers une liberté complexe de choix ou une capacité de jugement global. C'est parce que le choix des biens pour maximiser certaines formes d'utilité ou préférences individuelles se fait sur des composantes spécifiques, qu'il ne se transforme pas nécessairement en choix de bien-être. Paradoxalement, dans ces conditions, l'excès de choix ou la fragmentation excessive de l'offre nuit même à la liberté spécifique : aucune personne n'est en mesure de choisir de façon satisfaisante dans une gamme illimitée de biens. Et encore, cette liberté s'épuise dans le geste d'achat.

Une vision du bien-être de tous doit donc revisiter la question de la liberté de deux perspectives :

- comment transformer les choix du marché en créateurs potentiels de bien-être. Par exemple, lorsque les citoyens acceptent d'adhérer à des démarches collectives de consommation de produits de proxi-

mité ou d'énergie verte en acceptant les contraintes de la saison-
nalité ou de la fidélisation, ces contraintes raisonnées deviennent
génératrices de liberté : elles permettent de découvrir des champs
inexplorés d'expression des préférences qui vont enrichir la capacité
de jugement global de chacun et donc l'impact sur le bien-être de
tous ;

- comment démultiplier la capacité de choix dans l'espace civique ou
démocratique par l'exercice de la responsabilité. Il s'agit en effet de
combler la distance croissante entre augmentation du choix dans les
marchés et diminution du choix dans l'espace public[6].

c.   Une autre compréhension du concept de biens

En plus de l'exercice d'une liberté complexe et raisonnée, la vision du
bien-être de tous s'enracine dans la préservation et la (re)production des
biens publics et biens communs.

Une distinction s'impose entre biens d'intérêt général (par exemple, l'épanouissement de tous comme objectif politique avec la levée des obstacles
empêchant la pleine réalisation de soi[7]), biens communs et biens publics.

En général, sous biens communs, on classe ceux caractérisés par l'absence de rivalité dans la consommation (l'utilisation de la part d'un individu n'implique pas l'impossibilité pour un autre de le faire au même
moment) et de caractère excluant (une fois produit, il est impossible ou
difficile d'empêcher sa jouissance par les consommateurs)[8]. Les biens
publics (purs) – qui par définition sont non-excluants et non susceptibles
de soustraction – constituent une catégorie des biens communs. En effet,
tous les biens communs ne sont pas publics ni collectifs au sens large :
les communautés humaines trouvent des modes « combinés » de gestion
endogène adaptés pour éviter des conflits à cet égard.

Nous allons entendre par biens communs, matériels et immatériels, ceux
auxquels la société accède par héritage ou qu'elle construit/maintient en
commun, et qui sont à géométrie variable. Parmi les biens matériels on
distingue, par exemple, le territoire, l'environnement, les services d'uti-

---

6.   Pour l'impact de l'exercice démocratique dans le bien-être, voir les travaux de Bruno
Frey, entre autres Frey et Stutzer, 2000.

7.   Constitution italienne, article 3.

8.   Sur les biens communs, voir l'article de Bruno Amoroso dans ce volume.

lité publique, l'eau et parmi les biens immatériels, la connaissance, la sécurité, la légalité, la confiance dans les rapports sociaux, les formes de reconnaissance, les régulations du marché et de la vie ensemble, etc. Ils sont déterminants du bien-être puisque lorsqu'ils s'améliorent, le bien-être de tous s'accroît plus facilement et lorsqu'ils se dégradent, il s'amoindrit en conséquence (Donolo, 1997). Ils ont ainsi une incidence sur une vision égalitaire du bien-être : la conscience de leur valeur mène au rejet des inégalités et des abus qui mettent en péril le bien-être individuel. Etre égaux dans le bien-être, c'est jouir des mêmes capacités de s'insérer dans l'ensemble (Negri, 2006) et cela ne peut se faire en dehors du maintien et de la production de biens communs.

Contrairement aux conclusions des analyses fondées sur des données recueillies par enquête individuelle, qui mettent en lumière l'écart croissant entre la perception du « patrimoine et bien-être personnel » et celle du « patrimoine et bien-être national » (indice personnel de bien-être *vs* indice national de bien-être)[9], les citoyens participant à l'exercice proposé par le Conseil de l'Europe expriment le fait que l'appauvrissement des biens communs détruit le bien-être (ils sont peut-être moins conscients de l'augmentation de l'écart entre richesse privée et pauvreté publique). A cet égard, ils se sont montrés préoccupés par la dégradation des biens communs (excès de pollution, spéculation dans les ceintures vertes, insuffisance des transports et des crèches, manque de lieux de rencontre, exclusion de l'exercice de la responsabilité, etc.). Par ailleurs, ils perçoivent que le revenu individuel a plus ou moins de valeur selon que les biens communs sont abondants ou rares (Arena, 2008) et s'expriment en faveur d'une politique publique capable de stopper leur dépérissement et favoriser leur accroissement par l'inclusion active des citoyens dans de telles démarches.

Ces réactions suggèrent que l'écart perçu entre bien-être personnel et national est effectivement dû – en partie – à la rhétorique dominante du mythe des deux secteurs, comme J. K. Galbraith justement le relève (Galbraith, 2004), qui comporte une valorisation démesurée des biens privés par rapport aux biens publics (l'aspirateur personnel plutôt que les éboueurs qui ramassent les poubelles), mais en partie aussi à la confusion entre biens publics et biens communs : cette confusion produit un sentiment d'éloignement des citoyens de la gestion collective.

---

9. Voir l'article de Wolfang Glatzer dans ce volume.

En effet, les biens publics sont ceux administrés par l'Etat tandis que le concept même de bien commun renferme l'adhésion et l'inclusion de la responsabilité citoyenne active. A Rovereto (une des villes qui ont participé à l'expérimentation), par exemple, dans le cadre d'un engagement pour le bien-être, les citoyens proposent d'avoir en charge un quartier de la ville pour prendre soin des biens communs et du patrimoine public bâti pour en faire des lieux de rencontre ouverts à tous. Par ailleurs, la transparence dans l'administration publique est considérée comme composante clé du bien-être et, de surcroît, comme pivot essentiel pour engager la responsabilité des sujets dans la quête du bien-être de tous. Une vision du bien-être implique donc un lien fort entre biens publics et biens communs, mais pas leur confusion.

d. Le rôle déterminant des composantes immatérielles du bien-être dans le sentiment de bien-être

Les expérimentations réalisées avec les citoyens mettent en évidence l'existence de dimensions matérielles et immatérielles du bien-être et l'importance de ces dernières[10].

Dans des approches classiques, les dimensions immatérielles sont pratiquement ignorées et se limitent au sentiment individuel de bien-être, appelé «bien-être subjectif», sa mesure dépendant de fait du sujet. Le bien-être subjectif est ainsi le plus souvent assimilé à la satisfaction des préférences et de la vie en général que les individus obtiennent par leurs choix, en incluant la notion de maximisation du plaisir. Néanmoins, étant donné que d'autres composantes immatérielles du bien-être telles que la reconnaissance, l'empathie, la solidarité, l'esprit civique, font également partie du bien-être des individus en société, nous avons choisi de parler ici de «sentiment de bien-être» plutôt que de «bien-être subjectif».

Comment le sentiment de bien-être est-il abordé dans les approches conventionnelles ?

Le rapport entre croissance économique, bonheur individuel et sentiment de paix des personnes a été analysé dans des contextes, voire des pays, différents. Pour la plupart, ces travaux s'appuient sur des enquêtes individuelles, ayant comme fil conducteur l'approche hédoniste (flux entre plaisir et douleur).

---

10. A ce propos, voir l'article de Samuel Thirion dans ce volume.

Ayant fait le constat que les réponses individuelles sur la satisfaction globale peuvent varier en fonction des circonstances et par rapport à différents facteurs (Kahneman et Krueger, 2006) tels que la météo, le sentiment d'avoir de la chance, le fait d'un acte criminel ou de délinquance ayant fait la une des journaux les jours précédents, différentes méthodes ont été avancées pour mesurer le sentiment de bien-être dans la durée. D'une part, en faisant la distinction de ce qui est rétrospectif du réel en utilisant les concepts d'utilité instantanée et d'utilité vécue (Kahneman et Thaler, 2006), et d'autre part, pour relever des épisodes particuliers sans pour autant faire une évaluation générale de la vie, en demandant aux personnes concernées de se concentrer sur un fait concret en faisant abstraction du contexte, par exemple par la méthode de reconstruction de la journée (Day Reconstruction Method). L'index U (proportion du temps durant lequel les personnes vivent dans un état émotionnel déplaisant) qui en résulte a été proposé en tant que mesure du bien-être de la société (Kahneman et Krueger, 2006, p. 18-21).

Parmi les conclusions sur les manières de rendre possible le sentiment de bien-être tirées des études pour la constitution de cet index U (*ibidem*, p. 22)[11], certaines coïncident avec celles que l'on retire des exercices avec les citoyens, surtout pour ce qui est de l'influence possible de la sphère des politiques publiques dans les choix des individus.

- En premier lieu vient l'idée que rendre possible le sentiment de bien-être passe par une évolution des politiques d'incitation à l'augmentation de la consommation vers des politiques d'incitation au renforcement des contacts et des liens sociaux. Face à la pénurie de « biens relationnels » (Becchetti, 2005)[12], les citoyens sont demandeurs de politiques institutionnelles favorisant des espaces de rencontre et d'agrégation sociale, y compris avec les étrangers ou migrants, jusqu'au point de suggérer que le patrimoine public immobilier soit mis à disposition à cet effet.

- Puis on pense que rendre possible le sentiment de bien-être passe par l'évolution des politiques (implicites et explicites) qui mettent l'accent sur l'importance du revenu dans la détermination du bien-

---

11. Les auteurs parlent ici de «maximiser le bien-être subjectif».

12. Becchetti affirme justement que le bien-être individuel et collectif ne dépend plus uniquement de la production et de la consommation, mais aussi du pouvoir de jouir des biens relationnels et des biens environnementaux, considérés finalement en tant que biens en soi et non pas seulement en tant qu'*inputs* des processus productifs.

être de la personne vers des politiques de reconnaissance de la valeur de la personne et de son apport social. Le constat de la pénurie de vrais espaces démocratiques de reconnaissance de la dignité et de l'apport de chacun, amène les citoyens à invoquer le « droit à la reconnaissance » ainsi que le « droit à la prise de parole et à l'écoute » dans l'espace public.

- Enfin, en troisième lieu vient l'idée que même si la capacité d'adaptation des personnes est assez grande et les niveaux de satisfaction assez stables, les changements dans l'utilisation du temps affectent le sentiment de bien-être. En effet, le constat que l'incapacité de gérer le stress est source de mal-être et de déséquilibre conduit les citoyens à entrevoir dans une « ville à taille humaine », accessible sans trop d'investissement de temps, avec des réseaux de transport publics fonctionnels, et dans une certaine agilité et efficience bureautique sans longues files d'attente, autant de composantes du bien-être. Que la maîtrise du temps soit devenue un aspect clé du sentiment de bien-être se retrouve dans des expressions telles que « ne pas avoir de longues files d'attente dans les services », « avoir la possibilité de faire les choses avec calme » ou « avoir le droit à l'erreur ». Elles mettent en évidence la pression ressentie en termes de temps et d'énergie investis, par exemple, pour éviter la condamnation sociale de l'erreur… comme si l'on ne disposait plus du temps pour sa réparation.

Néanmoins, au-delà de ces convergences, d'autres dimensions du rapport entre sentiment de bien-être et environnement de vie n'émergent pas dans l'approche individuelle. Par ailleurs, il convient de questionner le sens même du processus et de s'interroger sur l'appropriation des conclusions. L'approche « raisonnée et partagée », quant à elle, est non seulement mobilisatrice du potentiel humain indispensable à la construction du bien-être de tous et de chacun, mais conduit également à expliciter les conditions de bien-être en tant que droits, c'est-à-dire en tant que fondements extensibles à tous. Ces deux questions seront abordées par la suite.

Pour l'instant, ajoutons deux aspects du sentiment de bien-être qui portent sur le droit à l'intimité et le droit à l'exercice de la responsabilité.

- D'une part, les citoyens sentent que l'interférence extérieure s'intensifie dans leurs vies et que leur vraie liberté de choix s'amoindrit. Ainsi parmi les critères de mal-être qu'ils expriment, on trouve « des mesures de sécurité qui empêchent la prise de risque », « être

constamment espionné, observé, influencé». Rendre possible le bien-être subjectif passe par la promotion d'espaces de réflexion et d'action sur les moyens d'améliorer la confiance sociale et personnelle pour contrer le sentiment que les comportements sont désormais produits de l'influence de la peur et/ou de la publicité.

- D'autre part, comme cela a été exprimé par les citoyens, «il n'y a pas pire aliénation que celle de ne pas exercer la responsabilité». Cette expression montre à quel point il leur paraît insupportable de ne pas pouvoir disposer d'espaces d'exercice de la responsabilité qui puissent ainsi influencer le parcours de la société. Le non-exercice de la responsabilité crée un sentiment de non-achèvement de la personne, de non-projection dans le futur. Rendre possible et améliorer le sentiment de bien-être passe par l'intégration des politiques de *welfare* universel avec des politiques de participation active et responsable à la gestion de la vie publique.

En conclusion, il semble difficile de résoudre – du point de vue des politiques – la question du sentiment individuel de bien-être sans prendre en compte le caractère interactif de la création de ses dimensions immatérielles, comme la possibilité de prendre des initiatives, l'exercice des responsabilités, le droit à l'erreur, le droit à la reconnaissance. La preuve en est qu'à partir des résultats d'expérimentations menées en approchant les personnes de façon isolée, les suggestions pour rendre possible la satisfaction ont été portées au champ des politiques. Si les changements à opérer se concentrent dans les fondements de la vie publique, pourquoi ne pas utiliser, dès le début, des méthodes permettant aux communautés de définir par elles-mêmes le contenu des aspects immatériels du bien-être ? Rendre possible pour tous le sentiment de bien-être passe par l'évolution des orientations dans le contenu et l'extension des droits – c'est-à-dire ces formes universelles de reconnaissance – et des biens communs.

Puisque le bien-être de tous est ainsi bien plus que la somme des bien-être individuels, songer à sa réalisation en l'absence d'engagement actif des concernés, c'est-à-dire des citoyens, c'est d'une certaine manière nier l'essence même du concept. Le partage au sujet de ce qui constitue le bien-être ouvre la voie à la définition de préférences communes (unanimes ou sur lesquelles l'unanimité peut se faire) qui ne résultent pas de l'agrégation des préférences ou des biens individuels. Ainsi, les citoyens ont une vision du bien-être dont les «biens» qui le rendent possible incluent ceux qui se produisent par l'interaction entre individus et collectivité, entre sujets et

environnement. En effet, lors de telles expérimentations, les participants ont traduit bien-être en « sens », « absence de peur dans l'avenir », « projets de vie », « exercice de la responsabilité », « reconnaissance de la valeur de chacun », « valeur de la parole dans l'espace public », en soulignant ainsi la nature interactive du concept et du processus pour le réaliser.

3. Une meilleure compréhension des rapports entre bien-être subjectif et bien-être objectif

Nombreuses références et analyses portent sur l'écartèlement entre bien-être objectif et subjectif. En fait il faudrait plutôt dire entre les dimensions matérielles du bien-être et le sentiment de bien-être. L'adaptabilité des personnes serait l'élément qui fait en sorte que les améliorations matérielles ont une courte vie dans la perception subjective du bien-être : l'augmentation des revenus ou de la richesse n'aurait ainsi pas d'effets détectables dans la durée. Des exemples expliquent[13] comment l'ajustement vers le haut des aspirations liées aux changements réels dans le pouvoir moyen d'achat annule le sentiment d'amélioration du bien-être subjectif.

C'est au sein des études sur l'économie de l'Etat social que le constat de la non-existence d'une relation directe ou linéaire entre indicateurs objectifs et subjectifs de bien-être s'est d'abord fait. Cette distinction serait le produit d'une césure inhérente à la condition humaine : le point de vue du sujet peut ne pas coïncider avec l'expérience publique objective, parce que commune à tous (Da Fonseca, 2001). Néanmoins on voit là qu'une confusion existe sur la différence entre bien-être objectif et subjectif. Cette question doit être considérée des trois points de vue suivants :

- le concept même de « bien-être » qui est subjectif par nature, dans la mesure où il appartient au sujet de le définir[14]. Néanmoins, le concept de bien-être de tous est une construction sociale ;

- les composantes du bien-être. Les composantes matérielles sont considérées dans une perspective quantitative – par exemple le revenu moyen par habitant, la surface d'habitat en m² par personne –, tandis

---

13. Par exemple, en Chine, lorsque le revenu moyen a augmenté de 250% entre 1994 et 2005, il a montré une diminution du pourcentage des personnes satisfaites et une augmentation de personnes insatisfaites (voir Kahneman et Krueger, 2006, *op. cit.*, p. 16).

14. Voir l'article de Samuel Thirion dans ce volume.

que les composantes immatérielles sont essentiellement perçues en tant que qualitatives ;

- enfin les critères du bien-être. Un critère objectif est ce qui fait le consensus, l'unanimité et qu'on partage en tant que vision avec les autres. Par exemple, le logement fait l'unanimité en termes de composante clé du bien-être (c'est objectif). Néanmoins, cela n'empêche pas que dans ce même domaine la « qualité » puisse différer d'un sujet ou d'un groupe à l'autre : les Rom/Tsiganes considèrent essentielles des places pour leurs caravanes, tandis que pour d'autres c'est l'espace couvert qui est important. Mais la « reconnaissance » aussi fait l'unanimité, etc.

Par conséquent, la forte corrélation entre objectif, matériel et quantitatif s'avère pertinente uniquement lorsque «objectif» est défini comme indépendant du sujet, tandis que lorsque «objectif» correspond aussi à «unanime», il est également immatériel et qualitatif.

Le sentiment de bien-être comme résultat d'interrelations complexes

Le constat du fait qu'à l'augmentation de la richesse peut correspondre une diminution des personnes satisfaites et même une augmentation de personnes insatisfaites, provoquant une stagnation du niveau perçu du bien-être – constat fait par de nombreux chercheurs – résulte de l'essai de rapprocher une mesure simple, quantitative et nationale (l'augmentation des richesses échangeables mesurées par leur prix) à un phénomène complexe, qualitatif, individuel et social (le sentiment de bien-être).

Dans les études sur l'économie du bonheur[15] – défini comme «le fait de se sentir bien, d'aimer la vie et de désirer que ce sentiment perdure » par Richard Layard –, la mesure du bien-être incorpore des éléments non quantitatifs, mais qui font l'unanimité, comme sécurité, stabilité, services publics efficients (Layard, 2005). D'autres auteurs ont aussi mis en évidence, dans le bien-être, le poids des composantes non-quantitatives propres à la gestion de la vie publique, tel que l'exercice démocratique (Frey et Stutzer, 2000). Ces travaux conduisent vers une définition complexe, multidimensionnelle du bien-être, notamment du bien-être de tous.

---

15. Pour une réflexion sur le sens de « bonheur » et « bien-être », voir l'article de Jean-Luc Dubois dans ce volume.

Il existe néanmoins ici d'autres explications sur l'écart entre augmentation de revenu et insatisfaction, notamment celles qui concernent le regard que les individus portent sur leur passé et leur futur. Selon certains analystes (Easterlin, 2001), les individus tendent à regarder le passé avec amertume et le futur avec optimisme, sur la base d'une hypothèse d'augmentation de revenu, ce qui les conduit à adapter leurs aspirations. Le niveau de vie passé serait jugé insatisfaisant compte tenu des aspirations présentes. En revanche, les perspectives futures seraient vues comme positives puisque la montée des aspirations qui en découle pourra être prise en compte. Par ailleurs, il a été également affirmé que le poids de l'expérience passée décline au profit des comparaisons sociales (relativisme), notamment dans les contextes où l'on dépasse un certain niveau de revenu : à partir d'un tel niveau, les individus ne s'occupent pas uniquement de leur bien-être absolu mais de leur position relative dans la société.

Ces observations se fondent pour la plupart sur des enquêtes guidées par un certain déterminisme dans le cycle de vie ainsi que par une idéologie qui ne laisse pas d'espace à la réflexion sur l'utilisation alternative des ressources (temps et revenu), et se situe dans les limites de l'augmentation de la consommation. De plus, elles s'épuisent avec le cycle de vie de l'individu sans prise en compte des relations intergénérationnelles : il n'y a pas de réflexion sur le bien-être qui découlerait de la capacité de prise en compte du bien-être des générations futures.

Ces a priori sont démentis par les faits. En Italie, par exemple, des sondages récents révèlent que les nouvelles générations ont le sentiment qu'elles seront plus pauvres que les précédentes et que leur bien-être matériel ne s'améliorera plus par rapport à celui des parents. La fragilisation de la certitude sur l'avenir ouvre une brèche sur la validité des appréciations déterministes des visions des individus sur le passé et le futur.

4. Faire du bien-être de tous un levier pour améliorer la vie ensemble

Les réflexions précédentes conduisent à nous demander s'il existe une hiérarchie, entre composantes matérielles et immatérielles, du bien-être de tous, en d'autres termes si des priorités s'établissent pour améliorer la vie ensemble, et quelle est la meilleure façon de se poser la question ?

Cette question a tout son sens lorsque le bien-être de tous est abordé du point de vue de sa complexité, considérant la multiplicité des aspects qui le composent. Les résultats des expérimentations menées par le Conseil

de l'Europe montrent en effet que les critères de bien-être sont multiples et se dégagent des différentes dimensions de la vie sociétale : de l'accès équitable aux droits et aux ressources ; des conditions (y compris esthétiques) de l'environnement ainsi que de la légalité ; des relations avec les institutions ; des interrelations personnelles et collectives ; de la gestion du temps ; des espaces d'épanouissement du potentiel de responsabilité, de solidarité et des compétences de chacun. Est-il possible d'établir des hiérarchies entre ces dimensions et par où commencer pour améliorer la vie ensemble ?

Nous soutenons qu'il n'existe pas d'amélioration matérielle à elle seule qui puisse satisfaire totalement les individus, bien que cette affirmation doive être considérée dans sa juste dimension lorsqu'on se réfère à des populations et personnes rendues vulnérables par les processus économiques. Le bien-être des pauvres passe par l'accès à ces conditions matérielles de vie décente qui font l'unanimité dans la conscience humaine : elles sont ainsi objectives et prioritaires.

Mais là où les conditions matérielles objectives (unanimes) sont satisfaites, l'accent sur la « reconnaissance » en tant que priorité apparaît. La « reconnaissance » est la promesse de nos sociétés démocratiques et axées sur des droits individuels, et l'absence de prise en compte de ce critère de bien-être démobilise les citoyens à tous les niveaux de la vie sociale et économique[16].

Prenons par exemple le cas d'analyse du bien-être dans une entreprise[17] : au-delà d'établir les critères pour le définir et les indicateurs pour le mesurer (tableau 1), les travailleurs (cadres et ouvriers) ont aussi attribué de la « valeur » plus ou moins positive aux indicateurs par rapport à la politique de l'entreprise (tableau 2). Comme on peut l'apprécier dans le tableau 2, l'écart le plus important entre les indicateurs émerge en comparant la perception de l'engagement (au-delà de l'obligation) des salariés avec le montant du salaire qui compense l'effort convenu par contrat. Le salaire, même s'il est par ailleurs reconnu comme équitable par rapport au contexte local, ne comble pas le besoin de reconnaissance de l'effort

---

16. Nous soutenons ici que, plutôt que de relativisme matériel, dans les sociétés où les besoins sont satisfaits, les populations se comparent par rapport au niveau de reconnaissance.

17. L'exercice a été mené dans l'entreprise Stracel – filiale d'UPM à Strasbourg.

fourni. C'est ainsi que, parmi les priorités[18] avancées en conclusion de l'analyse pour augmenter le bien-être dans l'entreprise, les participants ont signalé le besoin de politiques de gestion interne visant l'amélioration des relations hiérarchiques, la valorisation des idées des travailleurs et la transparence et efficience dans la communication (y compris celle des ordres). Il est vrai qu'ils ont aussi sollicité une plus grande individualisation du salaire, c'est-à-dire la reconnaissance de l'effort individuel de productivité.

Comme dans le cas de l'entreprise, la définition du bien-être dans les territoires a conduit à l'inclusion d'environ 30 indicateurs qui ont fait l'unanimité et que le Conseil de l'Europe a classés en huit familles[19]. Cette pluridimensionnalité est un atout pour la cohésion sociale, car elle permet de multiples possibilités de levier politique et de comprendre que toute action publique peut être évaluée à la lumière des effets sur le bien-être, plutôt que de restreindre son impact au champ immédiat d'intervention, en créant ainsi des cercles vertueux de bien-être par la prise en compte des «effets induits». En effet, une telle prise en compte peut amener à revoir en amont la conception et la mise en œuvre de l'action elle-même[20].

a. La capacité mobilisatrice du concept de bien-être de tous

Tandis que l'analyse du bien-être fondée sur l'augmentation du revenu moyen en tant que priorité conduit à ignorer les écartèlements et – par conséquent – l'immobilisme social que la croissance des disparités entraîne, le bien-être de tous est par essence un concept mobilisateur. En utilisant une méthodologie «de discussion» pour le définir, le bien-être de tous touche au potentiel que chaque individu a pour contribuer à la vie ensemble. Chacun pouvant y participer, il devient un concept inclusif dans le vrai sens du terme, y compris par la dimension de l'apprentissage mutuel et d'une compréhension affinée de la complexité.

---

18. A la suite de la construction participative d'indicateurs de bien-être chez Stracel, un plan d'action a été établi pour répondre aux «déficits» en bien-être, notamment dans le domaine de l'immatériel.
    Pour information/contact, voir : http://w3.upm-kymmene.com/upm/internet/cms/upmcmsfr.nsf/$all/AF429D46A847490FC2257069003E5287?Open&qm=menu,0,0,0

19. Ces huit familles sont : moyens de vie (droits individuels) ; cadre de vie ; rapports institutionnels ; rapports sociaux ; perceptions/sentiments ; équilibre social ; équilibre individuel ; participation/engagement.

20. A ce propos, voir le texte de Samuel Thirion dans ce volume.

Ainsi, la mise en avant du « bien-être de tous » plutôt que seulement du bien-être individuel, ouvre des perspectives d'action collective pour l'améliorer et une compréhension plus large de la valeur de l'interaction pour créer le bien-être, y compris l'épanouissement individuel.

b. La définition du bien-être en termes de droits extensibles à tous

Un des résultats les plus importants de l'expérimentation conduite sous l'égide du Conseil de l'Europe est la prise de conscience du besoin de l'étendre à tous. L'extension à tous implique que les critères du bien-être soient exprimés en tant que droits, c'est-à-dire en tant que références valables pour tous, indépendamment de toute autre condition. A noter que les droits pour le bien-être réclamés par les citoyens sont assez particuliers, puisqu'ils vont au-delà des droits fondamentaux déjà reconnus et structurés qui ont avant tout un caractère matériel pour inclure également les dimensions immatérielles. Ce sont, par exemple, les droits « à être reconnu », « à exercer la responsabilité », « à l'intimité », « à la seconde chance », « à l'initiative et à la prise des risques sans la peur du futur », « à s'exprimer en public et à être entendu », « à influencer les décisions qui concernent la vie ensemble », « à l'égalité de traitement », etc. Ils reflètent le ressenti des citoyens face aux promesses non-tenues de la démocratie et/ou sa dégradation en processus administratifs qui annulent le potentiel de la parole et de la responsabilité individuelle. Le bien-être en tant que droit de tous a besoin d'espaces publics dans lesquels la « parole » de tous et de chacun a de la valeur.

Conclusion

Le bien-être (de tous et de chacun) est le produit d'une multitude d'interactions personnelles, institutionnelles, professionnelles, économiques soumises toujours aux défis du changement. Dans ce sens il apparaît souvent comme instable (ou réversible). La stabilité du bien-être dans la durée n'est pas liée à l'élimination des aléas quotidiens par des méthodes différentes, mais à la construction et le maintien de biens communs, y compris des espaces de reconnaissance des droits intrinsèques à la promesse des démocraties et des sociétés. Une société de bien-être intègre une vision des biens communs ayant la double fonction d'atténuer les vulnérabilités et les peurs individuelles et démultiplier, voire protéger, des espaces de participation active dans la vie publique. Comme Hannah Arendt l'a fait remarquer (Arendt et Canovan, 1998), la peur de l'irréver-

sibilité dans nos sociétés ne peut se contrer que par deux mécanismes : le pardon (y compris, de notre point de vue, la reconnaissance du droit à l'erreur) et la tenue des promesses et des engagements (y compris ceux de la reconnaissance et du potentiel de responsabilité de chacun). Les biens communs sont un élément clé pour tenir les promesses et les engagements du bien-être : ils assurent qu'à terme chacun peut se sentir partie prenante et participer à la vie ensemble, y compris dans ses expressions de beauté et d'esthétisme.

L'expérimentation menée ou soutenue par le Conseil de l'Europe ouvre une voie à explorer. Il y a néanmoins des limites. En désignant les critères, les citoyens ne révèlent pas totalement le potentiel pour leur bien-être qui peut jaillir des changements dans leurs rapports individuels avec les marchés, notamment dans la consommation. La consommation est presque toujours perçue comme domaine de satisfaction personnelle à l'exception des conséquences en termes d'environnement (gestion des déchets, notamment). La pleine jouissance des multiples biens générés par les différentes dimensions de l'interaction humaine ne pourra avoir lieu sans passer d'un paradigme donnant priorité à la production des marchandises à un paradigme donnant priorité au bien-être de tous.

Bibliographie

Arena, G., La "tragedia dei beni comuni", Labsus, Laboratorio per la sussidiarietà, 3 mars 2008, http://www.labsus.org.

Arendt, H. et Canovan, M., *The Human Condition* (2ᵉ édition), University of Chicago Press, 1998.

Becchetti, L., *La Felicita Sostenibile – Economia della responsabilità sociale*, Donzelli Editori, 2005.

Da Fonseca, E. G., "Economia e felicità", https://nextonline.it/archivio/13/index/htm. Next n° 13, 2001.

Donolo, C., *L'intelligenza delle istituzioni*, Feltrinelli, 1997.

Easterlin, R. A., "Income and happiness : towards a unified theory", *Economic Journal*, Vol. 111, n° 473, juillet 2001, p. 465-484.

Finetti, B. de, "Sulle preferibilità", *Giornale degli Economisti*, Vol. XI, 1952, p. 685-709, cité par Rosaria Adriani, "Bruno de Finetti e la geometria del benessere", Università di Pisa, Dipartimento d'Economia (www. dse.ec.unipi.it/seminari/lunch/Paper_pdf/Adriani.pdf).

Frey, B.S. et Stutzer, A., "Happiness, Economy and Institutions", *The Economic Journal*, Vol. 110, n° 466, 2000, p. 918-938.

Galbraith, J. K., *The Economics of Innocent Fraud*, Houghton Mifflin, 2004.

Kahneman, D. et Krueger, A. B., "Developments in the measurement of subjective well-being". *Journal of Economic Perspectives,* Vol. 20, n° 1, Winter 2006, p. 3-24.

Kahneman, D. et T., Richard H., "Anomalies : utility maximization and experienced utility", *Journal of Economic Perspectives*, Vol. 20, n° 1, Winter 2006, p. 221-234.

Layard, R., *Happiness : lessons from a new science*, Allen Lane, Londres, 2005.

Negri, A., *Goodbye Mr Socialism*, Feltrinelli, 2006.

Annexe – Tableaux sur les indicateurs de bien-être en entreprise

Tableau 1 – Indicateurs de bien-être en entreprise

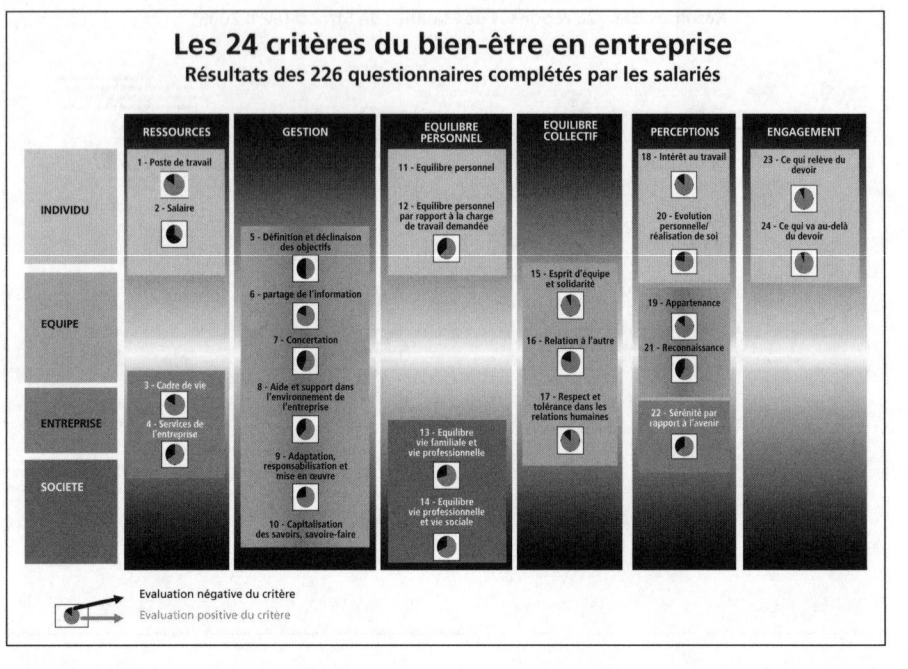

Les 24 critères du bien-être en entreprise
Résultats des 226 questionnaires complétés par les salariés

Source : Indicateurs de bien-être en entreprise. Rapport final élaboré par Cathie Fanton, consultante dans l'accord Stracel/Conseil de l'Europe/Chambre de et d'industrie de Strasbourg et du Bas-Rhin.

Tableau 2 – Evaluation des indicateurs de bien-être en entreprise par le personnel

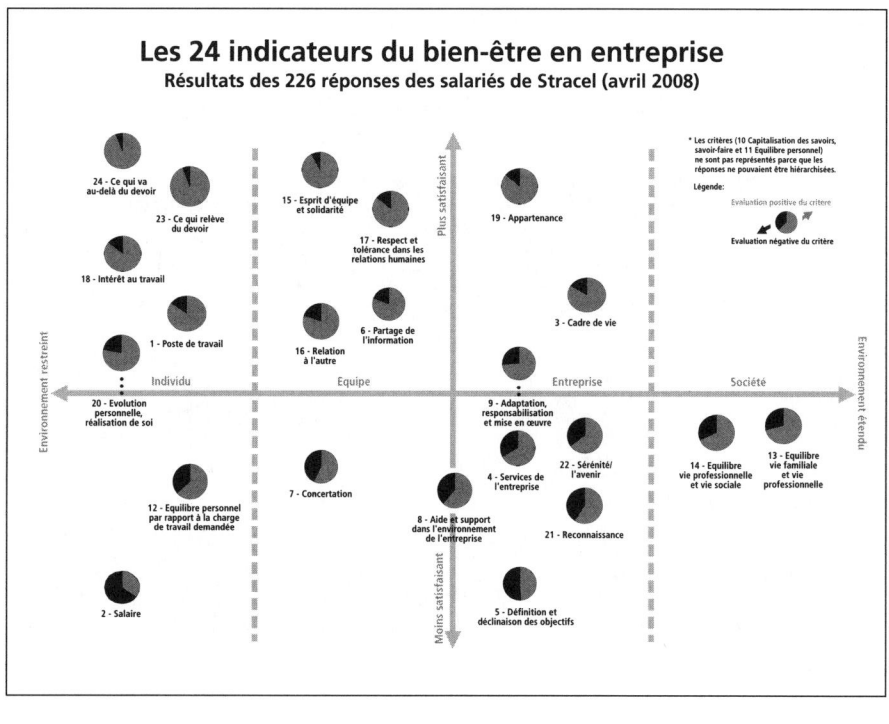

Source : Indicateurs de bien-être en entreprise. Rapport final élaboré par Cathy Fanton, consultante dans l'accord Stracel/Conseil de l'Europe/Chambre de commerce et d'industrie de Strasbourg et du Bas-Rhin.

II. Définir et mesurer le bien-être et le progrès avec les citoyens

Samuel Thirion[1]

Introduction

a. Le besoin de revoir les indicateurs de progrès de la société

Depuis l'émergence de la comptabilité nationale, la croissance du PIB sert d'indicateur de référence pour la mesure du progrès des sociétés modernes. Derrière ce choix, il y a un sous-entendu très largement accepté, selon lequel la croissance économique est intrinsèquement porteuse d'un meilleur bien-être global pour l'humanité. Cependant, cette croyance générale est aujourd'hui remise en cause par le constat des effets secondaires négatifs d'une croissance basée sur ce seul critère et d'une stagnation, voire une régression, des indicateurs subjectifs de bien-être des populations et de beaucoup d'indicateurs sociaux et environnementaux alors que le PNB ne cesse de croître.

Ces contradictions mettent à l'ordre du jour la redéfinition du progrès qui devient *de facto* une question de société. L'OCDE[2] a permis de relancer le débat sur cette question en y incluant un spectre étendu d'institutions publiques, notamment au niveau international. Reste que, s'agissant d'une question de société, elle doit aussi pouvoir faire l'objet d'un large débat démocratique, partant des citoyens eux-mêmes.

b. Le bien-être de tous comme point de référence

Prendre le bien-être de tous[3] comme point de référence d'une réflexion sur le progrès est un choix qui s'impose par sa propre logique. Le bien-être est en effet, dans sa définition même, l'expression de la satisfaction à laquelle aspire tout être humain et, plus généralement, tout être vivant.

---

1. Administrateur, Division pour le développement de la cohésion sociale, DG Cohésion sociale, Conseil de l'Europe.
2. Voir notamment : OCDE, « Global Project on Measuring the Progress of Societies – Towards a Strategic Action Plan », en cours de réalisation.
3. Voir l'article de Gilda Farrell dans ce volume.

Le bien-être de tous, y compris celui des générations futures (et, par déduction, celui de la planète), est donc l'expression de l'objectif ultime de la société, dans un monde globalisé. Tout indicateur de progrès doit pouvoir se référer à cet objectif.

La question fondamentale qui se pose alors est de savoir comment aborder le bien-être : comment le définir, le mesurer et s'en servir comme base pour développer des indicateurs de progrès de la société. Cette question est loin d'être banale car elle va bien au-delà de la recherche de techniques appropriées d'enquête ou de construction d'indices composites pour se positionner dans le domaine de l'épistémologie. Ne pas se poser la question sur ce plan conduit à en rester à des approches conventionnelles qui ne sont pas appropriées à la nature du bien-être.

C'est pourquoi, après avoir posé le cadre d'analyse (première partie), nous nous attacherons à comprendre la nature du concept de bien-être de tous et ce que cela implique dans la façon de le définir et de l'aborder (deuxième partie). Cela conduit à revisiter les méthodes d'analyse et à concevoir une approche appropriée qui, *de facto*, s'appuie sur les citoyens eux-mêmes.

c. L'approche du Conseil de l'Europe : une réponse possible

Cette approche est précisément celle que le Conseil de l'Europe a déve-loppée dans sa stratégie de cohésion sociale[4]. Celle-ci fait le constat qu'avec les évolutions en Europe et dans le monde à partir des années 1970 et la globalisation croissante de l'économie, il n'est plus possible de considérer que les droits de l'homme, notamment les droits sociaux et économiques, relèvent de la seule responsabilité des Etats comme cela est sous-entendu dans le concept d'Etat providence, mais plutôt de la responsabilité de l'ensemble de la société. Le passage d'un Etat providence à une société providence en appelle à une coresponsabilité des acteurs[5]. Le Conseil de l'Europe définit donc la cohésion sociale comme étant la capacité de la société à assurer le bien-être de tous et éviter les disparités, et met l'accent sur la nécessaire coresponsabilité des différentes parties prenantes de la société pour y parvenir. Or la promotion de la coresponsabilité pour le bien-être de tous suppose que l'on puisse le définir comme un objectif

---

4. Version révisée de 2004.
5. Voir l'article de Bruno Amoroso dans ce volume.

partagé, d'où l'idée d'une élaboration concertée d'indicateurs de bien-être et de cohésion sociale.

Un Guide méthodologique, *Elaboration concertée des indicateurs de cohésion sociale* (ci-après dénommé « guide ») a été produit et publié en 2005 (Conseil de l'Europe, 2005), suite à quoi un certain nombre d'applications ont été réalisées, que ce soit au niveau territorial (villes, quartiers, communautés locales) ou institutionnel (entreprises, écoles, etc.), dont nous rendons compte dans la troisième partie de cet article. Les premiers résultats mettent en évidence la multidimensionnalité de la notion de bien-être de tous. Ils en enrichissent le sens et permettent de poser les premiers jalons d'une compréhension de sa complexité. Ils révèlent le caractère interactif et systémique des différentes composantes du bien-être, donnant lieu, selon les cas, à des cercles vertueux (par exemple générateurs de bien-être) ou vicieux (générateurs de mal-être).

Cette vision globale et systémique du bien-être, encore très générale, est progressivement affinée par les expériences en cours et en la confrontant avec les recherches conduites par divers auteurs, dont certaines, essentielles, sont présentées dans les autres articles de ce volume. Sans prétendre affirmer des positions qui sont pour le moment encore plus au stade d'hypothèses, nous présenterons, dans la quatrième partie, les principales conclusions et questions qui ressortent de ce travail d'analyse sur le bien-être.

1. Le cadre d'analyse proposé

a. *Les éléments clés du bien-être : hypothèses de départ*

Le guide du Conseil de l'Europe propose une lecture de la cohésion sociale à trois niveaux, représentés par un « arbre de la cohésion sociale », avec un objectif propre à chacun de ces niveaux :

- premier niveau : la situation des personnes – représentée par le feuillage de l'arbre – avec comme objectif le bien-être de tous ;

- deuxième niveau : les activités humaines – représentées par le tronc de l'arbre – avec comme objectif la coresponsabilité ;

- troisième niveau : le capital social (confiance, liens, valeurs partagées, connaissance, etc.) – représenté par les racines de l'arbre – avec pour objectif son intégrité, c'est-à-dire sa pérennité et sa solidité, au-delà des conditions particulières de chaque moment.

Pour chacun de ces niveaux, un certain nombre d'éléments clés[6], essentiels pour développer un cercle vertueux du bien-être, ont été avancés (Conseil de l'Europe, 2005, p. 49-58) :

- au niveau un, ils sont au nombre de quatre : l'équité dans l'accès, la dignité et la reconnaissance de chacun dans la diversité, l'autonomie et le développement personnel, familial et professionnel et l'engagement/ participation citoyenne ;

- au niveau deux, l'élément clé mis en avant est la coresponsabilité des acteurs et les conditions pour l'assurer (partage de l'objectif de bien-être, citoyenneté, approche associative, compétences démocratiques et économie au service du bien-être individuel et collectif) ;

- au niveau trois, ce sont les valeurs citoyennes (sens de la justice et du bien commun, sens de la solidarité et de la responsabilité, tolérance/ouverture/intérêt pour la différence), les liens transversaux, la confiance et la connaissance partagée.

Avec les expérimentations que le Conseil de l'Europe a conduites dans différents territoires et institutions pour construire des indicateurs de bien-être avec les citoyens, ces hypothèses s'avèrent particulièrement utiles car elles apportent un éclairage sur les interactions entre les dimensions du bien-être (voir quatrième partie de cet article).

b. Bien-être et biens (communs)

L'analyse des facteurs et conditions de maximisation du bien-être et de minimisation du mal-être conduit à s'interroger sur les ressources sur lesquelles on peut s'appuyer pour développer le bien-être, c'est-à-dire ce que l'on appelle communément les biens.

Considérer que, par définition, un bien est toute ressource utile au bien-être de tous restitue les biens dans une fonction sociétale. Les biens peuvent avoir un caractère particulier – en général privé – comme un vêtement,

---

6. Au moment de la conception du guide méthodologique, l'identification de ces éléments clés ne reposait sur aucune analyse systématique ou scientifique, mais sur des observations et réflexions générales, relevant du bon sens et communément reconnues au sein de l'Institution et ailleurs. C'est pourquoi ces éléments clés ont un statut d'hypothèses, considérées certes comme vraisemblables et assez logiques, mais dont on ne peut pas vraiment dire qu'elles aient été systématiquement vérifiées et qu'on ait pu en saisir tout le sens et les raisons.

un agenda, un ordinateur personnel, etc., ou être des biens communs comme par exemple l'atmosphère, la confiance entre les personnes, les identités partagées, les droits sociaux, la protection sociale, etc. Et dans la catégorie des biens communs, il y a plusieurs niveaux : un parc est un bien commun des habitants qui le côtoient, tandis que l'atmosphère est un bien commun à toute l'humanité et tous les autres êtres vivants de la planète.

Partant de cette définition, nous considérerons six types de biens[7], dont les deux premiers relèvent du domaine matériel et les quatre suivants du domaine immatériel.

Ce sont :

- les biens économiques (infrastructures, équipements, entreprises, marchés…) ;

- les biens environnementaux (sous-sols, sols, ressources hydriques, biosphère – êtres vivants, biodiversité, écosystèmes –, atmosphère) ;

- le capital humain (population, savoirs, savoir-faire…) ;

- le capital social (relations humaines et liens, confiance) ;

- le capital culturel (valeurs communes, connaissances – de l'histoire, des sciences, etc.) ;

- le capital institutionnel et politique (institutions démocratiques, droits de l'homme, règles, formes de régulation, etc.)

Revenant à l'arbre de cohésion sociale dont il était question ci-avant, on peut reprendre cette image en ne limitant plus les racines de l'arbre au capital social, mais en y considérant l'ensemble des six types de biens/ capitaux, comme six racines, se divisant chacune en sous-racines. Il devient ainsi l'arbre du développement durable, défini comme étant la capacité de la société à assurer le bien-être de tous, y compris celui des

---

7.   Notons que l'on peut utiliser le terme capital, plutôt que biens (notamment quand il s'agit des dimensions non matérielles). Il y a dans le concept de capital l'idée de quelque chose d'utile qui s'accumule et persiste dans le temps pour être valorisé. Comme nous le verrons à la lumière de l'analyse des interactions entre dimensions du bien-être, c'est cette caractéristique qui distingue fondamentalement le bien du bien-être, non plus comme deux extrêmes d'une chaine linéaire de cause à effet allant des biens au bien-être, mais comme deux types d'éléments qui agissent de manière interactive dans un système non linéaire.

générations futures, dans une relation d'équité et par la coresponsabilité des différentes parties prenantes de la société.

En fait, il faut surtout retenir de l'image de l'arbre la structuration en trois étages qui est d'une aide pédagogique considérable pour comprendre comment s'articulent biens et bien-être (voir graphique 1).

Les trois étages sont de nature différente (état, action, ressources) et c'est la relation entre les trois étages avec les activités au centre qui permet de comprendre les relations entre biens et bien-être. Ainsi toute activité humaine quelle qu'elle soit (production, création, services, consomma-tion, loisirs, etc.) est plus ou moins consommatrice de biens, généra-trice d'autres biens et de bien-être. En retour, le bien-être/mal-être joue évidemment sur les activités.

Graphique 1 – Les trois étages de « l'arbre du développement durable »

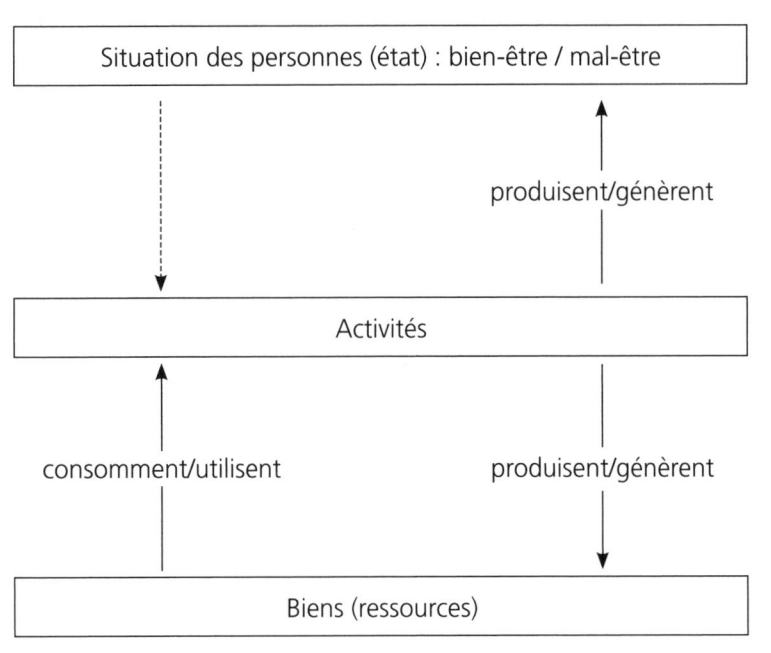

c. Bien-être, biens et indicateurs de progrès

Le concept de progrès porte en soi l'idée d'un rapprochement par rapport à un but, un état que l'on cherche à atteindre. On ne peut imaginer par exemple que l'on progresse sur une route si on ne sait où on souhaite aller. Un promeneur peut ne pas avoir d'autre objectif que celui de se promener et dans ce cas il ne parlera pas de progression, mais de déroulement, de plaisir que lui procure l'activité « promenade ». Même si on ignore où se trouve l'objectif et à quoi il ressemble exactement, il faut au minimum avoir conscience de son existence et la volonté de l'atteindre pour pouvoir parler de progrès. Et plus on connaîtra avec précision l'objectif, l'orientation qu'il faut suivre et les chemins possibles pour l'atteindre, plus le progrès sera une réalité appréciable et mesurable pour laquelle il est possible de construire des indicateurs.

Transposée au niveau de la société, cette réflexion nous conduit à considérer que sans s'être entendu sur l'objectif ultime de la société, toute recherche d'indicateurs de progrès risque d'être vaine et confuse, voire conduire à se tromper. C'est un peu comme vouloir se munir d'un mètre pour mesurer une distance parcourue sans savoir dans quelle direction il faut prendre les mesures. Et ce n'est pas parce qu'il est plus facile de mesurer dans une direction donnée que c'est la bonne direction à suivre !

Revenant aux réflexions antérieures, nous pourrions ainsi exprimer l'objectif ultime de la société comme étant sa capacité à assurer le bien-être des générations présentes et futures. En faisant le lien avec les biens, on peut l'exprimer comme étant la capacité de la société à assurer le bien-être de tous et la production et préservation des biens nécessaires à cet effet.

La mesure de progrès par rapport à cet objectif consiste donc à savoir dans quelle mesure la société est capable de développer (et développe effectivement) des activités (de production, consommation, loisirs, etc.) qui assurent le bien-être de tous, tout en générant et préservant les biens nécessaires à cet effet. A cette question de connaissance de la situation à un instant « t » (indicateur de progrès), il faut rajouter une deuxième question de connaissance de l'action dans le sens du progrès : que faut-il faire, dans une situation donnée, pour que la société développe effectivement des activités qui assurent le bien-être de tous, tout en générant et préservant les biens nécessaires à cet effet ?

On peut donc décomposer ces questions de la manière suivante, mettant en évidence les relations logiques entre six questions relatives au progrès de la société :

Tableau 1 – Les six questions relatives au progrès de la société

Connaissance de la situation par rapport au progrès (indicateurs de progrès)		Connaissance du chemin restant à parcourir	
1. Dans quelle mesure les activités humaines assurent-elles :	1.a. le bien-être de tous ?	2. Que faut-il faire pour que les activités humaines assurent :	2.a. le bien-être de tous ?
	1.b. la production des biens nécessaires à cet effet ?		2.b. la production des biens nécessaires à cet effet ?
	1.c. la préservation et la valorisation des biens, et donc au minimum un équilibre entre perte (notamment par l'utilisation) et régénération des biens ?		2.c. la préservation et la valorisation des biens, et donc au minimum un équilibre entre perte (notamment par l'utilisation) et régénération des biens ?

Ces questions permettent de mieux comprendre les apports et limites du PIB et les indicateurs de progrès complémentaires qu'il faut pouvoir développer. Mesurant l'activité économique monétaire, le PIB est en effet un indicateur qui ne concerne que la question 1.b et ce de manière partielle : il mesure de fait la production de biens échangeables sur le marché et donc mesurables par un prix, en excluant tous les autres biens (comme par exemple les biens publics immatériels – droits de l'homme, protection sociale, capital social, etc.). On peut rajouter à ces limites le fait que la mesure d'un bien par son prix implique plusieurs types de biais (non-prise en compte du travail domestique ou bénévole, variations des prix liés à des rapports entre offre et demande, non-prise en compte des progrès de productivité, etc.), qu'il reste un indicateur de performance globale en termes de production de biens (quantité de biens produits par an), et donc qu'il apporte un renseignement indirect sur la capacité à produire des biens (seulement ceux mesurables par un prix).

Le fait que les progrès de la société soient guidés uniquement par le PIB se retrouve dans le fort déséquilibre qui apparaît par rapport aux questions pour le bien-être de tous citées ci-dessus : tandis que des progrès considérables ont été accomplis en termes de production de biens échangeables (visibles dans l'augmentation drastique de la productivité du travail

et la quantité de richesses matérielles dont le monde moderne dispose), la performance dans la préservation est très faible, mettant en péril la préservation de biens essentiels pour le bien-être des générations futures – non seulement les biens environnementaux, mais également d'autres, aussi fondamentaux. Quant à la performance dans la génération de bien-être, elle reste aussi bien en deçà de ce qu'elle pourrait être au regard des biens disponibles. Nous y reviendrons ci-après.

Il existe un certain nombre d'aménagements et ajustements pour rendre le PIB plus adapté à un indicateur de progrès, notamment l'indicateur de progrès véritable (GDP : Genuine Progress Indicators) que d'autres indicateurs comme l'IDH[8] sont venus compléter. Cependant, comme le montre Takayoshi Kusago (2007), il n'est pas possible de construire un système d'indicateurs de progrès sans se référer à la question de la satisfaction globale. Plus encore, on pourra difficilement construire un système d'indicateurs de progrès satisfaisant si on se limite à des ajustements successifs par rapport au PIB et on ne prend pas comme point de départ une réflexion sur les objectifs.

On tire de cela plusieurs conséquences.

La première conséquence est qu'une réflexion sur les objectifs conduit à décliner un certain nombre de questions et de besoins de connaissance. Ainsi l'objectif de société tel que proposé ci-avant implique six questions qui elles-mêmes se posent à deux niveaux :

- au niveau de chaque activité humaine : Dans quelle mesure une activité contribue-t-elle au bien-être, est-elle génératrice de biens (utiles au bien-être) et participe-t-elle à la préservation des biens, et que faut-il faire pour qu'elle y contribue ?
- au niveau global de la société : Dans quelle mesure l'ensemble des activités permet-il d'assurer globalement le bien-être de tous et la production ainsi que la préservation des biens nécessaires à cet effet ? Comment faut-il faire pour y parvenir, et, question subsidiaire fondamentale, comment les acteurs se partagent-ils la responsabilité de cette performance globale ?

Pour répondre à ces questions il faut donc :

- savoir comment définir le bien-être ;
- pouvoir identifier les biens qui sont nécessaires au bien-être.

---

8. Voir l'article de Wolfang Glatzer dans ce volume.

On peut donc résumer cette « cascade » de relations logiques dans le tableau suivant.

Tableau 2 – Articulation entre objectif de société, questions et besoins de connaissances pour le progrès

Objectif de société		Capacité de la société à assurer le bien-être de tous ainsi que la production et la préservation des biens nécessaires à cet effet.
Six questions	Trois questions pour mesurer le progrès par rapport à l'objectif de société	1. Dans quelle mesure les activités humaines assurent-elles : a. le bien-être de tous ? b. la production des biens nécessaires pour y parvenir ? c. leur préservation ?
	Trois questions pour savoir que faire pour atteindre l'objectif de société	2. Que faut-il faire pour que les activités humaines assurent : a. le bien-être de tous ? b. la production des biens nécessaires pour y parvenir ? c. leur préservation ?
Deux niveaux auxquels se posent ces questions		– au niveau de chaque activité humaine – au niveau de l'ensemble des activités
Besoins de connaissances de base pour répondre à ces questions		– définir le bien-être – identifier les biens qui sont nécessaires au bien-être – connaître les conditions de leur production et de leur préservation

Il en résulte 12 types de connaissances à élaborer pour le progrès :

1. Définir ce qu'est le bien-être de tous (objectif de société).

2. Connaissance des situations présentes en termes de bien-être/mal-être (contribution globale des activités humaines).

3. Connaissance de la contribution des activités existantes.

4. Connaissance des améliorations possibles aux activités existantes.

5. Connaissance des améliorations globales à apporter.

6. Identification/choix des actions nouvelles les plus pertinentes/efficientes à mettre en place pour le progrès vers le bien être de tous.

7. Connaissance des biens nécessaires au bien-être.

8. Connaissance des biens existants (contribution globale des activités à la production et la préservation des biens).

9. Contribution des activités existantes à la production et préservation des biens.

10. Connaissance de ce qu'il faudrait faire pour concilier la génération du bien-être et la production et préservation des biens pour les activités existantes.

11. Connaissance des améliorations globales à apporter pour concilier l'objectif de bien-être de tous et celui de production et préservation des biens nécessaires au bien-être.

12. Identification/choix des actions nouvelles les plus pertinentes/efficientes à mettre en place pour le progrès vers le bien-être de tous et la production et préservation des biens nécessaires à cet effet.

Ces 12 types de connaissances pour le progrès des sociétés, numérotées de 1 à 12 peuvent être représentés dans le schéma suivant :

Graphique 2 – Schéma représentatif des besoins de connaissances pour le progrès

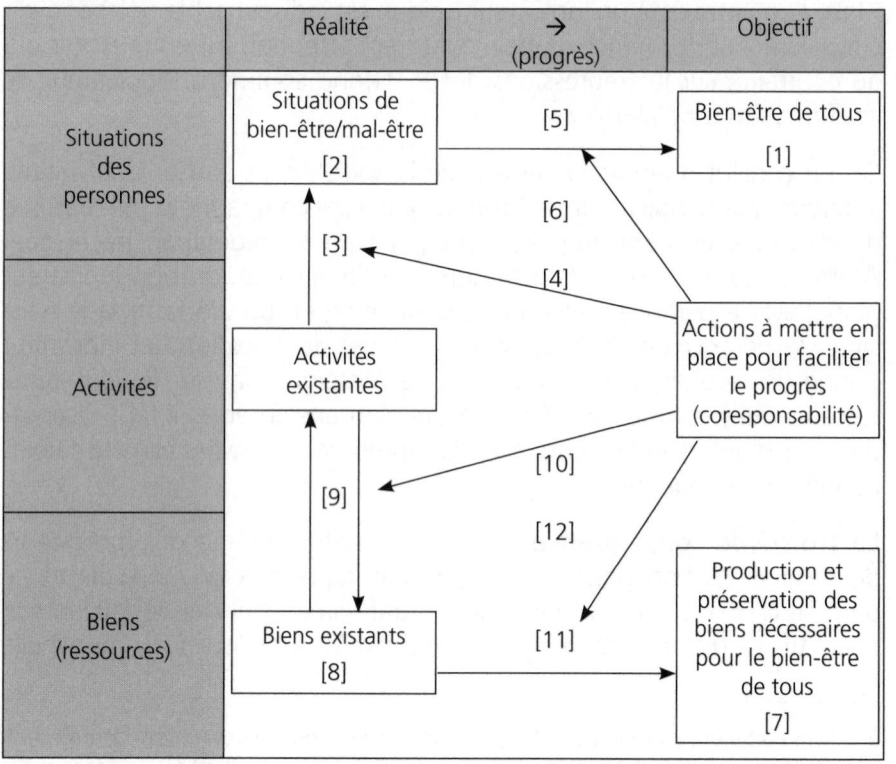

Note : les chiffres entre crochets sont les numéros des 12 types de connaissances pour le progrès défini ci-avant.

Les six premiers types de connaissances concernent le progrès en termes de bien-être et les six suivants le progrès en termes de biens[9]. Il est à noter qu'il s'agit bien de types de connaissances pour le progrès et non pas d'étapes du processus de progrès, car l'élaboration de ces connaissances est partiellement itérative. Par exemple la réflexion sur les biens immatériels nécessaires au progrès intervient tout au long du processus. Par ailleurs, ces types de connaissances ne concernent pas la mise en œuvre et le suivi des nouvelles activités.

La deuxième conséquence est que ces questions et défis conduisent à repenser la fonctionnalité même des indicateurs de progrès. Le progrès implique, par sa complexité, plusieurs types de régulation qui s'articulent les unes avec les autres. Or chacune de ces régulations a, pour pouvoir se réaliser, besoin d'au moins un indicateur. Un indicateur de progrès unique est donc insuffisant : il ne peut renseigner que sur le résultat global sans pouvoir être une aide efficace pour les différentes interactions nécessaires à l'obtention de ce résultat.

Mais d'un autre coté un indicateur unique est indispensable pour pouvoir connaître la performance globale et attirer l'attention sur les réussites ou, au contraire, sur les régressions. Il fonctionne comme un indicateur de confirmation ou d'alerte.

On en conclut que la progression de la société vers son objectif ultime impliquerait un indicateur de progrès global, accompagné d'une batterie d'indicateurs plus spécifiques à chaque type de régulation nécessaire. A titre de comparaison, dans le domaine de la santé, un bon indicateur global est l'espérance de vie de la population en bonne santé à la naissance (espérance de vie déduite des périodes de maladie). Cet indicateur donne un résultat d'ensemble mais ne renseigne pas sur les différents facteurs qui y contribuent. Pour progresser dans la santé, il faut disposer d'un set d'autres indicateurs pour comprendre ses points forts et faibles et agir en conséquence.

La troisième conséquence concerne la nature même des indicateurs de progrès. Si l'on parle de progrès par rapport à un objectif on ne peut se limiter à un indicateur quantitatif illimité (tel que le PIB ou son correctif, l'indicateur de progrès véritable-IPV) sans le lier à une échelle

---

9. Sans prétendre pouvoir répondre à chacune d'elles, nous chercherons à montrer comment les expérimentations conduites avec les citoyens apportent un éclairage sur la façon de les aborder et sur les grandes réponses à ces questions (voir les parties 3 et 4 ci-après).

d'appréciation qui ne soit pas uniquement « auto-relative » (un pays est plus avancé qu'un autre car son PIB est plus élevé, et un pays progresse si le PIB croît ou régresse s'il décroît). On doit pouvoir l'apprécier par rapport à un objectif (idéal) recherché et, à l'opposé, par rapport à la situation la pire, que l'on cherche à éviter. En introduisant un index avec une échelle limitée par un maximum et un minimum sur chacune de ses trois composantes (revenu, éducation, santé), l'indicateur du développement humain (IDH) des Nations Unies se rapproche de la notion de progrès. Cependant le chiffre obtenu (indice allant de 0 à 1) reste encore assez abstrait, étant, là aussi, essentiellement utilisé pour des comparaisons entre pays ou dans le temps.

Pour que ces indicateurs de progrès deviennent de véritables outils de repérage, de réflexion et de coresponsabilité, nous proposons qu'ils soient liés à une échelle d'appréciation qui fasse l'objet d'un débat aussi large et démocratique que possible. La construction de cette échelle consiste à définir pour chaque indicateur ce que seraient une situation idéale, une situation bonne, une situation moyenne, une situation plutôt mauvaise et une situation franchement mauvaise. Une telle échelle (définie ici à cinq niveaux mais dont le nombre peut être réduit ou accru à volonté) présente l'avantage de pouvoir s'appliquer à tous les types d'indicateur, quantitatifs ou qualitatifs. Elle permet notamment de construire des indicateurs qualitatifs multicritères, indispensables pour prendre en compte le progrès dans ses différentes dimensions. Elle permet également de traduire en indicateurs des *benchmarking* du progrès, par exemple en termes de gouvernance.

Nous présenterons dans cet article quelques exemples d'application expérimentale de cette échelle, notamment en ce qui concerne la construction des indicateurs de bien-être avec les citoyens. Au-delà de la particularité de chaque exemple, il ressort quelques repères transversaux sur ce qu'on appelle, en général, une situation idéale, bonne, moyenne, plutôt mauvaise ou franchement mauvaise. Ainsi une situation idéale est celle qui assure non seulement la réalisation de l'objectif recherché mais aussi sa pérennité dans le temps (et donc la sécurité/durabilité/sérénité par rapport à l'avenir). A l'opposé, une situation franchement mauvaise est une situation où, non seulement l'objectif est loin d'être atteint, mais les risques sont très élevés de voir la situation s'empirer chaque fois plus et/ ou devenir irréversible. Quant aux situations intermédiaires, elles sont des combinés de plusieurs variables.

Partant de ce principe général on entrevoit ce que pourrait être, à très grands traits, un indicateur de progrès qui permette de se situer globalement par rapport à l'objectif recherché :

- la situation idéale est celle d'une société capable d'assurer le bien-être de tous dans toutes ses dimensions et à long terme, donc avec une capacité de production/génération et préservation des biens nécessaires à cet effet ;

- la situation bonne pourrait être celle d'une capacité de production/génération et de préservation des biens nécessaires au bien-être mais sans être encore parvenu à l'idéal en termes de bien-être de tous ;

- la situation moyenne peut être celle où un certain bien-être est assuré mais les biens ne sont ni en croissance ni en dégradation ;

- la situation plutôt mauvaise pourrait être celle où le bien-être s'obtient au prix d'une dégradation/destruction des biens et ressources sans parvenir à en assurer le renouvellement, mais sans que cette situation ne soit encore irréversible ;

- la situation franchement mauvaise est celle d'une dégradation avec de forts risques de non-réversibilité et de coûts élevés légués aux générations futures dans le long terme.

Bien entendu il faut voir cette définition comme un exemple très général, illustratif de ce que pourrait être un indicateur global. Compte tenu de son importance un tel indicateur demanderait une échelle plus précise et plus détaillée et surtout devrait être complétée par d'autres indicateurs.

2. Aborder la question du bien-être (questions épistémologiques)

La définition et l'analyse du bien-être touchent, nous l'avons dit, à des aspects qui vont bien au-delà des questions d'ordre technique ou méthodologique. La nature même de ce concept nous invite à pousser la réflexion jusque dans le domaine de l'épistémologie. Sans vouloir entrer dans des considérations complexes, retenons trois idées clés qui apportent un éclairage déterminant sur la façon dont le bien-être doit être abordé.

Première idée : le bien-être est par définition un concept subjectif, seul le sujet lui-même peut le définir.

Le bien-être n'est pas un objet ordinaire que l'on pourrait étudier comme on le ferait pour n'importe quel objet dans une approche scientifique conventionnelle. Sans prendre en compte les caractères spécifiques de ce concept, on risque de se tromper d'orientation au départ dans la façon de l'approcher.

Tout d'abord le bien-être est un concept de nature intrinsèquement subjective, dans le sens où il appartient au sujet et à lui-seul de le définir et de l'apprécier. Cela ne veut pas dire que l'on ne peut le mesurer de manière objective. Par exemple, si un sujet dit qu'il est dans le bien-être en ayant une maison avec suffisamment d'espace pour lui et sa famille et qu'il peut quantifier cet espace en m², on pourra le mesurer objectivement. Il faut cependant faire une distinction entre le bien-être comme concept et la mesure du bien-être. La mesure peut être objective ou subjective selon que les critères sont mesurables objectivement (notamment tout ce qui concerne l'accès aux ressources matérielles) ou subjectivement (chaque fois que cela dépend de l'opinion d'une personne, notamment sur les critères immatériels comme la confiance, la reconnaissance, etc.). Mais le concept lui-même de bien-être est par nature subjectif.

Il est en effet impossible de dire à la place d'un sujet s'il est dans le mal-être ou le bien-être, de même qu'il est impossible de dire à la place d'une personne si elle ressent une douleur ou non, ou, à l'inverse, si elle ressent du plaisir ou non. A supposer que l'on puisse identifier précisément dans le cerveau la zone de manifestation du plaisir ou du bien-être et en mesurer l'activité par électro-encéphalogramme[10], quand bien même il y aurait une contradiction entre ce que la personne dit et la partie du cerveau qui est effectivement active, on ne pourrait pas dire qu'elle se trompe sur son plaisir, son bien-être ou le contraire. Tout juste pourrait-on la soupçonner

---

10. Par exemple, l'université de Wisconsin propose une batterie d'essais cliniques avec analyse des différentes zones et intensités d'activité du cerveau par Imagerie par résonnance magnétique (IRM) pour mesurer le degré de bonheur des personnes qui se soumettent à ces tests. Il va de soi que cela repose sur une hypothèse quant aux zones du cerveau qui sont habituellement actives et leur intensité, hypothèse préalablement établie sur une base expérimentale (répétition statistique des résultats de l'expérience). Supposons que l'hypothèse soit contredite par le sentiment réel exprimé par un sujet soumis à la mesure, c'est l'hypothèse qui demande à être revue ou nuancée et non le jugement du sujet, à condition bien sûr que celui-ci dise la vérité sur son sentiment.

de mentir. Et si elle dit vrai on devra en conclure que le bien-être se manifeste parfois autrement que ce qu'on avait pensé a priori, car le bien-être est par nature un ressenti personnel et non un phénomène que l'on peut décrire indépendamment du sujet. Cela démontre qu'il n'est pas possible de définir le bien-être de manière exogène.

Le fait que la définition du bien-être appartienne au sujet, et à lui seul, a des implications considérables, que ce soit sur le plan scientifique ou politique.

Sur le plan scientifique, on doit se résoudre à l'idée que toute connaissance du bien-être doit partir de ce que les sujets (citoyens) expriment sur ce concept. Toute démarche prédéfinissant a priori le bien-être, même partiellement, relève d'une démarche intellectuelle erronée dans sa conception. Cela se passe chaque fois que l'on mesure le bien-être des personnes à partir de questions spécifiques portant, par exemple sur leur niveau de satisfaction pour différentes catégories prédéfinies (logement, éducation, revenu, santé, etc.).

Sur le plan politique, le fait de considérer que le bien-être de tous, comme objectif final de la société, doit partir des citoyens eux-mêmes, met en avant la nécessité d'impliquer ces derniers dans la définition de ces objectifs, comme un préalable à la conception des politiques. Cela introduit un renversement « copernicien » dans la gouvernance, car, là aussi, il ne s'agit plus de penser et concevoir (la politique) à partir de catégories préétablies, mais de repenser globalement les objectifs et leur mise en œuvre à partir de paramètres définis avec les citoyens eux-mêmes.

Deuxième idée : subjectif ne veut pas dire irrationnel. La subjectivité peut être raisonnée.

Il existe cependant de multiples raisons pour lesquelles on n'étudie pas le bien-être de cette façon, mais plutôt en partant de définitions prédéterminées qui imposent un cadre exogène (par exemple produit par le chercheur, le statisticien, le politicien) aux personnes interrogées.

La principale raison tient au fait que l'on a tendance, souvent même inconsciemment, à considérer le bien-être comme un sentiment à un instant, traité comme une variable dépendant des conditions du moment où il se manifeste. On le voit par exemple dans certaines approches comme la méthode index U[11] consistant à étudier le bien-être en

---

11. Voir l'article de Gilda Farrell dans ce volume.

découpant la journée en types d'activité et en demandant aux personnes interrogées si elles éprouvent ou non du bien-être dans l'accomplissement de chacune d'elles.

Cette conception du bien-être part du principe que, relevant du subjectif, le bien-être est déconnecté de la raison et n'est qu'une réponse globale à un ensemble de stimuli endogènes et/ou exogènes immédiats, à la manière d'une lampe qui s'allume plus ou moins suivant le niveau d'intensité électrique qui passe dans un réseau.

Or chacun sait de sa propre expérience à quel point le bien-être est quelque chose de beaucoup plus complexe qui dépend de facteurs très divers. Les neurologues eux-mêmes mettent en évidence comment le niveau de satisfaction ne dépend pas uniquement des conditions du moment, mais est aussi le résultat d'un processus dans lequel interviennent non seulement le ressenti mais également la mémoire et la raison. Certaines découvertes jettent ainsi une lumière intéressante sur l'articulation entre ressenti, mémoire, raison et niveau de satisfaction.[12]

Déconnecter le bien-être de la raison est une erreur dangereuse car elle porte en soi une conception passive du sujet que l'on retrouve dans l'idée du sujet consommateur (de biens pour son bien-être) et qui évacue tous les processus endogènes, autoconstruits, de son propre bien-être, ainsi que les processus collectifs, actifs, citoyens pour le bien-être de tous.

Cette tendance à déconnecter bien-être et raison tient sans doute à un certain amalgame entre subjectif, ressenti et irrationnel. Ce raccourci, très courant, trouve lui-même sa source dans l'opposition qui est faite entre, d'un côté, objectif, rationnel, raisonné et de l'autre, subjectif et irrationnel, comme s'il n'était pas possible de raisonner sur du subjectif.

Nous ne détaillerons pas, dans le cadre de cet article, les raisons culturelles et historiques profondes qui ont conduit la pensée moderne à mettre en exergue cette opposition. Restons-en à ce constat et au fait que rien ne le justifie. Car bien au contraire, comme l'ont démontré les philosophes, puis les psychologues et les neurologues, le subjectif, le ressenti, l'émotion sont totalement partie prenante de notre raison. Ainsi le niveau de satisfaction à partir duquel un individu s'estime heureux ou a le sentiment d'être heureux est souvent fixé, ou en tout cas fortement influencé, par sa propre raison.

---

12. Voir, par exemple, Klingler et Théodule, 2008.

Le contrôle de la raison sur le niveau de satisfaction et le sentiment de bonheur est d'ailleurs une expérience que chacun peut conduire au niveau individuel comme le suggère Matthieu Ricard, ce moine tibétain d'origine française qui est considéré par des tests neurologiques comme étant l'homme le plus heureux du monde et qui conseille pour pouvoir être heureux de changer sa « ligne de base personnelle » par l'entraînement moral[13].

La raison élaborée, qui se place dans une perspective de rapport avec le monde, occupe une place centrale dans le sentiment de bien-être (bonheur) ou de mal-être (malheur)[14]. Elle est en quelque sorte ce qui fixe les règles du jeu et joue le rôle d'arbitre, à la manière d'un professeur qui décide des notes qu'il donne aux épreuves de ses élèves. Il peut, lui aussi, décider de changer son niveau de sévérité ou de satisfaction et il le fait en fonction de multiples facteurs qui interviennent dans sa raison : qualité de l'épreuve, mais aussi histoire de l'élève, nécessité ou non de l'encourager, évolution, etc. Le parallèle est d'ailleurs frappant car de même que le caractère personnel du professeur influence aussi la décision, suivant qu'il est plus ou moins sévère et tolérant, de même tout individu a une tendance naturelle à réagir plus ou moins positivement (sentiment de bien-être) ou négativement (sentiment de mal-être) face à une situation donnée.

Dans les deux cas l'histoire de la personne joue un rôle déterminant. Et de même que le professeur peut faire évoluer son caractère (par la raison, la sensibilité, etc.), de même tout individu peut travailler sur son niveau de réaction (la « ligne de base personnelle »). Enfin, de même que chaque professeur aura tendance à noter les épreuves selon des critères qui lui sont personnels et pourra avoir un jugement différent de celui d'un autre professeur sur ceux qu'il considère comme étant les meilleurs – dans les limites de certains paramètres communs essentiels –, de même les critères d'appréciation des situations génératrices de bien-être varieront d'un individu à un autre, tout en ayant des points communs à (presque) tous les individus. Ceux-ci correspondent aux caractéristiques humaines

---

13. « L'important avec l'entraînement moral – un terme sans doute plus pertinent que méditation –, c'est que vous changez votre ligne personnelle. C'est très différent de la sensation temporaire de bien-être que l'on peut éprouver quand on regarde un film des Marx Brothers. Ce qu'il faut faire, c'est relever cette ligne de base. » Extrait d'une entrevue de Matthieu Ricard par Robert Chalmers in *Courrier international* « Alors, heureux ? », supplément au n° 874-875, du 2 au 22 août 2007.

14. Voir l'article de Jean-Luc Dubois dans ce volume.

en général (par exemple rares seront les individus qui considèrent qu'une situation de grande souffrance physique ou de stress permanent génère du bien-être).

Troisième idée : le bien-être comme objectif de société doit être l'objet d'un débat démocratique raisonné.

Que la raison joue un rôle essentiel dans le bien-être est une vérité très importante à prendre en compte car elle a des conséquences multiples, à commencer dans le domaine de l'économie.

Elle met à mal en effet le présupposé, plus ou moins explicite en sciences économiques, selon lequel il existe une corrélation intrinsèque entre niveau de vie (et donc pouvoir d'achat et de consommation) et bien-être. Considérer que la raison joue un rôle essentiel dans le bien-être conduit à repenser l'économie différemment, en redonnant à la raison sa place entière de facteur générateur de bien-être, comme tout autre facteur de production et de croissance. Nous en tirerons plusieurs conséquences fondamentales.

La première est que cette hypothèse donne un éclairage intéressant au débat sur les indicateurs de progrès de la société au-delà du PNB : alors que le PNB ne prend en compte précisément que le seul niveau total et moyen de revenu par habitant et donc de pouvoir d'achat et de consommation (outre l'action publique), on voit clairement ici qu'il faudrait prendre en compte également la capacité des individus à raisonner sur leur propre bien-être et donc à vivre bien, individuellement et collectivement. La croissance de cette capacité est *de facto* un critère essentiel de progrès, au-delà du seul PNB. Nous y reviendrons plus avant.

La deuxième conséquence est le regard différent qui est jeté sur l'intelligence humaine. Dans une conception économique qui se limite à considérer que l'essentiel est le pouvoir d'achat et donc la capacité productive qui permet son développement, l'intelligence humaine, entendue comme capacité à satisfaire les besoins de l'humanité est vue avant tout du point de vue de l'intelligence technique et technologique ou de l'intelligence économique dans son sens conventionnel. A partir du moment où l'on considère que le raisonnement pour le bien-être fait partie aussi du cycle économique qui va des ressources (biens) au bien-être, l'intelligence humaine n'est plus seulement considérée du point de vue du savoir et du savoir-faire mais également du savoir-être et du savoir-agir.

La troisième conséquence, sans doute la plus importante, est que la raison pour accéder au bien-être ne peut être une démarche uniquement individuelle mais doit s'inscrire dans une dimension collective et sociétale. Cela est d'autant plus important à relever que l'on assiste aujourd'hui à une floraison d'approches raisonnées du bien-être à caractère principalement individuel, certes très utiles mais bien insuffisantes. C'est le cas notamment de la psychologie positive qui propose un certain nombre de conseils, principes, règles et pratiques pour permettre à chacun de parvenir au bonheur. Ses fondateurs, Martin Selligman et Christopher Peterson, ont ainsi établi en 2004 une liste de six vertus et vingt-quatre forces de caractère qui contribuent au bonheur.

Considérer que le bien-être peut être atteint par une réflexion personnelle est une vision du bien-être qui fait abstraction du rôle de toute réflexion élaborée en interaction entre les sujets. Or une approche de formalisation interactive du bien-être, et non plus seulement individuelle, est essentielle pour plusieurs raisons :

- pour une raison de justesse, tout d'abord, parce que le bien-être a une très forte dimension interactive et en faire abstraction conduit à en avoir une vision totalement tronquée, comme le démontrent toutes les expérimentations qui sont faites à ce sujet. « Le bonheur n'existe pas s'il n'est pas partagé » conclut, à la fin du film *Into the wild*, ce jeune qui quitte sa famille d'origine où il se sent malheureux pour aller vivre seul en pleine nature sauvage à la recherche du vrai bonheur ;

- pour les avantages directs que cette approche interactive comporte, notamment parce qu'elle contribue au propre bien-être de chacun : l'échange sur le bien-être est source d'éclaircissement de la position de chacun par rapport aux autres ; c'est aussi une aide fondamentale pour faire la part entre bien-être objectif et subjectif et retrouver une certaine cohérence entre les deux ;

- pour une raison politique, enfin, car elle est un processus indispensable de clarification des objectifs de société, permettant de construire une vision partagée du bien-être et de faire évoluer les visions à court terme, souvent influencées par des clichés ou des impressions immédiates, non raisonnées. C'est dans ce sens un exercice fondamental de concertation et de démocratie pour l'affirmation d'une vision commune raisonnée et partagée. Ainsi le bien-être de tous, comme objectif de société, doit pouvoir faire l'objet d'un débat démocratique ouvert.

Conclusion

En conclusion, la nature spécifique du bien-être en fait un objet qui n'est totalement définissable et appréhensible que dans une approche raisonnée à deux dimensions : individuelle et interactive entre sujets. Analyser le bien-être par des approches statistiques, neurologiques ou des approches réflexives/méditatives uniquement individuelles ne permet d'aborder qu'une partie du bien-être et produit donc des résultats partiels, voire tronqués et trompeurs. En d'autres termes, le bien-être est un concept subjectif qui doit pouvoir être appréhendé non pas uniquement par chacun des sujets individuellement, mais également par l'ensemble des sujets co-existants (dans un territoire, une entreprise, etc.).

Ainsi la définition du bien-être de tous est de nature fondamentalement démocratique. Elle doit pouvoir être construite avec les citoyens.

L'approche scientifique conventionnelle permettra, quant à elle, d'apporter des éléments de réponse à des questions complémentaires, telles que l'analyse comparée des critères de bien-être selon les contextes, les catégories sociales, etc., les corrélations existantes entre critères et d'autres questions qui peuvent éclaircir les facteurs déterminants du bien-être et du mal-être.

3. Construire la connaissance pour le progrès sociétal avec les citoyens – Premiers résultats des expérimentations

a. Définir le bien-être

Partant des caractéristiques du concept de bien-être qui viennent d'être exposées et de la notion de coresponsabilité des acteurs pour le bien-être de tous, le Conseil de l'Europe a conçu et proposé une méthode de construction de critères et indicateurs de bien-être avec les citoyens. Cette méthode a été expérimentée et affinée dans quelques territoires avec les municipalités et acteurs locaux concernés[15].

Le principe fondamental de cette méthode (dont on trouvera une présentation plus détaillée en annexe) est de laisser une totale liberté aux citoyens

---

15. Notamment dans la ville de Mulhouse (France), la ville de Timişoara (Roumanie), la ville de Rovereto (province de Trento en Italie) et le XIVᵉ arrondissement de Paris, ainsi qu'au niveau de quelques structures (entreprise, lycée, etc.).

dans la définition de leurs propres critères de bien-être, en faisant le lien entre la réflexion individuelle et interactive :

- individuelle pour respecter le droit à l'autodétermination de chacun ;

- interactive pour permettre une construction partagée et intégrer les dimensions sociales du bien-être.

L'application de cette méthode simple permet de dégager une grande diversité de critères de bien-être (et de mal-être) qui mettent en évidence la multidimensionnalité du bien-être (voir ci-après).

b. Connaître les situations de bien-être/mal-être

Ces critères conduisent à formuler ce que serait le bien-être dans une situation idéale et donc de définir l'objectif de bien-être pour tous où tous les critères seraient entièrement satisfaits.

Il faut, à partir de là, pouvoir mesurer la situation réelle par rapport à l'objectif, d'où la nécessité de disposer d'indicateurs de progrès par rapport à cet objectif.

Considérant que l'objectif (situation idéale) est celui où tous les critères sont positifs, on peut définir la situation la pire comme celle pour laquelle tous les critères de bien-être sont négatifs et un certain nombre de situations intermédiaires pour lesquelles certains critères sont positifs et d'autres négatifs ou dans des positions médianes. Par exemple le critère « avoir des amis » peut être positif (avoir beaucoup d'amis), négatif (ne pas avoir d'amis) ou intermédiaire (avoir peu, quelques amis, etc.). S'agissant de critères de bien-être on mettra surtout en avant la satisfaction, ce qui permet de simplifier en considérant deux positions : « avoir suffisamment d'amis » (position positive) ou « n'avoir pas suffisamment d'amis » (position négative).

Ces combinaisons de critères positifs ou négatifs supposent qu'ils soient corrélés entre eux. Dans certains cas les corrélations sont évidentes. Par exemple, la corrélation entre les critères « avoir un logement » et « avoir accès à l'eau courante » (il n'est pas possible d'avoir accès à l'eau courante à domicile si on n'a pas un logement). Dans d'autres cas les corrélations sont liées à des contextes locaux. Elles peuvent enfin reposer sur des choix de priorités.

Quoi qu'il en soit, la combinaison de critères suppose qu'ils soient regroupés par types d'objet auxquels ils se rapportent. Cela ne fait pas de sens en effet d'établir des corrélations entre critères relatifs à des objets différents (par exemple il n'y a pas de corrélation intrinsèque entre un critère de logement et un critère d'emploi). Pour cette raison les critères sont regroupés en indicateurs (par exemple un indicateur d'emploi avec tous les critères concernant l'emploi) et c'est sur chaque indicateur qu'est construite une échelle de progrès en considérant cinq niveaux : la situation idéale étant celle où tous les critères sont positifs, la situation très mauvaise celle où tous les critères sont négatifs et les situations intermédiaires des combinaisons de critères positifs ou négatifs suivant les corrélations logiques ou contextuelles existant entre eux.

Tableau 3 – Exemple d'indicateur de progrès pour le bien-être : indicateur d'emploi

Critères exprimés dans les réunions et variables correspondantes pour la construction de l'indicateur	Echelle de valeurs de l'indicateur pour caractériser la situation					
	-0-	-1-	-2-	-3-	-4-	-5-
	Nulle (pour mémoire)	Franchement mauvaise	Plutôt mauvaise	Moyenne	Bonne	Idéale (objectif atteint)
– Equité dans l'emploi – Emploi épanouissant → Variables : 1. Sécurité de l'emploi 2. Possibilités d'évolution professionnelle 3. Qualité de l'emploi (emploi épanouissant – horaires convenables, juste rémunération)	Exclus permanents du travail	Chômeurs de longue durée avec faibles possibilités de retrouver un travail	Emplois précaires entrecoupés de périodes de chômage, sans possibilité d'évolution professionnelle – qualité de l'emploi faible	Précarité : CDD (ou CDI temps partiel) mais possibilités de retrouver du travail facilement et possible évolution professionnelle – qualité de l'emploi faible	CDI avec difficultés de reconversion et d'évolution – qualité de l'emploi moyenne	CDI sur travail diversifié, épanouissant, horaires convenables, bien rémunéré, avec de bonnes possibilités de reconversion et d'évolution professionnelle.

Source : Résultats de l'expérimentation réalisée à Mulhouse.

On voit sur cet exemple les avantages que présente un indicateur de progrès en termes de bien-être construit sur une échelle d'appréciation :

- il donne une information plus fine de la réalité en prenant en compte plusieurs critères (par exemple, dans le cas de l'emploi, plusieurs critères interviennent dans le bien-être et non pas un seul comme le taux de chômage dans un indicateur conventionnel) ;

- il permet d'analyser la réalité sociale dans sa diversité sans se limiter à une moyenne, en identifiant qui/quels types de personnes correspondent à chacune des situations définies dans les échelons ;

- il permet de définir un chemin de progrès facilement compréhensible et appropriable par les citoyens et les autres acteurs ;

- il permet un débat démocratique et la construction d'un consensus sur le choix des échelons.

Par ailleurs l'élaboration de ces indicateurs permet de passer de cent ou plusieurs centaines de critères de bien-être à environ une trentaine, voire une quarantaine, d'indicateurs répartis en sept ou huit familles selon les cas, comme le montre l'exemple qui suit, présentant la liste des indicateurs établis à Timişoara (Roumanie).

Sur la base de ces indicateurs il est possible d'établir une photographie de la situation en termes de bien-être. Le principal problème qui se pose à ce niveau est la disponibilité des données, en général faible au niveau local. Pour y pallier on fait appel aux citoyens eux-mêmes en utilisant différents outils[16]. La participation des citoyens, et des acteurs locaux en général, à la production de données présente le triple avantage de collecter et valoriser les connaissances existantes (objectives et subjectives), de réduire les coûts et surtout de générer une connaissance partagée qui, elle aussi, participe à la cohésion sociale et la coresponsabilité.

---

16. Ces techniques seront précisées dans un prochain guide « Impliquer les citoyens/communautés dans l'évaluation et la promotion du bien-être et du progrès : vers des nouveaux concepts et outils » (groupes cibles, enquêtes réalisées par les propres intéressés, etc.).

Tableau 4 – Récapitulatif des indicateurs de bien-être à Timişoara (Roumanie)

1. Accès aux moyens de vie	2. Cadre de vie	3. Relations avec les institutions	4. Relations entre les personnes	5. Equilibres individuels et sociaux	6. Sentiments	7. Participation
1.1. Emploi	2.1. Environnement et espaces publics	3.1. Rapports institutionnels avec les citoyens	4.1. Respect	5.1. Famille	6.1. Confiance	7.1. Esprit civique
1.2. Pouvoir d'achat	2.2. Sécurité	3.2. Respect des droits et non-discrimination dans l'accès aux droits	4.2. Non-discrimination dans les relations humaines	5.2. Gestion du temps et du stress	6.2. Peur/tranquillité	7.2. Implication dans la vie civique
1.3. Logement		3.3. Respect et application de la légalité	4.3. Empathie et solidarité	5.3. Développement personnel	6.3. Sentiment d'appartenance	7.3. Responsabilité
1.4. Santé		3.4. Aides institutionnelles/services sociaux	4.4. Convivialité	5.4. Equité sociale		7.4. Respect des biens publics/biens communs
1.5. Alimentation		3.5. Dialogue civique et concertation dans les processus de décision		5.5. Paix et prospérité		
1.6. Education/formation						
1.7. Culture et loisirs						
1.8. Information						
1.9. Transport						

c. Connaître la contribution de chaque activité au bien-être de tous

L'évaluation de la contribution d'une activité donnée au bien-être de tous se fait de deux manières complémentaires :

- en analysant l'impact de l'activité sur chaque indicateur identifié. Cela peut se faire de manière simple par l'attribution d'une valeur +1, −1 ou 0 suivant qu'elle a un impact positif, négatif ou nul sur chacun des critères de bien-être identifiés avec les citoyens (cette échelle pouvant être élargie si on veut introduire des nuances dans l'impact). L'avantage d'une telle méthode, expérimentée à Mulhouse, est qu'elle conduit – en associant les différentes parties prenantes – à une plus grande appropriation du processus par les acteurs concernés et donc à une préparation de la coresponsabilité ;

- en analysant la pertinence de l'activité par rapport aux situations de mal-être identifiées : dans quelle mesure l'activité répond-elle à des critères et groupes de personnes pour lesquels il existe effectivement des situations de mal-être ?

Cette double analyse jette un regard intéressant car elle permet de saisir l'impact dans sa globalité et non plus par rapport à un objectif spécifique. Par exemple, dans une approche classique, une école est évaluée par rapport à un objectif d'éducation, une entreprise par rapport à un objectif d'efficacité et de pérennité économique, une action sociale par rapport à un objectif d'insertion, etc. La prise en compte du bien-être permet de mettre en évidence le caractère multiple de l'impact de chaque action.

Cet exercice, réalisé à titre expérimental à Mulhouse, a démontré, par exemple, comment des actions à caractère social dans leur conception peuvent avoir des effets tout aussi importants en termes économiques ou vice versa.

d. Identifier les améliorations possibles de chaque activité analysée

L'autre avantage de la méthode est qu'elle permet de trouver des formes d'amélioration qui vont au-delà de l'objectif spécifique de l'action et portent sur d'autres dimensions du bien-être. Par exemple, à Mulhouse, dans le cadre du plan municipal d'éducation à la santé, une action avait été conçue pour lutter contre l'obésité chez les populations les plus défavorisées, facteur de mal-être. Elle consistait pour l'essentiel à apporter

soutien et conseil aux personnes concernées dans leurs choix d'achats alimentaires et leurs pratiques culinaires. L'analyse multidimensionnelle sur la base des critères de bien-être a mis en évidence l'excellent ciblage par rapport à son objectif spécifique (alimentation équilibrée), mais la faible contribution de l'action dans d'autres domaines du bien-être pour lesquels elle pouvait être d'un apport intéressant en introduisant des modifications dans la façon de la conduire[17].

L'approche multidimensionnelle du bien-être de tous comme objectif de société ouvre donc la voie à une évaluation et une conception des actions transversales, permettant de développer des liens entre différentes approches et de les renforcer mutuellement. Elle est, déjà en elle-même, un facteur de promotion de la coresponsabilité entre les acteurs, permettant de dépasser les politiques sectorielles, souvent trop compartimentées par des objectifs spécifiques prédéfinis.

e. Connaître les améliorations globales à apporter

Comment passer d'une approche d'amélioration sur des activités spécifiques à une approche plus générale portant sur l'ensemble des activités.

Une première façon de procéder consiste à opérer par agrégation des impacts et pertinences des différentes activités réalisées ou en cours. Cela permet d'identifier :

- les critères de bien-être pour lesquels il existe peu d'impact et qui demanderaient donc une plus grande attention ;

- les groupes et situations de mal-être pour lesquelles il n'existe pas de réponse et qui méritent la conception de nouvelles actions ou l'ajustement des activités existantes.

---

17. Par exemple, si au lieu de concentrer tous les achats dans un supermarché, une partie était réalisée dans les circuits alternatifs comme celui des Associations pour le maintien d'une agriculture paysanne (AMAP) dans lesquels l'agriculteur fournit des paniers de légumes suivant un système d'abonnement collectif et solidaire, l'action deviendrait alors également porteuse de liens sociaux, de participation citoyenne, de meilleure connaissance du territoire de proximité, etc. Et elle contribuerait par conséquent à l'inclusion sociale et au bien-être des concernés.

Dans le deuxième cas, cette manière fait tout son sens. En revanche dans le premier elle pose une double question :

- dans quelle mesure est-il possible d'additionner les impacts des actions sur chacun des critères de bien-être pour en évaluer l'effet global ?

- dans quelle mesure l'amélioration du bien-être se pose-t-il uniquement en termes d'équilibrage entre les critères ?

Cela revient à poser la question de l'indépendance (*i.e.* inexistence d'interdépendance) des critères et indicateurs de bien-être. A supposer que les différentes dimensions du bien-être soient indépendantes les unes des autres, on pourrait en effet se satisfaire d'une analyse linéaire de l'impact de toute action sur le bien-être en l'étudiant séparément pour chacun des critères et en opérant ensuite une agrégation matricielle entre actions pour connaître l'impact global.

La consolidation des impacts peut se faire de manière simple, en additionnant les valeurs attribuées au croisement de chaque action et de chaque critère de bien-être, suivant la méthode présentée ci-avant. L'exercice, réalisé à Mulhouse à partir d'une analyse d'impact sur 70 actions choisies de manière relativement aléatoire, a permis de repérer les critères pour lesquels il existe un déficit d'actions et, parmi ceux-ci, ceux qui sont dans une situation critique, c'est-à-dire pour lesquels l'évaluation de la situation donne également un résultat négatif ou faible. Trois situations critiques ont ainsi été identifiées : l'insuffisance d'équité, de mixité sociale et d'égalité des chances. On pouvait alors penser que l'élaboration d'un plan d'action concerté devait focaliser les attentions sur des actions visant à les corriger.

Néanmoins ce raisonnement ne tient pas si on prend en compte les interactions entre les différentes dimensions du bien-être, quand elles existent. Rien ne prouve dans ces conditions que, par exemple, le déficit en termes de mixité sociale puisse être comblé par des actions spécifiquement ciblées sur cette question, comme la prise en compte de ce critère dans la construction de nouveaux logements. Sans doute cela pourra avoir un effet à court terme, mais dans le long terme il faut considérer les interactions existantes avec d'autres dimensions du bien-être, comme par exemple la reconnaissance, la non-discrimination, la création de liens sociaux transversaux entre couches sociales, le dialogue, etc.

4. Réflexions sur les éléments clés du bien-être de tous

On ne peut donc avancer plus dans les méthodes de construction des connaissances pour le progrès de la société sans mettre au clair les relations d'interdépendance des différentes dimensions du bien-être.

Pour répondre à cette question appuyons-nous sur l'analyse comparée du bien-être à partir des résultats des expérimentations réalisées.

a. Nature des dimensions du bien-être

Bien entendu l'exercice de construction des critères et indicateurs de bien-être donne des résultats différents d'un territoire ou d'une institution à l'autre. Néanmoins au-delà de la diversité des critères et, dans une moindre mesure, des indicateurs, on retrouve à chaque fois entre sept et dix grandes dimensions de bien-être qui constituent autant de familles d'indicateurs. Ce constat conduit à penser qu'il s'agit de dimensions universelles du bien-être, liées à la propre nature des sociétés humaines. Elles recouvrent des domaines très différents les uns des autres, incluant aussi bien des aspects matériels qu'immatériels, des aspects plus personnels ou plus collectifs, avec une forte dimension relationnelle et sociale. On retrouve notamment :

- le cadre de vie : l'environnement, les lieux de vie et de rencontre, la mixité sociale, et, plus généralement, l'aménagement de l'espace ;
- l'accès aux moyens de vie (droits socio-économiques) : alimentation, logement, santé, éducation, emploi, revenus, culture, transport, etc. ;
- les relations avec les institutions publiques : les formes de concertation, l'écoute des citoyens, la transparence, la qualité des services, etc. ;
- les relations humaines, que ce soit à un niveau général (reconnaissance, solidarité, convivialité, etc.) ou à un niveau plus personnel (amitié, famille etc.) ;
- les équilibres personnels : équilibre entre vie familiale, vie professionnelle et vie citoyenne, l'absence de stress permanent ;
- les équilibres sociaux : équité dans l'accès aux moyens de vie, la mobilité sociale, etc. ;
- la participation et l'engagement des citoyens et l'expression de la responsabilité individuelle et collective ;

- finalement les dimensions liées au sentiment de bien-être ou de mal-être, tels que la peur ou la sérénité et la confiance en soi, la confiance en l'avenir, etc.

Pour comprendre les articulations entre ces dimensions du bien-être, il convient de préciser la spécificité de chacune :

- les moyens de vie constituent les conditions de base de bien-être : aucune personne peut être bien en ayant faim, en étant malade, sans abri, sans accès à l'éducation, etc. ;

- la notion d'équilibre est fondamentale dans le bien-être et on la retrouve dans pratiquement toutes les situations. Elle exprime le besoin de diversité et de jouer sur plusieurs «ingrédients» pour être bien, par exemple l'équilibre entre la vie familiale, professionnelle et citoyenne, entre différents types d'activités, l'équilibre entre le niveau de sollicitation et sa propre capacité à y répondre, etc. ;

- la notion d'équilibre va au-delà du niveau individuel pour toucher également le niveau social. Elle joue un rôle fondamental car l'iniquité dans la répartition des ressources et des moyens de vie, l'injustice, l'absence d'ascenseur social pour ceux qui sont en bas de l'échelle sont les premières sources de sentiment de mal-être. Face à des situations où rien ne justifie que certains citoyens ou citoyennes bénéficient d'avantages considérablement plus élevés que les autres, le sentiment d'exclusion prend le dessus et «mine» toute possibilité d'amélioration du bien-être. C'est la principale explication de la divergence que l'on observe dans certains pays riches entre la croissance du bien-être objectif moyen (en termes de revenu et d'accès aux moyens de vie) et la décroissance du bien-être subjectif (sentiment de mal-être croissant) ;

- l'équilibre/déséquilibre social fait appel aux relations (d'une part entre les personnes et d'une autre part avec les institutions) et à tout ce qui concerne la participation/l'engagement de chacun, trois autres dimensions du bien-être. Celles-ci mettent en avant le caractère fondamentalement sociétal de la nature humaine : sentiment d'appartenance à une communauté, responsabilité collective et responsabilité vis-à-vis d'autrui, pratiques de partage sont des éléments clés d'une capacité à réguler les comportements sur la base de l'intérêt collectif et non pas seulement sur celle de l'intérêt individuel que l'on retrouve déjà dans le monde animal. A fortiori l'homme a véritablement développé cette conscience d'autrui, ce

qui remet en cause l'idée encore courante de l'*homo economicus* qui ne raisonnerait que par rapport à son intérêt personnel ;

- le cadre de vie intervient de manière transversale comme élément facilitateur du bien-être dans ses différentes dimensions, que ce soit en termes d'accès aux moyens de vie (habitat, infrastructures, espaces culturels et d'information, absence de pollution), d'équilibre (ville à taille humaine, bonne articulation entre les services – par exemple les différents types de transport – aménagement équilibré de l'espace, qualité de la vie) ou de relations humaines (espaces de convivialité, mixité sociale, lieux de rencontre et de débat, etc.).

Il ressort de cette rapide analyse quelques conclusions sur la signification du bien-être et ses implications :

- l'analyse des critères de bien-être avec les citoyens met en exergue le fait que le bien-être ne se retrouve pas uniquement dans des résultats mais aussi dans les processus (la façon de faire les choses) ;

- la notion d'équilibre illustre l'importance universelle de la recherche de l'optimum plutôt que du maximum. La recherche d'un revenu maximal et sans limite, non seulement ne produit plus de bien-être, mais fait naître un sentiment de mal-être par l'iniquité qu'elle génère ;

- repenser le revenu (et les autres dimensions) en termes d'optimum à partir de la multidimensionnalité du bien-être conduit à revoir le raisonnement économique. Prenons un exemple courant pour l'illustrer : raisonner la consommation uniquement par rapport à son utilité en termes d'accès aux moyens de vie conduit à maximiser la consommation dans les limites du revenu disponible. Si d'autres critères interviennent tels que la responsabilité, l'équité, le plaisir du partage, les choix de consommation ne visent plus un maximum mais un optimum qui se situera dans la possibilité de répondre à ces différents critères. Ceci se passe dans la vie courante : dans beaucoup de situations on préfère partager et avoir moins chacun que d'avoir beaucoup et n'avoir pas le plaisir du partage.

b. Affinement des hypothèses du Conseil de l'Europe à la lumière des résultats des expérimentations

On comprend donc, à la lecture des différentes dimensions de bien-être que leurs interrelations sont éminemment complexes, de sorte qu'on ne

peut les saisir qu'en les approchant d'une manière globale et non une à une.

Repartons pour cela des hypothèses du Conseil de l'Europe concernant les éléments clés du bien-être. Il y a derrière ce concept l'idée qu'un processus peut évoluer de manière positive ou négative en fonction des « éléments clés » qui jouent un rôle déterminant dans cette évolution. On observe en effet qu'il se produit, entre différentes dimensions du bien-être, des réactions en chaîne qui peuvent, selon les cas, avoir des effets d'entraînement vers le bien-être, ou, au contraire, vers un mal-être croissant. On parlera de cercles vertueux du bien-être, ou, à l'opposé, de cercles vicieux du mal-être.

Comment peut-on donc vérifier que les éléments clés qui vont déterminer l'évolution vers un cercle vertueux et non vicieux sont ceux qui sont avancés dans les hypothèses du guide du Conseil de l'Europe ? On remarque que des effets d'entraînement peuvent se produire entre différentes dimensions du bien-être, notamment entre l'accès aux moyens de vie, la façon dont les acteurs s'organisent pour assurer cet accès à tous par leurs relations, les équilibres ou déséquilibres personnels et sociaux qui en résultent, le sentiment de bien-être ou de mal-être que cela génère et la volonté d'engagement et de participation qui en découlera, celle-ci pouvant à son tour améliorer les relations entre les personnes et avec les institutions et les équilibres personnels et collectifs, etc.

Ces interactions sont représentées (en tant que cercles vertueux ou vicieux) dans le graphique 3 ci-après.

Graphique 3 – Représentation des interactions entre dimensions du bien-être avec quelques exemples d'indicateurs

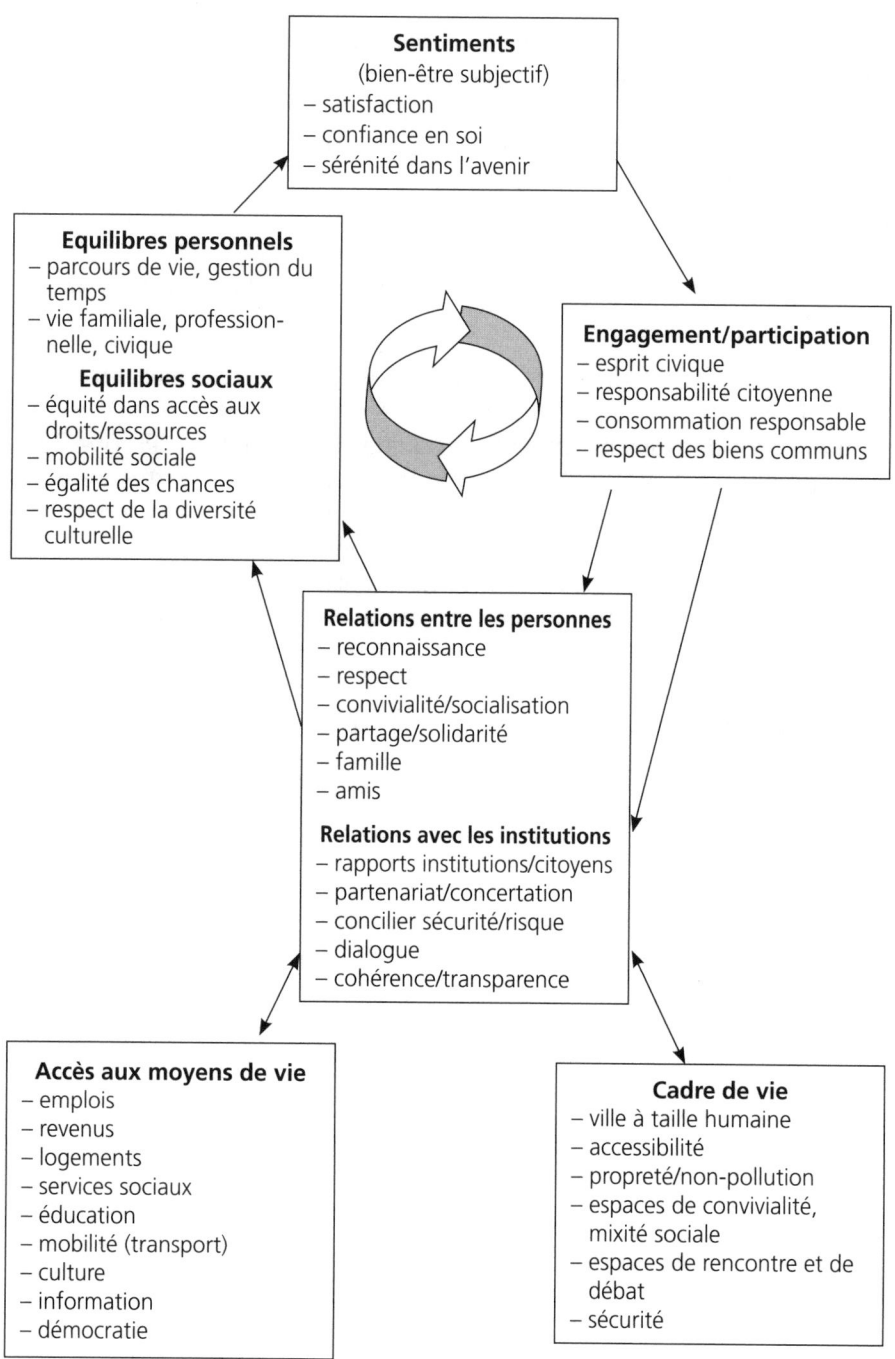

Sentiments
(bien-être subjectif)
– satisfaction
– confiance en soi
– sérénité dans l'avenir

Equilibres personnels
– parcours de vie, gestion du temps
– vie familiale, profession-nelle, civique
Equilibres sociaux
– équité dans accès aux droits/ressources
– mobilité sociale
– égalité des chances
– respect de la diversité culturelle

Engagement/participation
– esprit civique
– responsabilité citoyenne
– consommation responsable
– respect des biens communs

Relations entre les personnes
– reconnaissance
– respect
– convivialité/socialisation
– partage/solidarité
– famille
– amis
Relations avec les institutions
– rapports institutions/citoyens
– partenariat/concertation
– concilier sécurité/risque
– dialogue
– cohérence/transparence

Accès aux moyens de vie
– emplois
– revenus
– logements
– services sociaux
– éducation
– mobilité (transport)
– culture
– information
– démocratie

Cadre de vie
– ville à taille humaine
– accessibilité
– propreté/non-pollution
– espaces de convivialité, mixité sociale
– espaces de rencontre et de débat
– sécurité

Deux idées ressortent de cette représentation :

- le rôle central des relations dans les interactions entre composantes du bien-être, faisant le lien entre les dimensions matérielles (accès aux conditions de vie et cadre de vie) et immatérielles ;

- le fait qu'il peut se produire un cercle vertueux ou vicieux entre les composantes du haut du graphique ;

Ces idées tendent à montrer que les éléments clés du bien-être se situeraient au niveau des relations (entre les personnes et avec les institutions). Or celles-ci sont étroitement liées à la façon dont sont gérées la société et les activités en général, c'est-à-dire la gouvernance. Cela pourrait expliquer l'émergence de déconnexions entre bien-être objectif (essentiellement matériel, en bas du graphique) et bien-être subjectif (partie haute du graphique), comme le met en évidence Wolfang Glatzer[18]. En d'autres termes, même si les conditions matérielles sont réunies, une mauvaise gouvernance peut être la cause de déséquilibres générateurs de sentiments d'insatisfaction et de replis sur soi.

Quelles seraient donc les caractéristiques d'une gouvernance et de relations porteuses d'interactions positives (cercle vertueux) et celles qui, au contraire, généreraient un cercle vicieux vers le mal-être ?

Nous pouvons tenter de répondre en faisant appel à certains des résultats des expérimentations en cours.

Par exemple, la reconnaissance (être reconnu, être entendu) est le critère de bien-être le plus souvent avancé par les citoyens, Or être reconnu, entendu (comme personne, comme citoyen) se retrouve dans tous les types de relation, que ce soit entre les personnes ou avec les institutions. C'est l'expression même de l'inclusion dans la société (non pas uniquement inclusion économique, mais inclusion sociale/sociétale au sens d'être partie prenante de son fonctionnement). Une gouvernance génératrice de bien-être sera donc une gouvernance inclusive où chacun est partie prenante de la gestion de la société à son propre niveau et est reconnu comme tel, tandis qu'une gouvernance génératrice de mal-être est celle qui ne le permet pas ou difficilement.

Un deuxième constat est que les critères liés à l'équilibre (personnel ou social) sont souvent nombreux et apparaissent dans tous les exercices.

---

18. Voir son article dans ce volume.

Cela se comprend si on considère (comme suggéré dans le graphique) que les sentiments de bien-être ou de mal-être ont leur source dans des questions d'équilibre. On retrouve également ici l'idée de reconnaissance : il s'agit non seulement de reconnaître les citoyens comme parties prenantes de la société (ou de l'institution) mais également comme personnes ayant droit, comme toute autre, à un parcours de vie et des besoins d'équilibre personnel (gestion du temps, etc.). Quant aux équilibres sociaux (équité dans l'accès aux droits et aux ressources et ses corollaires : mobilité sociale, égalité des chances, respect des différences culturelles), ils sont l'expression même de la reconnaissance de tous comme personne à part entière, sans discrimination.

Si l'on revient maintenant aux hypothèses du guide du Conseil de l'Europe sur les éléments clés, la coresponsabilité pour le bien-être de tous exprime bien l'idée d'une gouvernance inclusive et orientée vers les équilibres sociaux et personnels de chacun. La coresponsabilité est en effet l'expression même de la prise en compte de l'intérêt de tous par tous et donc d'une gouvernance basée sur la participation et l'engagement de tous pour que chacun trouve sa place suivant ses besoins et sa capacité propre. Le concept de coresponsabilité peut être vu comme l'expression de la vie ensemble ou comme une relation que l'on peut appeler de co-sujets, chaque sujet raisonnant avec les autres sur l'ensemble des humains et êtres vivants et non plus seulement sur lui-même. Il rejoint l'idée d'approche associative à l'échelle de chaque espace de vie, institutionnel ou territorial, et à celle de la planète entière (concept également précisé dans le guide du Conseil de l'Europe comme élément clé de la cohésion sociale).

Quant aux quatre éléments clés au niveau des situations des personnes, ils expriment les objectifs vers lesquels tend un cercle vertueux du bien-être dans ses quatre dimensions : reconnaissance dans les relations humaines et de gouvernance ; autonomie et développement personnel, familial et professionnel dans les équilibres personnels ; équité dans l'accès pour les équilibres sociaux ; participation/engagement. Le sentiment de bien-être est la résultante de ces quatre objectifs.

En conclusion, la coresponsabilité permet de relier aspects matériels, formation d'équilibres et perceptions subjectives. Elle consolide la participation et l'engagement citoyen et est l'expression de la vie ensemble et d'une relation de co-sujets. A partir de ce travail on peut en quelque sorte reformuler le « triangle magique du bien-être » de Stefan Klein formé par le sens civique, l'équilibre social et la maîtrise de son propre

destin » (Klein, 2006), en ajoutant que tous ces aspects ont besoin d'une fonction de « régulation » tant sur les questions matérielles que sur celle de la reconnaissance de l'apport de chacun.

c. Sortir des « cercles vicieux »

Les éléments clés du bien-être autour de la notion de coresponsabilité tracent une ligne d'orientation vers une situation idéale de bien-être pour tous. Ils n'apportent cependant pas d'éclairage sur la façon de dépasser certains blocages pour sortir de situations de mal-être.

Les cercles vicieux vers le mal-être entraînent en effet des blocages qui nécessitent des interventions spécifiques. Par exemple, comme l'explique Catherine Redelsperger[19], si l'on se réfère à des individus dans des contextes de chômage de longue durée, relations difficiles au travail, surendettement (tous des processus répétitifs générateurs de mal-être), ils ont tendance à se replier sur eux-mêmes pour éviter de renouveler une expérience mal vécue. Parmi les cas les plus extrêmes il y a celui « d'auto-exclusion » des personnes qui ont été entraînées dans des processus d'exclusion à répétition sur un fond de culpabilisation.

Dans ces cas, la sortie passe par l'écoute d'un autre qui ne porte pas de jugement et propose d'autres chemins. Là encore les éléments clés de sortie du mal-être se retrouvent dans la relation à autrui, le dialogue, l'empathie, la solidarité, toutes ces formes relevant de la relation co-sujet dont il était question ci-avant.

Cependant les obstacles à l'exercice de la (co)responsabilité au niveau de la société sont immenses. Notamment dans le cas des exclus et des pauvres, la culpabilisation de leur situation évite d'avoir à exprimer la responsabilité mutuelle. La culpablilisation des autres est *de facto* l'expression première de la déresponsabilisation de soi-même et donc l'inverse de la coresponsabilité.

Outre la culpabilisation, d'autres phénomènes sociaux induisent des blocages dans le mal-être : l'absence de reconnaissance de l'apport social de chacun, la négation de la valeur de la parole dans l'espace public à moins d'appartenir à des groupes de pouvoir, au monopole de l'information, etc.

---

19. Voir son article dans ce volume.

d. Raisonner sur une éthique de la coresponsabilité

La culpabilisation et la négation de l'opportunité d'exercer la responsabilité tendent à recouvrir plusieurs sphères de la vie en société. Dans le domaine social notamment, les théories et pratiques basées sur le rejet de la responsabilité de la pauvreté sur les pauvres eux-mêmes se substituent à l'idée de l'Etat social et de la solidarité citoyenne.

Pour comprendre les raisons du phénomène, il faut se référer à la légitimation des tendances négatives, c'est-à-dire de celles qui vont dans le sens de l'égoïsme, de l'égocentrisme et de la défense de ses propres intérêts par rapport à autrui (approches dissociatives), à l'opposé de l'empathie et de la solidarité (approches associatives). A partir du moment où ces tendances et pratiques sont reconnues comme légitimes – et il n'existe pas de règles qui les condamnent ou les interdisent –, elles s'imposent aisément car elles sont l'expression d'un choix plus facile que celui de la coresponsabilité.

Dans l'histoire de l'humanité, on retrouve des périodes où la légitimation (ou simplement la non-condamnation) de ces tendances a conduit à des régressions, voire des désastres, suivis de périodes où, tirant les leçons de ces conséquences, la société a intégré de nouvelles règles et formes de régulation basées sur la coexistence responsable. L'exemple le plus parlant dans l'histoire européenne moderne est celui de la période 1920-1945 où la légitimation de la non-tolérance et de la dictature a conduit à des atrocités, suivie d'une période d'apprentissage du respect des différences, de la dignité, de l'autonomie de chacun et de la participation citoyenne, à partir de la mise en avant des droits de l'homme et de tout le processus qui s'en est suivi, dans lequel le Conseil de l'Europe et d'autres institutions nationales et internationales ont joué un rôle essentiel.

Aujourd'hui la légitimation de la déresponsabilisation et de son corollaire – la culpabilisation – conduit à des situations de mal-être généralisées qui, à leur tour, entraînent des phénomènes de rejet et de négligence faisant courir le risque d'un désastre lorsque la rareté des ressources demande une capacité accrue à savoir partager et coexister. Plus que jamais une nouvelle éthique de la coresponsabilité pour le bien-être de tous, facette complémentaire des droits de l'homme pour la coexistence, doit être développée.

Tandis que les droits de l'homme et les règles qui lui sont liées sont de nature juridique et institutionnelle et relèvent avant tout du domaine public, des Etats et des organisations gouvernementales et intergouvernementales,

la coresponsabilité est de nature éthique car elle est inséparable de la pratique des relations entre acteurs : elle ne se décrète donc pas, mais fait l'objet d'un apprentissage itératif entre règles et pratiques. Le sens qu'on donne ici à l'éthique est donc celui d'un savoir qui se bâtit de manière raisonnée, par l'interaction entre sujets et structures. C'est en quelque sorte le savoir-vivre ensemble qui s'élabore sous forme de règles entre les acteurs (d'un territoire – local, régional, national – ou d'une institution – entreprise, service, etc.) en son sein et/ou dans ses rapports avec l'extérieur. On parlera d'éthique raisonnée, construite dans l'interaction entre sujets, en la distinguant de la morale qui est plutôt un ensemble de règles données à soi-même, et en général définies par une entité supérieure.

Conclusions

L'analyse précédente nous permet de mieux comprendre comment répondre aux besoins de connaissances pour le progrès.

Revenons tout d'abord aux besoins de connaissances concernant le bien-être (voir le graphique 2). La prise en compte des éléments clés du bien-être conduit à introduire une deuxième dimension de l'analyse de pertinence des activités (existantes ou conçues pour être mises en œuvre), à savoir la pertinence en termes de contribution au renforcement de ces éléments clés. Ce critère d'évaluation est particulièrement important car il met en avant la plus-value particulière des activités qui sont génératrices de coresponsabilité et des autres éléments clés qui lui sont liés, notamment l'équité dans l'accès. Il introduit par ailleurs une orientation dans l'identification des améliorations à apporter à chaque activité prise individuellement. Finalement il conduit à considérer deux dimensions dans la recherche de cohérence des activités (connaître les améliorations globales à apporter) :

- pour s'assurer que les situations de mal-être sont effectivement prises en compte ;

- pour permettre la pleine expression de la coresponsabilité pour le bien-être de tous.

Pour ce qui est des connaissances pour le progrès en termes de biens, l'état d'avancement des expérimentations en cours depuis 2006 n'est pas encore suffisant pour apporter des réponses méthodologiques confirmées. Néanmoins certaines conclusions ressortent assez clairement.

Ainsi relativement à la connaissance des biens nécessaires au bien-être, on déduit de l'analyse précédente le rôle essentiel des biens immatériels, et plus précisément la vision et les règles que les sujets (citoyens, acteurs) élaborent et se donnent pour assurer, ensemble, le bien-être de tous. C'est cette vision et ces règles communes qui permettront d'identifier les biens nécessaires au bien-être et de répondre aux questions concernant les biens. Au contraire, sans vision, chacun fonctionne pour soi, « à l'aveugle », et tend à chercher des formes de compensation au mal-être immatériel dans les biens matériels, sans repères sur le sens de la satisfaction recherchée.

Plus que des règles il s'agit d'une véritable culture du vivre ensemble. Elle se construit progressivement. Les processus de réflexion sur le bien-être de tous et la façon d'y parvenir ensemble, tels que décrits ci-avant peuvent être des catalyseurs.

Cependant, on l'a vu également, cette culture du vivre ensemble est fragile. Des formes de déresponsabilisation et de culpabilisation peuvent prendre le dessus notamment dans des contextes de tension, et entraîner des mal-être. Plus généralement toutes les formes de non-reconnaissance, discrimination, mépris, non-transparence, ou l'iniquité dans l'accès aux ressources, etc. peuvent être la cause de cercles vicieux vers le mal-être (méfiance, insécurité, etc.), vont à l'encontre d'un savoir-vivre ensemble et peuvent détruire en peu de temps des années d'efforts dans ce sens.

Pour cette raison – assurer dans la durée le bien-être de tous –, le vivre ensemble ne peut pas se limiter à une culture commune informelle. Il doit faire l'objet de formalisations précises avec des espaces et instruments socio-institutionnels d'affirmation, de suivi et de recours.

Les droits de l'homme et les droits qui y sont attachés (démocratie, Etat de droit) sont des acquis fondamentaux dans ce sens car ils inscrivent les limites à ne pas franchir pour éviter de tomber dans les cercles vicieux du mal-être et de la destruction des biens communs.

Cependant, nous l'avons dit, les droits ne sont qu'une facette des règles de vivre ensemble. Ils doivent être complétés par les responsabilités qui en sont le pendant et qui doivent faire l'objet d'une éthique raisonnée construite par les interactions propres à une gouvernance qui laisse la place à l'expression de la coresponsabilité, notamment à la concertation et au principe d'autonomie contre responsabilité.

Outre les biens immatériels, le bien-être suppose la préservation des biens matériels et des conditions qui permettent à chaque communauté humaine d'assurer l'accès à tous aux besoins de base (logement, éducation, santé, emploi, etc.).

Identifier les biens nécessaires au bien-être est une tâche complexe mais essentielle, pour disposer d'un cadre de référence (situation idéale) permettant l'évaluation des biens effectivement existants (septième étape). Les écarts entre les biens existants et ceux qui sont nécessaires au bien-être doivent pouvoir être connus non seulement en termes statiques mais également en termes de tendances (tendance à la capitalisation ou, au contraire, dégradation). Cela afin de pouvoir apprécier l'impact et la pertinence des activités existantes, et identifier ce qu'il faudrait faire, que ce soit pour chaque activité ou au niveau global.

A ce point deux questions fondamentales se posent :

- comment partager les responsabilités pour la production et la préservation des biens ? Ici la notion d'équité dans l'accès aux biens et dans la responsabilité dans leur préservation est essentielle. Elle est à la base notamment d'une coresponsabilité dans les actes de consommation, de production et de préservation, l'un des défis majeurs de la société actuelle (production et consommation responsables) ;

- comment concilier la production et la préservation des biens avec la génération du bien-être ? Cette question est déjà au centre des débats quand le travail sur les critères et indicateurs de bien-être avec les citoyens est réalisé au sein d'institutions qui ont pour vocation la production de biens matériels ou immatériels (entreprises, écoles, etc.). Si cela paraît être, au départ, une équation difficile à résoudre, tant les efforts pour la production de biens sont souvent assimilés à l'idée de sacrifices et de mal-être (mal-être dans le travail, l'effort éducatif, etc.), il apparaît ensuite, dans l'application de la méthode, que le bien-être de tous est un facteur de performance dans la production de biens, inscrivant de fait cette question de la conciliation dans une logique de « gagnant-gagnant ».

En conclusion, le processus de construction d'une coresponsabilité pour le bien-être de tous ouvre la perspective d'une nouvelle gouvernance, plus associative, créant des ponts non seulement entre acteurs, entre institutions et citoyens, mais également entre secteurs par sa transversalité et entre grands objectifs de société qui ont pu pendant longtemps apparaître comme difficilement conciliables.

Les expérimentations en cours ont permis de tracer des voies essentielles dans ce sens, que ce soit au niveau territorial local ou dans les institutions (entreprises, écoles). Cet article en fait un premier bilan tout en mettant en évidence l'ampleur des questions qu'il reste à traiter. C'est en quelque sorte un « bilan d'étape ». Notamment les indicateurs de progrès concernant les biens restent une tâche essentielle non encore mise en pratique.

Cela étant, on dispose d'ores et déjà d'une méthode simple de définition de critères et de construction des indicateurs du bien-être de tous, facilement applicable et aisément transmissible qui devrait permettre son transfert à plus grande échelle dans les prochaines années[20].

---

20. Voir les Recommandation 207 (2007) et Résolution 226 (2007) du Congrès des pouvoirs locaux et régionaux du Conseil de l'Europe (27 mars 2007) sur l'élaboration d'indicateurs de la cohésion sociale – L'approche territoriale concertée.

Bibliographie

Chalmers, R., interview avec Matthieu Ricard : "Alors, heureux?", publié dans *Courrier international*, supplément au n° 874-875, du 2 au 22 août 2007.

Conseil de l'Europe, *Elaboration concertée des indicateurs de la cohésion sociale – Guide méthodologique*, Editions du Conseil de l'Europe, 2005.

Klein, S., *The Science of Happiness : How our brains make us happy – and what we can do to get happier*, Marlowe, mars 2006.

Klingler, C. et T., M.-L., "Pourquoi le cerveau devient dépendant", *La Recherche*, n° 417, mars 2008, p.36.

Kusago, T., "Rethinking of economic growth and life satisfaction in post-World War II Japan – A fresh approach", *Social Indicators Research*, mars 2007.

Annexe – Eléments de méthode

Elaboration des critères de bien-être avec les citoyens

L'élaboration des critères de bien-être avec les citoyens peut se faire en une séance de trois heures avec un grand nombre de citoyens (au moins 60) en ayant recours à une méthode d'animation de groupes qui s'inspire des *World café* utilisés dans les *Future Search*[21], en adaptant cette méthode à la réflexion sur le bien-être.

Dans un premier temps les citoyens sont invités à se répartir en petits groupes de huit à dix personnes, constitués de manière homogène, en termes d'âge, de sexe, d'origine ethnique et/ou de catégorie professionnelle selon les cas (par exemple un groupe de jeunes, un groupe d'immigrés, un groupe de personnes handicapées, un groupe de personnes âgées, un groupe de femmes au foyer, un groupe de minorités ethniques, etc.). Chacun de ces groupes définit ses propres critères de bien-être à partir de trois questions :

- Qu'est pour vous le bien-être ?

- Qu'est pour vous le mal-être ?

- Que faites-vous ou que pouvez-vous faire pour votre bien-être ?

(Les questions peuvent être légèrement différentes selon les cas, mais en ayant soin de ne jamais prédéfinir les catégories du bien-être[22]).

Au sein de chaque groupe, la réflexion sur ces questions est conduite en premier lieu au niveau individuel en invitant les participants à inscrire leurs critères de bien-être sur des post-it. On passe ensuite à une phase de réflexion collective en reportant les post-it sur une grande feuille ou tableau visible par tout le groupe et en en opérant une synthèse du groupe. Au total la séance demande environ une heure.

---

21. Méthode utilisée notamment par le Neighborhood Assemblies Network : http://www.sfnan.org/

22. Une quatrième question a été introduite dans les dernières expérimentations (Rovereto, Trento, Paris) consistant à demander ce qu'il faudrait faire pour le bien-être. Cette quatrième question qui sort de la propre définition du bien-être présente l'avantage d'inciter à réfléchir à ce que serait une situation idéale et donc permet d'élargir l'échelle des indicateurs (voir ci-après).

Dans un deuxième temps des groupes hétérogènes arc-en-ciel sont constitués avec une personne de chacun des groupes homogènes. A supposer par exemple que l'on ait huit groupes homogènes de huit personnes, on pourra constituer huit groupes arc-en-ciel. Ces groupes hétérogènes s'attachent à définir les critères de bien-être de tous, en élaborant une synthèse inclusive des critères des différents groupes homogènes dans le sens où la diversité des points de vue est bien prise en compte. A supposer par exemple qu'un des critères concernant le logement est le fait de disposer d'un logement en dur suffisamment spacieux et qu'un groupe homogène de Rom-Tsiganes ait exprimé la possibilité de vivre dans des caravanes, la synthèse devra bien prendre en compte ces deux situations. La synthèse inclusive doit pouvoir ainsi concilier les points de vue différents, comme par exemple concilier la volonté des jeunes de disposer d'espaces et moments de fête tard le soir et la volonté des personnes âgées d'avoir le calme en retenant comme critère de bien-être de tous l'existence d'espaces différenciés.

Partie II – Compréhension et perception du bien-être : les sujets et les biens

I. Comprendre le bien-être pour l'assurer de manière équitable

Jean-Luc Dubois[1]

Introduction

La croissance mondiale s'est traduite par l'émergence de nouveaux acteurs sur la scène internationale. Cela soulève bien des espoirs concernant l'amélioration durable des conditions de vie et, plus généralement, du bien-être pour des millions d'être humains qui en étaient jusqu'alors privés. Cependant, elle a aussi un coût, car l'augmentation de la pollution qui en résulte, l'accroissement des déchets domestiques comme industriels, les effets sur la biodiversité et sur le climat induisent de nouveaux risques qui sont l'expression de ces coûts environnementaux. Sur le plan social, si l'on assiste à une réduction de l'extrême pauvreté de long terme, on constate, en parallèle, un accroissement des différentes formes d'inégalité, l'augmentation de la vulnérabilité face à ces nouveaux risques et le maintien d'une forte précarité qui favorise la constitution de nouvelles trappes à pauvreté engendrant de l'exclusion sociale. Sur le plan humain, on remarque un certain mal-être qui est relié à l'obligation de réussite et de rendement collectivement partagée, à des formes de délitement social et à l'apparition de solitudes nouvelles, qui induisent des conséquences d'ordre psychologique touchant aussi les populations les plus favorisées.

Dans ce contexte, la poursuite de la croissance amène à se poser un certain nombre de questions. Peut-on protéger un environnement naturel qui se trouve mis à mal par les modes de production au point d'en réduire la biodiversité et de menacer les équilibres écologiques ? Quelles devraient

1. Centre d'économie et d'éthique pour l'environnement et le développement (C3ED) de l'université de Versailles Saint-Quentin-en-Yvelines (UVSQ) et Institut de recherche pour le développement (IRD). L'auteur remercie François-Régis Mahieu, professeur émérite au C3ED, pour ses conseils sur l'orientation de cette recherche et Hanitra Randrianasolo, doctorante au C3ED, pour son appui à la rédaction finale de ce texte.

être les modalités d'un savoir-vivre ensemble qui permettrait de lutter, de manière équitable, contre les inégalités et l'érosion de la cohésion sociale dans un monde globalisé ? Comment lutter contre le mal-être des individus, sur le plan humain, en valorisant leurs potentialités et en promouvant leurs capacités d'innovation. Les réponses à ces questions demandent de réfléchir à une croissance qui relèverait ces défis tout en continuant à améliorer le bien-être.

Il y a, en effet, une aspiration au bien-être qui semble universellement partagée et qui se révèle être, en même temps, un formidable moteur de changement, au sein des sociétés, dans l'agencement des liens et rapports sociaux. Cela demande de s'accorder sur la définition même du bien-être et, ensuite, de voir comment l'améliorer tout en veillant à ce qu'il soit réparti de manière équitable.

Nous tenterons d'aborder, dans cet article, ce double questionnement. Notre réflexion se déroulera en deux parties. La première portera sur la définition du bien-être en examinant ses relations avec le bonheur des philosophes et la recherche de sens des psychologues. La seconde se penchera sur la possibilité d'instaurer des processus d'action collective, impliquant la responsabilité des acteurs sociaux, pour tenter de satisfaire de manière équitable à l'aspiration au bien-être, qui concerne tout être humain.

1. Une aspiration générale au bien-être

Il y a actuellement une aspiration universelle à parvenir à un niveau de bien-être considéré comme satisfaisant. Elle suscite une revendication si forte qu'elle en vient à bouleverser les équilibres démographiques, économiques, sociaux, écologiques, etc. Elle se traduit par des stratégies de développement mobilisant la communauté internationale comme, par exemple, les objectifs du millénaire (ODM) qui concernent la réduction de la pauvreté et de certaines formes d'inégalité.

En fait, cette recherche de bien-être s'inscrit dans une longue et ancienne tradition philosophique qui est relative à la « quête du bonheur ». Les premiers penseurs de l'Antiquité, qu'ils soient grecs, chinois ou indiens, se sont penchés sur cette question dès le Ve siècle av. J.-C. Mais, la plupart des économistes modernes n'en ont retenu qu'une vision réductrice qui insiste sur la gestion optimale des biens et des services qui se dégagent de l'équilibre des marchés. Pourtant de nombreux auteurs ont introduit les notions de biens publics, de besoins fondamentaux, de liens sociaux,

d'accomplissement et même de liberté de réalisation. Avec pour conséquence d'élargir les frontières de la vision économique du bien-être.

Des travaux récents de psychologie permettent d'aller encore plus loin en intégrant le vécu personnel dans l'analyse du bien-être. Ils visent à conférer du sens à la notion de bien-être en fournissant les moyens de lutter contre le mal-être qui se développe parallèlement à l'accroissement du bien-être (matériel). On articule ainsi, à travers la notion de sens (psychologique), le concept de bien-être économique et celui de bonheur philosophique.

a. A l'origine, la vision philosophique du bonheur

A l'origine du questionnement sur le bonheur, il y a les réflexions des philosophes de l'Antiquité. Chez les Grecs, Aristote (382-322 av. J.-C.) fait le double constat que tous les hommes veulent être heureux, mais que tous ne sont pas d'accord sur les moyens d'y parvenir et sur les approches qu'il conviendrait de suivre pour cela. On retrouve ailleurs, en Chine notamment, des réflexions assez proches chez des penseurs comme Mencius (Meng Zi, 371-289 av. J.-C.) et Mo Zi (479-392 av. J.-C.).

Face à cette aspiration humaine au bonheur, considérée comme universelle, deux écoles de pensée se sont rapidement opposées, proposant des définitions différentes de ce que devrait être le bonheur.

La première, dite «école hédoniste», met l'accent sur la recherche du plaisir comme source de bonheur. Ses fondements viennent de la philosophie hédoniste (Aristippe, 435-356 av. J.-C.) selon laquelle une vie ne peut être considérée comme bonne que si elle procure le plus possible de plaisir ou de satisfaction. Cette vision est atténuée par la définition épicurienne (Epicure, 342-271 av. J.-C.) selon laquelle le bonheur résulte d'un équilibre réfléchi entre la dimension positive issue du plaisir et une dimension négative liée à la souffrance. Il tient à la personne humaine d'être capable de gérer intelligemment cet équilibre entre les deux, à travers le temps et l'espace.

Cette vision a influencé la philosophie utilitariste (Bentham, 1748-1832) selon laquelle les comportements des individus résultent d'un calcul hédoniste visant à maximiser la quantité de plaisir et à minimiser la quantité de peines, le bonheur se définissant alors comme la différence entre les deux. Au niveau collectif, le bonheur global résulte alors de la somme des bonheurs individuels et la meilleure société est celle qui est capable d'offrir «le plus grand bonheur au plus grand nombre».

Une telle doctrine a été reprise sur une base économique par Stuart Mill (1806-1873) qui en a fait une philosophie capable d'évaluer, en termes d'utilité, les conséquences des actions entreprises sur le bien-être. L'utilité, ou satisfaction objective, retrace le fait qu'un bien ou une action puisse engendrer du bien-être sous forme de plaisir, de joie, d'avantages, etc., permettant de déboucher, même indirectement, sur le bonheur. Ce qui permet d'assimiler bien-être et bonheur. Le but de toute action est alors de rechercher le maximum de satisfaction afin de maximiser le bien-être général. Ce qui importe c'est la quantité globale de bien-être produit, quelle qu'en soit la répartition entre les individus. Dans ce cadre, tous les individus se valent également et le bonheur de chacun dépend de celui des autres. Il convient alors de considérer le bien-être de tous et non le bien-être de quelques-uns en particulier.

La pensée économique actuelle, bien qu'elle soit parcourue par de nombreux autres courants hétérodoxes, demeure toujours fortement influencée par cette vision. Elle considère que la croissance de la consommation et du revenu est la condition de l'amélioration du bien-être, l'utilité mesurant toujours l'aptitude d'un bien à satisfaire les besoins d'un agent économique. Ainsi, par exemple, la théorie de la décision qui fait appel à des procédures d'analyse coûts-avantages pour l'évaluation de projets ou de politiques publiques, se réfère toujours à un calcul de type hédoniste.

La vision d'Aristote se trouve à l'opposé de cette vision utilitariste, fortement influencée par l'hédonisme. Son école de pensée, dite «eudémoniste», privilégie l'accomplissement, personnel ou social, comme source de bonheur, en se référant à des valeurs éthiques comme la prudence, la générosité, etc. Pour Aristote, ce qui importe c'est d'instaurer, en relation avec les autres, une éthique du possible au sein de la Cité, afin de réaliser, de manière concertée, des objectifs de devenir commun ; et, à travers cette forme de liberté, d'améliorer le bonheur de vivre dans la cité. Cette philosophie, dite de «la vie bonne», refuse que l'équilibre des plaisirs soit le seul critère de définition du bonheur et s'appuie sur le fait que si l'individu est un sujet autonome, rationnel et raisonnable, il doit aussi être capable de faire le lien entre sa capacité d'action propre et la possibilité d'atteindre le bonheur à travers des actions adaptées à son environnement, tant social que naturel.

Le philosophe Robert Misrahi (2003), notamment dans ses réflexions sur le bonheur, illustre clairement cette façon de voir. Le bonheur n'est pas le fruit spontané d'événements agréables qui surviennent dans la vie, c'est

plutôt l'aboutissement d'une construction personnelle réfléchie. C'est, en effet, à l'individu de construire le bonheur par ses propres actions. Cependant, l'accès au bonheur ne sera possible que si la société assure auparavant aux individus les opportunités économiques et sociales minimales qui leur permettront de vivre normalement.

Cette vision rejoint celle de Sen (1999) qui montre que, en économie, c'est la « capacité d'action » dans un environnement de liberté – ce qu'il appelle « l'agencéité » – qui permet aux individus d'atteindre les finalités auxquelles ils accordent de l'importance. Le rôle des politiques publiques est alors de veiller à ce que soit assuré un accès aux ressources et opportunités qui permette de choisir, parmi un ensemble d'accomplissements possibles, ceux qui portent à atteindre une vie épanouie.

Tout en demeurant dans le même cadre de pensée, on peut alors considérer que les individus sont insérés dans des réseaux de droits et d'obligations sociales, ce qui les oblige à combiner la liberté de leurs choix avec la responsabilité de leurs obligations sociales (Ballet et al., 2005). Ce qui implique d'élargir « l'agencéité », ou capacité d'action des individus, aux responsabilités personnelles en allant au-delà de leurs seules libertés et finalités. Cet apport supplémentaire se réfère à l'approche phénoménologique qui considère les interactions sociales en lien avec les intentions existentielles des personnes, les formes de responsabilité qui les animent, les rapports de force ou de domination auxquels elles participent dans un contexte donné. On aborde ainsi, de manière plus pertinente, la complexité humaine dans son aspiration au bonheur.

En conclusion, cette philosophie de « la vie bonne » montre donc que, par le biais d'une démarche raisonnée et construite, s'appuyant sur la responsabilité, il est possible de faire en sorte que les capacités de réalisation, individuelles comme collectives, des personnes se traduisent en capacité à construire une vie épanouie, source de bonheur commun. C'est en ce sens que Ricœur parle de « la vie bonne, avec et pour les autres, dans des institutions justes » (Ricœur, 1995).

b. Elargir la vision très restrictive du bien-être économique

Face aux philosophes, qui raisonnent en termes de bonheur, les économistes utilisent plutôt le concept de bien-être. Un bien-être qui est le résultat d'une gestion équilibrée de biens et de services matériels, consommés, ou accumulés sous forme de capital. La définition a été élargie par l'introduction récente des relations que l'individu entretient

avec son environnement social, à travers notamment la prise en compte du capital social et de l'altruisme.

Pour parvenir à un certain niveau de bien-être, il faut prendre des décisions concernant l'allocation des ressources disponibles face aux nombreuses contraintes techniques et aux comportements sociaux. Comme on raisonne essentiellement sur des biens et des services, on peut rechercher les manières d'allouer de façon efficiente ces moyens limités à des finalités qui ont été auparavant évaluées, le plus souvent en termes monétaires. Et, dans ce contexte, la démarche économique consiste à gérer de manière optimale les ressources disponibles en décidant où les affecter pour atteindre le plus rapidement possible une finalité donnée, comme celle d'accroître le bien-être.

La vision utilitariste trouve sa validation dans les théories de l'équilibre général et de l'économie du bien-être. Toutes deux cherchent à répondre à la question : entre plusieurs situations économiques possibles, chacune étant caractérisée par une certaine répartition des ressources et des revenus, laquelle peut être considérée comme la meilleure ? Il s'agit, en effet, d'une question fondamentale de l'économie publique qui s'appuie sur des comportements individuels pour analyser les problèmes relatifs aux biens publics, à la fiscalité, aux choix collectifs, à l'optimum social, au traitement des formes de pauvreté et d'inégalités, aux aspects de justice et d'équité (Jarret et Mahieu, 1998).

La théorie de l'équilibre général montre, sur la base d'un certain nombre d'hypothèses, que lorsque les consommateurs maximisent de manière rationnelle leurs satisfactions individuelles sous contraintes de revenu, et que les producteurs maximisent de même leurs productions sous contraintes techniques, on débouche sur un système unique de prix et de quantités qui assure l'équilibre de l'offre et de la demande sur l'ensemble des marchés, la satisfaction optimale des agents économiques et la production technique la plus efficiente. Les hypothèses sont relatives au comportement supposé égoïste et rationnel des individus, dans un système de concurrence pure et parfaite. De plus, selon l'économie du bien-être, cette situation d'équilibre peut être considérée comme optimale (au sens de Pareto) c'est-à-dire que l'on ne peut accroître la satisfaction d'un agent économique sans diminuer celle d'un autre.

Cette approche formalisée et monétaire, intéressante par sa rigueur et sa cohérence, repose sur des hypothèses extrêmement restrictives. Elles sont de nature individualiste, tant au niveau du consommateur que du producteur, et donc n'intègrent pas les interactions sociales, comme

l'engagement vis-à-vis d'autrui ou l'alliance entre producteurs, qui pourtant sont à la source de l'innovation sociale et du progrès technique, engendrant par là même des rendements croissants. Il y a, certes, un intérêt à de tels modèles pour comprendre, sur une base didactique, comment différentes variables peuvent interagir entre elles dans un cadre cohérent, mais le risque est celui d'une déconnection totale de la théorie face à la réalité des choses vécues. Ce qui, dans le cas de la prédiction de politiques publiques, peut conduire à des erreurs de ciblage en termes de bien-être des populations concernées.

Dans ce cadre, le Produit national brut (PNB) ou le revenu national par tête servent d'indicateurs pour mesurer le niveau de bien-être à l'échelon macroéconomique. Ils présentent de multiples faiblesses, car s'ils intègrent bien la consommation des biens et services et le revenu, issu de la production, qui permet cette consommation, ils ne tiennent pas compte de la nature des biens produits ou consommés, ni des nuisances dues à la production (encombrement urbain, coûts sociaux, insécurité) et, de plus, ils oublient bien des formes de production (travail domestique, bénévolat).

Face à la vision utilitariste, la vision de la vie bonne met l'accent sur les réalisations des personnes en termes de conditions de vie, sur leurs comportements et sur les accomplissements qui peuvent en résulter. Ce qui importe, ce n'est pas tant la satisfaction obtenue, que la capacité d'action des personnes, c'est-à-dire la capacité à faire un certain nombre d'actions (ou de fonctionnements) qui leur permettent d'atteindre un objectif qui n'est pas forcément la recherche de son propre bien-être, mais qui traduit un certain accomplissement personnel (Sen, 1985).

Cette approche dite « approche par les capacités » permet de dépasser une économie basée sur la seule gestion de ressources, biens et services consommés, notamment, pour penser une économie qui met l'accent sur les potentialités et les fonctionnements des personnes afin de les rendre plus capables de faire les choix de vie qu'elles souhaitent, pour elles-mêmes et avec les autres. Cela correspond à l'ajout dans l'analyse économique d'une réflexion sur les comportements, parallèlement à celle habituelle sur le niveau et les conditions de vie.

Par définition, cette « capacité » de la personne recouvre deux composantes. La première, retrace ce qu'elle est effectivement capable d'accomplir dans le contexte actuel, face aux contraintes et opportunités qu'elle rencontre, en fonction de ses caractéristiques propres, et en utilisant les ressources dont elle dispose. Cela peut se mesurer par des indicateurs

classiques issus notamment des enquêtes auprès des ménages. La deuxième composante exprime – et c'est là son aspect original – la capacité potentielle de la personne, c'est-à-dire ce qu'elle pourrait accomplir dans un contexte différent et qui démontrerait sa capacité à choisir et à réaliser des actions particulières, non initialement prévues. Cela traduit, en fait, son degré de liberté dans le choix de réaliser ce qu'elle aspire à faire. Il y a là une forme de « liberté de faire et d'être » qui s'avère bien plus difficile à mesurer par des indicateurs, mais elle permet de considérer la « capacité » de la personne comme sa liberté d'accomplissement.

Dans un tel cadre, la pauvreté devient l'expression d'une privation de capacités, et même de liberté de choix, et la lutte contre la pauvreté se traduit par des politiques économiques qui viseront à accroître les capacités des personnes pour qu'elles puissent avoir la liberté de mener la vie qu'elles désirent. Le développement humain durable, préconisé par le Programme des Nations Unies pour le développement (PNUD), s'inscrit dans ce courant de pensée. Il vise à renforcer les capacités individuelles et collectives, à travers le lien à l'autre, tout en luttant contre les inégalités de capacités intra et intergénérationnelles qui freinent la réduction de la pauvreté.

De même, la vulnérabilité d'une personne vient d'une insuffisance dans les capacités qu'elle aurait besoin de mobiliser pour faire face aux conséquences de la concrétisation de risques. Accroître son éventail de capacités individuelles, comme collectives, permettrait d'améliorer sa capacité de résilience face aux chocs imprévus.

Dans ce contexte, le bien-être prend alors le sens « d'être-bien » (*wellbeing*) dans une vision multidimensionnelle qui s'oppose au bien-être monétaire (*welfare*) retraçant l'utilité. La lutte contre la pauvreté, prise dans sa dimension multidimensionnelle et non uniquement monétaire, la réduction de la vulnérabilité, la lutte contre l'exclusion, etc., s'inscrivent dans cette dynamique qui privilégie le développement (Perroux, 1952), et le développement humain durable (PNUD, 2005), à la seule croissance économique exprimée par le PNB.

Cette vision économique de « l'être-bien » reflète mieux la réalité humaine observée où les relations économiques de production, consommation, épargne, etc. s'effectuent entre personnes appartenant à des réseaux sociaux et ayant des obligations et contraintes à satisfaire. Elle considère leur capacité de compassion ou d'engagement, ce qui en fait des acteurs sociaux raisonnables, des citoyens responsables, ou des personnes capables de dépassement. On s'intéresse alors autant aux liens sociaux et

aux accomplissements des personnes qu'à la gestion des biens et services qui permettent ces accomplissements. Dans ce cadre, c'est la capacité d'action et d'accomplissement de la personne qui devient la source de bien-être, bien avant la satisfaction ou l'utilité (Sen, 1999).

La mesure macro-économique de ce bien-être est alors l'indicateur de développement humain (IDH) qui présente lui aussi bien des limites. Il se réfère à un petit nombre d'accomplissements essentiels, relatifs au revenu, à l'éducation (alphabétisation, scolarisation) et à la santé (espérance de vie). Ces quelques accomplissements ont cependant le mérite de pouvoir être évalués dans tous les pays du monde permettant ainsi à l'IDH d'être régulièrement confronté au PNB.

c. Les apports nécessaires de la psychologie

Les psychologues, à travers les différents courants de la psychologie positive, clinique et sociale, apportent à la vision du bien-être une nouvelle dimension. Celle-ci permet d'élargir la vision économique en faisant le lien avec le bonheur philosophique. Le courant positif ou humaniste, représenté par Eric Fromm, Abraham Maslow, Carl Rodgers ou Victor Frankl, considère la capacité des personnes à donner du « sens » à la vie (Lecomte, 2007) par l'intensité des relations sociales, la référence à un certain nombre de valeurs et de connaissances, et la capacité personnelle ou collective d'action. La construction du bonheur, au sens philosophique, se réalise alors par la combinaison du bien-être, au sens « d'être-bien » des économistes, et du « sens ».

Dans le cas de la psychologie clinique, et en lien avec la psychanalyse, l'accent est plutôt mis sur la recherche des causes qui sont à l'origine du mal-être, de la souffrance qui en résulte et qui bloque la possibilité de bien-être. Si certains préconisent des solutions médicamenteuses pour lutter contre le mal-être (Layard, 2005), on ne peut s'empêcher de remarquer que ces situations sont souvent issues de relations humaines difficiles, en termes de hiérarchie et de partage de l'information, face au maniement de technologies plus sophistiquées, à une compétition internationale accrue, à des modes de communication nouveaux.

La psychologie sociale étudie les effets de l'environnement social et des institutions sur le comportement des personnes, en tenant compte des interactions des individus au sein de groupes, des perceptions et motivations en société, de l'influence des représentations sociales, des situations de conflit, etc.

Ces différentes approches permettent de mieux cerner les concepts de bien-être, de sens et de bonheur. On peut ainsi éviter d'assimiler le bien-être au bonheur, comme le font les utilitaristes. Et considérer que le bonheur se construit à travers la recherche de bien-être, exprimé en termes de niveau de vie, de conditions de vie, de liens sociaux, auxquels se rajoute la recherche de sens, qui s'appuie sur la capacité d'accomplissement des personnes. Certains vont jusqu'à parler d'un « être-bien humain » pour retracer cette vision du bien-être élargie qui intègre les dimensions économiques et psychologiques, et se rapproche ainsi de l'idée de bonheur.

Avec cette expression, on répond à l'interrogation fort pertinente du sociologue Edgar Morin qui demandait s'il ne valait pas mieux considérer le « bien-vivre » plutôt que le bien-être.

2. Assurer le bien-être : à la recherche d'une nouvelle éthique

Une réponse à cette aspiration universelle au bien-être a été apportée dès le XVIIIᵉ siècle (Sismondi, 1773-1842) avec la mise en place des premières politiques publiques. Elles se sont poursuivies au XXᵉ siècle à travers la recherche d'une croissance économique régulière et d'un développement programmé. L'idée était que la croissance bénéficierait à tous quels que soient les mécanismes de redistribution envisagés. Or la question sociale du XIXᵉ siècle dans les pays industrialisés, puis les questions du développement dans les pays du tiers-monde et, enfin, la construction européenne à la fin du XXᵉ siècle, ont bien montré que seules des politiques de croissance accompagnées de mécanismes de redistribution volontaristes pouvaient garantir des niveaux minima de bien-être accessible à tous.

L'Etat providence, à travers des mécanismes de redistribution sociale spécifiques, a été le garant de cette stratégie en veillant à protéger les plus vulnérables. Une partie de la responsabilité face à l'accès au bien-être a ainsi été assurée par l'Etat qui garantissait, d'un côté, les moyens d'une croissance régulière du niveau de vie et de l'amélioration des conditions de vie, et de l'autre, la réduction du risque de pauvreté et la correction des inégalités par des mécanismes de redistribution appropriés. De telles politiques ont permis une réduction régulière de la pauvreté et, dans nombre de pays, l'émergence d'une nouvelle classe moyenne.

Or actuellement, si la croissance se poursuit au niveau mondial, on remarque cependant un fort accroissement des inégalités qui va jusqu'à

freiner la réduction de la pauvreté alors que c'est la condition première pour accéder au bien-être. De plus, au-delà d'un certain seuil, cette croissance ne s'accompagne plus d'une amélioration dans la perception subjective qu'ont les populations de ce bien-être. Comme si la croissance économique ne contribuait plus à l'amélioration du bien-être.

a. La croissance économique ne garantit plus le bien-être

En effet, les enquêtes qui évaluent le bien-être, sur une base subjective à partir de questions posées aux individus, montrent que, si le sentiment de bien-être s'accroît très fortement lors de la sortie de la pauvreté, résultant d'un accroissement de consommation en biens et services, ce sentiment s'affaiblit ensuite au fur et à mesure que s'accroît cette consommation.

Tout se passe comme si la croissance économique, tant qu'elle permet d'échapper à la pauvreté et d'atteindre un niveau de vie perçu comme correct, améliorait le sentiment subjectif de bien-être. Au-delà, l'amélioration du niveau de revenu ou de la consommation ne modifie plus guère le niveau de bien-être ressenti (Lecomte, 2007).

On trouve des résultats similaires dans tous les pays riches, que ce soit aux Etats-Unis, où le phénomène s'est manifesté dès le milieu des années 1960, en Angleterre et au Japon où il est apparu plus tardivement, vers la fin des années 1970[2]. Cette déconnection peut aussi s'expliquer par le fait que la poursuite de la croissance économique engendre des coûts sociaux et humains supplémentaires qui sont de moins en moins acceptés. Pour accroître ce bien-être, il faut alors se pencher sur sa forme élargie de « l'être-bien ». D'autant plus que les références psychologiques montrent que des suppléments de bien-être peuvent être trouvés dans l'intensité des relations sociales, dans l'accès à la connaissance et la pratique de certaines valeurs, et dans la capacité d'action des personnes. Autant d'éléments qui apportent du sens et un sentiment d'accomplissement. Autrement dit, l'insertion dans des réseaux d'appartenance sociale, avec ce que cela implique d'engagement et de compassion, d'obligation de responsabilités, contribue à accroître le sentiment subjectif de bien-être.

Cela pose néanmoins la difficile question du passage d'une approche en termes de bien-être individuel à une situation de bien-être au niveau

---

2. L'analyse comparée des pays montre qu'au-delà d'un seuil de revenu annuel d'environ 20 000$US par tête, le sentiment subjectif de bien-être cesse de s'accroître avec son augmentation (Layard, 2005).

collectif en tenant compte de l'interaction sociale. Il y a là un sérieux problème agrégatif sur lequel se penchent notamment les économistes du choix collectif. Mais il n'y a pour l'instant guère de solution universelle car il demeure difficile d'évaluer le bien-être issu de l'interaction de plusieurs personnes, autrement qu'en considérant chaque situation de façon particulière.

Or, en ce qui concerne la mesure du bien-être, la question est de savoir comment le caractériser et en évaluer le niveau. Il existe bien les indicateurs liés au revenu ou à la consommation, mais ils s'avèrent insuffisants. La solution consiste à adopter une démarche pragmatique en se reportant aux différentes dimensions du bien-être élargi et en rajoutant les aspects de mal-être[3].

Pour évaluer les capacités d'action et de réalisation des personnes, ainsi que les difficultés et contraintes rencontrées lors de ces réalisations, la liste de capacités fondamentales proposée par la philosophe Nussbaum (2000) peut servir de référence pour ouvrir de nouvelles voies. Enfin, l'approche psychologique, plus proche des dimensions existentielles, impose de considérer les interactions sociales, les perceptions et la confiance, les aspects de mal-être, les comparaisons et représentations sociales, etc.

b. Assurer l'équité dans la réduction de la pauvreté et des inégalités

Le désir d'échapper à la pauvreté peut-être considéré comme le premier des accomplissements à réaliser en priorité dans l'aspiration au bien-être. Il en est de même en ce qui concerne l'exclusion sociale, surtout si l'on considère qu'elle résulte de l'impossibilité d'accéder à certains biens, services et relations sociales. C'est cette pauvreté d'accessibilité qui engendre l'exclusion sous ses différentes manifestations (Dubois et Mahieu, 2002).

La croissance économique est un moyen efficace pour réduire la pauvreté. Cependant, on montre, notamment en termes monétaires, que la croissance réduit bien moins la pauvreté si les inégalités augmentent en parallèle. Autrement dit, l'augmentation des inégalités, à un niveau de croissance donné, freine la réduction de la pauvreté, le supplément de revenu ne se reportant pas sur les catégories les plus pauvres. La correction de cette situation demande la mise en œuvre de mécanismes de redistribution

---

3. Voir à ce propos l'article de Samuel Thirion dans ce volume.

spécifiques de manière à ce que les fruits de cette croissance permettent d'échapper de la pauvreté.

Le problème est qu'il y a de multiples formes d'inégalité qui sont, notamment d'ordre social, spatial, sexué, etc. Elles se déclinent en termes de différence d'accès aux biens et services, d'écarts dans la formation d'actifs et de potentialités, d'inégalités d'opportunités ou de chances, de capacité à être partie prenante, de résultats, etc. Or, toutes ces formes d'inégalité s'accumulent souvent autour des mêmes catégories, constituant alors des structures d'inégalités difficiles à combattre par des mécanismes de redistribution.

Face à la variété des situations socioéconomiques, le problème demeure de savoir sur quelles inégalités mettre l'accent, et lesquelles doivent être combattues en priorité. D'autant plus que, selon les domaines d'intervention retenus, il arrive que le fait de réduire certaines formes d'inégalités spécifiques ait pour conséquence d'en générer ou d'en accroître d'autres.

La notion d'équité répond à ce dilemme car elle permet de distinguer parmi les inégalités, celles qui sont considérées comme inacceptables, car injustes ou illégitimes, et celles qui peuvent être considérées comme acceptables à un moment donné, car tolérées pour des raisons sociétales, ou reconnues comme source de bénéfices globalement positifs.

Les principes d'équité définissent des sphères de justice, au sein desquelles la confiance peut s'établir entre acteurs sociaux, facilitant l'émergence d'initiatives individuelles – ou collectives – qui sont sources d'innovation. On voit ainsi que l'équité joue un rôle fondamental. Elle permet d'articuler, dans un cadre de croissance et de développement pérenne, la lutte contre la pauvreté et les inégalités avec le respect de la liberté des acteurs sociaux.

Dans ce contexte, l'objectif premier est bien d'assurer une équité dans l'accès au bien-être. Ce qui implique de garantir un accès minimal aux biens et services essentiels pour tout le monde, puis de faire en sorte que chacun dispose des moyens de pouvoir viser une situation de bien-être qu'il estime correcte. Ensuite il conviendra de s'attaquer aux situations de mal-être, et aux facteurs qui en sont à l'origine.

c. S'appuyer sur une éthique de la responsabilité

La mise en œuvre des processus visant à promouvoir le bien-être et, plus précisément, l'équité dans l'accès à ce bien-être, pose des problèmes de responsabilité morale. Une responsabilité vis-à-vis de ceux auxquels on a promis une amélioration de la situation et qui attendent un résultat à leurs aspirations. Mais aussi une responsabilité en tant que co-auteurs de règles d'équité ou de processus visant à la réalisation et la répartition du bien-être. Ces deux formes de responsabilité permettent de distinguer deux visions de la responsabilité qui s'expriment par le fait de « répondre devant autrui » ou le fait de « répondre d'autrui » (Thirion, 2004).

Dans le premier cas, le fait de « répondre devant autrui » concerne la responsabilité vis-à-vis de ses propres actes et donc des conséquences a posteriori (on dirait *ex-post* en économie) qui en résultent. Cette responsabilité est habituellement définie par les pratiques sociales, ce qui permet d'en parler comme d'une responsabilité sociale ou rétroactive (Jonas, 1979). Ce qui importe, dans ce cas particulier, c'est la liberté d'action que détient la personne et qui induit sa responsabilité vis-à-vis d'autrui.

Dans le second cas, « répondre d'autrui », ce qui importe c'est la responsabilité de répondre à des obligations, qui peuvent être imposées par un statut particulier, par d'autres ou par soi-même. Cette responsabilité se situe a priori (on dirait *ex-ante* en économie). Le modèle en est la responsabilité parentale. On parle alors de responsabilité personnelle ou prospective, et elle a pour effet de réduire sa propre liberté.

Un auteur comme Sen ne considère que la responsabilité rétroactive, du moins de manière explicite, car il est plus facile à travers elle de mesurer a posteriori les conséquences des actions entreprises. Les philosophes Jonas, Levinas et Ricœur insistent, au contraire, sur la responsabilité prospective, ou personnelle, comme élément de solution le plus pertinent face aux défis naturels comme sociaux du monde actuel. Il est certain, qu'à part quelques situations précisément définies, comme la responsabilité parentale, la responsabilité des chefs d'entreprise, et parfois la responsabilité politique, il n'y a pas de règle morale générale permettant de couvrir tous les cas représentés par cette forme de responsabilité.

En étendant l'exemple de la responsabilité parentale, Jonas (1979) insiste sur la responsabilité vis-à-vis des générations à venir et vis-à-vis d'un milieu naturel fragilisé par la sophistication technologique issue du progrès technique. Une situation qui induit un principe de responsabilité qui peut être concrétisé par l'établissement de principes de précaution ou de prudence.

On rejoint ainsi la vision vertueuse d'Aristote pour lequel la prudence était la vertu associée à toute capacité d'action.

Cette même attitude se retrouve chez Levinas (1982) pour lequel c'est la confrontation aux plus fragiles et vulnérables, qu'on les connaisse déjà ou pas encore, qui fait qu'on doit leur accorder la priorité en restreignant, en conséquence, sa propre liberté. La responsabilité personnelle vis-à-vis des autres devient alors première sur la liberté d'action personnelle.

Ricœur précise mieux la responsabilité face à la capacité d'action des personnes. Pour lui, c'est la faillibilité des individus, le fait qu'ils puissent se tromper, qui induit les situations de vulnérabilité. Poursuivant la démarche des deux auteurs précédents, il montre que la responsabilité prospective se traduit par le fait d'être capable de s'imputer une responsabilité a priori face à des actions et à des personnes précises, en se considérant « responsable de… ». Cela conduit à une démarche volontaire d'auto-contrainte de sa propre liberté face à des obligations sociales qui deviennent comme prioritaires. Or, cette capacité volontaire à s'autocontraindre caractérise la personne, en tant que sujet responsable.

On retrouve, derrière la pensée concomitante de ces trois auteurs, la démarche compréhensive de la réflexion phénoménologique qui met l'accent sur les intentions des personnes, leurs interactions sociales, l'articulation de leurs droits et obligations afin d'assurer la cohésion sociale d'une société considérée comme socio-culturellement située.

Le fait d'insister sur la responsabilité personnelle amène ainsi à quitter la stricte définition de l'individu utilitariste, cherchant à maximiser de manière rationnelle son intérêt, pour aller vers une définition plus large, celle de la personne capable de transcendance, c'est-à-dire de dépassement de soi pour les autres, notamment les plus vulnérables. La personne devient le sujet de l'analyse qui est le plus englobant car elle est tout à la fois capable de rationalité, de raison, de responsabilité et de dépassement.

Il y a donc, entre l'individu rationnel, tel que perçu en économie, et la personne capable de dépassement, de multiples manières de considérer le sujet en action, tantôt comme agent économique, acteur social raisonnable, citoyen responsable, etc.

Ce qui confère, de nos jours, à la responsabilité personnelle une importance croissante par rapport à la responsabilité sociale, pourtant mieux définie et instituée, c'est la confrontation aux grands défis, naturels comme sociaux, du monde actuel. L'importance des problèmes à résoudre, dans

une société qui s'est complexifiée, fait qu'une multiplicité d'acteurs se trouve concernée par les risques existants et qu'une démarche de prévention, effectuée a priori, devient préférable à une démarche de guérison des conséquences a posteriori ; démarche qui dans certains cas peut même ne pas s'avérer possible.

Dans le même temps, on assiste à une prise de conscience accrue des acteurs sociaux, face aux défis qui menacent le bien-être, sous sa forme élargie. Ce qui soulève la question, plus générale, du partage des responsabilités entre les différents acteurs concernés. Face au rôle habituel de l'Etat et des institutions formelles, apparaissent les particuliers, divers groupes sociaux, des collectivités locales, des associations concernés par les problèmes environnementaux, la réduction de la pauvreté, la montée des inégalités, la cohésion sociale, etc. Autant d'aspects à prendre en compte lorsqu'on est impliqué dans une dynamique d'amélioration du bien-être.

Dans tous les cas, il faut faire face à un partage des responsabilités. Cela peut se faire sur la base d'un cadre légal et institutionnel qui définit les responsabilités respectives de chaque acteur. Ou, à l'inverse, on peut considérer la coresponsabilité des acteurs comme un processus qui s'applique mieux à la responsabilité prospective en permettant aux acteurs de se sentir responsables en fonction de règles établies par eux. Un processus que l'on peut appliquer au cas de la promotion équitable du bien-être élargi. Il permet ainsi la mise en place « d'institutions justes » au sens de Ricœur, c'est-à-dire des institutions qui, parce qu'elles se sentent coresponsables, veillent à une promotion équitable du bien-être en renforçant, notamment, les capacités d'action des personnes.

Dans ce cadre, les critères de répartition, n'étant pas instaurés de manière légale ou institutionnelle, ne peuvent que résulter, à l'issue d'une discussion, d'un accord entre les différents acteurs concernés. L'éthique de la discussion (Habermas, 2003) fournit alors les conditions d'une mise en débat entre parties prenantes qui permet de déboucher sur un compromis autour d'une solution de répartition durable.

Cette approche permet d'arriver à des décisions collectives importantes comme celles consistant à s'accorder sur les dimensions du bien-être ou mal-être, sur les priorités concernant les *capabilities* à renforcer pour articuler libertés et responsabilités, sur les critères d'équité concernant la répartition du bien-être. La mise en débat de ces questions permet de construire une capacité d'action collective, sous la forme de coopération et d'engagement, en s'appuyant sur les *capabilities* des parties prenantes,

tout en considérant aussi leurs choix de valeurs. Elle devient alors un formidable instrument pour déterminer de manière effective le niveau de coresponsabilité des différents acteurs concernés.

Il ne faut cependant pas nier qu'il existe un certain nombre de difficultés pour mettre en œuvre une telle approche. Des difficultés qui résultent de la présence de situations d'exclusion, de discrimination, de hiérarchie de pouvoir ou d'asymétrie d'information, et qui traversent toute société. Un savoir-faire particulier, qui est surtout le fait des psychosociologues ou des spécialistes du coaching social, permet de surmonter les risques correspondants de blocage.

Conclusion

Face à des aspirations au bien-être universellement partagées, l'Etat et les institutions peuvent veiller à ce qu'un niveau minimal de bien-être soit assuré pour tous, ainsi qu'une répartition équitable dans les moyens et capacités à atteindre ce bien-être. La recherche du bonheur, à travers la vision élargie qui articule bien-être économique et sens psychologique, relève plus des personnes et des acteurs sociaux, qui, à travers leurs choix, peuvent tirer parti des opportunités qui leur sont directement offertes par la croissance et le progrès technique, afin d'agir dans le sens d'un plus grand accomplissement.

Dans ce contexte, le fait de partir des aspirations des personnes, et de leurs moyens d'expression, pour inspirer des politiques publiques concertées apparaît comme une démarche plausible, dès lors que le bien-être ne se réduit pas à la seule recherche de satisfactions personnelles, issues de la consommation de biens et services, mais intègre les dimensions d'accomplissement individuelles et collectives qui résultent d'un système de droits et d'obligations réciproques. Cela a aussi pour effet de conférer du sens aux actions entreprises.

On rejoint ainsi la formulation éthique de Ricœur relative à l'instauration d'une « vie bonne, avec et pour les autres, dans des institutions justes ». Elle fournit, en effet, le cadre éthique qui justifie la promotion d'une vision du bien-être élargi, de manière équitable, et sur la base d'une coresponsabilité des acteurs sociaux. Une praxis peut découler de cette vision, qui se fonde sur l'expression concertée de parties prenantes considérées comme coresponsables des situations de bien-être, comme de mal-être, et qui mettent en œuvre dans une démarche de bas en haut (*bottom-up* en anglais) des processus d'amélioration et de répartition du bien-être.

Sur cette base, on peut identifier, de manière pragmatique et à travers la mise en débat, la panoplie d'indicateurs permettant de caractériser les situations de bien-être comme de mal-être. Et, ainsi, envisager des actions et politiques publiques qui auront pour objet d'agir sur les facteurs d'amélioration du bien-être, tout en luttant contre ceux qui sont sources de mal-être.

De nombreux problèmes demeurent, cependant, dans la mise en œuvre d'une telle vision. Ils sont autant d'ordre théorique qu'empirique. Ainsi, par exemple, la réflexion sur le sujet économique considéré comme personne responsable, car capable de réduire sa liberté pour respecter ses obligations sociales et économiques, implique d'évaluer les coûts d'une telle responsabilité à travers des travaux de mesure spécifiques.

De même, le fait que les personnes puissent s'associer pour accomplir des actions collectives dans le but d'améliorer leur bien-être implique de savoir comment résoudre le problème de l'agrégation des effets de ces actions, car il est souhaitable que l'amélioration du bien-être au niveau local puisse aussi contribuer à l'amélioration du bien-être à un niveau plus global.

Ce sont là autant d'investissements méthodologiques à mettre en œuvre et qui tirent leurs légitimités des nouvelles interrogations conceptuelles, d'ordre phénoménologique, visant à intégrer les perceptions, aspirations et intentions des acteurs sociaux dans l'analyse économique. On rejoint, de ce fait, par l'accent mis sur les interactions sociales, la vision plus générale du développement socialement durable qui est directement concerné par les aspects de responsabilité et d'équité (Ballet *et al.*, 2005).

Bibliographie

Ballet, J., Dubois, J.-L. et Mahieu, F.-R., *L'autre développement, le développement socialement soutenable*, L'Harmattan, Paris, 2005.

Ballet, J. et Mahieu, F.-R., *Ethique économique*, Ellipses, Paris, 2003.

Dubois, J.-L. et Mahieu, F.-R. , « La dimension sociale du développement durable : lutte contre la pauvreté ou durabilité sociale ? » in Martin, J.-Y. (Ed.), *Développement durable ? Doctrines, pratiques, évaluations*, IRD, Paris, 2002, p.73-94.

Habermas, J., *L'éthique de la discussion et la question de la vérité*, Grasset, Paris, 2003.

Jarret, M-F. et Mahieu F-R., *Economie publique : théories économiques de l'interaction sociale*, Ellipses, Paris, 1998.

Jonas, H., *Le principe responsabilité*, Champs, Flammarion, Paris, 1990 pour la traduction française de *Das Prinzip Verantwortung*, Insel Verlag Francfort, 1979.

Layard, R., *Happiness: Lessons from a New Science*, Penguin Book, New York, 2005.

Lecomte, J., *Donner un sens à sa vie*, Odile Jacob, Paris, 2007.

Levinas, E., *Ethique et Infini*, Fayard, Paris, 1982.

Misrahi, R., *Le sujet et son désir*, Editions Pleins Feux, Paris, 2003.

Nussbaum, M., *Women and Human Development: The Capabilities Approach*, Cambridge University Press, Cambridge, 2000.

Perroux, F., *L'économie du XXe siècle*, P.U.F., Paris, 1952.

PNUD, *15 années de publication du Rapport mondial sur le développement humain 1990-2004*, CD-Rom base de données statistiques, Programme des Nations Unies pour le Développement, New York, 2005.

Ricœur, P., *Le Juste*, Esprit, Paris, 1995.

Sen, A.K., *Commodities and Capabilities*, Elsevier, Amsterdam, 1985.

Sen, A.K., *Un nouveau modèle économique : développement, justice et liberté*, Odile Jacob, Paris, 2000 pour la traduction française de *Development as Freedom*, New York, Knopf, 1999.

Thirion, S., «Indicateurs de cohésion sociale et contribution de l'économie solidaire», in *Engagement éthique et solidaire des citoyens dans l'économie : une responsabilité pour la cohésion sociale*, Tendances de la cohésion sociale n° 12, Conseil de l'Europe, Strasbourg, 2004.

Pour en savoir plus

Aristote, *Ethique à Nicomaque*, Garnier-Flammarion, réédition 1965, Paris.

Ballet, J., Dubois, J-L., Bigo, V. et Mahieu, F-R., «Happiness, Responsibility and Preference Perturbations», in J. Ballet et D. Bazin (dir.), *Essays on Positive Ethics in Economics*, Transaction Publishers, Londres, 2006, p. 225-238.

Bebbington, A., Danis, A., de Haan, A. et Walton M., *Institutional Pathways to Equity : Adressing Inequality Trap*, The World Bank, Washington DC, 2008.

Beck, U., *La société du risque. Sur la voie d'une autre modernité,* traduction française 2001, Flammarion, Paris, 1986.

Deneulin, S., Nebel, M. et Sagovsky, N. (eds), *Transforming Unjust Structures : The Capability Approach*, Springer, Dordrecht, The Netherlands, 2006.

Mahieu, F-R., *Responsabilité et crimes économiques*, L'Harmattan, Paris, 2008.

Misrahi, R., «Construire son bonheur», in *Philosophies de notre temps*, Editions Sciences Humaines, Paris, 2000, p. 287-289.

Ricœur, P., *Parcours de la reconnaissance*, Paris, Stock, 2005, pour la traduction française de *The Course of Recognition*, Harvard University Press, Cambridge, Mass, 2004.

Sen, A.K., «Equality of What ?» in *Choice, Welfare and Measurement*, Blackwell, Oxford, réédition Harvard University Press, 1982, p. 353-369.

II. Perception et mesure du bien-être

Wolfgang Glatzer[1]

Introduction

Bien-être et qualité de vie sont deux concepts assez proches en ce sens que ces objectifs fondamentaux de la société sont beaucoup plus larges que le seul bien-être matériel. L'un et l'autre correspondent en effet à des conditions de vie « objectives » et, en même temps, à leur perception « subjective » par les individus.

Dès lors qu'on établit une corrélation entre différentes composantes d'origine « objective » et « subjective », le tableau de la société présente toujours une certaine complexité. La perception des biens publics, en particulier, semble suivre des règles propres, mais elle est présumée importante pour la cohésion sociale de la population. Suivant la nature des biens, l'Etat peut exercer sur l'offre une influence plus ou moins grande, qui diffère selon les modèles d'Etat providence.

Le problème sera illustré par trois exemples :

1. Les différences d'appréciation entre les biens publics et les biens privés ;

2. Les différences d'évaluation entre les caractéristiques individuelles et les caractéristiques collectives ;

3. Les différences de niveau entre bien-être personnel et bien-être national.

Dans tous ces cas de figure, le constat est celui d'une moindre satisfaction et appréciation des composantes lorsque la responsabilité de l'individu est faible. Le problème de l'évaluation des biens publics par la population est ainsi démontré et un enjeu se dégage : la nécessité d'éviter les conséquences sociales négatives.

---

1. Professor Dr. Wolfgang Glatzer, J. W. Goethe-Universität, Frankfurt a. M. – Institut für Gesellschafts- und Politikanalyse.

1. Bien-être et perception du bien-être

a. Les concepts du bien-être et de la qualité de vie

Le bien-être, ou bien-être social, est l'un des objectifs ultimes de l'humanité. C'est un concept en vogue dont on parle beaucoup, mais qui lui-même n'est pas historiquement très ancien. Pour autant que l'on puisse en juger, c'est l'Organisation pour la coopération et le développement économiques (OCDE 1973, 1976) qui a généralisé le terme et le concept du bien-être au début des années soixante-dix et qui l'a utilisé jusqu'à ces derniers temps. Outre l'OCDE, plusieurs auteurs, tout particulièrement américains (notamment Andrews et Withey, 1976), l'ont choisi comme terme directeur et ont présenté des recherches relatives au bien-être et à la qualité de la vie. Ces termes, semble-t-il interchangeables, étaient utilisés indistinctement dans leurs ouvrages et travaux.

Bien sûr, la question du bien-être existait déjà dans les temps anciens et n'a jamais cessé d'être posée, mais souvent en d'autres termes et avec des préoccupations différentes. L'OCDE indique utiliser le terme bien-être social comme un abrégé de « bien-être global des individus. Le cœur du problème est le bien-être de chaque individu et la manière dont il est affecté par ses rapports avec autrui et avec l'environnement physique. » (OCDE, 1976, p. 12) [Traduction non officielle]. Le bien-être s'inscrit dans un cadre de référence élargi : le champ de la recherche sur les indicateurs sociaux. Si l'on prend les 17 premiers articles dans *Citation Classics from Social Indicators Research : The Most Cited Articles* (Michalos, 2005), le concept de bien-être (subjectif) revient sept fois. Le bien-être est lié à la réalité objective ainsi qu'à sa perception et à son évaluation subjectives. Les « éléments subjectifs du bien-être » (OCDE, 1973), ou « bien-être subjectif » (Strack, Argyle et Schwarz, 1990), font l'objet d'une attention grandissante de la part des chercheurs et de la classe politique. Ce concept a remporté un tel succès que des auteurs ont récemment parlé de « l'universalité des indicateurs du bien-être subjectif » (Gullone et Cummins, 2002).

Au sens large, le bien-être est fondamentalement défini comme une constellation de composantes pouvant consister en conditions de vie objectives ou en aspects subjectifs de la vie tels qu'ils sont ressentis.

Figure 1 – Composantes du bien-être et de la qualité de vie

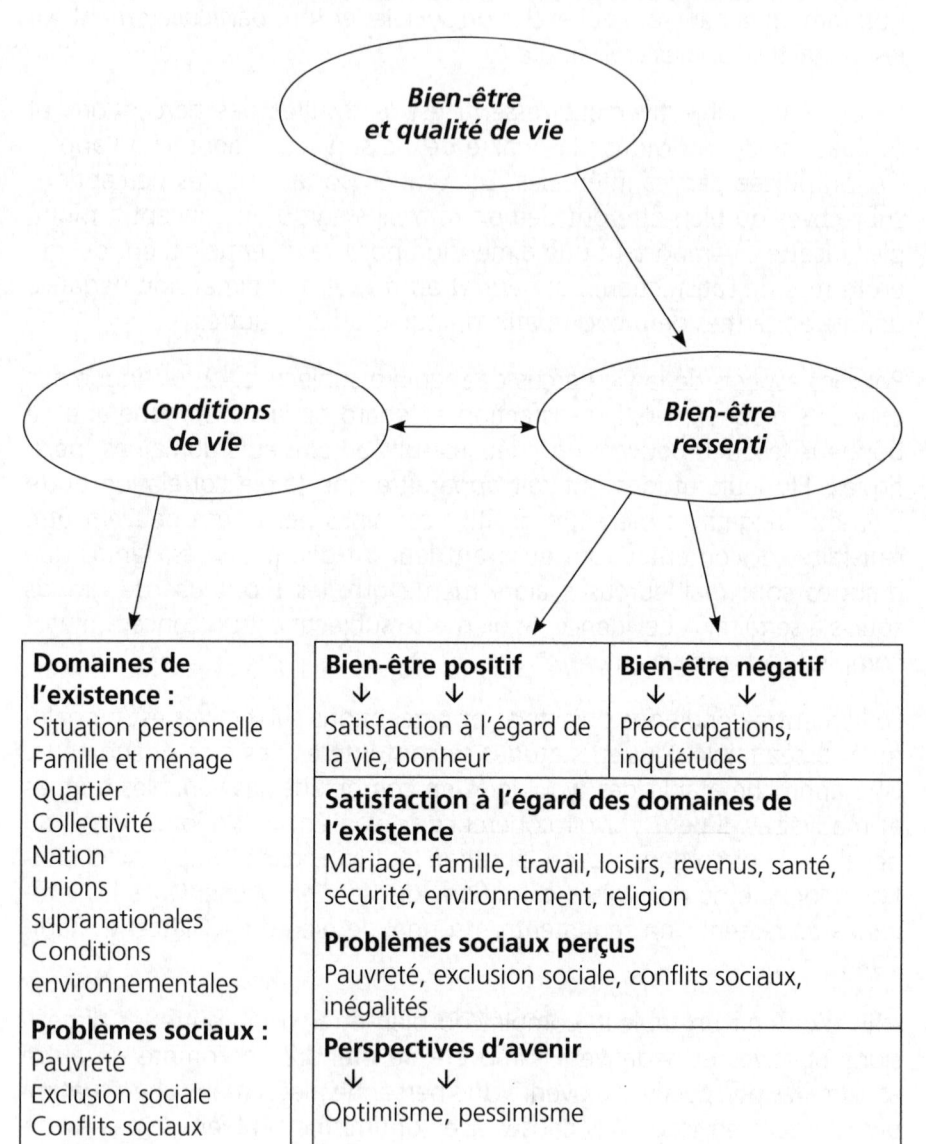

Les conditions de vie objectives sont généralement suivies par les spécialistes des sciences sociales et naturelles. Elles existent, que les populations concernées en aient conscience ou non. L'éventail en est large : depuis les situations personnelles *stricto sensu*, replacées dans le cadre collectif, jusqu'aux conditions environnementales à l'échelle de la planète.

Certaines approches préfèrent mettre l'accent sur les problèmes sociaux, notamment la pauvreté et l'exclusion sociale, et tout particulièrement sur les inégalités sociales (voir figure 1).

Le bien-être subjectivement ressenti est le résultat des perceptions et évaluations des individus ; la qualité de vie subjective tient ici à l'appréciation portée par les intéressés. Les études portant sur les perceptions subjectives du bien-être ont démontré qu'il s'agit d'un concept à multiples facettes, comportant une dimension positive essentiellement décrite en termes de satisfaction, bonheur et autres, et une dimension négative définie en termes de préoccupations, inquiétudes et autres.

Pour les aspects de la vie perçus de manière subjective, on distingue des concepts globaux, tels la satisfaction à l'égard de la vie en général et le bonheur, lesquels peuvent être déconstruits en plusieurs domaines spécifiques. Plusieurs études ont fait apparaître une faible corrélation entre bien-être négatif et bien-être positif : certaines personnes peuvent être satisfaites et contentes tout en ayant leur lot d'inquiétudes, tandis que d'autres sont malheureuses alors même qu'elles n'ont pas de grands soucis à se faire. A l'évidence, le bien-être subjectif est un concept plutôt compliqué et ambivalent.

Le lien entre conditions objectives et perceptions subjectives est globalement assez faible. Plusieurs études se sont intéressées à ce phénomène. Une approche établit des typologies en combinant des variables bonnes et mauvaises. Il peut y avoir cohérence (« bien-être », « déprivation ») ou décalage (« discordance », « adaptation »). Il y a, par exemple, « adaptation » lorsque de mauvaises conditions de vie n'empêchent pas les intéressés de ressentir un sentiment personnel de bien-être (Glatzer et Zapf, 1984).

Afin d'obtenir un tableau complet du bien-être social, outre les dimensions positives et négatives, il importe de prendre en compte un autre aspect : les perspectives d'avenir. Une personne placée dans une situation difficile peut envisager les choses avec optimisme ou bien ne pas savoir comment s'en sortir. Cela fait une grande différence. C'est pourquoi l'accent a été mis sur le fait que les perspectives sont aussi une composante du bien-être et, partant, l'optimisme et le pessimisme sont devenus une part essentielle de la notion de bien-être.

Selon les Etats et les enjeux auxquels ils sont confrontés, on constate une assez grande disparité dans les réponses apportées au problème de la définition du bien-être. Aux Etats-Unis, une forte préférence pour

l'approche subjective a recueilli l'adhésion générale. En Europe – du moins en Scandinavie et à un certain point dans d'autres parties –, on a plutôt privilégié des indicateurs objectifs qui mesurent les conditions sociales du point de vue des experts en statistiques. En Allemagne, plus particulièrement, les chercheurs ont adopté une position médiane et préféré une combinaison de données objectives et subjectives (Zapf, 1987). Ce n'est que récemment que l'approche subjective a été adoptée pour les pays en voie de développement (Camfield, 2004). En Europe, une attention grandissante a été accordée à l'évaluation et au suivi du bien-être. C'est aujourd'hui une discipline établie et appréciée qui fait partie des sciences sociales.

Le concept de bien-être est lié à des objectifs d'une grande importance pour notre société : liberté[2] et démocratie, protection sociale et sécurité, solidarité et participation politique, équité et développement durable, et autres notions du même ordre. Parmi les valeurs conceptualisées de notre société, le bien-être s'inscrit dans le cadre des valeurs de la plus haute importance.

b. La différence entre aspects objectifs et subjectifs

La distinction entre aspects objectifs et subjectifs (et leurs composantes respectives) est fondamentale dans la recherche sur le bien-être. Le problème soulevé est de savoir dans quelle mesure ces deux perspectives sont justes ou fausses : les aspects objectifs de la réalité sont-ils plus corrects que les aspects subjectifs ? Ou l'inverse ? Si l'on décide que les deux présentent un intérêt, la question se pose de savoir s'ils sont à mettre sur le même plan ou si l'un a une plus grande signification que l'autre. Au fil des années, diverses solutions pragmatiques ont été élaborées afin de pouvoir mesurer les concepts objectifs et subjectifs. Disposant de plusieurs indicateurs objectifs et subjectifs – comme c'est le cas aujourd'hui –, il devient possible d'appréhender les lacunes et les contradictions. Aux différents niveaux – le monde, les nations, les individus –, on constate qu'il n'y a pas de correspondance exacte entre les composantes objectives et les composantes subjectives.

---

2. Par analogie avec la mesure de la qualité de la vie, il existe aujourd'hui des mesures de la liberté et de concepts analogues. Voir par exemple Holmes *et al.*, 2008.

2. Les mesures du bien-être

a. Les mesures du bien-être entre pays

Les nouvelles mesures du bien-être objectif sont l'Indicateur du développement humain (IDH), le *Human Well-being Index* (HWI) ou indicateur de bien-être, et le *Weighted Index of Social Progress* (WISP) ou indice pondéré de progrès social. Dans l'IDH, qui comporte essentiellement trois composantes, le traditionnel PIB compte pour un tiers. Le HWI est fortement axé sur les aspects environnementaux et a dix composantes. Enfin, avec ses quarante composantes, le WISP est un indice qui intègre plusieurs autres domaines d'un Etat social. Les mesures du bien-être subjectif sont *l'Overall Life Satisfaction with Life* (OSL) ou indicateur de satisfaction à l'égard de la vie, et *l'Affect-Balance Scale* (ABS) ou échelle d'évaluation du bien-être psychologique. L'OLS comporte un seul item. L'ABS en comporte dix explicitement liés à des expériences quotidiennes positives ou négatives.

Enfin, le *Happy Life Expectancy* (HLE) mesure l'espérance de vie heureuse. Il s'agit d'un indicateur mixte qui intègre dans un seul indice des aspects objectifs et subjectifs, notamment la longévité et les satisfactions à l'égard de la vie. Ces indicateurs me semblent être les plus importantes mesures du bien-être et de la qualité de vie, mais il en existe d'autres dans la littérature scientifique et publique, bien qu'ils soient parfois insuffisamment documentés.

Afin de pouvoir dresser un tableau, la présente étude a été limitée à un échantillon choisi de pays. Aux fins de la comparaison, il y a toujours deux pays représentatifs d'une zone plus large : deux pour l'Europe du Nord (Norvège, Danemark), deux pour l'Europe centrale (Allemagne, France), deux pour l'Europe méridionale (Italie, Espagne) et deux pour l'Europe de l'Est (Pologne, Roumanie). A ces pays européens ont été ajoutés deux pays représentatifs du monde moderne extérieur à l'Europe (Etats-Unis et Japon).

Figure 2 – Indicateurs de la qualité de la vie pour certains pays

Indicateur	IDH	HWI	WISP	OSL	ABS	HLE
Norvège	1 0,97	1 82	2 104	3 79	1 2,31	2 59,4
Danemark	3 0,94	2 81	1 107	1 86	3 1,93	1 62,7

	IDH	HWI	WISP	OSL	ABS	HLE
Allemagne	6 0,93	4 77	3 100	2 80	4 1,47	4 56,1
France	4 0,94	5 75	6 94	6 66	6 1,33	8 51,4
Italie	5 0,93	6 74	4 98	5 70	7 1,24	5 54,2
Espagne	7 0,93	7 73	5 96	7 65	8 0,73	6 53,4
Pologne	9 0,89	8 65	7 85	8 50	5 1,47	9 43,2
Roumanie	10 0,83	9 50	10 77	10 38	9 0,71	10 38,0
Etats-Unis	2 0,94	7 73	7 85	3 79	2 2,21	3 57,0
Japon	8 0,92	3 80	7 85 (1995)	9 53	10 0,93	7 53,0

IDH : Indicateur du développement humain (ONU, 2005)
HWI : Human Well-being Index (Prescott-Allen, 2001)
WISP : Weighted Index of Social Progress (Estes, 2004)
OSL : Overall Satisfaction with Life (Halman *et al.*, 2008)
ABS : Affect Balance Scale (Bradburn, 1969, Veenhoven, 2008)
HLE : Happy Life Expectancy (Veenhoven, 1996)

Suivant la construction des indicateurs de bien-être, les dix pays considérés se positionnent comme suit. Les meilleures valeurs sur chaque échelle sont essentiellement atteintes par la Norvège et le Danemark. Les pays scandinaves et d'Europe du Nord obtiennent des résultats exceptionnels quel que soit l'indice utilisé. Les Etats-Unis sont les seuls à obtenir parfois des évaluations aussi élevées que les pays d'Europe du Nord. L'Europe dans son ensemble montre un biais favorisant l'Europe du Nord et l'Europe centrale par rapport à l'Europe du Sud et de l'Est. Concernant les pays de comparaison, les Etats-Unis se situent parfois dans la partie supérieure de l'échelle, le Japon étant le plus souvent dans la partie inférieure. Les Etats-Unis présentent les écarts les plus grands, passant de 2 pour l'IDH à 7 pour le WISP. On observe le plus souvent une stabilité plutôt que d'importants changements. Les écarts constatés entre les valeurs les plus hautes et les plus basses se maintiennent au fil des années. Les valeurs IDH sont assez proches des valeurs OSL et globalement, les écarts sont moins importants qu'on aurait pu s'y attendre. Il y a lieu d'ajouter que les séries de données chronologiques sont toujours très stables dans le temps

pour les pays dans leur ensemble. Enfin, il est évident que la société d'un pays a une influence sur la qualité de vie (Böhnke, 2008).

b. La mesure du bien-être au sein des pays

La mesure du bien-être contribue à une meilleure compréhension des différences existant entre les pays mais aussi au sein des pays, où la répartition du bien-être est souvent décrite en termes d'écarts (divergence durable et significative entre deux variables). Ces écarts peuvent prendre plusieurs formes : écarts entre les sexes, les âges, les générations, les régions (Bergheim, 2007), en matière d'éducation, de chômage (Luechinger, Meier, Stutzer, 2008), de migration, de composition familiale. Des cartes exhaustives retracent la distribution du bien-être au niveau des pays dans leur ensemble (Bergheim, 2007).

Figure 3 – Conditions de vie et exclusion sociale en Europe (2003)

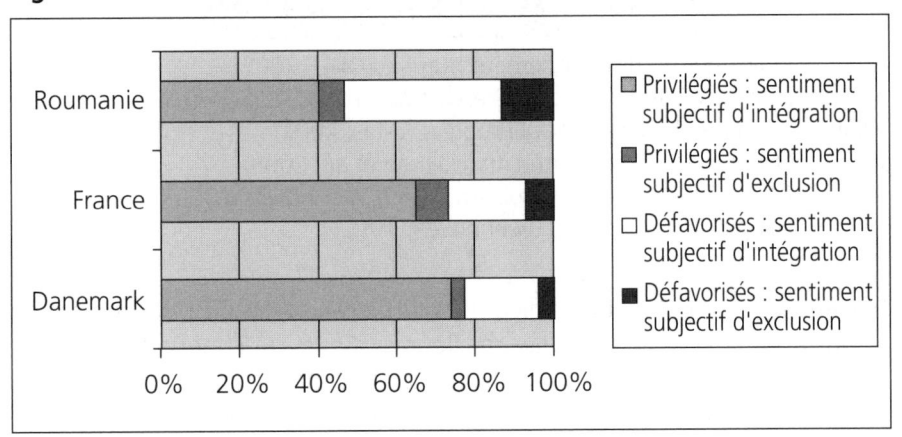

Conditions des privilégiés et des défavorisés : index des conditions objectives.
Intégration subjective et exclusion subjective : index des sentiments d'exclusion sociale.
Source : Böhnke d'après Alber, Fahey, *European Survey, Percentage of population in the age between 15 and 65*, 2008, p. 22.

Bien évidemment, la plupart des personnes aisées privilégiées par la vie se sentent intégrées socialement. Parallèlement, il y a tout le lot des personnes défavorisées qui se sentent exclues. Le plus remarquable, cependant, sont les catégories n'entrant pas dans ce schéma : des personnes privilégiées peuvent éprouver un sentiment subjectif d'exclusion et des personnes défavorisées un sentiment subjectif d'intégration. Au total, cela concerne encore près de 25 % de la population dans un pays riche comme le Danemark et 60 % dans un pays plus pauvre comme la Roumanie.

Les personnes défavorisées ayant un sentiment subjectif d'intégration sont beaucoup plus nombreuses que les personnes privilégiées ayant un sentiment d'exclusion. Cela favorise l'intégration sociale de la société.

Il existe de nombreux écarts de la sorte, et chaque aspect de l'inégalité sociale peut avoir une incidence en termes objectifs et subjectifs. Les écarts au sein d'une société ont des conséquences sociales sur le développement de la société. Le point auquel les différences objectives deviennent des divergences subjectives, articulées, diffère suivant les sociétés et les cultures.

c. Bien-être individuel

Sur un autre plan, la notion d'écart est liée à l'individu et à son processus de perception. Cela a donné lieu à un très large débat depuis le début des recherches sur le bien-être (voir essentiellement Michalos, 2005 ; Diener, Lucas, 2000). Une hypothèse habituelle dans la plupart des travaux est que l'insatisfaction est toujours motivée par un écart entre ce que l'on a et ce que l'on souhaiterait avoir. C'est dans les deux cas une question de définition : la personne définit sa situation et ce qu'elle préférerait. L'écart entre ces deux points de référence détermine le degré de satisfaction. On distingue plusieurs points de référence : les attentes et aspirations, les expériences passées, les perspectives d'avenir, la situation des proches, amis et voisins, la classe moyenne, les riches et les pauvres. Divers travaux s'intéressent à ces aspects. L'écart est à ce jour la théorie la plus importante pour expliquer la satisfaction et l'insatisfaction[3].

3. Biens publics, caractéristiques de l'environnement et bien-être national dans l'Etat social

Dans l'approche de la mesure du bien-être, une démarche habituelle est d'inclure la perception de l'ensemble des biens et caractéristiques sans se limiter aux biens marchands et à la production domestique. De notre point de vue, il faut ainsi prendre en compte les biens publics et collectifs comme le réseau routier ou la sécurité sociale, les caractéristiques de l'environnement comme la santé moyenne dans la région, mais aussi le bien-être national, par exemple la satisfaction concernant divers indicateurs de performance nationale.

---

3. Cette approche mise à part, la théorie la plus débattue est la théorie des ensembles.

La prospérité repose sur la production de biens (ou de maux). Les biens et services sont produits dans le cadre des quatre sphères suivantes : le marché et ses entreprises, l'Etat et ses activités, les ménages et leur production, les intermédiaires et leurs prestations. Chaque bien est essentiellement produit par un type de fournisseur. La production des biens marchands, par exemple, relève du marché. Néanmoins, on trouve souvent différents types de combinaison. Les soins de santé, par exemple, sont assurés à la fois par l'Etat et par le marché. La production mixte est souvent considérée comme particulièrement productive. Les biens politiques sont des biens fournis par l'Etat ou parfois en partenariat avec l'Etat.

Il y a un débat complexe sur plusieurs types de biens : biens publics, biens communs, biens collectifs, biens sociaux, biens tutélaires, biens politiques et autres biens infrastructurels et environnementaux. Tous sont définis d'une manière ou d'une autre par opposition aux biens privés, personnels, individuels ou marchands. Les « biens » apportent une contribution positive à la vie au sens matériel ou symbolique. On les oppose aux « maux », qui ont une incidence négative. S'agissant des inégalités dans la société, les maux sont un facteur tout aussi important que les biens, même s'ils sont beaucoup moins mentionnés. Au sens classique, le critère de définition des biens publics et des biens collectifs se rattache aux notions de non-rivalité et non-exclusivité, les biens publics étant parfois conçus en termes de non-rivalité et les biens collectifs en termes de non-exclusivité. Mais c'est là une définition théorique. Pour parler des biens fournis par l'Etat, nous utiliserons plutôt l'expression « biens politiques ».

Certains biens sont partagés par l'ensemble de la population, comme l'air, le climat, la sécurité sociale ou le réseau routier. Les conditions de vie moyennes d'un pays sont aussi assimilables au bien commun, comme le niveau de vie moyen, le degré de satisfaction moyen, etc. On pourrait dire que les biens particuliers s'inscrivent dans le cadre des biens environnementaux. Les biens personnels sont toutefois accessibles au seul individu tandis que les biens collectifs sont au service de tous. Le bien commun résulte de l'agrégation des biens individuels.

Elaborée au cours du siècle dernier, l'institution de l'Etat social offre un large éventail de biens et services publics à la population, notamment des biens symboliques comme la solidarité et la justice. Il existe différents modèles d'Etat providence : conservateur, social-démocrate et libéral. Une autre terminologie établit une division entre les Etats providence pauvres et limités et les Etats providence élaborés. L'influence de l'Etat providence sur le bien-être est difficile à apprécier car elle s'exerce directement et

indirectement. L'Etat social élaboré est imbriqué dans la structure sociale qui est elle-même garantie et façonnée par l'Etat social.

4. Différenciation public/privé et bien-être

L'importance des biens publics et collectifs pour le bien-être ne suscite aucun doute sur le principe. Dans le détail, le problème n'est pas pour autant résolu. Aucun ouvrage ou article exhaustif n'en donne un aperçu instructif. Ici ou là, cependant, certains aspects du problème sont abordés : de nombreux ensembles de données renferment des informations à ce sujet. Les trois exemples présentés dans cet article donnent un nouvel éclairage sur la différenciation public/privé selon différents points de vue. Procéder à une étude plus large et systématique irait au-delà des possibilités du présent document. Aussi ne donnons-nous ici que quelques indications, à titre d'illustration.

Les premières études sur le bien-être (Andrews, Withey, 1976, p. 433) et la qualité de vie (Campbell *et al.*, 1976, p. 63) avaient déjà abordé le problème du faible degré de satisfaction concernant des aspects relevant des pouvoirs publics. Les indicateurs montrent que « l'immense majorité des gens dans ce pays sont satisfaits de la vie aux Etats-Unis aujourd'hui » mais font aussi apparaître que « des millions d'Américains ont de sérieux griefs à formuler à l'égard de leur société » (p. 285-286). La question a donc été soulevée, mais ce point n'a pas été traité plus avant, probablement parce que très peu de dimensions publiques avaient été incluses dans les questionnaires.

Des constats analogues peuvent être dégagés dans plusieurs travaux. En Europe, une étude s'intéresse explicitement à la qualité du secteur public (Office de planification sociale et culturelle des Pays-Bas, 2002). De nombreuses dimensions du secteur public sont examinées, mais la comparaison avec le secteur privé reste des plus limitées. Globalement, elle confirme ce sentiment de satisfaction modérée envers les biens publics : « Il n'est pas difficile de dénoter chez la population un sentiment diffus mais généralisé d'insatisfaction à l'égard du secteur public aux Pays-Bas » (*Ibid.*, 2002, p. 56,). L'exemple ci-après porte sur la comparaison des sphères public/privé (tableau 1).

a. Bien-être privé/Bien-être public

Dans l'étude des domaines de l'existence et des domaines de la société, certains aspects semblent relever davantage de la sphère privée et d'autres

de la sphère publique. Une division apparaît clairement, sans réserve. Les aspects relevant du privé sont mieux notés que ceux relevant du public. Les données exploitées ici sont extraites du *German Welfare Survey* de 1998, représentatif de la population allemande. Cette enquête englobait en effet plus de domaines que d'autres lors de l'entretien. L'Allemagne de l'Ouest a été dissociée de l'Allemagne de l'Est car les données obtenues pour cette dernière témoignent d'une logique particulière, bien que la division public/privé soit la même.

Le tableau 1 montre que la fourchette de la moyenne générale s'établit entre 8,8 et 5,8, soit un différentiel de 3 entre les domaines se situant plutôt dans la partie supérieure de l'échelle et ceux situés plutôt dans la partie inférieure. Ceux situés au-dessus de 7 sont la satisfaction à l'égard du mariage ou de son partenaire, de la famille, du quartier, du lieu de travail, du niveau de vie, du logement, de la santé, des revenus du ménage. En dessous de 7, on trouve sécurité sociale, démocratie, participation politique, sûreté publique, protection de l'environnement. La première impression est claire : on observe un moindre degré de satisfaction pour les aspects relevant de la sphère publique et une plus grande satisfaction pour ceux relevant de la sphère privée.

Ces résultats ne sont pas propres à une époque, mais sont stables dans le temps (en Allemagne, depuis 1978). De plus, un autre type de données tend à corroborer ces observations. Si l'on prend le *German Socio-Economic Panel*, dans plusieurs domaines la sécurité sociale affiche la valeur la plus faible (Statistisches Bundesamt, 2006, p. 445). Là encore, les évolutions dans le temps sont particulièrement intéressantes. On observe une baisse de la satisfaction vis-à-vis de certains domaines, notamment concernant la protection de l'environnement et – ces dernières années – la sécurité sociale.

Les différents groupes de population montrent souvent le même niveau de satisfaction, mais on relève néanmoins des différences. Ainsi, les femmes sont moins satisfaites que les hommes s'agissant de la démocratie et de la participation politique. Cela pourrait s'expliquer par des considérations historiques. Les plus âgés apparaissent plus satisfaits de la sécurité sociale, sûrement parce qu'ils en profitent davantage. On ne constate pas de grandes différences suivant les niveaux d'études. Les retraités sont les plus satisfaits à l'égard de la sécurité sociale et les chômeurs les moins satisfaits. Les personnes situées dans la tranche supérieure des revenus expriment un plus grand degré de satisfaction que celles situées dans la tranche inférieure concernant la sécurité sociale, la démocratie et la

Tableau 1 – Degré de satisfaction à l'égard de divers domaines de la sphère publique et de la sphère privée, pour certains groupes (1998, Allemagne de l'Ouest)

Satisfaction* à l'égard de ...	Total	Sexe		Age			Niveau d'études			Situation professionnelle			Niveau de revenus (par quintiles)		Nationalité	
		Homme	Femme	18-34 ans	35-59 ans	60 ans et plus	Formation profession-nelle	Niveau brevet	Enseignement secondaire	Emploi	Sans emploi	Retraite	Tranche inférieure	Tranche supérieure	Allemande	Autre
Mariage/ partenaire	8,8	9,0	8,6	8,8	8,7	8,9	8,8	8,8	8,6	8,8	8,5	9,0	8,7	8,7	8,8	8,8
Famille	8,5	8,7	8,4	8,3	8,5	8,9	8,6	8,7	8,3	8,6	7,5	8,9	8,3	8,6	8,5	8,5
Logement	8,3	8,1	8,3	7,8	8,2	8,8	8,3	8,2	8,2	8,1	7,2	8,7	7,6	8,5	8,3	7,3
Quartier	8,1	8,0	8,1	7,6	8,0	8,5	8,1	8,0	8,0	8,0	7,0	8,4	7,9	8,1	8,1	7,3
Lieu de travail	7,7	7,7	7,6	7,6	7,6	8,5	7,6	7,7	7,6	7,7	-	-	8,1	8,1	7,7	7,1
Temps de loisirs	7,6	7,6	7,5	7,2	7,2	8,3	7,6	7,5	7,5	7,2	6,7	8,4	7,3	7,7	7,6	7,0
Situation économique	7,4	7,4	7,4	7,1	7,3	7,7	7,2	7,4	7,8	7,5	5,2	7,7	5,3	8,3	7,4	7,0
Santé	7,4	7,6	7,3	8,4	7,3	6,5	7,0	7,8	7,9	8,0	7,4	6,2	7,0	7,6	7,4	7,9
Revenus	7,0	7,0	7,0	6,7	7,0	7,4	6,8	7,0	7,3	7,1	4,9	7,4	5,0	8,2	7,0	6,2
Sécurité sociale	6,5	6,6	6,4	6,2	6,4	7,0	6,5	6,5	6,6	6,4	5,5	7,1	6,4	6,9	6,5	7,0
Démocratie	6,5	6,7	6,3	6,4	6,5	6,7	6,3	6,4	6,8	6,6	5,9	6,7	6,3	6,9	6,5	6,6
Protection de l'environnement	6,1	6,3	6,0	6,0	6,1	6,4	6,3	6,1	5,9	6,2	6,2	6,3	6,0	6,3	6,1	6,5
Sûreté publique	5,9	6,0	5,9	6,1	5,9	5,9	5,8	5,8	6,2	6,0	5,6	5,9	5,9	5,9	5,9	6,3
Participation politique	5,8	6,0	5,5	5,5	5,8	6,0	5,5	5,8	6,3	5,9	4,7	6,0	4,9	5,8	5,8	4,4

* Échelle de satisfaction de 0 (pas du tout satisfait) à 10 (tout à fait satisfait)

Base de données : Wohlfahrtssurvey, 1998.

Source : Statistisches Bundesamt 2000, p. 432 et suivantes.

participation politique. D'une manière générale, les Allemands notent mieux leur participation politique que la sécurité sociale. A l'évidence, les conditions d'existence influent sur la satisfaction en fonction des intérêts de chacun. Nous en examinerons les raisons au dernier chapitre. Contre toute attente, les plus riches sont plus satisfaits des biens publics que les plus pauvres. On peut supposer qu'ils pallient les insuffisances des biens publics en utilisant leur revenu privé.

b. *Caractéristiques individuelles/Caractéristiques collectives*

Dans toute entité collective, on peut distinguer les caractéristiques individuelles des caractéristiques de l'ensemble, par exemple la richesse d'un individu par opposition à la richesse de la collectivité. Chaque individu a une perception des caractéristiques qui lui sont propres et de celles de sa collectivité d'appartenance.

L'exemple le plus courant est l'opposition entre la perception que les individus ont de leur situation personnelle et leur perception de la situation globale. Le problème est que l'on a tendance à valoriser la première au détriment de la seconde. Les biens publics entrent dans la même catégorie que les biens collectifs, au sens où ils échappent à l'emprise de l'individu. Dans bien des cas, on observe des différences de perception, par exemple :

- satisfaction personnelle concernant sa propre vie/satisfaction à l'égard de la vie au niveau national ;

- sentiment personnel de la justice/évaluation de la justice dans le pays ;

- évaluation de la situation économique personnelle/conditions économiques nationales ;

- perception des conflits personnels/intensité générale des conflits ;

- satisfaction quant à sa propre sécurité sociale/satisfaction concernant le niveau général de la sécurité sociale dans la région.

Quel que soit le point soulevé, on obtient des résultats différents pour les caractéristiques individuelles et les caractéristiques de l'ensemble. Et l'on constate une tendance manifeste à évaluer plus positivement les conditions personnelles que les conditions collectives.

c. Bien-être personnel et bien-être national

Dans les débats à propos du bien-être, un discours revient toujours selon lequel un seul item ne saurait décrire le bien-être subjectif. Certes, un seul item ne pourra jamais rendre compte de la différenciation ni de la complexité du bien-être subjectif. Cela permet néanmoins d'en brosser un tableau sommaire véhiculant le principal message. Un petit nombre d'items pourrait fournir une représentation plus instructive du bien-être subjectif. Une approche intéressante, dans la ligne de la déconstruction du bien-être, nous est fournie par le *Personal Well-being Index* (PWI) et son complément, le *National Well-being Index* (NWI) (Cummins, 2007 ; voir figure 4 ci-après). Le PWI comporte sept items relatifs à la perception qu'ont les individus de leur vie, tandis que les six composantes du NWI se rapportent à la vie de la nation en général.

Figure 4 – Indice du bien-être personnel et national
Représentation du bien-être personnel par sept items à partir de la question suivante :
Dans quelle mesure êtes-vous satisfait des aspects suivants ?

❏ niveau de vie	77,8
❏ santé	75,1
❏ réussite dans la vie	74,8
❏ relations personnelles	81,3
❏ sentiment de sécurité	79,0
❏ sentiment d'appartenance à votre communauté	71,2
❏ sécurité future	71,4
Indice du bien-être personnel	**75,8**

Représentation du bien-être national par six items à partir de la question suivante :
Dans quelle mesure êtes-vous satisfait des aspects suivants ?

❏ situation économique dans votre pays	66,1
❏ état de l'environnement naturel dans votre pays	59,6
❏ conditions sociales	62,6
❏ gouvernement de votre pays	55,8
❏ activité commerciale dans votre pays	60,9
❏ sécurité nationale dans votre pays	65,2
Indice du bien-être national	**61,6**

Source : Cummins, 2007

Les réponses sont données sur une échelle de onze points numérotés de 0 à 10, où 0 = « pas du tout satisfait » et 10 = « tout à fait satisfait ». Plusieurs tests conduits dans différents pays sur la base de cette

échelle témoignent de sa bonne capacité de mesure. Les items considérés semblent pertinents dans la quasi-totalité des pays (Lau, Cummins et McPherson, 2005).

L'intérêt est la distinction établie entre bien-être personnel et bien-être national. Le bien-être national se situe en moyenne un peu en dessous du bien-être personnel, et les plus hautes valeurs du NWI sont toujours au-dessous de la plus basse valeur du PWI. Les composantes des deux indices ne sont pas sur le même niveau mais dans chaque cas elles se situent dans la limite supérieure ou inférieure de l'intervalle de dispersion.

Pour l'heure, le PWI est disponible dans des pays comme l'Australie ainsi que dans plusieurs pays d'Europe. Il est démontré que la hiérarchie des pays européens reste la même que pour la mesure de la satisfaction générale à l'égard de la vie. Ainsi, le PWI de l'Irlande est supérieur à celui de l'Italie et de l'Espagne, ces deux pays se situant à leur tour au-dessus de la Roumanie. Dans chaque pays, le NWI est inférieur au PWI.

Conclusions

Les données présentées ici et de nombreuses autres démontrent que les perceptions des biens et caractéristiques varient : la valeur associée à un bien est d'autant plus élevée qu'il est proche de l'individu et moins élevée dès lors que l'on ne se situe plus sur le plan individuel. Différentes terminologies rendent compte de ce problème : le degré de satisfaction vis-à-vis des biens publics est inférieur au degré de satisfaction vis-à-vis des biens privés, la satisfaction relative aux caractéristiques collectives est inférieure à celle relative aux caractéristiques individuelles, le niveau de bien-être national est inférieur au niveau de bien-être personnel. Il y a manifestement une perception déséquilibrée, qui se maintient dans le temps et reste stable entre les groupes de population. Toute chose qui, dans un sens social, est loin de l'individu semble être moins satisfaisante que si elle en est proche. Certaines hypothèses pourraient expliquer une telle différence :

- Les divers degrés de satisfaction pourraient traduire des différences dans le niveau réel de fourniture des biens (par ex. richesse privée/ pauvreté publique). Les biens publics sont souvent plus rares que les biens privés. En conséquence, la satisfaction envers les aspects du domaine public est moindre. On remarquera, cependant, que la note moyenne qui leur est attribuée est supérieure à la moyenne numérique de l'échelle de satisfaction : d'une manière générale, les

gens sont globalement satisfaits. Cela étant, il ne faut pas négliger le fait que certains biens publics obtiennent des scores plus élevés et d'autres des scores moins élevés. Autrement dit, il y a des différences entre les niveaux de satisfaction suivant les biens publics.

- Un aspect à prendre en compte pour expliquer cette différence entre biens privés et biens publics est que l'acquisition des premiers répond à un désir, alors que les seconds sont donnés. S'agissant des biens privés, chacun se trouve certes limité par son budget, mais s'agissant des biens publics, leur fourniture est principalement une décision politique sur laquelle les particuliers n'exercent pas d'influence directe.

- Les biens privés ont un coût tandis que les biens publics sont payés indirectement par le biais des impôts et taxes ou des contributions sociales. Le coût est nul pour l'usager. Or selon une vieille théorie, une chose qui ne coûte rien est moins appréciée ; en revanche, s'il faut y mettre le prix, elle est très appréciée.

- Les aspirations et attentes sont plus importantes pour les biens publics que pour les biens privés. Dans la mesure où ils ne coûtent rien, le budget ne constitue pas un frein, d'où une augmentation sans limite des attentes.

- Selon une autre théorie le processus d'appropriation est important pour les degrés de satisfaction. Lorsqu'une personne ne considère pas un bien comme le produit de son activité, elle est plus facilement insatisfaite que si elle se sent concernée. Quand la personne a prise sur la situation, elle peut modifier sa perception. Un sentiment de responsabilité peut conduire à une plus grande satisfaction.

- Il est facile de se séparer des biens privés que l'on n'apprécie plus, par exemple une vieille voiture ou un mariage malheureux. Dans chaque cas, il est possible d'échapper aux risques liés à la voiture ou aux déboires du mariage. Dans le cas des biens publics, ce n'est généralement pas possible. On ne peut pas non plus améliorer la situation par des actions individuelles.

- La question de l'information se pose. Le rapport aux biens privés relève essentiellement d'une expérience ou d'une observation directe. En revanche, les biens publics sont utilisés dans certaines circonstances : les crèches lorsque l'on a des enfants en bas âge, l'allocation retraite lorsque l'on est suffisamment vieux pour la percevoir, etc. Souvent,

l'on doit répondre à des questions sur l'avenir à long terme, notamment en matière de retraite. Mais on n'en a généralement qu'une vague idée à un horizon de trente ou quarante ans. Les gens se font souvent une idée erronée des biens publics, ce qui pourrait expliquer leur grande insatisfaction.

- Les médias ont une influence sur la connaissance des biens publics et de toutes les caractéristiques n'entrant pas dans le champ individuel. En règle générale, ils privilégient les messages négatifs car cela retient davantage l'attention. Ce faisant, ils contribuent inévitablement à entretenir un faible niveau de satisfaction vis-à-vis des biens publics.

- Au-delà de tous ces facteurs d'irritation, il existe manifestement des différences de satisfaction à l'égard des biens publics, au sein de la population comme à des périodes différentes. Les politiques devraient en tenir compte. Quel que soit le modèle d'Etat providence, ces questions sont essentielles car le jugement des populations (bon ou mauvais) a un impact sur la politique et la société. C'est évidemment important pour la cohésion sociale. L'évaluation des biens publics constitue ainsi un nouvel enjeu pour la recherche et l'élaboration des politiques.

Bibliographie

Références bibliographiques

Alber, J. et Fahey, T., « Wahrnehmung der Lebensbedingungen in einem erweiterten Europa », *Europäische Stiftung zur Verbesserung der Lebens- und Arbeitsbedingungen*, Dublin, 2004.

Andrews, F. M. et Withey, S.B., *Social Indicators of Well-being*, Plenum Press, New York et Londres, 1976.

Bergheim, S., « Deutschland zum Wohlfühlen », in *Deutsche Bank Research*, 14 novembre 2007.

Böhnke, P., « Does Society Matter ? Life Satisfaction in the Enlarged Europe », in *Social Indicators Research*, Springer, 2008, p. 189-210.

Bradburn, N. M., *The Structure of Psychological Well-Being*, Aldine, Chicago, 1969.

Camfield, L., « Subjective measures of well-being in developing countries », in Glatzer, W., von Below, S. and Stoffregen, M., *Challenges for Quality of Life in the Contemporary World*, Social Indicators Series, vol. 24, Kluwer Academic Publisher, Dordrecht, Boston et Londres, 2004, p. 45-60.

Campbell, A., Converse, P. E. et Rodgers, W. L., *The Quality of American Life. Perceptions, Evaluations and Satisfactions*, Russell Sage Foundation, New York, 1976.

Cummins, R. A., *Australian Unity Wellbeing Index – Survey 18,* Deakin University & Australian Unity Limited, 2007.

Diener, E. et Lucas, R. E., « Subjective emotional well-being» in Lewis M. et Haviland J.M. (dir.), *Handbook of Emotions* (2e éd.), Guilford, New York, 2000, p. 325.

Estes, R., « Development Challenges of the New Europe », in *Social Indicators Research*, Kluwer Academic Publishers, 2004, p. 123-166.

Glatzer, W. et Zapf, W., *Lebensqualität in der Bundesrepublik Deutschland*, Campus Verlag, Francfort et New York, 1984, p. 25.

Gullone, E. et Cummins R. A. (dir.), « The Universality of Subjective Well-being Indicators », *Social Indicators Series*, vol. 16, Kluwer Academic Publisher, Dordrecht, Boston, Londres, 2002.

Halman, L. *et al.*, *Changing Values and Beliefs in 85 Countries. Trends from the Values Surveys from 1981 to 2004*, Brill, Leiden et Boston, 2008.

Holmes K. R., Feulner E. J. et O'Grady M. A., *The 2008 Index of Economic Freedom*, Dow Jones Company, New York, 2008.

Lau, A. L. D., Cummins R. A. et McPherson, W., « An investigation into the cross-cultural equivalence of the Personal Well-Being Index », in *Social Indicators Research*, n° 72, 2005, p. 403-430.

Luechinger, S., Meier, S. et Stutzer, A., « Why does unemployment hurt the Employed ? Evidence from the life satisfaction gap between the public and the private sector », in *Boston Public Policy Discussion Paper*, n° 08-1, 2008.

Michalos, A.C. (dir.), *Citation Classics from Social Indicators Research*, Springer, Dordrecht, 2005.

OCDE, *Subjective elements of Well-being*, Paris, 1974.

OCDE, *Measuring social well-being*, Paris, 1976.

Prescott-Allen, R., *The Well-being of nations. A Country-by-Country Index of Quality of Life and the Environment*, Island Press, Washington, Covelo et Londres, 2001.

Office de planification sociale et culturelle des Pays-Bas, in *The Quality of the Public Sector*, La Haye, 2002.

Statistisches Bundesamt (éd.), *Datenreport 1999*, Bonn, 2000.

Statistisches Bundesamt (éd.), *Datenreport 2006*, Bonn, 2006.

Strack, F., Argyle, M. et Schwarz, N., *Subjective Well-being*, Pergamon Press, Oxford, 1990.

PNUD, Rapport mondial sur le développement humain, New York, 2005.

Veenhoven, R., « Happy life-expectancy. A comprehensive measure of quality of life in nations », in *Social Indicators Research*, 2003, p. 1-58.

Veenhoven, R., *World Data Base of Happiness*, 2008.

Zapf, W., « German Social Report. Living conditions and subjective well-being », in *Social Indicators Research*, vol. 19, n° 1, 1987, p. 1-171.

Pour en savoir plus

Böhnke, P. et Kohler, U., « Well-being and Inequality », in *WZB Discussion Paper*, SP I 2008-201, 2008.

Ferris, A.L., « The 2008 Index of Economic Freedom », in *SINET*, n° 93, 2008, p. 1-3.

Glatzer, W., « Quality of life in the european Union and the United States of America. Evidence from comprehensive indices », in *Applied Research of Quality of Life*, vol. 1, 2006, p. 169-188.

Glatzer, W., « Der Sozialstaat und die wahrgenommene Qualität der Gesellschaft », in *Zeitschrift für Bevölkerungswissenschaft*, 2006, p. 183-204.

Glatzer, W., von Below S. et Stoffregen M., « Challenges for Quality of Life in the Contemporary World », in *Social Indicators Series*, vol. 24, Kluwer Academic Publisher, Dordrecht, Boston et Londres, 2004.

OCDE, *Panorama de la société. Les indicateurs sociaux de l'OCDE,* Editions OCDE, 2006.

Veenhoven, R., « Return of Inequality in Modern Society ? », étude présentée à la conférence de l'Institut mondial pour la recherche sur l'économie du développement (WIDER) sur l'inégalité, la pauvreté et le bien-être humain, Helsinki, 2003.

I. Bien commun, bien-être et responsabilités des collectivités locales

Iuli Nascimento[1]

1. Bien commun et intérêt général

Les crises sociales et les fractures civiques occupent aujourd'hui la scène du paysage politique de la plupart des pays européens. Les citoyens se sentent de moins en moins représentés par leur système de représentation politique. Depuis les années soixante-dix, le taux d'abstention a ainsi presque doublé pour chaque type d'élection : présidentielles, législatives, municipales, européennes (et même régionales à partir de 1986, date de leur création), induisant, au moins en France une diminution de participation des citoyens envers le système de représentation politique. Cette fracture civique atteint toutes les couches de la population, et devient même massive dans les territoires où se concentrent les couches populaires les plus concernées par les effets de la crise sociale (Dapaquit, 2007). Ainsi, la participation des citoyens dans le processus d'une démarche participative et de cohésion sociale se trouve en perte de vitesse.

S'agit-il réellement d'un phénomène d'apolitisme ou s'agit-il plus exactement d'un manque d'identification des citoyens par rapport à leur représentation politique et à leur modèle de développement social en usage ?

Ne s'agirait-il pas également d'une perte de confiance des individus dans le corps politique face à l'augmentation du chômage et des inégalités sociales ?

Sans vouloir apporter de réponses exhaustives, il semblerait que c'est une réelle remise en cause du système du pouvoir politique actuel, de son autorité, de son efficacité et de ses résultats, ainsi que de la remise en cause de l'intégrité de ses représentants, qui est probablement à la base de cette fracture civique. Face aux changements des bases culturelles,

---

1.　Institut d'aménagement et d'urbanisme de la région Ile-de-France (IAURIF).

les anciens modèles de représentativité politique sont en train de s'effondrer. On assiste ainsi, dans plusieurs pays d'Europe et à chaque niveau de représentativité de l'autorité politique, à des efforts pour mettre en place des démocraties participatives. Cette aspiration des collectivités locales vers une démocratie participative ne doit pas rester qu'un simple effet d'affichage politique. Elle doit conduire à un nouveau processus d'apprentissage afin de nous permettre d'élaborer de nouvelles théories et de nouveaux systèmes d'information pour faire face aux changements de la société.

L'objectif doit être de donner une vraie place aux citoyens dans le processus de décision afin de répondre aux vraies questions et aux attentes des citoyens. La responsabilité des collectivités locales dans ce processus est de contribuer à créer un cadre favorable au développement durable, où les notions de «bien commun» et d'intérêt général ne se limiteraient plus aux populations locales, mais s'étendraient à la population mondiale actuelle, ainsi qu'aux générations futures au nom de la solidarité inter-générationnelle. Les collectivités locales doivent contribuer à éviter toute menace de désagrégation sociale afin justement de garantir la cohésion sociale et d'assurer ainsi le bien-être des citoyens. La cohésion sociale d'une société moderne correspond en effet à son pouvoir «d'assurer de façon durable le bien-être de tous ses membres, incluant l'accès équitable aux ressources disponibles, le respect de la dignité dans la diversité, l'autonomie personnelle et collective et la participation responsable» (Conseil de l'Europe, 2005).

La société actuelle connaît une accélération dans sa transformation avec une perte des anciens repères et l'apparition de nouveaux. La crise présente est une crise d'identité dont il faut essayer de comprendre les mécanismes plutôt que faire des corrélations simples entre montée du chômage et violence urbaine, ou mondialisation et désagrégation sociale, par exemple. Les mutations dans les sociétés existent depuis toujours. Elles entraînent obligatoirement des changements et peuvent ainsi créer des problèmes au sein des groupements humains. Afin de s'adapter et de faire face à ces changements, les collectivités locales doivent donc apporter des réponses aux défis que constituent ces mutations.

Dans le contexte actuel de la mondialisation, le modèle économique rend peu transparente la gestion démocratique des pouvoirs locaux et fragilise la légitimité de son action au niveau du territoire. L'économie mondialisée et l'exercice de la démocratie demandent en effet des rythmes et des supports distincts. La première exige l'existence d'un marché global

et se développe à un rythme accéléré. La seconde nécessite l'existence d'un territoire bien défini et géographiquement localisé, qui se développe à un rythme lent. Le contraste entre ces deux rythmes et espaces de développement, qu'il soit économique ou social, peut mettre en cause la confiance en un avenir personnel et collectif de qualité, et induire à une quasi-immobilité du développement social des populations les plus modestes. Le développement d'un libre-échange mal maîtrisé, et sans outil de régulation, peut plonger les sociétés modernes dans une situation d'incertitude et faire disparaître les projets collectifs mobilisateurs.

En général, dans le processus de mondialisation de l'économie, la croissance rapide devrait apporter un surplus de la production, maximiser les bénéfices en faveur des consommateurs et accroître le bien-être des populations. Mais l'imperfection des marchés ne permet pas que ce surplus de la production de biens apporte le bénéfice escompté à l'ensemble de la population mondiale. Tout d'abord, les producteurs de biens et services peuvent jouer avec la justification d'une meilleure « recherche d'efficacité » dans la production, et augmenter ainsi leur surplus au détriment de celui des consommateurs. Ensuite, les producteurs se trouvent de plus en plus concentrés dans un nombre réduit de pays, contrairement aux consommateurs qui eux se retrouvent dispersés sur l'ensemble de la planète. Ce phénomène dilue ainsi la notion de «bien commun». Dans ce contexte, il faut donc veiller à ce que des outils de régulation permettent de compenser les dysfonctionnements du processus de mondialisation.

La mise en place du processus de mondialisation a bouleversé le cadre conceptuel de nos sociétés aussi bien sur le plan culturel et sociétal que sur le plan des échanges commerciaux et financiers. Nous vivons dans un monde où les activités humaines sont en constante accélération, et où les conséquences de l'économie internationalisée ont des répercussions sur la vie des sociétés, exigeant une réflexion sur le contenu et l'évolution des notions de bien commun et de bien-être des populations. Pour ce faire, il faut bâtir de nouveaux cadres de référence afin d'évaluer leurs conséquences et s'ils correspondent à nos exigences et à celles des futures générations. Repenser la notion du bien commun dans le contexte actuel de la mondialisation est donc indispensable pour maintenir la cohésion sociale à l'intérieur de nos sociétés.

La notion de bien commun est une notion proche de celle de « l'intérêt général ». Elle correspond à la satisfaction des besoins des personnes vivant dans un espace donné et qui partagent un projet commun.

Le bien commun est le résultat de leurs propres actions individuelles à l'intérieur et à l'extérieur de cet espace. Les membres de cette société sont donc volontairement solidaires et interdépendants de fait avec l'extérieur. L'espace commun de vie pour la consommation et la satisfaction de leurs besoins doit devenir pertinent avec l'espace de prise de décision des agents économiques qui, à leur tour, vont assurer ces échanges entre groupes de personnes ou sociétés différentes. « Le bien commun est donc, ce qui donne sens au corps social, et par-là, ce qui donne du sens à l'homme en tant qu'individu comme acteur social » (Rochet, 2001). Dans ce contexte, les collectivités territoriales ont un rôle majeur à jouer.

2. Bien-être et mondialisation

a. L'internationalisation de l'économie, un processus entamé de longue date

Il ne s'agit pas ici de faire de l'historicisme ou du déterminisme entre la mondialisation et le bien-être des populations, mais il est nécessaire de faire un bref point sur l'émergence du processus de mondialisation de l'économie. Elle résulte d'un processus commencé depuis fort longtemps. La planète a vécu des phases successives d'internationalisation de l'économie. La première phase couvre la période qui va de 1840 à 1914. Cette phase est marquée par une tentative de normalisation des prix des produits du commerce des biens standards (commodités), et aussi par des phénomènes tels que les migrations humaines et les déplacements des capitaux qui se sont manifestés au sein de l'espace atlantique et sur les marchés asiatiques. Cette phase se termine lors de la guerre 1914-1918. Cette première phase de mondialisation a entraîné de nombreux sacrifices à cette époque, mais de nombreux consommateurs ont tiré profit du marché qui s'est ainsi créé.

Pendant les années suivant la première guerre mondiale, et jusqu'en 1945, naît un esprit de revanche et sont apparues les guerres idéologiques et commerciales, le développement de l'exploitation des colonies et le partage de leurs ressources naturelles, accompagnés de tragédies telles qu'Auschwitz, Hiroshima... Pour réguler les relations économiques internationales, des institutions ont été créées afin d'instaurer des règles du jeu en matière commerciale, monétaire et financière. En 1947, une nouvelle phase de mondialisation de l'économie débute et une vingtaine

d'Etats signent la Charte de la Havane[2] pour libéraliser leurs échanges dans un cadre multilatéral. Depuis la signature de cette charte, 139 pays ont rejoint le GATT[3], aujourd'hui l'OMC,[4] avec pour objectif d'assouplir leurs politiques commerciales. Depuis cette époque, l'expansion du volume des échanges a une contribution sans précédent à la croissance de la production mondiale.

Depuis les années 1970, l'internationalisation de l'économie a pris de l'ampleur et les peuples ont pris conscience de leur interdépendance. Parallèlement, les entreprises ont étendu leurs activités au-delà des frontières nationales. Aujourd'hui différents types d'interconnexion (télécommunication, transports aériens, nouvelles technologies…) se matérialisent et maillent l'ensemble de la planète. Des agences et organisations scientifiques, culturelles, politiques, internationales et nationales, intergouvernementales et non gouvernementales prolifèrent sur la scène internationale. Le développement des techniques de communication met en lumière le rôle grandissant des entreprises multinationales et, à l'opposé, l'affaiblissement du rôle de l'Etat dans l'économie internationalisée. Au XXe siècle le rôle de l'Etat était prépondérant dans les innovations majeures : l'instauration du libre-échange, les transports routiers, le creusement des canaux, les chemins de fer, les câbles transocéaniques…

Le résultat de ce processus est la mondialisation telle qu'elle est apparue dans les décennies 1960 à 1980 : celle du « village global » décrite par McLuhan (1968) ou celle de la « globalisation des marchés » (Levitt, 1983), ou bien encore celle du « monde sans frontières » (Ohmae, 1999). C'est-à-dire, un village planétaire diversifié et modifié par la réduction de l'effet de distance et l'information généralisée ; un monde sans barrières s'accompagnant d'une prise de conscience progressive d'un patrimoine et de valeurs communes apportées par les bienfaits du progrès scientifique. Les

---

2. La charte de La Havane, signée le 24 mars 1948, proposée par les USA à la fin de la seconde guerre mondiale. Les règles ne sont pas suivies immédiatement, mais la charte prévoit la création d'une Organisation internationale du commerce (OIC). Il s'agit d'un réel accord puisqu'il institue une véritable organisation.

3. General Agreement on Tariffs and Trades : Accord général sur les tarifs douaniers et le commerce, signé à Genève en 1947, afin d'organiser les politiques douanières des signataires. En 1955, l'Organisation de coopération commerciale complète le GATT.

4. L'Organisation mondiale du commerce (OMC) (World Trade Organization, WTO). Organisation internationale qui s'occupe des règles régissant le commerce entre les pays. Elle doit aider les pays importateurs et exportateurs à mener leurs activités, par la réduction d'obstacles au libre-échange.

effets du « progrès » accompli depuis 1990 peuvent conduire à contester cette mondialisation, car l'abondance apportée par la croissance économique mondiale à certains, n'a pas apporté le bien-être à la grande majorité de la population de la planète. C'est un fait que la mondialisation est aujourd'hui une réalité qui va au-delà des systèmes politiques et idéologiques et qui est marquée par l'emprise du capitalisme, du marché, du néolibéralisme[5] et de technologies toujours à la recherche d'une meilleure productivité. Cette réalité a conduit à des modifications rapides dans les relations entre certaines parties du monde et le monde globalisé.

Les changements considérables qui s'opèrent actuellement dans le monde, induits par le libre-échange et la concurrence marchande, exigent une réflexion sur la relation entre la mondialisation de l'économie et le bien commun, entre la mondialisation et l'intérêt général des populations, et entre la mondialisation et le rôle des états au niveau des enjeux économiques. Est-ce que « l'état de libre-échange » du processus actuel de mondialisation crée les conditions nécessaires pour que l'économie atteigne un optimum et apporte ainsi le maximum de satisfaction aux populations ? Est-ce que l'ampleur des conflits d'intérêts que les Etats doivent arbitrer entre les protagonistes de ces conflits met en cause la notion de «bien commun» ou d'intérêt général ?

Les avantages du libre-échange et de l'ouverture du monde à l'économie peuvent être illustrés par le postulat de « l'équilibre concurrentiel[6] » qui définit un monde sans Etat, des entreprises sans pouvoir de marché et un appareil de production totalement malléable. Par ailleurs, les imperfections du marché international et les réglementations publiques nationales freinent une dynamique équilibrée du libre-échange. En effet, les états membres de l'OMC dirigent un processus exposant les dirigeants politiques aux pressions des groupes d'intérêts économiques. Autrement dit, l'OMC est une agence intergouvernementale où les représentants officiels des pays poursuivent une double mission : négocier au mieux les intérêts de leur propre pays et essayer d'éliminer les pratiques protectionnistes de leurs partenaires.

---

5. Intervention limitée de l'Etat.

6. L'équilibre général de concurrence parfaite permettrait le plein emploi de tous les facteurs de production. C'est-à-dire que toute la population active serait occupée et que tous les capitaux seraient utilisés pour permettre de satisfaire toutes les demandes solvables (Léon Walras, 1834-1910).

Il faut souligner que la mondialisation contemporaine dépasse les frontières des biens matériels. Elle intègre des échanges internationaux avec une part importante de prestations de services, incorporées ou non aux marchandises. Ces services sont tributaires d'informations transmises par satellites, qui relèvent de la responsabilité de l'Etat. Le caractère immatériel d'internet modifie l'efficacité de toute forme de contrôle sur les négociations commerciales des services financiers, des services des transports, des industries culturelles, des industries cinématographiques, des droits de propriété intellectuelle… Dans un tel contexte, où faut-il mettre la barrière entre ce qui est du domaine de la puissance publique et celle qui est du marché ? Ainsi, à force de promouvoir la libre concurrence, la mondialisation empêche les pouvoirs publics d'apporter des aides financières aux politiques industrielles de chaque pays. De ce fait, les politiques économiques nationales ne peuvent plus s'appuyer sur la demande interne en raison des répercussions qu'elles peuvent avoir sur le commerce extérieur. Enfin, la libre circulation des capitaux limite l'autonomie et la marge de manœuvre des pouvoirs publics nationaux en matière de politiques fiscales et monétaires.

Un des paradoxes de la mondialisation orientée par l'OMC est une constante revendication de libre accès aux marchés étrangers et la dénonciation des barrières à l'importation de façon unilatérale sans aucun esprit libre-échangiste. De ce fait, la mondialisation entretient certes la croissance économique, mais génère des inégalités et des exclusions sociales. La société actuelle est ainsi le théâtre de trois grandes transformations : le pouvoir de l'Etat, la distribution des responsabilités en matière de choix publics et le contenu de la notion de «bien commun» et d'intérêt général.

Dans ce contexte, l'ensemble des services publics doit être repensé et réorganisé pour harmoniser la dimension citoyenne et la dimension commerciale de la mondialisation. C'est là que se trouve l'enjeu majeur de la démocratie participative. L'affaiblissement de la représentativité des élus par une diminution de la participation des citoyens aux élections doit être compensé par un appel à une autre forme de participation à la décision publique pour défendre l'intérêt général des citoyens et les politiques publiques en général. Les associations de consommateurs-usagers et les associations non gouvernementales sont a priori les partenaires principaux des concertations entre les pouvoirs publics et la population. Par ce biais, les citoyens peuvent avoir une part importante de responsabilité dans le processus de décision politique.

b. La mondialisation et la notion de «bien commun»

Le processus de mondialisation actuelle est marqué par une croissance inégalement distribuée entre les zones urbaines et rurales, entre les régions, entre les pays et entre les continents. Cette croissance inégalement répartie est de toutes natures : économique, démographique, des connaissances, des revenus, de l'augmentation de la durée de vie... Ces inégalités au regard des fruits de la croissance affectent les modes de vie des populations et ne peuvent pas durer éternellement (Dollfus, 2007).

En Europe, les directives européennes ont force de lois. Cependant les responsabilités des Etats n'en ont pas été allégées pour autant. Elles ont, au contraire, été complexifiées par la notion de «bien commun» dégagée par ces directives. Les services publics doivent concilier leur mission d'intérêt général et celle d'ouverture à la concurrence. Dans le cadre du développement durable, les notions de bien commun et d'intérêt général ne se limitent plus à la population mondiale actuelle, mais s'étendent également aux générations futures au nom de la solidarité intergénérationnelle. Penser «le bien commun» suppose donc d'organiser diverses composantes autour d'un projet : les composantes matérielles (les ressources physiques et financières), les composantes immatérielles (l'identité et le sentiment d'appartenance) et le projet lui-même qui fédère les deux composantes (le long terme).

La Stratégie de Lisbonne a proposé sans succès de faire de l'économie européenne une économie plus compétitive, s'appuyant sur la connaissance et l'innovation technologique, afin d'assurer un niveau élevé de protection sociale, donc de bien-être. D'autres voies doivent continuer à être explorées dans la recherche en faveur de « l'Etat de bien-être » des populations. Ainsi, le nouveau traité européen modifié et signé le 13 décembre 2007 à Lisbonne par les chefs d'Etat et de gouvernement des 27 pays membres de l'Union européenne est, selon certains, une occasion manquée : les enjeux « environnementaux » ont été passés sous silence et aucune des réformes institutionnelles proposées ne permettra de mieux prévenir les crises majeures qui s'annoncent et que confirment, rapport après rapport, les experts[7].

Le rapport de la Stratégie de Lisbonne reprend pour l'essentiel les dispositions précédentes du Traité de Maastricht sur le développement durable sans laisser de marge de manœuvre à la participation des citoyens

---

7. *Le journal de l'environnement*, 14 décembre 2007.

européens dans les enjeux environnementaux. Le seul moyen de participer donné aux citoyens européens est le droit de pétition qui requiert un million de signatures. Ce droit ne représente qu'une proposition à l'Union européenne et n'est pas une obligation de prendre en compte les propositions des citoyens. Par contre, sur le plan de l'énergie, la politique de l'Europe clairement définie est de continuer à promouvoir le développement des énergies nouvelles et renouvelables. Dans ce contexte, peu de place est donnée à la participation citoyenne.

Force est de constater que la dernière édition du rapport sur le développement humain montre que le monde n'a jamais produit autant de richesse et que paradoxalement la pauvreté augmente au sein même des pays les plus développés. La réflexion de « l'Etat sur le bien commun » doit faire partie de toutes stratégies de développement, qu'elles soient européennes, nationales, régionales... car c'est cette notion qui donne un sens au corps social, donc qui donne une existence à l'homme en tant qu'individu et acteur social.

Les outils statistiques dont nous disposons actuellement ne sont pas capables de mesurer les avantages et les satisfactions réels apportées par la mondialisation (libre-échange) à la notion de bien commun. La réalité est plus complexe. La satisfaction des consommateurs (citoyens) et la notion de bien commun ne se réduisent pas à l'addition d'intérêts d'individus ou de petits groupes séparés les uns des autres, et cela au détriment de la majorité de la population mondiale.

Récemment, le Grenelle de l'Environnement en France a rappelé qu'un grand nombre de nos activités induisent des émissions de gaz à effet de serre contribuant ainsi au réchauffement planétaire. Le quotidien français *Les Echos* du 21 novembre 2007 a publié un article intitulé « La désertification s'empare des sols fertiles » illustrant ainsi la responsabilité de l'activité humaine dans la dégradation de l'ensemble des sols agricoles dans le monde. Le constat est assez inquiétant : les zones de désert ainsi que l'érosion des sols augmentent considérablement. *L'International Soil Reference and Information Center* (ISRIC) annonce que 200 000 km^2 de sols sont érodés chaque année, ce qui correspond à l'équivalent de la surface du Royaume-Uni. Les équilibres sociaux et écologiques s'effondrent et induisent des perturbations de plus en plus rapides et importantes :

- désertification ;

- changements climatiques (réchauffement planétaire) ;

- forte et rapide expansion urbaine (opposition entre zones urbaines et zones rurales) ;

- augmentation de l'exclusion sociale (accès à l'eau potable, aux services de santé, à l'habitation, à l'éducation,…) ;

- changements démographiques importants (vieillissement des populations, immigration et pression de l'augmentation de la population mondiale) ;

- augmentation de la pauvreté dans le monde ;

- impacts sanitaire et environnemental des pesticides ;

- catastrophes naturelles et technologiques à répétition…

Pour faire face à la crise planétaire, l'économie mondialisée envisage plusieurs solutions concernant la production d'énergies renouvelables, telles que le développement des biocarburants provenant des huiles végétales et des céréales, présenté par certains groupes comme étant le remède miracle. Pour développer ce type de combustible, l'agriculture industrielle doit faire un appel massif à l'utilisation d'engrais chimiques et de pesticides. Ce modèle de développement économique est un moteur de croissance mais n'apporte aucune réponse aux problèmes de cohésion sociale et de bien-être des populations. L'augmentation de la pauvreté et de la faim dans le monde en est la preuve. La rapidité des mutations favorisée par la technologie, ne génère plus le bien-être et la cohésion sociale de l'ensemble du système socio-économique. Il est donc grand temps d'affiner et d'adapter la notion de bien commun aux projets collectifs pour affirmer la légitimité des collectivités locales à délibérer sur l'avenir des populations, l'amélioration de leur cadre de vie et sur l'avenir du monde en général.

3. Rôles, responsabilités et outils à la disposition des collectivités territoriales – L'exemple de la France et de la région Ile-de-France

a. Les responsabilités des collectivités locales et le bien-être des populations

La mise en place effective du concept de développement durable peut redonner un sens à la responsabilité des collectivités locales et rendre efficace les actions pour mettre en œuvre un modèle de développement

socio-économique plus équitable, puisqu'il peut être décliné en de multiples domaines sectoriels. Partant du concept suffisamment global et polymorphe de développement durable, la notion de bien-être peut se décliner dans presque toutes les politiques publiques locales. L'approche systémique de l'action humaine dans l'ensemble biophysique de la planète doit permettre de réfléchir à l'avenir des sociétés : traiter les parties (les territoires) en interaction avec le milieu naturel et l'activité de l'homme. C'est le message principal du Sommet de la Terre (Rio de Janeiro, 1992) et le principal enjeu de développement durable mis en évidence par l'Agenda 21 de Rio, donnant lieu aux agendas 21 locaux.

L'exemple d'articulation, illustré ci-après par les outils réglementaires mis à disposition des collectivités locales susceptibles de garantir à la population une qualité de vie et de bien-être acceptable, sera celui d'Ile-de-France.

Deux schémas régionaux principaux définissent le rôle de la région Ile-de-France afin d'assurer son développement de façon intégrée. Il s'agit du Schéma régional de développement économique et du Schéma directeur régional d'Ile-de-France. Le rôle du premier est de coordonner sur son territoire les actions de développement économique des collectivités territoriales et de leurs groupements, sous réserve des missions incombant à l'Etat. D'après l'article L. 1511-1 du code général des collectivités territoriales, l'Etat peut confier à la région le soin d'élaborer un schéma régional de développement économique. Ce schéma expérimental définit et promeut les orientations stratégiques pour un développement économique équilibré. Il vise à développer l'attractivité de son territoire et veille à prévenir les risques d'atteinte à l'équilibre économique de tout ou partie de la région. Ce schéma une fois adopté par délégation de l'Etat, la région devient compétente pour attribuer des aides aux entreprises.

Le rôle du Schéma directeur régional d'Ile-de-France est de définir l'aménagement du territoire dans son ensemble. Il peut être modifié par le président du Conseil régional en accord avec l'Etat et à condition que ces modifications ne portent pas atteinte à l'économie générale du schéma de développement économique. Après enquête publique, le projet de schéma directeur peut être modifié afin de prendre en compte les observations des citoyens et les avis émis par les personnes publiques consultées. Il est adopté par le Conseil régional et approuvé par l'autorité administrative. En cas d'opposition d'un département, les modifications sont approuvées par décret en Conseil d'Etat.

La déclaration d'utilité publique ou la déclaration de projet est prononcée après examen de la validité du schéma en concertation avec l'Etat, la région

Ile-de-France, le Conseil économique et social régional, les départements et les chambres consulaires. La « déclaration d'utilité publique » correspond à l'approbation des nouvelles dispositions du schéma directeur de la région Ile-de-France. Elle est prise par décret en Conseil d'Etat en cas d'opposition de la région. La déclaration de projet ne peut intervenir qu'après mise en compatibilité du schéma par l'autorité administrative et, en cas de désaccord de la région, par décret en Conseil d'Etat.[8] Ensuite le schéma est soumis à enquête publique pendant deux mois. Ainsi tous les acteurs dans le périmètre d'une région peuvent intervenir en ce qui concerne les lignes directives du schéma directeur régional.

A partir de ces deux schémas régionaux, la notion de bien-être peut être déclinée selon six grands thèmes du développement durable, et qui sont de la responsabilité des politiques publiques locales : l'organisation et l'aménagement de l'espace, le développement social, le développement des activités économiques et de l'emploi, les déplacements et la mobilité, l'écogestion des ressources naturelles, l'énergie et les déchets, la coopération décentralisée ainsi que la lutte contre les menaces globales. Dans ces grands thèmes il est possible de développer la notion de bien commun et de bien-être des populations. Une bonne articulation des outils réglementaires mis à disposition des collectivités locales devrait permettre d'éclaircir leurs responsabilités à l'égard de ces deux notions et de rendre effective la mise en place du développement durable aux différents niveaux des territoires.

En ce qui concerne l'organisation et l'aménagement de l'espace, des procédures existantes en France peuvent constituer des outils efficaces pour garantir le bien-être des populations et faire émerger une politique de développement durable : le Schéma de cohérence territoriale (SCOT), le Plan local d'urbanisme (PLU), le Plan d'aménagement et de développement durable (PADD), le Programme local d'habitation (PLH), la loi Solidarité et renouvellement urbain (SRU) et le Plan de déplacements urbains (PDU).

Le SCOT est conçu par les élus. Il remplace l'ancien Schéma directeur d'aménagement et d'urbanisme local et doit mettre en cohérence les politiques d'urbanisme, d'habitat, de déplacements et d'équipement commercial à l'échelle d'une aire urbaine. Il fixe les objectifs d'aménagement et d'urbanisme afin d'articuler toutes les démarches de planification

---

8.   Article 2 du code de l'urbanisme L. 141-1-2 – Projet de loi relatif aux libertés et responsabilités locales (texte définitif).

et de programmation. Il est conçu pour assurer : d'une part, l'équilibre entre la maîtrise du développement, du renouvellement urbain et du développement des territoires ruraux ; d'autre part, la préservation des espaces agricoles et forestiers, ainsi que la protection des espaces naturels et des paysages.

Enfin, il se doit en outre de respecter la diversité des fonctions urbaines et la mixité sociale dans l'habitat et l'emploi. En résumé, il doit assurer une mise en valeur économe et équilibrée des espaces urbains, périurbains, naturels et ruraux.

Le PLU, remplace le Plan d'occupation des sols (POS). Il détermine l'affectation des espaces à l'échelle communale ou intercommunale. Il doit comporter un PADD définissant l'organisation générale en termes d'urbanisme et d'aménagement du territoire communal. Il peut éventuellement fournir des indications précises sur la vocation de certains espaces ou quartiers. Ce document est conçu à l'échelle de la commune et constitue le référentiel pour les actions d'aménagement en matière de politique d'habitat, de traitement des espaces publics et de préservation des paysages. Il se doit aussi d'identifier et de donner un caractère opérationnel aux secteurs qui ont vocation à se renouveler ou à être protégés.

Le PLH, outil de programmation, définit l'offre de logements sociaux (il définit surtout l'équilibre entre logements sociaux et logements non sociaux) et planifie pour une durée de cinq ans les efforts de la collectivité dans la construction de logements neufs ou dans la réhabilitation de logements anciens. La loi SRU encourage l'élaboration de PLU intercommunaux afin de permettre la définition d'une politique d'habitat à une échelle géographique adéquate à la demande d'un « bassin d'habitat » et en cohérence avec le SCOT. La loi SRU renforce les procédures de concertation autour de la révision d'un PLU ou d'un POS.

Dans le cadre du développement social, le traitement des grands dysfonctionnements sociaux, comme la pauvreté, le chômage, l'habitat dégradé ou insalubre, la violence... est pour une petite partie de la responsabilité des collectivités locales ; le chômage et la pauvreté relèvent plutôt de politiques nationales et non locales. Cette responsabilité s'étend aux dysfonctions dans le domaine de l'environnement, de l'économie et du social. Dans le domaine de l'environnement, ces dysfonctionnements sont de plusieurs ordres : l'exposition des ménages aux nuisances sonores, la présence de friches industrielles, les pollutions des sous-sols, la présence des déchets inertes, la dégradation des milieux naturels... Dans le domaine de l'économie, ce sont l'augmentation du chômage,

la diminution des ressources financières locales… Dans le domaine social, les difficultés de reclassement des anciens salariés, la dévitalisation du tissu social, l'augmentation de la pauvreté… L'article L. 214-12 du code de l'éducation confie à la région le rôle de mise en œuvre de la politique régionale d'apprentissage et de formation professionnelle des jeunes et des adultes à la recherche d'un emploi ou d'une nouvelle orientation professionnelle. La région est ainsi censée organiser sur le territoire les réseaux et points d'information et de conseil sur la validation des acquis de l'expérience professionnelle, parallèlement à l'organisation des actions destinées à répondre aux besoins d'apprentissage et de formation.

Le développement des activités économiques et de l'emploi est l'une des responsabilités majeures des collectivités territoriales. Cependant, les pratiques actuelles ne favorisent pas une approche intégrée avec les aspects environnementaux et sociaux lors de l'implantation d'entreprises ou de projets de valorisation économique des ressources locales.

La responsabilité des collectivités locales dans le domaine des déplacements et de la mobilité de la population est assez importante. Elles disposent des leviers d'action, définis dans le PDU, pour infléchir la tendance à la croissance des déplacements individuels en automobile que l'on constate depuis plusieurs dizaines d'années.

A l'échelle d'une agglomération, le PDU, tel qu'il est défini dans la loi sur l'air et l'utilisation rationnelle de l'énergie, est obligatoire pour les agglomérations de plus de 100 000 habitants. Son ambition est de réduire à terme la part des déplacements automobiles au bénéfice de celle des transports en commun, du vélo et de la marche à pied.

Les collectivités locales doivent donc mettre en place un certain nombre de mesures pour favoriser un rééquilibrage des déplacements et de la mobilité :

- aménager des sites propres pour les transports en commun, les vélos, les piétons ;

- agir sur le stationnement par la réglementation, la tarification, la création de parcs relais… ;

- optimiser le transport de marchandises en centre-ville par la création de plates-formes de livraison en périphérie, par les livraisons avec des véhicules non-polluants… ;

- articuler l'urbanisme et les déplacements par le positionnement des nouvelles zones à urbaniser le long des infrastructures des transports collectifs.

La responsabilité des collectivités locales dans le domaine de l'écogestion des ressources naturelles, de l'énergie et des déchets est au premier rang pour réaliser les objectifs qui lui sont assignés. Il s'agit notamment de maîtriser les impacts du développement économique et social sur l'environnement. Cette responsabilité doit se traduire par la recherche de la protection des écosystèmes fragiles, par la gestion économe des ressources naturelles, par une réduction de la consommation des matières premières et d'énergie et par une réduction de la production de déchets.

Un certain nombre de ces actions ont des incidences directes sur la qualité de vie et le bien-être des populations. Par exemple, la préservation des espaces naturels au milieu et/ou aux abords des villes contribue à la protection et à la valorisation de la faune et de la flore locales, atténuant ainsi les effets de la pollution atmosphérique (parcs naturels, ceintures vertes, aires d'agriculture périurbaine…).

Ces actions apportent une amélioration directe très importante aux conditions de vie des populations urbaines, grâce à la proximité d'espaces récréatifs et à la possibilité de se fournir à peu de distance en produits agricoles de qualité. D'autres actions peuvent paraître de moindre importance mais elles apportent également des bénéfices indirects, comme le tri des déchets, les économies d'eau ou la lutte contre la crise du climat et le réchauffement planétaire, etc.

Les mesures en faveur du traitement des déchets ont permis de diminuer le nombre de décharges sauvages en France. D'autres mesures favorisent également de façon indirecte une meilleure qualité de vie, comme la valorisation des déchets (recyclage, compost individuel, valorisation énergétique…) ou la mise en place de moyens pour la maîtrise de l'énergie (isolation des logements, construction HQE). Elles peuvent aussi correspondre à des opérations pilotes en faveur des énergies renouvelables (éolienne, biomasse, solaire…) contribuant au bien-être des collectivités locales.

Par ailleurs, un plan local de lutte contre l'effet de serre peut apporter des résultats significatifs en combinant des mesures pour la réduction des émissions polluantes produites par les transports et des mesures en faveur de l'économie de l'énergie dans l'habitat et les bâtiments publics.

Dans le cadre de la coopération décentralisée et de la lutte contre les menaces globales, une collectivité locale peut développer des projets visant à stimuler le développement des régions moins favorisées dans le monde. La production d'électricité à partir de panneaux photovoltaïques, de la micro-hydraulique, de la biomasse et d'éoliennes, accompagnée de la formation de techniciens locaux, peut remplacer l'installation de groupes électrogènes à carburants fossiles. Cela permet d'alimenter en énergie une activité artisanale et de réduire la pollution, tout en contribuant à une amélioration de la qualité de vie et de bien-être d'une population défavorisée.

b. Vers un processus d'amélioration du développement durable au niveau des territoires

Affirmer une volonté de mettre en place «le bien commun», c'est affirmer la capacité de l'homme à décider de son avenir et de celui de la planète. La prise en compte du «bien commun» améliore également la créativité, la productivité et la compétitivité des entreprises. Pour penser un développement réellement durable, il faut apprendre à évaluer le profit à long terme. Il faut éviter des conclusions rapides au sujet de la disparition des frontières, de la libéralisation des échanges de biens et de services, de la circulation des capitaux et de l'innovation technologique. L'innovation technologique et la mondialisation peuvent ainsi représenter des possibilités d'ouverture culturelle à condition qu'elles soient conditionnées par un libéralisme raisonné.

Les sociétés humaines sont des systèmes complexes en constante évolution et en déséquilibre. Pour que de tels systèmes fonctionnent, il faut faire des ajustements en permanence. Les collectivités locales doivent être garantes du bon fonctionnement de ces systèmes afin d'éviter une régression sociale. Les associations non gouvernementales représentatives de la société peuvent et doivent contribuer à assurer le bien-être des citoyens. Le transfert du pouvoir de décision à des autorités indépendantes peut par ailleurs être assez nuisible à une collectivité. Il faut éviter que le modèle de développement économique actuel ne devienne plus compliqué que complexe, et que seuls les lobbys soient entendus.

Sur cet aspect, « c'est la politique qui a le plus grand besoin de complexité. Elle produit des idées de plus en plus simplifiantes pour des sociétés de plus en plus complexes. Elle produit des visions de plus en plus unidimensionnelles pour des sociétés de plus en plus multidimensionnelles.

Elle produit des idéologies de plus en plus rationalisatrices pour une réalité de plus en plus incertaine » (Morin, 2004).

L'homme doit être l'acteur actif et responsable dans l'organisation et la gestion de son environnement. Les relations de l'homme avec son territoire permettent de prendre en compte simultanément les intérêts individuels et l'intérêt commun pour la pérennité de ce territoire et la survie du groupe qui y vit. Cela ne peut être effectif qu'avec une coordination des actions des collectivités locales et celles des associations non gouvernementales. Les agendas 21 locaux peuvent ainsi être fort utiles pour mettre en place un développement durable et cohérent au niveau des territoires.

Dans la perspective d'un développement durable, le bien-être de la population et la qualité de l'écosystème apparaissent comme des objectifs incontournables à atteindre à toutes les échelles, l'échelle régionale occupant une position clé. Se fixer des indicateurs de bien-être est un des moyens à mettre en œuvre pour y parvenir. Cela nécessite la réorganisation et l'interopérabilité des systèmes d'information à toutes les échelles (nationale, régionale, départementale et communale) et avec les données ad hoc qui permettent tant des approches techniques approfondies (notamment en termes d'évaluation de la qualité de l'écosystème) que des approches plus simples destinées aux médias et au grand public afin de les sensibiliser aux différents aspects du bien-être humain.

Cet objectif implique que les systèmes existants de recueil de données statistiques puissent fournir un ensemble de données comparables et déclinables aux différentes échelles. Outre les analyses statistiques, dans le cadre des projets de territoire, il est essentiel d'être en mesure de définir des « zones de bien-être » selon différents critères (par exemple, le calme, le patrimoine, la biodiversité sauvage et domestiquée…), afin de maintenir une bonne qualité de vie et de bien-être des populations dans des zones à utilisations mixtes (urbain bâti et ouvert – zones cultivées – aires de nature sauvage…). L'indicateur de qualité de vie et de bien-être développé par la région Ile-de-France, est, parmi d'autres indicateurs du développement durable, un exemple d'effort d'une collectivité territoriale pour mieux saisir la notion de bien commun et ainsi rendre effectif le projet d'écorégion.

L'indicateur composite de bien-être développé par la région Ile-de-France, n'est pas seulement un indicateur, c'est un véritable outil adaptable à différentes échelles territoriales, et qui grâce à sa structure en arborescence transparente et évolutive, permet :

- d'évaluer et de comparer des territoires à un instant donné ;

- de suivre l'évolution de ces territoires ;

- de se fixer des objectifs de bien-être et de cibler les secteurs et les acteurs qui permettraient de les atteindre ;

- de faire des simulations en faisant varier tout ou partie des indices qui le composent ;

- d'évaluer globalement une politique à partir d'un panel d'indicateurs de développement durable, ou plus particulièrement, d'orienter une politique (en développant des arborescences spécifiques).

Le projet politique du Conseil régional de faire de la région Ile-de-France une écorégion, représente une excellente opportunité pour la mise en place d'un développement durable au niveau régional. Bien que le concept de développement durable puisse paraître flou au premier abord, il a le mérite de proposer une approche transversale du développement régional en intégrant l'économie, la sociologie et l'environnement, qui le rend à la fois riche et complexe. Il intègre, en outre, l'échelle temporelle (le long terme) avec la notion de responsabilité vis-à-vis des générations futures, ainsi que le principe de la participation citoyenne et de la gouvernance (l'écologie politique). Transcrire le concept de développement durable au niveau des territoires n'est pas toujours aisé, et son application exige un effort particulier aux spécialistes des différentes disciplines. Les sciences humaines, les sciences de la terre et le développement durable se trouvent ainsi parfois en conflit au regard des objectifs sectoriels. Cependant, le développement durable offre la possibilité de mieux comprendre le fonctionnement des systèmes urbains dans leur globalité et d'aller dans le sens d'une vraie démarche d'écologie urbaine. Etre des citoyens responsables correspondrait tout à fait aux aspirations des Franciliens.

Conclusion

Dans les années 1970, Nicolas Georgescu-Roegen (1995) avait démontré dans sa théorie de la « décroissance », appuyée sur la thermodynamique[9] et l'entropie des systèmes[10], que la croissance économique était le résultat

---

9. Domaine de la physique qui étudie les phénomènes thermiques.

10. En thermodynamique, l'entropie correspond à l'état de désordre d'un système. Elle augmente lorsque celui-ci augmente.

de la productivité d'une société et que cette productivité était fonction de la disponibilité en ressources naturelles et de la force de travail utilisée pour la transformation de ces ressources en biens de consommation. Il résultait de ses travaux le constat que les ressources naturelles n'étaient pas inépuisables et que leur exploitation ne se faisait pas dans le respect de la capacité de résilience[11] des milieux et de l'environnement. Comme il a été dit précédemment, le modèle de développement économique d'après-guerre a eu des conséquences graves sur les sociétés actuelles : les changements climatiques, l'augmentation des risques naturels, la perte de la biodiversité, l'exclusion d'une catégorie de la population mondiale des biens élémentaires à la survie… La croissance correspond à l'accroissement de l'activité économique et ne se traduit pas toujours au niveau de la qualité du cadre de vie et du bien-être des populations. Par contre, le développement correspond à une extension de l'épanouissement de l'être humain et doit conduire à l'approfondissement de la réflexion sur la notion de bien commun.

Le modèle économique fondé sur la croissance industrielle a apporté un préjudice indéniable aux économies rurales et aux ressources naturelles. La mondialisation, telle qu'elle est conduite actuellement, ne fait qu'accélérer le processus d'exclusion des petits centres urbains et des zones rurales du réseau économique mondialisé. Il faut donc veiller à ce que la mondialisation de l'économie ait des externalités positives pour l'ensemble des pays et des régions du monde.

Il importe, pour la région Ile-de-France, de veiller à ce que les aires rurales ne restent pas isolées du réseau économique mondialisé, sans pour autant rompre avec l'équilibre économique et culturel de ces aires. Afin de réorienter le modèle de développement de l'activité humaine au niveau régional, il conviendrait de proposer une nouvelle forme d'organisation de l'espace qui puisse être génératrice de bien-être pour la population. L'écorégion semble être un cadre spatial approprié pour atteindre cet objectif.

Une écorégion se décompose en sous-secteurs géographiques (bassins de vie). Ces bassins de vie sont les lieux de développement et des vecteurs de bien-être de la population. L'ensemble correspond à l'écosystème régional. Ces sous-secteurs géographiques sont les fondements de toute vie sociale, économique et culturelle au sein de l'entité territoriale qu'est la région Ile-de-France. Son équilibre repose à la fois sur son aptitude à

---

11. Ici, la résilience correspond à la capacité de régénération d'un milieu.

répondre aux besoins légitimes de sa population et sur sa capacité à réagir face aux comportements de cette population, qui peuvent être nuisibles au développement durable. Donc, repenser la notion de bien commun dans le contexte actuel de la mondialisation est indispensable pour maintenir la cohésion sociale à l'intérieur de nos sociétés, car en effet, le bien commun est le résultat d'actions individuelles et collectives à l'intérieur et à l'extérieur de l'espace sociétal.

Bibliographie

Références bibliographiques

Conseil de l'Europe, *Elaboration concertée des indicateurs de la cohésion sociale – Guide méthodologique,* Conseil de l'Europe, 2005.

Dapaquit, S., « Crise sociale et fracture civique – Le système d'autorité en question », Forum de la gauche citoyenne, février 2007.

Dollfus, O., *La mondialisation*, La bibliothèque du citoyen, Presses de Sciences Po, 3ᵉ édition, 2007.

Georgescu-Roegen, N., *Demain la décroissance*, Editions Pierre-Marcel Favre. 2ᵉ éd., Sang de la terre, Lausanne et Paris, 1995.

Levitt, T., «The globalization of markets», *Harvard Business Review*, Vol. 61, n° 3, 1983, p. 92-102.

McLuhan M., Fire Q., *War and Peace in the Global Village*, Bantam, New York, 1968.

Morin, E., *Pour rentrer dans le XXIᵉ siècle*, Le Seuil, avril 2004.

Ohmae, K., The Borderless World, power and Strategy in the Interlinked Economy, Rev. ed. HarperCollins Publishers, New York, 1999.

Rochet, C., *Gouverner par le bien commun. Un précis d'incorrection politique à l'usage des jeunes générations*. Cahiers pour la liberté de l'esprit. François-Xavier de Guibert, 2001.

Pour en savoir plus

Bienaymé, A., *Bien commun, concurrence et mondialisation*, Montréal, mai 2001.

Boyer, R., Actes du colloque « Etat et régulation sociale » 11-13 septembre 2006, *L'Etat social à la lumière des recherches régulatrices récentes*, Paris, 2006.

Brachet, Ph, « Le "service public", enjeu de citoyenneté active », Forum de la gauche citoyenne, septembre 2001.

Conseil de l'Europe, *Engagement éthique et solidaire* – Tendances de la cohésion sociale n° 12, Editions du Conseil de l'Europe, décembre 2004.

Nascimento, I., Indicateurs stratégiques de développement durable « un indice de qualité de vie et de bien-être », IAURIF, novembre 2007.

Nascimento, I., « L'Ile-de-France et l'écorégion », in *Notre Planète* : www. notre-planete.info, juin 2006.

O'Neill William, « Remettre sur le métier le bien commun », Ceras - revue *Projet* n° 68, décembre 2001, URL : http://www.ceras-projet.com/index. php?id=1868.

II. Du mal-être au bien-être : responsabilités personnelles et collectives

Catherine Redelsperger[1]

Introduction

Le monde du travail est un lieu de lutte entre des forces qui tentent de créer de la solidarité, du décloisonnement, du dialogue, de l'intégration, de la symbolisation, de la vision partagée et d'autres qui tentent de classer en catégories, en territoires, en expertise close, en langage hermétique, en repli sur soi, en désintégration du collectif.

Partant de l'hypothèse que l'expérience du monde du travail peut contribuer à comprendre, questionner, trouver des pistes sur les processus d'apprentissage d'équilibres et de déséquilibres personnels et collectifs générant du bien-être ou du mal-être, l'auteur se propose de définir trois expressions clés :

- les processus d'apprentissage ;
- les équilibres/déséquilibres personnels et collectifs ;
- les sentiments de bien-être/mal-être.

Elle abordera ensuite ce qu'elle a appris sur ces processus dans le contexte de la recherche d'emploi et dans celui du monde salarié sur trois dimensions : personnelle, collective, et sur la posture de celui qui vient de l'extérieur et agit sur le système.

---

1. Théologienne protestante de formation, Catherine Redelsperger est intervenante pour les entreprises et les associations sur des sujets comme le management, les équipes apprenantes, la gouvernance par des actions d'accompagnement des personnes, des équipes, des organisations.
   Elle est aussi l'auteur d'un thriller philosophique sur les questions de filiation et de bioéthique, *Dayly, Texas*, Hachette littératures, 2007 ; d'une pièce de théâtre, *Le Sauvage*, créée par la compagnie Nie Wiem en avril 2008, pièce dont le thème est le délitement d'une société fondée sur la peur de l'autre ; et de *Météo mélancolique* à paraître fin 2008, Edon éditeurs (graphisme de Nicolas Famery).

1. Propositions de définitions[2]

a. Les processus d'apprentissage

Un processus d'apprentissage est l'explicitation (a priori pour un processus connu, a posteriori pour un processus aléatoire), au fil du temps, de la transformation d'un état initial en état final que vit un individu :

- par observation et confrontation du monde, des autres, de lui-même. De ses observations et de ses confrontations, il induit des lois générales, de la connaissance ;

- par transmission de savoir, de connaissances qui lui permettent d'interpréter les faits.

Ces observations et ces savoirs, l'individu les mémorise, il agit, il s'adapte pour le meilleur (il améliore, il crée pour lui et pour autrui du mieux-être) et pour le pire (il s'enferme, il se détériore, il emporte autrui dans un cercle de mal-être).

La condition nécessaire de l'apprentissage est que l'individu soit en lien avec un autre. On n'apprend pas seul, mais en interaction avec un autre. Parfois l'autre est un animal, parfois il est un objet, parfois il est une invention imaginaire.

Un processus d'apprentissage est celui de vivre. Ce sont des chemins, des détours, des rencontres, des tâtonnements, des questions, des dialogues, des tensions, des erreurs voire des conflits.

Les processus d'apprentissage sont divers en fonction des individus. Ils sont réversibles, des bifurcations sont possibles.

Le contenu du processus d'apprentissage peut-être aussi bien du mal-être que du bien-être. On apprend aussi à mal-être.

---

2. Les définitions proposées ici s'appuient sur *Le Trésor : dictionnaire des sciences*, Michel Serre et Nayla Farouki (dir.), Flammarion, 2000 ; sur un article de Barbara Cassin sur le « esti » et « einai » du poème de la nature de Parménide dans *Vocabulaire européen des philosophies*, Le Seuil, 2004 ; sur diverses lectures sur la complexité et la systémie, et sur l'expérience professionnelle de l'auteur.

b. Les équilibres/déséquilibres personnels et collectifs

Nous nommerons équilibre pour un individu, ou pour un collectif, la combinaison adéquate entre plusieurs «ingrédients». Choisissons par exemple, pour un individu, la combinaison entre sa vie professionnelle et sa vie privée. Si sa vie professionnelle l'envahit, l'absorbe par le volume horaire (ou par son absence de temps de travail dans le cas du chômage), par le stress, par les soucis, au point que sa vie personnelle en est atteinte, il vit un déséquilibre général.

Prenons un autre exemple à l'échelle collective : un département, dans une entreprise, choisit une démarche ouverte, participative, partant de la base pour un projet touchant de près les participants puisqu'il s'agit de dessiner les potentiels de leur parcours professionnel en fonction des évolutions de cette entreprise et de ses besoins de compétences à l'avenir. Des volontaires s'engagent dans cette démarche et découvrent le plaisir de travailler collectivement et leur capacité à prendre des responsabilités. Mais dans ce même département, au quotidien, le fonctionnement est cloisonné, hiérarchique, infantilisant. Au bout de quelques mois, la domination du quotidien sur le mode déresponsabilisant étouffe littéralement les volontaires qui vivent, à cause de cette contradiction, un déséquilibre et un mal-être.

C'est là une première définition du déséquilibre qui se fonde sur une combinaison déréglée par la domination abusive d'un élément générant du mal-être ou par la contradiction entre deux éléments, voire l'injonction paradoxale (le célèbre « Je te donne l'ordre d'être spontané »). Et, par conséquent, une définition de l'équilibre basée sur une combinaison d'éléments de vie, de conditions de vie vécus par l'individu ou le système comme générant du bien-être.

Nous intégrerons aussi dans notre propos la dynamique du rapport équilibre/déséquilibre.

Les scientifiques nous disent que le rapport équilibre/déséquilibre peut être dynamique. Cette notion dynamique nous rend sensibles au fait qu'un équilibre de nature A peut devenir un équilibre de nature B. Le passage de l'un à l'autre passe par un déséquilibre de passage ou de crise. Un exemple très simple peut illustrer ce propos : la crise d'adolescence, déséquilibre physiologique et psychologique, passage de l'enfant à l'adulte.

Ce déséquilibre de transition est nécessaire au processus de bien-être. La culture occidentale y est particulièrement sensible ; les mythes de la création sont ceux de la séparation créatrice : Dieu sépare les eaux du ciel et celles de la terre, il sépare la lumière… Et la psychanalyse nous dit une évidence : pour que l'enfant qui vient de naître vive, il faut qu'il soit séparé de sa mère par la coupe du cordon ombilical. Cette séparation est un déséquilibre de transition qui permet de créer un nouvel équilibre.

Dans le rapport du personnel au collectif, je pose l'hypothèse que si je suis mal avec moi-même, j'ai du mal à générer du bien-être avec les autres ; par contre, je peux le reconstruire avec quelqu'un ou quelques-uns qui génèrent du bien-être. Se pose ici la question de qui est pro-actif, dans le sens de qui prend l'initiative dans la dynamique de passage du déséquilibre à l'équilibre ?

La régulation des équilibres/déséquilibres du collectif à une plus grande échelle (organisation, institution) se fait par la loi (sous ses diverses formes), dont la modification est la résultante de rencontres de personnes et de leurs intérêts (par exemple l'équité salariale hommes-femmes dans les entreprises) ou par des organismes régulateurs.

c. Le sentiment de bien-être/de mal-être

La définition de sentiments de bien-être et de mal-être est complexe. La question de l'être est l'une des questions majeures de la philosophie européenne. Elle l'est par l'usage exceptionnel du verbe « être » qui a un usage syntaxique et lexical, et qui, dans la langue, sert à la cohésion entre sujet et prédicat. Le texte de référence est le *Poème* de Parménide. Nous pouvons retirer de l'interprétation du poème par les philosophes deux enseignements clés pour la suite de notre questionnement :

- Etre c'est vivre, s'épanouir, demeurer (dans le sens de la maison).

- Etre c'est exister, penser et parler.

J'en déduis que le bien-être serait de l'ordre du « c'est » et le mal-être de l'ordre de la négation « ce n'est pas ».

Reste la question du sentiment. « Le sentiment de bien-être et de mal-être » nous met dans le registre de l'émotion, de l'appel aux sens et de la représentation subjective de ce qui est vécu comme bien-être et mal-être. Il est immédiatement sous-entendu la relativité de ce sentiment.

Si l'on s'attarde simplement sur la question de la maltraitance, on comprend très vite qu'il y a deux réalités : celle qui est vécue, et le discours tenu sur elle. Tant qu'il n'était pas dit que faire travailler des enfants était de la maltraitance, ce n'était pas de la maltraitance, y compris pour celui qui la vivait. Il n'avait pas les mots pour le dire, et tous ses points de repère étaient construits sur cette normalité. Ce qui signifie que les sentiments de bien-être et de mal-être sont subjectifs et sociaux, et nécessitent une écoute de l'autre, des autres, en suspension de jugement sur des plans divers comme le sujet parlant, la société parlant au travers du sujet (ce qu'il est censé dire), la stratégie du sujet le traversant (l'intelligence mise au service d'une stratégie de surendettement par exemple). Mais aussi une connaissance de soi, de ses propres représentations et de son propre vécu par rapport au bien-être et au mal-être de la part des praticiens, des décideurs, des penseurs, des experts.

Une question est importante : Qui parle et qui décrète qu'il s'agit là de bien-être ou de mal-être ? Est-ce que je parle ou est-ce que je suis parlé par autrui ?

d. De l'utilisation de ces propositions de définition dans la suite du propos

Les propositions de définition ne sont pas définitives. Elles sont ouvertes, riches par leur dynamique et par les différents points de vue (scientifiques, philosophiques). De plus, les définitions sont en cours de construction. Dans la suite du propos, vous retrouverez des liens avec un ou des aspects des définitions proposées. Elles sont en quelque sorte un arrière-plan du propos qui va être illustratif, et tâtonnant.

2. Processus apprenants pour un retour vers le bien-être : les dimensions personnelles et collectives

Dans la ligne des définitions proposées, le propos qui suit est de décrire des processus de passage d'un mal-être à un bien-être. Le mal-être étant associé à un déséquilibre (par exemple l'absence de travail, la chute de revenu, de considération de soi, de vie sociale) et le processus apprenant pouvant générer momentanément un déséquilibre dans le déséquilibre, c'est-à-dire un déséquilibre de passage (par exemple, sortir de la croyance «je ne pourrai plus trouver de travail»). Le bien-être est associé à un équilibre.

a. La dimension personnelle

L'expression de l'attente et la prise de responsabilité,
ou comment je sors de la fatalité pour reprendre mon destin
en main

J'ai accompagné des demandeurs d'emploi d'une durée supérieure à deux ans vers la reprise d'emploi. Il était difficile à la Direction régionale de l'ANPE de trouver des consultants acceptant ce type de mission. Je l'avais accepté non pas parce que j'étais une superwoman ou un chevalier au panache blanc, mais parce que je savais qu'à partir du moment où une personne s'inscrit, au bout de deux ans de chômage, dans un dispositif d'accompagnement, elle émet une demande (même si elle a répondu à la contrainte d'un(e) conjoint(e) ou de l'ANPE). En tout cas c'est cette personne-là qui est face au conseiller, et non un agent de l'ANPE ou son conjoint(e). Le premier travail dans le processus est de redonner la possibilité à l'autre de dire quelle est son attente et de lui faire prendre ses responsabilités. Ainsi la personne arrête d'invoquer l'action funeste des astres ou le désastre du fatalisme, pour exprimer un désir de changement dont elle sera acteur. C'est une première transition vers le bien-être, une étape de ré-appropriation de soi. Car il ne faut pas omettre que les êtres humains s'adaptent à leur malheur. C'est un effort que d'exprimer dans ces circonstances le désir de vivre autre chose, car le risque est énorme.

La normalisation et la sortie de la culpabilisation,
ou comment je comprends ce qui m'arrive

Le fonctionnement de notre société étant fortement basé sur la culpabilité et non sur la responsabilité, le processus apprenant passe par une chasse à cette culpabilité, sentiment efficace qui permet d'être narcissique, centré sur soi et bloqué. La culpabilité a la plupart du temps son origine dans l'éducation ; elle est vécue comme une souffrance par celui qui en éprouve le sentiment et n'arrive pas à s'en défaire. Ce qui est aidant pour le demandeur d'emploi c'est de l'aider à comprendre ce qui lui arrive, qu'il n'est pas l'unique, que d'autres vivent un enchaînement similaire (la rupture, le deuil, la re-projection), et qu'il a une part de responsabilité dans sa représentation de ce qui lui arrive aujourd'hui et dans sa représentation de son rôle dans la construction de son avenir. Bref, on ne traite pas la question de la culpabilité en l'approfondissant et en en recherchant les causes, mais en se centrant sur la responsabilité qui favorise l'action.

*L'estime de soi, ou comment l'autre m'estime
et me rend à mon estime de moi*

L'estime de soi est usée :

- par le regard qui a été porté sur la personne au moment de sa rupture avec l'entreprise (sur un curseur de ++ si elle n'a pas choisi de partir, de -- si elle a été acteur de la rupture) ;

- par le regard qui est porté par son entourage (regard fantasmé ou réel) ;

- par le regard qu'elle porte sur elle en rapport à son système de valeur et à sa vision du monde.

Quand l'usure est très forte, un sentiment d'exclusion est exprimé. Il peut être associé à un déni de la situation auprès de l'entourage (mensonge sur la situation réelle), à un abattement tel que l'interlocuteur a peu d'espoir de « valoir » encore quelque chose, à un esprit revanchard si violent qu'il en devient intolérable, ou à une révolte inassouvie contre l'ex-employeur....

La reconquête de l'estime de soi est une étape d'apprentissage de retour à un bien-être dans l'équilibre vis-à-vis de soi et des autres, de retour à l'inclusion.

Cette reconquête nécessite un certain nombre d'ingrédients :

- une institution qui reconnaisse la personne et que la personne reconnaisse. (Ici je note une difficulté : en France, une institution comme l'Agence nationale pour l'emploi-ANPE n'est de loin pas reconnue comme légitime auprès des entreprises, donc des salariés, et ses agents sont souvent eux-mêmes en difficulté dans leur estime de soi. Le miroir de l'estime de soi ne fonctionne pas bien.) ;

- une fonction et une personne. Les objectifs quantitatifs en nombre de rendez-vous par jour fixés aux agents augmentent la difficulté d'être au-delà de la relation d'une fonction (le conseiller) à un demandeur/chercheur, à donc être dans une relation d'une personne authentique et sincère qui reconnaît une autre personne ;

- le temps de la connaissance, qui manque. Rappelons ici que le processus de reconnaissance ne se fait pas sans une première étape de connaissance.

Il ne s'agit pas de parler ici des vertus de l'ANPE à générer un retour à l'emploi au regard de la concurrence avec des cabinets privés (il n'y a pas moins de réussite pour les uns que pour les autres), mais de ce qui se passe pendant la phase d'exclusion du marché de l'emploi du travail actif.

L'inclusion, ou comment je m'identifie à un collectif

Dans le processus est proposée, dans un laps de temps très rapproché, une démarche à la personne de manière individuelle et collective. Le premier collectif auquel elle est confrontée est composé de ses pairs : d'autres chômeurs. La dénomination englobante de chômeurs ne doit pas masquer à l'intérieur de ce groupe les différences considérables : des personnes de métiers différents dont ils ne côtoyaient pas les homologues dans leurs emplois antérieurs, des personnes qui ne sont pas dans le même état psychologique, des personnes de positions hiérarchiques différentes. C'est une première étape importante, même si elle est, pour certains, déséquilibrante et désagréable (s'exposer devant autrui, sortir de soi, de ses habitudes…) : c'est une première étape d'inclusion, savoir se coltiner autrui et être dérangé.

L'inclusion par la professionnalisation

Pour certaines personnes, l'inclusion ne peut passer que par une professionnalisation dans un autre métier. La personne vit un renoncement à un métier pour se reprojeter sur un autre. Là encore le déséquilibre et le temps de mal-être du renoncement sont nécessaires pour se plonger radicalement dans autre chose. Il est nécessaire pour que ce déséquilibre soit vertueux, qu'il soit un déséquilibre de transition. Autre cas de figure : l'alphabétisation (lecture calcul de base) sans laquelle un opérateur ne peut participer aux opérations qualité, suivre les consignes, etc. ou la réussite au permis de conduire (le financer et obtenir le permis) sans lequel certaines professions ou bien la mobilité sont impossibles.

Pour d'autres, la situation est beaucoup plus compliquée. Je veux parler ici des personnes qui dans leur mode de relation à autrui sont rigides, fonctionnent sur un seul mode autoritaire hiérarchique binaire alors que les entreprises recherchent davantage des personnes capables de travailler à la fois dans une ligne hiérarchique, et dans une ligne dite transversale, et matricielle. Dans ce cas, la mue est douloureuse, mais pour autant déterminante pour un retour à l'emploi.

b. La dimension collective

Je propose de développer cette dimension collective, toujours dans le contexte du chômage. Concrètement la dimension collective s'organise par la formation de groupes d'une dizaine de personnes, demandeurs d'emploi et hétérogènes, autour d'ateliers (CV, lettre de motivation, mailing, entretien, prospection téléphonique, réseaux). Les vertus de ces ateliers, au-delà d'un apprentissage de méthode, d'outils, de déclencheur de passage à l'action, sont de générer un processus de rééquilibrage pendant leur durée.

La mesure aux autres : comment retrouver des points de repère sur une échelle bien-être/mal-être

La normalisation, la sortie de la culpabilisation, la reconquête de l'estime de soi que nous avons traitées dans la dimension personnelle, sont amplifiées, accélérées par la confrontation collective. Car les individus peuvent se mesurer les uns aux autres ; ils mesurent leur malheur, leurs ressources, leurs chances, leurs solutions. Ils se constituent une échelle et se situent sur cette échelle. Souvent d'ailleurs, leur appréciation évolue au fur et à mesure qu'ils comprennent ce qui se passe pour les autres. Une sensibilité à autrui, des brèches s'ouvrent pendant ses ateliers, car il n'y a pas d'enjeu d'intérêt entre eux (sauf dans des cas extrêmes de retour à des sentiments concurrentiels très forts quand, par exemple, il y a une crise sur le marché des informaticiens et qu'ils sont nombreux dans l'atelier).

L'interaction avec les entreprises

Dans ma pratique, j'ai observé que la démarche est plus opérante quand elle inclut les entreprises et ne se limite pas à un agent de l'ANPE animateur ou un intervenant du privé et le groupe de demandeurs d'emploi. Un atelier de prospection téléphonique, après une période d'apprentissage de la méthode – de tests en jeux de rôle – aboutit, pendant l'atelier, à une mise en pratique réelle : les demandeurs d'emploi appellent des entreprises. Le fait de parvenir à décrocher des entretiens de recrutement pendant l'atelier, et cela dans l'émulation du groupe, est un facteur d'inclusion puissant : « J'ai réussi par ma pro-activité à décrocher un rendez-vous sans avoir attendu avec angoisse l'arrivée d'une réponse dans ma boîte aux lettres (qu'elle soit physique ou virtuelle).» Le visage éclairé et triomphant de celui qui décroche un rendez-vous est le signe d'un retour vers l'estime de soi.

L'espace diviseur : la reproduction des divisions sociales dans la recherche d'emploi

La question de l'espace est ambivalente. Aussi bien l'ANPE que les cabinets d'outplacement jouent sur la reproduction des divisions sociales dans le monde du travail. Les cadres et les non-cadres pour l'ANPE, les non-cadres, les cadres, et les cadres dirigeants pour les cabinets d'outplacement,. Bref « on ne mélange pas les torchons et les serviettes ». Je parlais d'espace car les lieux ne sont pas identiques, on y côtoie ses pairs, l'espace mis à disposition n'est pas le même, les prestations sont différentes. L'effet tout à fait positif est que les conditions sont réunies pour contribuer à la reconquête de l'estime de soi : on continue à jouer dans la même cour, celle des grands (ce sont d'ailleurs les cadres qui sont narcissiquement souvent les plus fragiles).

Mais l'imperméabilité est étonnante. Comment ne pas penser qu'un directeur du développement des ressources humaines pourrait aider des non-cadres dans leur recherche d'emploi par ses conseils et son propre carnet d'adresses. Pourtant, à ma connaissance, ce genre de passerelles n'est quasiment jamais établi (je serais heureuse de découvrir des expériences dans ce sens). Ces passerelles pourraient contribuer à changer les représentations mentales une fois que les personnes se retrouvent prises dans l'organisation de l'entreprise : « Je sais maintenant qu'un directeur des ressources humaines n'est pas seulement le bras armé de la direction, qu'il est aussi capable d'aider, etc. » « Je sais qu'un ouvrier n'est pas simplement un matricule de plus, j'ai vu l'être humain, etc. »

La solidarité au fil du temps : l'amnésie des ex-demandeurs d'emploi

Il est rare dans l'entreprise que je rencontre des personnes qui sont ouvertes à parler de leur période de chômage, ou à s'investir auprès de demandeurs d'emploi, ou, quand il s'agit de recruteurs, de ne pas vouloir absolument recruter quelqu'un qui est déjà en activité.

Les ex-demandeurs d'emploi sont amnésiques, peu tolérants envers les demandeurs d'emploi qui leur semblent suspects comme si leur propre période de chômage était suspecte, qu'il y avait là une honte, un stigmate. Cette période est rarement valorisée comme une phase de meilleure connaissance de soi, d'apprentissage. Et quand elle est explicitée ainsi, les interlocuteurs le perçoivent souvent comme un habillage pour mieux se vendre.

Il y a au niveau collectif une double perte : celle de la reconnaissance de l'apprentissage, et celle de la solidarité.

c. Le cas particulier du surendettement

Je souhaite évoquer un cas particulier qui est l'un des effets possibles du chômage de très longue durée : le surendettement, qui est un sujet complexe. Il met en cause à la fois des éléments de systèmes macro (les banques, les organismes de crédit, les lois, le marché de l'emploi…) et aussi de système personnel qui met en jeu la responsabilité de la personne surendettée. J'aimerais tout d'abord insister sur une conviction basée sur mon expérience : je ne crois pas que toutes les personnes surendettées se sentent en situation de mal-être ni en déséquilibre. Elles peuvent y avoir trouvé un système de confort avec des bénéfices secondaires considérables et choisir de répondre au discours ambiant sur le mal-être pour s'adapter tout en ne cherchant ni à raisonner différemment, ni à développer d'autres stratégies que d'instrumentaliser les nouvelles ressources d'aide. Une question très importante se pose : Est-ce que la personne surendettée est prête à changer sa posture ?

La confrontation : pour une vision partagée

Il m'apparaît capital que toutes les fonctions «aidantes» se réunissent avec la personne (ou le couple) surendettée pour aligner la vision partagée sur la situation et la demande. Cette confrontation permet de sortir des jeux de «je te dis ce que tu veux entendre de moi en fonction de ta mission auprès de moi». Cette confrontation au réel est dure pour les professionnels et pour la personne (ou le couple) surendettée. Pourquoi ? Parce que tous autour de la table sont contraints de s'avouer qu'ils se sont aveuglés sur la situation.

L'unité de temps et de lieu

Pour sortir des jeux de miroir de séduction, cette confrontation se joue dans une unité de temps et de lieu. Elle brise les possibilités de jeu de triangulaire «vous, vous me comprenez, mais pas les autres», et les réponses ciblées en fonction des interlocuteurs.

La question paradoxale
Comment est-ce que je réussis à être surendetté ?

Les approches systémiques mettent en évidence des paradoxes apprenants et valorisants. En effet, l'expression de sa réussite par la personne surendettée permet de mettre en évidence des compétences, des qualités,

des stratégies aboutissant au surendettement, puis de mettre au service d'une autre stratégie, celle de la sortie du surendettement, ces mêmes compétences et qualités en passant par toutes les propositions expérimentées dans le cadre du contrat social multipartite.

3. Le processus apprenant de bien-être/mal-être dans le contexte du salariat

Nous partons de l'hypothèse que ce qui se joue en matière de processus apprenant d'équilibres/déséquilibres générant du bien-être et du mal-être dans le contexte de l'entreprise, nous permet, par analogie, de prendre du recul sur l'ensemble de la société.

a. La dimension personnelle

Le divorce entre les salariés et leurs entreprises

Le constat a été fait par les ethnologues d'entreprise : les salariés sont avertis, peu dupes des systèmes de marketing et de propagande mis en place dans les entreprises. Les salariés jouent le jeu, font semblant, et surtout se protègent en ne livrant aux entreprises qu'une partie de leur intelligence, de leur créativité, de leur culture. Leur chemin de bonheur, ils se le construisent en dehors d'elle. Il semblerait qu'en France ce phénomène se soit intensifié depuis le passage aux 35 heures.

Pour exemple, de nombreux pères prennent leur congé de paternité à la naissance de leur enfant. C'est encore plus flagrant chez les plus jeunes qui envisagent de « traverser » les entreprises ; ils les instrumentalisent comme leurs parents ont été instrumentalisés par elles (des parents qui ont connu des périodes de chômage, des mères coincées par des horaires de travail à temps partiel rendant leur vie quotidienne infernale et absurde). Leur vie privée est devenue plus importante que la vie professionnelle.

Je décris là le cas de figure d'équilibres personnels trouvés, mais qui engendrent des fragilités collectives considérables, des replis sur soi et de l'individualisme fort. Certaines entreprises tentent de développer ce qu'elles appellent de l'intelligence collective, de la coresponsabilité, avec plus ou moins de bonheur en fonction des contradictions ambiantes : par exemple développer de la coresponsabilité quand un patron n'assume pas ses erreurs et rend la tâche impossible.

Certaines situations de « divorce » sont liées à une confusion génératrice de mal-être et de frustration, quand le salarié projette sur l'entreprise l'ensemble de sa vie. J'ai observé ce cas chez de jeunes femmes célibataires engluées dans des horaires de travail qu'elles ont rendus délirants (60 à 70 heures par semaine), et qui finissent par reprocher à l'entreprise de ne pas leur laisser le temps de trouver l'âme sœur et, souvent aussi, se plaignent du peu de reconnaissance de l'entreprise face à leur investissement professionnel. Pour sortir de cette confusion et remettre chaque chose dans la bonne case, le chemin le plus efficace est de renvoyer à l'individu la responsabilité de son problème. J'évoque ici des situations, où dans des circonstances de travail similaires, certains travaillent dans des amplitudes horaires anormalement étendues alors que d'autres trouvent des systèmes de régulation très simples à décrire (à savoir : travailler moins) mais difficiles à mettre en œuvre par quelqu'un qui est « piégé ».

Les zones de non-être

Nous parlons de bien-être et de mal-être, et je me permets ici d'introduire la notion donnée par Virginia Woolf : les zones de non-être.

Je traduis le non-être par une sorte d'évanescence, de perte de soi, du temps qui passe, de perte du lien au monde. L'évènement y est non-évènement. « Rien ne m'arrive, rien n'est grave ». Cette banalisation de soi ravale l'individu à pas grand-chose.

Cette zone de non-être est une absence d'être qui n'est ni du bien-être, ni du mal-être : c'est une négation de l'être. Comme elle sous-entend une souffrance, la tentation serait de la ranger dans la catégorie de mal-être. Mais ce serait passer à côté d'une notion qui dévoile une situation d'auto-mise en parenthèse, comme une sorte de situation de refuge, d'échappatoire, une zone de non-atteinte des cercles vicieux de mal-être dans la société.

Je me retrouve parfois face à des personnes qui sont en état de non-être quand elles travaillent. Elles agissent par automatisme, mais « elles n'y sont pas ». C'est une forme d'auto-exclusion au monde. Là aussi, grâce au dialogue avec un autre, peut se reconstruire la possibilité d'un lien à soi et à l'autre. C'est ce dialogue qui remet en perspective et en valeur les évènements quotidiens de la vie de cette personne en auto-exclusion.

Matérialisme et individualisme

La tristesse assumée de personnes désabusées qui auraient un potentiel d'investissement de solidarité envers autrui de par leurs compétences et leur capacité d'initiative professionnelle, est questionnante. Je
croise régulièrement des cadres approchant la quarantaine, avouant être
matérialistes, individualistes, tristes de l'être et en même temps disant
combien ils sont lucides sur eux-mêmes : ils aiment leur confort et ne
veulent pas choisir un chemin vers plus de bonheur qui passerait par une
baisse de revenu (pour changer de métier, créer une entreprise), l'argent
leur servant à acheter des compensations (dit textuellement). Il est difficile d'imaginer que ces personnes en position « conservatrice » vis-à-vis
d'elles-mêmes puissent spontanément prendre le risque de se préoccuper
d'autrui. Elles ont pourtant conscience des exclusions sociales. Reste à
savoir comment stimuler leur désir d'être acteur de changement ? Là
encore, la clé est dans la rencontre avec un autre qui ne les juge pas et
leur propose d'autres chemins.

Dire non

Dans le processus apprenant vers le bien-être, le fait d'apprendre à dire
non est l'une des clés de la reprise de la pro-activité. Bien entendu, il
arrive l'inverse, le « dire oui » pouvant être une clé. Mais de manière majo-
ritaire, je rencontre des personnes soumises à leur envie de faire plaisir,
d'être parfaites, d'être obéissantes, d'être surchargées. Parfois, quand
je les rencontre, fatiguées, mal dans leur peau, elles n'en ont pas pris
conscience par elles-mêmes, car c'était devenu leur état normal. C'est un
autre (un membre de leur famille, un manager, un collègue) qui a provoqué
cette prise de conscience qu'il lui serait possible de vivre autrement. Vient
après cette prise de conscience l'apprentissage de se poser des limites
et de les expliciter aux autres, d'assumer un changement d'image de
« gentille bonne poire ». L'apprentissage peut se faire, entre autres, par
des méthodes de renversement (« je prends la place de l'autre et je me
rends compte qu'entendre dire non ne déclenche pas un conflit »). C'est
l'apprentissage de la rhétorique (l'argumentation du non).

b. La dimension collective

Je me propose de développer ici uniquement les principes des processus
apprenants du bien-être en exposant les limites et difficultés de ces
apprentissages. Ces principes sont essentiellement issus d'expériences

intra-entreprise. Ils sont expérimentés de plus en plus dans des contextes mixtes (associations, projets de création d'activité, entreprises, région).

La diagonale

La « diagonale » signifie ici de proposer de devenir acteurs à des personnes issues de différentes entités, de niveaux hiérarchiques différents, de cultures différentes, bref de chercher l'hétérogénéité et de créer des conditions de parité. C'est-à-dire, dans des organisations hiérarchiques, créer des espaces « a-hiérarchiques » ou « hétérhiérarchiques ». Dans le premier cas il n'y a plus de hiérarchie, dans le second la hiérarchie est tournante, chacun à tour de rôle est en position de leader. L'intérêt est de pouvoir créer des conditions de co-responsabilité, d'empathie, d'inventivité et de mise en œuvre. Pour que le principe fonctionne, des efforts d'humilité sont nécessaires aux experts et aux décideurs qui devront accepter d'écouter des personnes moins sachantes qu'eux, mais pour autant co-créatrices de solutions dont tous seront les acteurs.

Le volontariat

Le volontariat est également une des clés de la réussite, et permet à partir d'un groupe de provoquer un effet de contagion progressif. La limite dans le monde de l'entreprise est qu'à un moment donné la règle du volontariat soit bousculée par l'impératif du temps court-termiste et qu'un décideur finisse par désigner les volontaires.

La coresponsabilité

Parler de coresponsabilité est un autre moyen de dire que tous sont acteurs, que tous sont interactions, que tous ont des effets les uns sur les autres. Les entreprises, comme les états, ont de forts niveaux de complexité. Pour vivre cette complexité, non pour imaginer la dissoudre, il est nécessaire que tous les acteurs mesurent qu'ils sont acteurs. Dans la pratique, une des clés pour y arriver est le décentrage.

Le décentrage

Pour qu'il y ait coresponsabilité, il faut soit qu'il n'y ait plus de centre, soit que celui-ci se déplace au fil des rencontres, des réflexions, des actions. Tant qu'un individu – ou un groupe d'individus – peut être identifié de manière constante comme étant le centre, ce phénomène diminue les possibilités

des acteurs à se voir sur la scène ; ils redeviennent si souvent spectateurs qu'ils finissent par laisser faire ceux ou celui qui est au centre.

Concrètement, le décentrage implique une circularité de l'exercice du pouvoir (chacun à son tour, avec un changement fréquent, dicté non pas par un règlement mais par la nécessité du réel qui est observé chemin faisant).

Chemin faisant

Ce dont nous venons de parler ne génère pas de bien-être au départ mais plutôt un trouble, un dérangement des habitudes (dire mon opinion, écouter des personnes différentes de moi, m'engager, briser des barrières).

L'une des autres caractéristiques est la nécessité de prendre en compte le réel : Comment agissons-nous ? Comment pourrions-nous faire autrement ? Que provoquons-nous comme effet ? Ce qui signifie de sortir d'une logique unique de planification pour la combiner avec une acceptation des imprévus, des effets secondaires plus intéressants que les résultats visés, etc. Cette prise en compte du réel, de ce qui arrive et de ses conséquences, conforte chacun dans ses possibilités d'agir à son échelle. C'est un processus d'expérimentation, dont l'intérêt est sa singularité d'être vécu par ce groupe-là, à ce moment « t ».

Le dialogue

La manière dont les personnes se parlent est capitale dans un processus apprenant générant le bien-être. Plusieurs conditions sont requises :

- c'est une personne qui parle et non pas la fonction ou l'institution ;

- ce n'est pas de la communication ;

- c'est de la parole ;

- la suspension de jugement ;

- l'hospitalité de l'autre ;

- l'empathie ;

- la curiosité ;

- l'association d'idées…

Et tout cela s'apprend en le faisant et en étant guidé au départ pour développer cette manière de sortir des monologues de sourds, des « je veux avoir raison », de la conversation policée de salon.

Les objectifs partagés et la vision partagée

La vision partagée, terme fort usité dans l'entreprise, sous-entend la possibilité de créer une image commune, un concept, un *logos* commun.

Le vocable est utilisé pour désigner la possibilité de construire collectivement une stratégie commune (par exemple « la santé » pour une entreprise fabriquant et vendant des produits alimentaires), un projet commun (par exemple, fabriquer une voiture coûtant moins de 10 000 euros destinée aux marchés dits émergents). Dans cette dimension, le vocable « vision partagée » sous-entend une mise en marche de tous dans la réalisation de cette stratégie, de ce projet, et donc un moyen de fédérer des métiers, des logiques, des personnes différentes.

Un mouvement de « cocréation » de valeur autour de la vision partagée englobant les salariés, les clients, les actionnaires s'impose depuis une dizaine d'années dans de très grandes entreprises. Voici un exemple pour illustrer ce propos. Une entreprise internationale d'agro-alimentaire cotée en bourse a pour stratégie « la nutrition ». Elle englobe symboliquement l'actionnaire (nourrir l'actionnaire), en pratique le client et les salariés (avec une notion d'éducation). Destiné aux salariés, un programme de nutrition spécifique a été créé pour les opérateurs postés, dont les habitudes alimentaires liées aux conditions de travail alternant nuit et jour, ne sont pas optimales et peuvent générer des ennuis de santé. De plus, les entreprises sensibilisées à « leur responsabilité planétaire » englobent de plus en plus l'environnement naturel (écoresponsabilité).

Mais, en même temps, dans certaines de ces très grandes entreprises, les salariés perçoivent souvent cette volonté de cocréation de valeurs comme une nouvelle manière (à la mode) de leur faire accepter encore plus de changements dans des conditions de stress.

Cependant la perception de la vision est celle de l'optique et d'une partie de la philosophie rationnelle. La vision partagée ne va pas avec la dimension du chemin faisant et de son bricolage. C'est davantage la *metis*, concurrente du *logos*, qui serait à prendre en compte. La *metis* c'est la ruse, la pensée courbe. Il s'agit d'entendre, de partager des représentations mentales et les objectifs des individus, des collectifs, de les entendre

et de composer collectivement un devenir commun, une tension vers un avenir dans l'action.

Aujourd'hui dans les entreprises, ces deux logiques du *logos* et de la *metis* se combinent avec plus ou moins de réussite.

A titre d'exemple, je cite une réussite : une entreprise internationale fabriquant des composants industriels regroupe deux sites dans un nouveau site. 110 personnes vont devoir travailler à 50 km de leur lieu de travail actuel. L'entreprise a voulu se donner toutes les chances de générer le moins de mal-être possible, et elle a pris cette occasion comme opportunité de favoriser l'expression des salariés. Le directeur général, le directeur des usines, la direction des ressources humaines, le comité d'entreprise, les syndicats, l'ensemble des 110 salariés opérateurs et chefs d'équipe ont, durant six mois avant le déménagement, vécu une expérience multiple :

- des entretiens individuels avec tous les salariés pour comprendre leur besoin ;
- l'expérience du transport (covoiturage, bus d'entreprise, bus de collectivités locales) choisie par d'autres entreprises ;
- le travail à partir de cartes routières pour calculer les coûts (péage d'autoroute) ;
- le travail en commun avec des agents immobiliers, l'architecte.

Le pari est extraordinaire car le nouveau site a été choisi à la fin de cette démarche. Ce nouveau site d'usine a offert une aventure étonnante, qui des années après cette expérience, soude encore les gens de cette nouvelle usine. Elle leur a donné confiance en eux-mêmes. Les collaborateurs se sont sentis écoutés, pris en compte, et ont été les acteurs de la décision. Dans des entreprises reines de la planification et de la centralisation, une telle coconstruction d'un choix partagé serait impossible. Après un rapide sondage des salariés, le directeur financier et le dirigeant prendraient la décision et communiqueraient leur décision.

c. Des clés ?

L'attitude des accompagnateurs : ne pas savoir

Le vocable de « coaching sociétal » désigne une action d'accompagnement au niveau du système, donc des interactions entre les éléments

du système. Le coach sociétal en serait l'un des acteurs avec d'autres acteurs. La posture d'accompagnateur est fondamentalement celle d'un non-sachant.

L'accompagnateur a une position basse (a contrario, un décideur a une position haute) ; il ne sait pas quelles seront les solutions, le contenu, le résultat ; son savoir-faire porte sur les conditions de réussite à réunir (dont certaines sont décrites dans cet article) pour que les interactions dans le système se tissent différemment, que certains éléments du système disparaissent et que d'autres – neufs – s'y introduisent et qu'ainsi, le système dans son entier se transforme. L'accompagnateur n'est pas le décideur ni l'expert en termes de contenu.

La perception du système : les interactions

Autant il est facile de dire que regarder le système c'est regarder les interactions, autant il est difficile de le faire. Nous avons tendance à nous regarder le nombril et à voir l'autre comme un problème à résoudre. Regarder l'interaction et les effets générés par l'autre sur moi, et par moi sur lui, nécessite une grande rigueur, une quête de sortie de la « self-illusion », cela à l'échelle des personnes. Et à l'échelle des institutions, regarder les interactions nécessite de les regarder ensemble et de se parler de « comment on fait pour réussir à travailler ensemble (mal ou bien) ».

Un point aveugle

Quand une personne s'engage à travailler en rapport à plus faible, plus démuni que lui, le point aveugle majeur est sa propre générosité. L'excès de générosité a des effets négatifs, car la générosité est une manière de rendre l'autre dépendant, en dette vis-à-vis de moi. Bref je me fais plaisir en étant généreux, supérieur à l'autre. Cette générosité, dont Edgar Morin parle fort bien dans son *Ethique*[3], doit être contrebalancée par un égocentrisme et une conscience des effets de sa générosité. Ici, je parle d'un des risques majeurs d'aveuglement des accompagnateurs.

À l'échelle de la société, l'affichage de la générosité doublée d'un intérêt égoïste fort peut être une perte de vue de l'équité du bien-être de tous. En effet, ce rapport égoïsme/générosité pourrait être le germe d'un clientélisme : « Je suis généreux envers toi, mais tu devras en réciprocité un jour

---

3. Morin, Edgar, *La méthode – Tome 6, Ethique*, Le Seuil, 2004.

me rendre un service ». Toute personne n'étant pas « à la hauteur » ou ne voulant pas rentrer dans ce jeu est exclue.

Conclusion

Les quelques exemples présentés dans cet article démontrent combien les processus apprenants d'équilibres et de déséquilibres générant du bien-être ou du mal-être sont faits de chausse-trappes, de faux-semblants, de paradoxes, d'illusions, et que la vigilance et l'humilité sont des qualités indispensables à tout acteur intervenant au fil de ce processus.

PARTIE IV – PLAIDOYER POUR UNE SOCIÉTÉ
DU BIEN COMMUN AU SERVICE DU BIEN-ÊTRE

De l'Etat providence à la société de bien-être

Bruno Amoroso[1]

1. Imaginaire collectif et bien-être : deux utopies

L'imaginaire collectif, qui nourrit le projet de vie et de société des citoyens, s'exprime, notamment, au travers des notions d'éducation, d'instruction, de culture et de religion. Il transparaît dans la place qu'occupent la famille, la société civile, le travail et les institutions. L'imaginaire collectif a souvent donné naissance à de nouvelles utopies lorsque les utopies précédentes s'estompaient ou étaient intégrées à d'anciennes philosophies remaniées. Chaque utopie est propre à une période donnée de l'histoire et favorise la réunion des conditions nécessaires à une transformation radicale. Elles sont indispensables aux individus, dans la mesure où elles matérialisent l'imaginaire collectif dans le temps et l'espace. Toute mutation économique, politique ou religieuse suppose une révolution culturelle préalable. Les utopies ont précisément la faculté de légitimer les révolutions et les contre-révolutions. La révolution keynésienne s'est appuyée sur l'utopie de l'économie sociale (règne d'une équité mêlant efficacité et égalité), tout comme la contre-révolution néolibérale a puisé dans l'utopie de la mondialisation (« le village planétaire »).

La mondialisation a très rapidement montré qu'elle ne tenait pas ses promesses. Le village planétaire est devenu un apartheid planétaire ; face à ce phénomène, un nouvel univers de philosophies, d'aspirations et de rêves se met en place. L'évolution quotidienne à laquelle on assiste à l'échelon local et à l'échelle de la planète (comme la mondialisation de l'économie, l'explosion de l'information et de la communication, l'augmentation des inégalités et de l'exclusion sociale, la marginalisation économique et la déstabilisation politique des communautés et des pays, la « révolution » biotechnologique, la recrudescence du chômage

---

1. Chaire Jean Monnet. Maître de conférence émérite, Département société et mondialisation, université de Roskilde, Danemark.

et de l'esclavage professionnel au Nord comme au Sud, la pollution de l'environnement, les changements climatiques constatés sur l'ensemble de la planète) impose à nouveau de repenser la situation actuelle et les grands objectifs de notre mode de vie.

Parce que la mondialisation avait été présentée comme l'aboutissement ultime du modèle occidental de la modernisation, « le point d'accostage de l'histoire de l'humanité », le mécontentement à son égard a entraîné la réouverture à la fois du dossier de la mondialisation et de celui de l'ensemble du système mis en place depuis plus de deux siècles d'histoire européenne. Une fois encore, l'imaginaire collectif donne naissance à une nouvelle utopie, « un autre monde est possible », qui repose sur la renaissance des communautés et de leur vie en commun. Elle se définit par la réintégration du marché dans la collectivité, la désinstitutionnalisation de ses principales attributions, qui doivent être reprises par la société civile, ainsi que le retour à une éducation associée à l'instruction et à la formation. L'existence, les individus, la vie en commun et la créativité représentent à nouveau de grandes questions qui doivent être analysées et étudiées et sur lesquelles il convient de s'interroger.

a. Utopie européenne et mondialisation

Les utopies européennes ont accordé depuis le XVIIIe siècle une place de premier plan à la science et aux technologies ; elles ont par ailleurs reconnu la suprématie de l'Etat sur les collectivités et des institutions sur la société civile. En outre, la mondialisation se définit comme une « société de la connaissance », dans la mesure où l'on considère que son économie est de plus en plus régie par la connaissance (« la connaissance est le moteur de l'économie ») et où la tendance dominante du moment est à une conception technoscientifique et utilitaire de la recherche et de l'éducation. L'éducation et la connaissance ont tout d'abord été expulsées de la vie familiale et communautaire (la société civile) par l'Etat (qui régissait un nouveau cadre appelé société) ; elles sont à présent expulsées de la société et de l'Etat par la mondialisation capitaliste. La connaissance et les établissements qui en sont le siège (écoles, universités, centres de recherche) sont devenus un instrument au service des objectifs du marché capitaliste et de la transformation qui l'a conduit à privilégier l'aide au travail à l'aide sociale (1980-1990), puis à passer de l'aide au travail à l'état de guerre (2000-2008).

Ces processus ont, à l'évidence, un effet déstabilisant sur l'université et le système éducatif. L'université tend à se spécialiser dans des domaines

et des disciplines « utiles », pour mieux servir les intérêts économiques de la compétitivité nationale. Cette attitude resserre de plus en plus les liens qui l'unissent aux entreprises privées pour le financement d'une recherche dont elles tirent profit et la mise en place de formations de pointe. La mercantilisation et la privatisation de l'enseignement supérieur, et notamment de l'enseignement universitaire, s'en trouvent du coup renforcées. Dans une telle logique, l'éducation ne fait plus partie des biens et services non commerciaux. Les étudiants se transforment en clients et les divers acteurs de l'enseignement sont considérés comme des « parties prenantes » au sein de cette « entreprise d'enseignement » que devient l'université.

Il lui faut avant tout s'adapter à l'objectif de mondialisation, en dispensant un enseignement aux « ressources humaines » les plus qualifiées et les plus compétentes, pour permettre aux entreprises de conserver et de renforcer leur compétitivité sur les marchés mondiaux. Cette adaptation s'accompagne d'un processus de financiarisation et de la création d'une technostructure, qui recourt de plus en plus à la science et à la technologie pour orienter les systèmes de production et le comportement des consommateurs en fonction de ses intentions et pour mettre en place un contrôle inégal de la conception, de la production et de l'utilisation des nouvelles technologies de l'information et des communications (l'univers internet) par certains pays et catégories sociales.

Ce processus a été qualifié de « fracture de la connaissance » : elle désigne le fossé qui se creuse inexorablement entre, d'une part, les personnes, les catégories sociales et les pays qui « produisent » et, d'autre part, ceux qui ne produisent pas les connaissances de plus en plus sophistiquées et complexes qui façonnent les domaines militaire, spatial, biotechnologique, agricole et les multimédias. Vu la puissance que leur confère cette capacité, les premiers ont peu intérêt à partager avec les seconds leur savoir. Ils ont plutôt avantage à étendre et à consolider leur influence et leur contrôle de l'économie mondiale à partir d'un échelon local. C'est ce qui explique l'importance stratégique acquise par les droits de propriété intellectuelle et la course aux brevets qui en découle.

b. Les voies européennes de l'émancipation

La renaissance de la collectivité, qui se matérialise par les millions de personnes désireuses, en Europe et dans le reste du monde, de diriger elles-mêmes leur existence conformément aux choix et aux valeurs qui leur sont propres, s'est produite de manière récurrente au cours de

l'histoire européenne. Toutes les formes de protestation et de révolte contre l'imposition de processus économiques et politiques ont été extrêmement salutaires. Cette opposition était essentiellement l'expression d'un rapport difficile avec la modernité et les diverses formes prises par la modernisation à l'échelon institutionnel (politiques et décisions étatiques) et économique (banalisation et financiarisation des économies de marché). Ces choix et ces décisions étaient systématiquement présentés comme des « contraintes », dictées par les besoins de l'économie et les promesses de développement faites par diverses forces sociales et politiques ; les populations et les collectivités locales devaient, pour leur part, se contenter de s'y soumettre.

Les Anciens s'en remettaient à Dieu et à l'interprétation des oracles lorsqu'ils avaient des choix à faire et des décisions à prendre ; ce rôle est désormais dévolu à la science et aux laboratoires. Une fois tracées les grandes orientations futures, la collectivité n'avait plus qu'à les suivre. L'abandon de « l'éducation » à… au profit de « la formation à… », de l'expérience et de la connaissance au profit de la science, tout comme l'impératif de conformation des exigences locales à l'intérêt général, sont ainsi devenus les règles du jeu admises. La philosophie traditionnelle, penser à l'échelon local et agir à l'échelle planétaire (de bas en haut), sur laquelle reposait naturellement et depuis toujours la pérennité de la collectivité, s'est muée en une conception exactement inverse, penser à l'échelle planétaire et agir à l'échelon local (de haut en bas), source d'un inévitable appauvrissement.

Ces positions, qui transparaissent dans l'orientation politique des organisations européennes et internationales, ainsi que dans divers mouvements, se résument en deux courants de pensée :

- l'un est partisan de l'adaptation des collectivités locales, des régions et des Etats à l'impératif d'intégration et d'innovation industrielle qu'impose de plus en plus la mondialisation. Cette position, adoptée par les institutions européennes et internationales, est partagée par un certain nombre de gouvernements ;

- l'autre recherche le moyen d'adapter le processus d'intégration et d'innovation technologique aux besoins de la collectivité. Cette conception, à laquelle souscrivent certains gouvernements et les mouvements dits « néo-mondialistes », ne remet pas en cause les choix et les orientations de la doctrine précédente, mais tente d'en atténuer les conséquences négatives.

En dépit de leurs différences, ces deux positions sont favorables au développement, dont elles assument les orientations et la teneur, et se montrent optimistes sur l'issue de la modernisation. La première considère l'adaptation de la collectivité aux besoins des entreprises comme une simple résultante du développement mondial, auquel il est indispensable de prendre autant part que possible. La seconde se montre plus critique à l'égard des risques d'exclusion sociale et du coût social élevé de cette orientation ; elle conserve cependant la possibilité de surmonter ces difficultés en recourant à des politiques adéquates. Les deux courants partagent l'idée que le développement local est un facteur résiduel, qui s'intègre dans des objectifs plus vastes. Il en existe un troisième, défendu par les mouvements antimondialistes et altermondialistes, qui remet en cause la mondialisation et la notion plus générale de développement. Il se rapproche d'une conception inverse de la mondialisation, dans la mesure où, contrairement aux deux positions précédentes, il considère la collectivité comme une variable indépendante et l'entreprise et le marché comme des variables dépendantes.

Les événements qui ponctuent l'existence de nos collectivités et sociétés suivent systématiquement deux voies au moins, parallèles et souvent imbriquées : une voie tracée, juridique et institutionnelle, et une voie spontanée, qu'empruntent les individus, les mouvements et les associations. De par leur diversité et leurs interactions, ces deux cheminements provoquent des conflits, tout en s'influençant l'un l'autre et en créant des synergies ; il convient par conséquent de les analyser soigneusement et de les suivre attentivement, pour vérifier la cohérence de leurs objectifs respectifs.

c. Grandeur et décadence du modèle social européen

L'Etat providence a été, pendant les vingt années qui ont suivi la deuxième guerre mondiale, le projet de société mis en œuvre par les politiques européennes et une réussite des sociétés européennes. La crise de ce modèle s'explique par un manque d'innovations au cours des années soixante et par les conséquences de la mondialisation depuis les années soixante-dix. Sa structure et sa dynamique interne ont été mises en place grâce au « pacte social », qui conférait aux entrepreneurs le droit de gérer et d'organiser la production pour assurer l'efficacité du système et qui attribuait aux travailleurs le pouvoir de diriger, en fournissant les biens publics indispensables et une redistribution des revenus financée par un régime fiscal progressif, afin d'assurer l'équité des revenus et une répartition de la protection sociale.

La voie étroite de la redistribution sociale était cependant dictée par une logique et une intention : compenser le « coût social » du progrès capitaliste. Le défi lancé par le système économique n'a pas été relevé par des politiques visant à intégrer ce coût social dans les entreprises, mais, au contraire, par celles qui s'attachaient à atténuer ses conséquences négatives sur les travailleurs et les citoyens en général. Paradoxalement, l'intervention de l'Etat dans ces domaines et la compensation partielle qui l'a accompagnée ont entraîné une externalisation accrue des coûts de production par les entreprises.

Cette crise interne est à l'origine de l'échec de l'Etat providence. Plusieurs auteurs (Archibugi, 2000) donnent une illustration de ses diverses dimensions : i. une crise fiscale ; ii. une crise d'efficacité ; iii. une crise d'affection. Son incapacité à réagir face à ces tendances et à la résistance rencontrée lors de la mise en œuvre de réformes indispensables (démocratie professionnelle et économique) a permis aux nouvelles politiques économiques des années soixante-dix et quatre-vingt (néolibéralisme) d'entreprendre, grâce au Consensus de Washington, un travail de sape de la légitimité des « pactes sociaux », de démanteler par la privatisation la fourniture des biens publics et de rétablir des régimes fiscaux à faible prélèvement.

Dans l'intervalle, la transformation des systèmes de production, passés du fordisme au postfordisme, a fait disparaître le cadre qui avait permis la constitution d'une classe ouvrière et d'une classe moyenne, sur lesquelles reposaient les institutions et la participation démocratiques. Ces changements structurels ayant entraîné un glissement du pouvoir de l'industrie vers les groupes financiers et technologiques, la reconstruction du système de protection sociale ne peut plus être du ressort de la première. Comme le fait très justement remarquer Archibugi :

> « de ce point de vue, l'expression "société du bien-être" ne saurait être uniquement considérée comme *intégrant* et *complétant* la notion d'Etat providence, puisqu'elle serait également *antinomique* de cette dernière : l'existence d'une société du bien-être suppose, d'une manière ou d'une autre, la « destruction » préalable de l'Etat providence, qui a jusqu'ici assumé la tâche de généraliser le bien-être, en recourant uniquement à une *redistribution* toujours croissante et/ou à la fourniture de fonctions génératrices d'un bien-être divisible et indivisible, individuel et collectif. » (Archibugi, 2000, p. 177).

Le projet de bien commun fait à présent son apparition à cause de la crise que traverse l'Etat providence, dont la Commission de l'Union européenne a souligné le déficit démocratique, économique et social. Cette crise

prend sa source dans une double pénurie : une pénurie économique, qui se traduit pas la « crise financière de l'Etat », et un manque de ressources, dû à la disponibilité limitée des ressources naturelles.

La pénurie économique découle de l'incapacité des systèmes de protection sociale à gérer correctement les processus de socialisation et de démocratisation qu'ils avaient mis en place (Caffè, 1986). Le principe de durabilité économique (énoncé par les entreprises) et sociale (énoncé par les citoyens), qui devait limiter les conséquences du coût social sur les finances publiques et la population, n'a pas produit les résultats escomptés. Le comportement induit par le système capitaliste a conduit à l'externalisation des « coûts sociaux » (« la privatisation du profit et la socialisation des coûts »). Le marché capitaliste est de plus en plus devenu un « système de coûts impayés » (Kapp, 1950) qui a rendu l'économie inefficace et a provoqué le déséquilibre des finances publiques. L'aide publique aux entreprises a systématiquement été utilisée non pas pour renforcer l'économie proprement dite, mais pour couvrir le déficit structurel et les erreurs de gestion. Les mesures prises en matière d'aide sociale n'ont pas servi à améliorer la qualité de vie des familles et de la population, mais à accroître leur dépendance vis-à-vis du marché du travail. En outre, l'augmentation des revenus et de la protection sociale n'a pas amélioré la qualité et la durée de vie des produits, mais a au contraire renforcé la propension à consommer des citoyens et leur comportement de consommateurs.

La pénurie de ressources provient du conflit entre l'idéologie de la croissance illimitée et le caractère limité des ressources naturelles. Au cours des années 1970, un certain nombre de rapports ont abordé la question des « limites de la croissance » (par exemple le rapport produit par le Club de Rome ; Meadows *et al.*, 1972) et ont renforcé la conscience sociale de leur dimension planétaire et de leur corrélation. Divers rapports ont ainsi souligné la problématique de la répartition des ressources (CMED, 1988) et des disparités régionales.

Les deux phénomènes ont donné naissance ces dernières années à plusieurs mouvements et à de nouvelles organisations, qui ont dépassé le stade de la réalisation des objectifs mentionnés, en étendant leur implication à la forme de l'organisation du marché, des systèmes de production et de la coopération internationale. La mobilisation de la société civile sur ces sujets représente certes une intervention constructive dans la réflexion sur l'Etat providence, mais elle accélère dans le même temps la nécessité de le réformer et de le transformer radicalement. La conscience de

l'interconnexion entre les personnes et la collectivité, due à l'augmentation des problèmes environnementaux, au gaspillage scandaleux de l'énergie et des matières premières, aux migrations croissantes, aux conflits et aux guerres, représente ce que nous appelons la « mondialité ». Ces inter-dépendances sont renforcées et étendues par la diffusion des nouvelles technologies de transport, des nouvelles communications et des nouveaux matériaux. Enfin, l'augmentation des communautés immigrées au sein des Etats nationaux attire l'attention sur les questions de la diversité cultu-relle et du polycentrisme dans les pays européens.

d. L'Etat social, symbole du bien commun, hier et aujourd'hui

Avant l'objectif de société du bien-être dont il est aujourd'hui question, les sociétés européennes ont pendant quarante ans privilégié le modèle de l'Etat providence. Ses objectifs et ses attributions étaient coordonnés par les biens publics. L'Etat providence avait été mis en place au cours du siècle dernier pour faire face à la crise économique et politique qui secouait le système capitaliste. A l'issue de la deuxième guerre mondiale, il avait été conçu pour procéder à la reconstruction d'une bonne partie des infrastructures civiles et économiques, dont l'éducation, la santé, les transports, les services postaux, le logement, l'industrie, etc. A l'époque, les gouvernements démocratiques ou non représentaient la seule auto-rité compétente en la matière. L'Etat a par conséquent pris le contrôle de nombreuses attributions de l'économie de marché et a mis en place une « économie mixte », qui se caractérisait par l'existence de puissantes entreprises publiques dans les principaux secteurs stratégiques de l'éco-nomie. La modernisation de l'économie reposait principalement sur le modèle fordiste et son système de production et de consommation de masse.

Cet industrialisme hégémonique, transposé en Europe à partir des Etats-Unis, est devenu le principe directeur du nouveau modèle de reconstruc-tion européen, pénalisant du même coup les sociétés et les traditions rurales. Le cadre institutionnel et politique (partis politiques, syndicats, etc.) a été aménagé autour de cette nouvelle organisation de l'économie et de l'Etat : le « syndicat » industriel et le parti politique « de classe » découlent tous deux d'un modèle d'entreprise fordiste à grande échelle. Ce processus a négligé la culture et les traditions rurales, qui étaient au cœur des sociétés européennes, et les a marginalisées en les considérant

comme des formes « précapitalistes » ou « prémodernes » d'organisation de la société.

La quête d'un nouveau bien-être mondial compatible avec l'objectif de « vie en commun » sur terre a vu le jour il y a plusieurs dizaines d'années ; ce projet de société se caractérise par une moindre intervention des gouvernements, mais une autonomie et une participation renforcées des citoyens et des communautés locales. J. M. Keynes avait déjà souligné les limites du « laisser-faire » et du libéralisme, ainsi que la nécessité de veiller au bien commun, dans deux ouvrages : *National Self-reliance (1933)* et *The economic possibilities for our grandchildren* (1932). Au cours des années 1960, Gunnar Myrdal a estimé qu'une transition de l'Etat providence à la société du bien-être s'imposait (Myrdal, 1960), tandis que Gunnar Adler-Karlsson a dénoncé le « barbarisme culturel » des idéologies du consumérisme et de la croissance (Adler-Karlsson, 1976).

Ce besoin de dépasser le modèle national de redistribution du bien-être social a été analysé récemment par Franco Archibugi :

> « La société du bien-être n'intègre ni ne complète l'Etat providence ; elle ne peut naître, au contraire, que sur les ruines de ce dernier : les limites de l'Etat providence sont définies par l'utopie du dualisme fonctionnel entre la politique sociale et le système économique, ainsi que par la nécessité de mettre un terme à la logique de compensation des coûts sociaux du « développement » (Archibugi, 2000, p. 177).

Comme l'a fait remarquer William Robson :

> « L'Etat providence est l'œuvre des pouvoirs publics. La société du bien-être, quant à elle, est le fruit de l'attitude que les citoyens adoptent à l'égard du bien-être en général, ainsi que de la manière dont ils le ressentent et le conçoivent. Atteindre les objectifs de l'Etat providence est impossible si la population tout entière ne traduit pas, dans son comportement et ses actes, les politiques et la conception de l'Etat providence. Lorsqu'un pays industriel devient un Etat providence, le besoin d'un sens aigu de la responsabilité individuelle, collective et institutionnelle, ainsi que la nécessité d'une discipline sociale, se fait beaucoup plus fortement sentir » (Archibugi, *ibidem*, p. 303).

L'importance et la complexité de ce changement de paradigme tiennent au fait que, au terme de trois siècles de modernisation européenne,

la création d'une nouvelle culture s'impose. L'Etat providence représente, à bien des égards, la forme la plus aboutie des transformations économiques et institutionnelles réalisées par la Révolution française. Le glissement de pouvoir provoqué par la bourgeoisie européenne s'est opéré par la déstabilisation de toutes les formes de pouvoir en place, qui reposaient sur la société civile (la famille, la religion, les collectivités locales, etc.) ; elle a ainsi transformé les « personnes » en « individus », puis en « citoyens » libérés des liens et des obligations qui les attachaient à leur communauté. Le vide créé par cette mutation a été comblé par l'Etat, qui a repris le rôle des anciennes structures communautaires, en proclamant les droits de l'individu et en mettant en place l'Etat social sous ses diverses formes. Cette transformation a individualisé le rapport entre les gouvernements et les citoyens, tout en ôtant aux personnes la responsabilité sociale qu'elles avaient à l'égard de la communauté dans son ensemble. « L'intérêt général », obtenu par la somme des intérêts individuels, a remplacé le « bien commun de la collectivité ». Les conflits entre des « groupes d'intérêts particuliers » ont succédé au souci du bien commun.

L'Etat est ainsi devenu, pour ses citoyens, le fournisseur de biens et de services « du berceau à la tombe ». C'est pourquoi la crise de l'Etat providence est particulièrement profonde dans les sociétés où cette transformation s'est opérée avec le plus de succès. Il n'existe aucune solution de repli, ce qui pousse bien souvent les citoyens au désespoir et, parallèlement, à tenter de restaurer de nouveaux modes de vie communautaires. L'essor récent de la société civile et la mise au point de systèmes économiques alternatifs à caractère communautaire sont l'expression de ce nouveau désir de transformation sociale.

2. La société du bien-être, un nouveau projet en faveur du bien-être

La société du bien-être est une alternative à la mondialisation, guidée par une nouvelle conception du bien commun des communautés et leur capacité à vivre ensemble. Il est indispensable qu'elle élabore des méthodes d'éducation et de fonctionnement conformes à ses principes, fondées sur le développement local, qui représente la principale cellule des réseaux mondiaux de solidarité, et sur de nouvelles institutions de coopération à l'échelon mesorégional, qui redéfinissent les frontières communes que les Etats ne représentent plus. Ces méthodes doivent privilégier la participation, depuis l'élaboration jusqu'à la mise en œuvre

du projet. Elles doivent par ailleurs être capables d'unifier la connaissance segmentée, qu'a entraînée la spécialisation, dans une perspective trans-disciplinaire, en accordant à nouveau une place centrale, aujourd'hui limitée, à l'interculture, afin qu'elle passe de l'écoute réciproque et du dialogue véritable à une méthode d'enseignement des valeurs et modes de vie propres aux uns, aux membres d'autres cultures.

Cette nouvelle utopie du bien commun repose sur l'idée que la connaissance représente le patrimoine commun de l'humanité et que le partage de cette connaissance est d'une importance primordiale. Déposséder les communautés de la connaissance accumulée au fil des ans par leur action collective et privatiser les résultats obtenus grâce aux investissements publics dans l'éducation et la recherche est contraire à la logique du bien commun et de la vie en commun. La rémunération des résultats obtenus par les chercheurs peut se faire autrement que par leur privatisation, puisque le véritable objectif est dans ce cas uniquement d'assurer les bénéfices les plus élevés aux actionnaires des sociétés titulaires des brevets.

Le bien commun de chaque collectivité doit être étayé par un principe de « vie en commun » au sein d'un système polycentriste mondial de communautés et de mesorégions, capables de coopérer à tous les échelons, et qui s'oppose ainsi à la tendance du XXIᵉ siècle à la multiplication des conflits et des guerres entre les Etats et, au sein des Etats, entre les catégories sociales. La majorité de ces conflits prennent naissance dans des systèmes économiques, politiques et sociaux qui ont généré un « mode de vie » non durable, en opposant les citoyens entre eux dans une confrontation justifiée par le besoin de survivre. La promotion de ces « modes de vie » et des systèmes économiques sur lesquels ils reposent, dans une nouvelle forme de civilisation, de même que l'affirmation répétée qu'ils ne sauraient faire l'objet de marchandage ni être partagés à cause de leur durabilité, ont donné naissance à un discours occidental selon lequel le monde est entré dans une ère de « guerre des civilisations » où se heurtent, d'une part, un système de connaissance jugé évolué, moderne et ouvert et, d'autre part, un système archaïque accusé d'être rétrograde et obscurantiste.

Les objectifs du bien commun et de son utopie diffèrent de ceux de la mondialisation. La mondialisation n'est pas durable, dans la mesure où elle prétend instaurer une durabilité mondiale qui profite à 800 millions de personnes, mais exclut plus de 6 milliards d'individus qui composent le reste de l'humanité. Il n'en va pas de même pour l'utopie du bien commun : il s'agit d'un projet de mondialisation qui ambitionne

de permettre à 8 milliards d'êtres humains de vivre ensemble. Il favorise le dialogue entre les communautés et la participation au sein de celles-ci, en vue de créer un système planétaire composé de modes de vie divers, respectueux les uns des autres et tous préoccupés par l'utilisation durable des ressources naturelles.

L'utopie du bien commun peut-elle aboutir au projet mondial suivant,

> « qui permet à un groupe de personnes de constituer une communauté d'êtres humains, de former une société et de vivre ensemble, de manière à garantir à chacun de ses membres le droit à une existence décente (conforme à la dignité humaine) et la sécurité collective, dans le respect « d'autrui » et de la solidarité avec les autres communautés d'êtres humains et les générations futures, tout en sauvegardant la vie sur terre » ? (The University for the Common Good)

Ce projet s'enracine dans la philosophie et l'existence concrète de millions de personnes dans le monde, qui, en s'opposant à la réponse donnée à la mondialité par la mondialisation, mettent en place de nouvelles formes de vie et de coopération communautaires (mondialisation). « Un autre monde est possible », dans la mesure où il se réalise déjà à travers la vie de communautés, de familles et de personnes aujourd'hui privées de la possibilité de s'exprimer, frustrées dans leurs aspirations collectives et dépossédées de la faculté de diriger leur existence. L'essor d'une « citoyenneté » mondiale s'est toutefois manifesté, au cours des dernières décennies, au travers des mouvements de la société civile (Seattle, Prague, Göteborg, Gênes, Québec, Porto Alegre, Florence), malgré les difficultés et les contradictions auxquelles ils étaient confrontés. La tâche n'est pas facile. Il faut pour cela s'employer de manière responsable à repenser la dynamique du monde, à remettre en question les paradigmes dominants, à ouvrir le débat sur l'actuelle homologation culturelle planétaire et à prendre les mesures qui s'imposent à l'égard du processus de mondialisation. Il est indispensable de rétablir la capacité de penser le bien commun à l'échelon local et mondial ; de redéfinir les fondements sur lesquels reposent le monde et la valeur qu'on lui accorde, en respectant différents mots clés ; enfin, de replacer « autrui » dans la dynamique des rapports interpersonnels, au sein des communautés humaines et dans l'ensemble des relations entre la société mondiale et l'écosystème planétaire.

a. Les liens entre le bien-être et les ressources/le bien commun

Le projet de société du bien-être a vu le jour suite à la mise en place, en dépit du succès rencontré par le modèle antérieur de l'Etat providence, d'un système de production et de consommation qui n'est pas viable, à cause de son prélèvement brutal des ressources naturelles et de sa répartition inéquitable de la richesse et de l'énergie. Mais ce projet suppose de repenser nos modèles de production et de consommation, ainsi que les principes sur lesquels se fonde notre cadre institutionnel. Les premiers doivent viser au développement durable et à la coopération entre les Etats et les communautés. Les deuxièmes doivent être réappréciés en fonction de l'autonomie et de la participation accrues qu'il est indispensable de réaliser à l'échelon local, afin de renforcer la coopération entre les pays voisins et les entités mésorégionales. Le bien commun repose sur deux éléments : la conciliation de l'homme et de l'ensemble des autres êtres vivants et de leur environnement naturel, ainsi que leur capacité à vivre ensemble.

Le bien commun n'est pas la forme du singulier des biens communs, ni la somme des richesses individuelles d'un pays ; il représente :

> « *l'esprit communautaire*, c'est-à-dire un troisième facteur à la fois invisible et intégrateur, qui ne se réduit pas à la somme des parties et ne peut être détenu par quiconque. Nul ne saurait, dès lors, lui accorder une importance supérieure à celle que lui reconnaît chacun. Son identité renferme la diversité d'autrui. Il établit une relation familiale invisible et irréductible, qui unit les êtres malgré leurs différences et à cause d'elles. Il forme une structure de réciprocité, qui prévient toute initiative de privatisation et entrave la concurrence, l'accumulation de la richesse et l'exploitation ; il empêche par conséquent l'apparition des classes sociales » (Vachon, 1988).

Le bien commun est l'essence du projet, le noyau dur autour duquel s'articulent les activités et les objectifs économiques, sociaux et culturels des personnes et de la collectivité. Le bien commun prône les valeurs et les principes qui inspirent la forme et le contenu de la vie en commun au cours d'une période spécifique de l'histoire, ainsi que le choix des biens communs nécessaires à leur mise en œuvre. Comme le précisent d'autres auteurs :

« le « bien commun » fait intégralement référence aux :

- *principes* (comme le principe du droit de toute personne à la vie, le principe de précaution, le principe d'égale citoyenneté, le principe d'épuisabilité de la plupart des ressources de la planète, etc.) ;

- *institutions* (comme la démocratie représentative, les institutions des collectivités locales, les syndicats libres, etc.) ;

- *ressources* et *moyens* (comme l'air, l'eau, le sol, l'éducation, l'information, etc.) ;

- *pratiques* (les pratiques du partage en commun, de la solidarité individuelle et collective, etc.) » (The University for the Common Good).

b. De l'Etat providence à la société du bien-être

Le passage de l'Etat providence à la société du bien-être, fondé sur le nouveau pacte social du bien commun, impose la définition exacte de trois domaines : i. *le bien-être collectif* ; ii. *le bien-être associatif et coopératif* et iii. *le bien-être personnel*.

i. *Le bien-être collectif* « est constitué par l'ensemble des principes, institutions, moyens et pratiques auxquels la société recourt pour garantir à l'ensemble de ses citoyens le droit à une existence décente et à une « vie en commun » pacifique, satisfaisante et coopérative, afin de préserver la sécurité de leur « foyer » c'est-à-dire la durabilité de l'écosystème local et planétaire, ainsi que la prise en compte globale du droit à la vie des générations futures » (Petrella, 1999). Le bien commun est le fondement du bien-être collectif, à partir duquel peut se construire le bien-être associatif et personnel.

ii. *Le bien-être associatif et coopératif* « est constitué par l'ensemble des principes, institutions, moyens et pratiques auxquels la société recourt, en vue de promouvoir une coopération volontaire entre les personnes et/ou les groupes qui partagent les mêmes objectifs, en mettant à leur disposition commune et en partageant les ressources matérielles et immatérielles selon les usages de la mutualité et de la coopération » (*ibidem*). La déprivatisation suppose d'étendre le domaine de la démercantilisation aux nouvelles formes d'organisation du secteur privé capables de promouvoir et de mettre en place des modèles économiques de coopération et d'association qui s'inscrivent dans les notions de « l'alteréconomie », « l'économie de la solidarité » et de « districts de solidarité ».

Ces nouveaux secteurs d'activité et de socialisation, qui englobent les formes de production, de consommation et de service, peuvent se développer à condition de créer un espace autonome, à l'intérieur et à l'extérieur de l'économie de marché, qui soit propice

au renforcement de la participation et à divers types d'avantages sociaux conformes aux idées qui les inspirent. Ces formes sociales d'organisation et de gestion de l'économie doivent se défaire des contraintes juridiques imposées par les institutions pour protéger les situations de monopole qui existent sur le plan aussi bien économique qu'institutionnel.

iii. *Le bien-être personnel et privé* : « Le bien-être personnel est constitué par l'ensemble des principes, institutions, moyens et pratiques auxquels recourt la société, en vue de permettre à toute personne, en concurrence avec toutes les autres, d'optimiser sa propre utilité personnelle sur le plan de la richesse pécuniaire et de la liberté d'action » (*ibidem*). Ce secteur de l'économie privée doit recouvrer ses forces au sein de l'économie de marché, en rétablissant ses liens avec l'économie véritable grâce à la quête d'un profit d'entreprise dans les canaux de production et de services, qui soit libéré des « chaînes » et des « contraintes » imposées par les systèmes financiers et la charge inutilement excessive que fait peser l'Etat sur le coût et la gestion des entreprises. La création d'une culture d'entreprise capable d'analyser les coûts sociaux, de demeurer dans les limites de la production en temps de paix, de prendre part à l'établissement d'un juste rapport entre la production, la distribution et la consommation au sein de la société, ainsi que d'être ouverte au dialogue avec la collectivité et la société à laquelle elle appartient, semble un objectif réaliste.

Ces lignes directrices permettent à un groupe de personnes de constituer une communauté, « de créer la société » et de vivre ensemble de manière à garantir à chacun une existence décente (conforme à la dignité humaine) et la sécurité collective, dans le respect « d'autrui » et en se montrant solidaire des autres communautés d'êtres humains et des générations futures, tout en sauvegardant la vie sur terre.

c. *La constitution de nouveaux biens communs matériels et immatériels pour le bien-être citoyen*

Les biens communs sont des instruments indispensables à une société du bien-être ; ils doivent être le reflet de la teneur et de la forme de l'objectif de solidarité poursuivi en vue de parvenir au bien commun. Il s'agit des biens nécessaires à l'existence matérielle, ainsi qu'aux nouvelles activités et aux nouveaux rapports jugés essentiels à la vie de la collectivité. C'est la raison pour laquelle leurs caractéristiques doivent être distinctes de celles des biens (marchandises) privés, soumis aux principes de la concurrence

et de l'exclusivité de l'accès et de l'utilisation, qui s'appliquent au système du marché capitaliste. L'économie publique et l'économie coopérative fonctionnent, au sein de l'économie de marché, d'une manière différente de celle du capitalisme.

On peut ainsi établir une première liste de biens communs ; celle-ci comprend l'air, l'eau, le domaine foncier de l'Etat, les mers et les forêts, l'espace, l'énergie, la connaissance, les transports, l'éducation, la santé, les communications et l'information, la sécurité, la justice, les activités financières essentielles et les institutions politiques. On y trouve également le travail et la culture, dont le rôle, les attributions, la durée et la forme sont étroitement imbriqués avec d'autres formes de vie sociale. Les biens communs d'importance planétaire devraient faire l'objet d'un dialogue entre les communautés, afin qu'ils soient entretenus et utilisés dans la perspective d'une « vie en commun » (tableau 1).

Le projet de société du bien-être, inspiré par le bien commun, dispose ainsi d'un certain nombre de ressources :

- des valeurs et des principes ;

- une législation et des institutions ;

- un financement ;

- des acteurs et des usages.

La récente tendance à la segmentation des biens communs et à leur gestion par les organisations internationales (« la gouvernance ») reproduit les effets négatifs constatés à l'occasion de l'administration par l'Etat des biens publics, laquelle avait entraîné la déresponsabilisation des communautés et des individus. Aussi convient-il de rétablir, face à l'Etat et aux institutions internationales, le principe de la souveraineté de la collectivité dans le choix et l'administration des biens communs. Cela suppose la mise en place de nouvelles formes de propriété et de gestion, fondées sur une large autonomie et une participation importante, capables de mobiliser les collectivités locales et la société civile.

L'économie ne saurait demeurer à l'écart et hors d'atteinte de ce système, tout comme elle n'avait pas échappé à l'Etat providence, bâti sur le dualisme entre Etat et marché. Ce dualisme est aujourd'hui doublement contesté. La mondialisation, par la privatisation croissante à laquelle elle conduit, transforme le dualisme en un système unique, fondé sur les principes et la suprématie de la finance et de la technologie, qui s'accompagne

Tableau 1 – Biens communs, acteurs et usages, bien-être

Biens communs	Acteurs et usages	Bien-être
– *l'air* – *l'eau* (de surface et souterraine, saumâtre et douce, consommée non seulement sous forme d'eau potable, mais également pour tout autre usage, comme l'agriculture, indispensable à l'existence de la collectivité). – *les énergies renouvelables*, comme l'énergie solaire, éolienne, etc. – *les terres et forêts domaniales de l'Etat* – *les espaces célestes et extraterrestres* – *la connaissance* (sous ses formes diverses) – *l'éducation* (sous toutes ses formes) – *l'habitat* (depuis le logement jusqu'à l'administration du territoire) – *la santé* – *la culture* (spécifiquement les biens culturels) – *les transports en commun* – *les communications et l'information* – *la sécurité publique* (police, armée, protection civile) – *la justice* · – *les institutions financières publiques* (Trésor public, caisses d'épargne, etc.) – *les institutions politiques* (parlement, gouvernement, administration publique)	Acteurs : – *les institutions* (comme la démocratie représentative, les institutions des collectivités locales, les syndicats libres, etc.) – *les entreprises sociales* (PME, coopératives, coopératives sociales, etc.) – *les organisations de la société civile* (ONG, associations, etc.) Usages : – *les principes* (comme le principe du droit de toute personne à la vie, le principe de précaution, le caractère épuisable de la plupart des ressources de la planète, etc.) – *les usages* (les usages du partage commun, de la solidarité individuelle et collective, etc.)	Durabilité : – environnementale – sociale – culturelle – politique – économique

d'une marginalisation de domaines toujours plus nombreux de la société. Le bien commun offre une solution de remplacement, qui dépasse le dualisme du système précédent, en restituant sa place centrale à une vie communautaire assise sur ses principales composantes : le territoire, la population, les systèmes de production et les institutions (figure 1).

Inspirée par le bien commun, la vie des communautés exige une cohésion et une mobilisation globale de l'ensemble de ses composantes et de ses ressources. Les biens communs créent les conditions de départ de son fonctionnement général et de celui de chacun de ses principaux facteurs : le territoire, les systèmes de production, la population et les institutions. Son indispensable structure, assise sur ces quatre piliers, forme un diamant qui la symbolise. La mondialisation repose sur des systèmes de production déterritorialisés, le nomadisme de la population et des institutions centralisées. Les cellules de la société du bien-être sont représentées par les communautés, dont le fonctionnement exige, au sein de leurs limites respectives, l'existence d'institutions propres qui gouvernent un territoire, une population et des systèmes de production spécifiques.

Figure 1 – Le diamant de la communauté

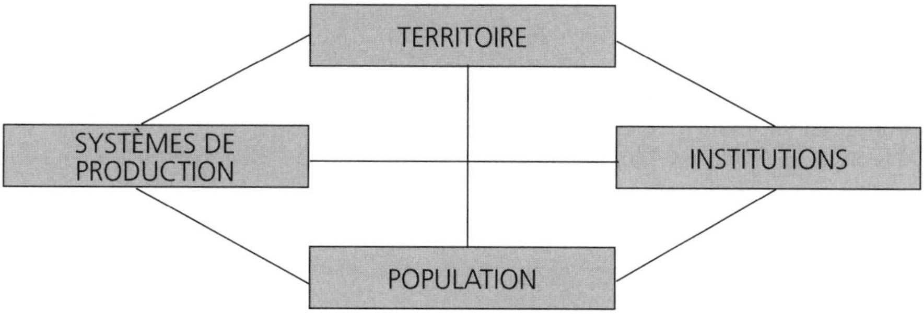

A la différence de la mondialisation, le bien commun poursuit un but de resocialisation, c'est-à-dire qu'il vise à étendre, en partant du secteur coopératif de l'économie, le domaine de la démercantilisation aux autres formes de l'économie privée, sensibles à l'attrait de « l'alteréconomie », en se fondant, notamment, sur divers types de coopération, les réseaux de solidarité et les districts sociaux. Il s'agit de créer une économie à nouveau intégrée dans la communauté, où le marché retrouve le rôle subordonné d'un service fourni aux producteurs et aux consommateurs, dépourvu de tout esprit « lucratif » capitaliste et guidé par un principe excédentaire (sans idée de profit) capable de préserver sa durabilité. Ces nouveaux domaines

d'activité et rapports sociaux peuvent se développer dans leur espace autonome à l'échelon local, au sein et hors de l'économie de marché.

Leur succès peut aller jusqu'à améliorer le comportement des entreprises privées. Aussi la réussite de ce nouveau modèle économique a-t-elle été étendue au secteur privé, grâce à la notion d'entreprise sociale : toute entreprise, indépendamment de sa forme juridique, exerce son activité à l'échelon local et adopte un comportement qui définit sa fonction sociale. L'entreprise sociale est ainsi enracinée dans sa communauté et poursuit ses objectifs de durabilité (économique, sociale, institutionnelle et environnementale).

Dans toutes formes d'organisations sociales, le système de production et le marché peuvent jouer le rôle essentiel d'instrument de mise en commun sociale et culturelle des expériences, ainsi que de lieux de rencontre et de réflexion. Mais cela est uniquement possible s'il existe un solide lien entre le territoire, la population, les systèmes de production et les institutions et s'il se maintient sans qu'aucun de ces facteurs ne s'amoindrisse ou disparaisse. C'est pourquoi la place centrale accordée à la dimension locale dans la définition du tracé des nouvelles frontières de la communauté (en remplacement de la dimension nationale de l'Etat) ne correspond pas à un choix de spécialisation au sein d'un domaine plus vaste, mais à des domaines de référence privilégiés auxquels les autres dimensions, comme l'Etat, les régions et les institutions internationales, doivent être liées de manière fonctionnelle (tableau 2, page suivante).

d. Rôle de la propriété collective et du patrimoine commun

L'économie européenne a évolué en deux étapes au cours de la deuxième moitié du siècle dernier. Les deux premières décennies, c'est-à-dire les années 1950 et 1960, ont été le théâtre de l'application du système de planification en Europe centrale et orientale, tandis que l'Europe occidentale suivait le modèle du marché capitaliste et de l'économie mixte. Ces deux systèmes ont été la source d'une croissance économique et d'un développement des institutions et des services publics. Au cours de cette étape, les économies planifiées et de marché étaient en mesure de répondre à l'essentiel de la demande de biens et de services et ne laissaient guère de place pour l'élaboration d'autres modèles économiques. Le mouvement coopératif qui existait à l'Est et à l'Ouest était coincé entre le marché et l'Etat ; il parvenait à survivre dans un espace extrêmement étroit, en s'adaptant bien souvent au mouvement du système économique dominant.

Tableau 2 – Etat providence, mondialisation et bien commun

	État providence	Mondialisation	Société du bien-être
Objectifs (a)	Individuels et matériels	Individuels - Statut	Sociaux - relationnels
Objectifs (b)	Croissance nationale	Apartheid mondial	Bien commun
Instruments	Biens publics : Acier Electricité Transports Ecole Santé	Biens privés : Finance Technologie Commerce Connaissance Société	Biens communs : Eau Environnement Habitat Education Santé Espace
Acteurs	**Individus - droits**	**Consommateurs - choix**	**Individus - adhésion**
Institutions	Etat national	Pouvoir triadique	Collectivité, région, Etat et mésorégion
	Gouvernement	Gouvernance	Autonomie et participation
	Développement national	Du planétaire au local	Du local au mésorégional
Systèmes de production	Entreprises publiques et privées (grandes entreprises) Districts industriels	Transnationaux (de type Toyota)	Entreprises sociales PME Réseaux Institutions publiques

La situation a radicalement changé au cours des trente années qui ont suivi (1970-2000), dans la mesure où la mondialisation est devenue le paradigme majeur de l'économie et de la politique. La chute du mur de Berlin a permis l'unification des sociétés d'Europe de l'Est et de l'Ouest, ce qui a favorisé la concentration de la croissance et réduit le marché aux grands axes d'un apartheid planétaire (Amoroso, 2004). En outre, la mise en œuvre du néolibéralisme a mis fin aux politiques économiques keynésiennes, qui favorisaient la production et la consommation de masse à l'époque du capitalisme national. Dès lors, les politiques de secteur public

et les biens publics qui les accompagnaient n'étaient plus nécessaires et ont commencé à disparaître.

Paradoxalement, ces deux éléments négatifs de l'histoire des sociétés européennes sont également à l'origine de l'apparition des principales innovations du siècle actuel. En se retirant de vastes régions et secteurs pour se concentrer sur les segments riches du marché, le capitalisme, qui aborde ainsi la question du développement durable de la planète, a délaissé certains espaces du marché et des activités sociales. La société civile s'est alors mobilisée et a décidé, après une brève période de résistance à la mondialisation pour défendre le système de protection sociale, d'essayer de nouveaux modèles d'organisation économique et institutionnelle : c'est ainsi que les coopératives sociales et les entreprises sociales ont accompagné la revitalisation du développement local, constituant du même coup le socle indispensable à la renaissance des communautés (Amoroso et Zandonai, 2007). La devise de la mondialisation, « du mondial au local », a été inversée, pour devenir « du local au mondial ». La première considère la mondialisation comme le modèle dont il convient de s'inspirer à l'échelon local et auquel la communauté locale doit s'adapter. La seconde, en revanche, oppose à ce point de vue monocentriste une conception polycentriste, dans laquelle la durabilité de chaque communauté et son projet de société déterminent les formes et l'étendue du dialogue avec les autres communautés, et qui est indispensable à la réalisation du bien commun dans le monde. Aussi ce nouveau paradigme considère-t-il l'entreprise sociale comme la réponse à la question de la durabilité de la production des biens et des services de la nouvelle économie.

En résumé, les critères de l'entreprise sociale sont les suivants :

- un enracinement territorial et local, condition préalable d'un choix efficace du secteur d'activité et de l'utilisation des ressources locales ;

- une appartenance à la communauté, qui lui permet de ressentir les exigences auxquelles elle est confrontée, ainsi que de mesurer les répercussions de son activité sur la communauté en matière de production et sur le plan social ;

- le caractère hybride des ressources et des formes de travail dont dispose le projet d'entreprise, qui peut avoir recours à tous les types d'emploi, en dépassant les frontières d'une définition juridique, axée sur le marché, de l'emploi et des formes de propriété ;

- l'implication de l'ensemble des acteurs de l'entreprise, grâce à de véritables formes de codécision et de participation à la gestion de l'entreprise ;

- le fait de porter attention aux relations entre les organisations à l'échelon local et à un échelon élargi, et s'y investir comme il convient, de manière à conjuguer coopération locale et coopération avec les producteurs et les marchés des autres communautés et pays.

Le modèle de l'entreprise sociale s'inscrit naturellement dans le cadre des questions soulevées par la mondialisation.

Conclusion : la question de l'accès aux ressources et aux droits et de leur utilisation

Les thèmes de «l'accès à» et de «l'utilisation de» ont été, au cours de ces dernières années, les mots clés du contrôle et de l'évaluation de l'efficacité d'un système démocratique au sein de la politique européenne et des organisations internationales. Ces deux notions ont été largement employées pour établir l'étalonnage des processus de démocratisation. A l'époque de l'Etat providence, leur mise en œuvre reposait sur la fourniture par le secteur public des infrastructures essentielles, indispensables à la réalisation de ces objectifs et sur une série de « droits » garantis à l'ensemble des citoyens sous la forme de déclarations de principe (droit au travail, droit au revenu, etc.). Cette stratégie des droits était étroitement imbriquée à l'échelon international avec celle des « droits de l'homme », mais elles sous-estimaient toutes deux le problème posé par les prépositions «à» et «de», qu'elles croyaient clairement définies et parfaitement maîtrisées.

Or les quelques résultats obtenus ont été systématiquement inférieurs aux attentes. Depuis les années 1970, certaines questions que l'on croyait enfin réglées, comme la pauvreté, l'inégalité, les mauvaises conditions de travail, la sécurité, etc., se sont à nouveau posées à une plus grande échelle. Elles ont provoqué, auprès de la population et de ses différents mouvements, diverses réactions, qui exprimaient une désaffection générale à l'égard des institutions et de la politique, et qui ont été à l'origine des initiatives prises par les institutions et la société civile. Le nouveau maître mot est devenu celui de la « participation », qui s'est généralisé à tous les échelons des institutions et auxquels certains secteurs de l'économie se sont également essayés. La participation a cependant une limite : elle ne remet pas en question les objectifs et les formes des institutions politiques

et économiques en vigueur ; elle vise à renforcer l'adhésion en faveur de leur fonctionnement. La participation peut certes améliorer « l'accès à » et « l'utilisation de », mais elle ne remet pas en cause l'objectif et la forme des institutions dans lesquelles elle doit s'inscrire.

Cela nous ramène au problème crucial de la forme et du contenu du modèle de développement qu'il convient de choisir. La tendance dominante est aujourd'hui à un modèle monocentriste (eurocentrisme et occidentalisation), en dépit des déclarations et des politiques attentives à la question de la diversité dans le développement européen, qu'elles considèrent à juste titre comme une valeur positive et proprement européenne. Cette diversité n'est pas devenue la clé qui permet de comprendre la nécessité d'un développement polycentriste, fondé sur les régions et les communautés – où les valeurs, les objectifs et les formes partagés demeurent différents – mais qui, comme nous l'avons déjà dit, va du planétaire au local, en adaptant ce dernier au premier.

Bibliographie

Adler-Karlsson *G., The Political Economy of East-West-South Co-Operation*. Springer-Verlag, New York, 1976.

Amoroso, B., *Global Apartheid,* Economics and Society, Federico Caffè Center, Roskilde, Città di Castello, 2004.

Amoroso, B. et Zandonai, F., *Oltre i confini : percorsi di internazionalizzazione dell'impresa sociale*, CGM Brescia, 2007.

Archibugi, F., *The Associative Economy*, Macmillan Press, London, 2000.

Caffè, F., "Umanesimo del welfare", *Micromega*, n° 1, 1986.

CMED (Commission mondiale sur l'environnement et le développement – Commission Brundtland), *Notre avenir à tous*, Editions du Fleuve, Québec, 1988.

Kapp, K. W., *The Social Costs of Private Enterprise*, Harvard University Press, Cambridge, Mass., 1950.

Keynes, J. M., "National Self-Sufficiency", *Yale Review*, 1933.

Keynes, J. M., "Economic possibilities for our grandchildren" in Keynes, J.M., *Essays in Persuasion*, 1932.

Meadows, D. H., Meadows, D. L., Randers, J. et Behrens, W.W., *Limits to Growth*, Universe Books, 1972.

Myrdal, G., *Beyond the Welfare State. Economic Planning and its International Implocations*, Yale University Press, New Haven, Conn., 1960.

Petrella, R., *Le Manifeste de l'Eau*, Pour un Contrat mondial, Lausanne, 1999.

The University for the Common Good, Federico Caffè Centre, Roskilde University, Denmark, 2004. http://www.ruc.dk/upload/application/pdf/f51d6748/The_UNIVERSITY_for_the_COMMON_GOOD.pdf.

Vachon, R., "La pensée de Dominique Temple", *Interculture*, n° 98, Montréal, 1988.